D0871881

Women and Self-Esteem

Other books by Linda Tschirhart Sanford

IN DEFENSE OF OURSELVES: A Rape Prevention
Handbook for Women (with Ann Fetter)

THE SILENT CHILDREN: A Parents' Guide to the
Prevention of Child Sexual Abuse

Women and Self-Esteem

*Understanding and Improving the Way
We Think and Feel About Ourselves*

by

LINDA TSCHIRHART SANFORD

and

MARY ELLEN DONOVAN

ANCHOR PRESS/DOUBLEDAY
Garden City, New York   1984

"Fight Back," words and music by Holly Near, published and reproduced by permission of Hereford Music, copyright © 1978. All Rights Reserved.

Library of Congress Cataloging in Publication Data

Sanford, Linda Tschirhart.
   Women and self-esteem.

   Includes index.
   1. Women—Psychology.   2. Self-respect.   3. Feminism.
I. Donovan, Mary Ellen. II. Title.
HQ1206.S24   1984   305.4'2   82–45269
ISBN 0-385-17310-5

ACKNOWLEDGMENTS

This book could not have been written without the resources and helpful staffs of the Schlesinger Library at Radcliffe College and of Baker Library at Dartmouth College. At the Schlesinger special thanks to Pat King and Ruth Hill, who generously provided office space and moral support during a critical period. Special thanks for the office space provided by Baker, too, and to Baker's extremely accommodating and efficient circulation staff.

This book also could not have been written without the hundreds of women who either participated in our self-esteem groups or granted us interviews. To them our deepest thanks.

Various friends and colleagues helped us greatly by reading and criticizing portions of the manuscript in progress, providing insights and new ideas, suggesting invaluable sources, and/or serving as sounding boards for our ideas as we struggled to clarify and organize them. We are especially grateful to Robin Barnett, Claudia Black, Ellen Cole, Susan Dentzer, Terrence Des Pres, Beth Dingman, Roger Gottlieb, Ann Grobe, Marcia Germaine Hutchinson, N. P. Kannan, Beth Kindl, Claudia Lamperti, Leslie Madden, Linda Markin, Francine Rainone, Judy Rowan, Donna Sweaney, Carole Trickett and Nancy Wasserman. Ann Watson did more than her share of reading and is a "most excellent" friend. David Coburn served as courier and cook in addition to helping with ideas and organization. We are also grateful to Margarita Ascencio, Mary Fitzgerald, Anne Slade Frey, Barbara Harrington, Sandra Lowe, Helen Boulware Moore, Valerie Mullen, Kesa Noda, Grace Paley, Barbara Palmer-Litchfeld, Holly Porter, Eleanor Swaim and Sheila Ward—all of whom gave us guidance in better understanding the experience of women of different cultures, classes, ages, and life circumstances.

Marcia Putnam put in many long hours over several years typing manuscript in various stages. We thank her for the excellent job she did and for her cheerfulness and constant enthusiasm for the project. Hedy Anderegg and Jesse Piaia also did fine and enthusiastic jobs typing; we thank them too, and are especially grateful to Hedy for the ideas and insights she added. Thanks as well go to April Pinard, who took on typing at the last minute and completed it with speed. And we owe thanks to the staff at Gnomon Copy in Hanover, New Hampshire, who over the years always provided us with fast and friendly service.

Frances Goldin, our agent, has worked relentlessly on behalf of us and this book in the three-plus years it took to write it. She is tenacious and professional, and we're grateful that she's been on our side.

Finally, thanks from both of us go to Lindy Hess and Felecia Abbadessa, this book's editors. Lindy gave us encouragement during an important stage of the writing, and was generous with her considerable intelligence and skills as an editor. Felecia did an outstanding job taking care of the line editing and many important details, and has been a genuine pleasure to work with.

In addition to those we both want to thank, there are certain persons each of us is individually indebted to.

Linda gives special thanks to:

—Carl Cooley, Trudi Lanz, Linda Ross, Florence Rush, Rich Snowdon, Kathleen Vogel and Bill Young for their special support and friendship during my work on this book.

—Joanne, Peter, Brian, Sara, Sheila, Michelle, Judith, Phil and Willa from Upper Valley Youth Services in Lebanon, New Hampshire. All contributed to my self-knowledge and self-esteem during the time I was a foster parent.

—Ruth, Anne, Jessa, Judith and Marge from the Black Women's Oral History Project at Schlesinger-Radcliffe. You not only shared work space with me, you gave me the support and sense of belonging that only a work family can give.

—Tom Davidow, for whom I want especially to express my affection and respect. You will no doubt recognize in these pages much of your wisdom and spirit, along with many of the bad jokes we exchanged in our work together. You have contributed greatly to my sense of well-being, and for that I will always be grateful.

—Janet LeBrun Cosby and Joe Cosby, who generously took a chance on me and gave me the kind of support I needed most.

—Janice DeLange, PhD., deserves credit and thanks as my professor at the University of Washington Graduate School of Social Work. In 1977 Janice introduced me to the theory of self-esteem development and several clinical techniques. Her work inspired mine; she is a great scholar and teacher.

Mary Ellen gives special thanks to:

—All the friends whose love and support helped me through the three years I have worked on this book. In addition to those already mentioned, this includes Linsey Abrams, Jeff and Sue Grobe, Roberta Hathorn, Helen Hertzog, Sandi Hulon, Mary Koen, Marie Lapre-Grabon, Heather Mates, Sean Mullen, Laurie Ridgeway, Amy Semmes, Amanda Smith, Diane Stevenson and Emily Quimby.

—Nancy Baker, who helped me through a particularly rough time.

—Daniel Donovan, especially for helping out with cash-flow problems.

—The women with whom I worked while waitressing at the Owl's Nest restaurant during the final phase of writing this book. Thanks also to Bob at the bar, who provided moral support.

—Esther and Mitch Lipson and Allan and Nenette Harvey, in whose homes I did much of my work on this book.

—My sister Liz and brother Pat, who let me know they believed in this project.

—My dear friend David, who put up with a lot while I was working on this book, but who nevertheless was always loving, understanding and supportive.

CONTENTS

PREFACE: ABOUT THIS BOOK

> . . . studies of women have repeatedly shown disturbing patterns: lack of self-esteem, an inability to feel powerful or in control of one's life, a vulnerability to depression, a tendency to see oneself as less talented, less able than one really is. The myriad studies that have been done over the years give the district impression of constriction, a crippling, a sense of being somehow not quite as good, not quite as able, not quite as bright, not quite as valuable as men . . . Certainly there are many women who have escaped that blight, who have lived full and happy lives, but when you leaf through the studies you can sense, floating in the air, ghosts of unborn dreams, unrealized hopes, undiscovered talents. The tragedies are the "might have beens," and they are the most poignant.
>
> —Caryl Rivers, Rosalind Barnett and Grace Baruch,
> in *Beyond Sugar and Spice*

This book is about the millions of women whose lives and happiness have been constricted because of lack of self-esteem. How and why have so many women come to see themselves as less able, less bright, less valuable than they really are? What effects does lack of self-esteem have on individual women's psychological health, relationships, work performance and attitudes toward others and the world in general? What effects does low self-esteem among large numbers of women have on women as a group, politically, economically and socially? These are the questions we attempt to answer in this book. Equally important, we also offer suggestions for what women can do, starting right now, to increase their self-esteem and take more control of their lives, and thus make their own existences more happy and fulfilled and the history of women a brighter one.

Two women collaborated on this book. Linda is a psychotherapist who has worked extensively with victims of sexual violence and has been conducting Self-Esteem Enhancement Groups for women since

1978. Mary Ellen is a journalist-writer with a special interest in women's issues and experience in political activism. For the record, both of us were born after World War II, were raised in middle-class Catholic families and are white; both of us are also feminists. Although we arrived at our common interest in the topic of women and self-esteem via different routes and bring to this book different perspectives, our various personal and professional experiences have led us to a shared awareness of the crucial and complex role of self-esteem in the lives of women.

Amazingly little of depth has been said so far about women and self-esteem. Self-esteem and the experience of those who are members of religious and racial minorities have been written about at length. Gunnar Myrdal, Gordon Allport, Kurt Lewin and others, for example, have explored in detail the question of whether the Jews' status as a despised and persecuted group has led to "group self-hatred." And Frantz Fanon, in *Black Skin, White Masks* has written with great fervor about the black man's *(sic)* self-esteem problems as consequences of racism, colonialism and a heritage of enslavement. As yet, however, only scattershot and indirect attention has been given to the relationship between self-esteem and women's life experience in a society and culture that holds us to be second-class. Although many of the books about women to appear in recent years touch on women's self-esteem problems, they do so only obliquely, through examination of another aspect of women's lives. And although other writers have examined some of the more obvious symptoms of low self-esteem among women (e.g., depression, nonassertiveness, negative body image), the root cause of these symptomatic manifestations—namely, lack of self-esteem—remains inadequately explored.

We see this book as an exploration of self-esteem and women's experience. Although we have tried to be comprehensive in our approach, we do not pretend that this book stands as the definitive statement. On the contrary, our hope is that it will not be the last word on this subject.

Our exploration of self-esteem and female experience rests on four related premises. The first is that low self-esteem among women is largely the result of female oppression in male-dominated culture and society,* and constitutes an insidious form of oppression in its own

---

* The words "culture" and "society" are often used interchangeably, but throughout this book we will use them to mean two different things. By "society" we mean the structures, rules and formal relationships by which groups of people live together; by "culture" we mean the beliefs, values and expressive creations of people bound by social arrangements.

right. A woman whose career opportunities, for example, are restricted because of sex discrimination is externally oppressed. But a woman whose career opportunities are restricted because she had been taught to think of herself as lacking in capabilities and not worth much is also internally oppressed.

Our second premise is that low self-esteem is at the bottom of many of the psychological problems that plague individual women today, and attempts to "cure" these problems without addressing what underlies them can often lead to other problems. For instance, a woman who compulsively overeats or is dependent upon alcohol may be able to change her behavior in that specific regard. But when she does, the low self-esteem behind the original problem will probably manifest itself in other ways.

Our third premise is that low self-esteem and the psychological problems it gives rise to facilitate the continuation of women's external oppression in a male-dominated world. A woman who is taught from childhood that she is of less value than males, for instance, easily may come to believe it, and her lack of faith in her own value will predispose her to depression and passivity, which, in turn, will make it easier for others to keep her down—down being her "proper place."

Our fourth premise is that the development of self-esteem in individual women is necessary for the advancement of women as a group. Male-dominated culture and society can continue only if women accept and internalize the notion that women naturally are and deserve to be second-class. For a woman to hold herself in high esteem in a world where women are held in low esteem is to tacitly challenge the prevailing social, political and economic order.

In expanding upon these premises in this book, our intent is not to either allege or attempt to prove that all women have self-esteem problems; we know some women who, fortunately, are relatively free of such problems. Nor do we mean to suggest that all men have high levels of self-esteem, all women lower levels by comparison; just as there are women with high self-esteem, there are men with low self-esteem. What we do mean to suggest is that there are often very different reasons for low self-esteem among men and women, and that, overall, the average man has a decided advantage over the average woman in developing and maintaining self-esteem. For there are great differences in the experience of males and females in the world, and the fact that ours is a world in which men have a monopoly on power and prestige provides individual men with an enormous hedge against feelings of self-devaluation. No matter how downtrodden, humiliated, "alienated" or otherwise bad about himself a man may feel, he can always find a measure of self-worth in remembering and asserting that he is, after all, a man. By contrast, women have no similar defense against self-devaluation; we are devalued by definition.

The relationship between women's lowly social status and women's self-attitudes is circular and extremely complex. In exploring it, our guiding principle has been this: as women we cannot understand ourselves and our attitudes toward ourselves unless we understand the dynamics of the family situations in which we were raised and the culture and society in which we interact; and we cannot understand either our individual upbringing and experience or the larger culture and society without some understanding of history and women's consistently ignored place in it.

The book breaks down into four parts. In Part One, we explain why self-esteem is important, and identify the most common self-esteem problems we have found among women. In Part Two, we look at how women's self-attitudes are shaped by interpersonal relationships with family members, friends, lovers and spouses, and women's own children. In Part Three we look at how women's self-attitudes are further shaped as we leave the intimate sphere and venture into the larger world; here we look at the influence of religions, schools, the work experiences and government, among others. In Part Four, we examine the common ways low self-esteem is manifested in women's individual psychology; here we look at such problems as emotional suppression and depression, self-fulfilling prophecies, negative body image, and hatred of others.

At the end of Part One and many chapters throughout the book, the reader will find sections suggesting ways to cope with the problems addressed in the preceding pages. We call these sections "Blueprints for Change," and they contain information about dealing with street harassment, for example, and/or psychological exercises effectively used over the years in self-esteem enhancement groups. We have included these sections in the hope that they will be helpful to women reading this book, and also out of a sense of responsibility. Too many books about women, we fear, demoralize women by concentrating solely on how poorly women have been treated, offering no glimmer of hope for change short of full-scale social and political revolution. We believe there are many things we women can do, beginning now, to improve our individual and collective situations, and we offer the "Blueprints for Change" as various means to those ends.

A word of caution about the psychological exercises in many of the Blueprints: these exercises constitute tools which may help women build self-esteem, but they are not guarantees of self-esteem, and they are certainly not quick and easy formulas for a happy, successful life. Many authors and pop psychologists today contend that they have a "secret" or foolproof method for instant self-esteem and happiness. We have no such secrets or magical solutions, and we distrust those who claim they do. For a problem so deeply rooted in social and cultural forces, there are no overnight solutions or individual cure-alls.

We have stated that two women collaborated on this book. But in another, and very real, sense this book is the product of collaboration among many women. These are the 120 women who have participated in our self-esteem enhancement groups since 1979, and the more than 200 other women who took the time to discuss with us the role of self-esteem in their lives and the lives of women they know. All these women are contributors to this book, and we use their voices to illuminate theoretical points or clinical observations.

In talking to women, we found a wide-ranging diversity of experience and viewpoint, and we have tried to keep this diversity in mind while writing. All women, just by virtue of our status as the "other" group in this society, share a thread of common experience. Still, there is no such thing as *the* female experience or *the* women's perspective. Race, social class, economic status, sexual preference, educational level, geographical origin and residence, ethnicity, religious background and affiliation, age, and varying physical abilities—all these and other factors distinguish women from one another, making it ludicrous to speak as if all women's experiences can be lumped together as one and the same.

But if diversity was a theme that came through in our interviews, so was commonality. Even women very unlike one another often found that along with their differences existed similarities of experience, perception, and feeling. Some women had thought their self-esteem problems were unique to them, and were relieved and consoled to find that other women had them too. Moreover, the discovery of common bonds was a boon to many women's self-esteem.

While we had no difficulty finding women willing to share their thoughts and experiences pertaining to self-esteem, we have had considerable difficulty coming up with scientific evidence that validates women's experience. Although myriad studies measuring women's self-esteem levels have been done over the years, most have been of white women, thus they cannot be considered representative of all women. Moreover, the bulk of the existing studies simply establish the fact of low self-esteem among the women studied and do little to explain its causes or dynamics. Finally, many studies are gender-comparative: instead of linking women's self-esteem levels to women's experience in the world, women's self-esteem levels are compared to men's levels. This sort of approach is problematic, for it enforces the notion that males are the norm, and ignores the fact that from the moment of birth, male and female experience in the world is very different.

Finding scientific evidence to validate women's experience or "prove" our clinical observations has been further hindered by the androcentric bias that permeates most of the existing research and literature of self-esteem. Although several hundred studies of female subjects have been performed, these studies constitute only a small portion of the total research on self-esteem. Looking through the clinical work on self-esteem, we've found that nearly all the supposedly general studies have been performed on male subjects, and it is from the study and/or observation of males, and males alone, that universal conclusions about *human* psychology, behavior and experience have been drawn. Similarly, most of the vast theoretical and speculative literature on self-esteem either deals specifically with males or speaks in vague abstractions about "man" and "the individual." What about women? Do writers who talk about "man" and "the individual" mean women too? These are questions one is forced to ask in reading the literature on self-esteem, and in most cases the answer is no.

The work of Stanley Coopersmith and Morris Rosenberg, two of the leading American authorities on self-esteem, well illustrates the androcentrism of most of the research. In Coopersmith's *The Antecedents of Self-esteem* and Rosenberg's *The Adolescent Self-image,* both men make generalized statements about "students," "children," and "adolescents," when, in fact, their studies are of *male* students, *male* children, *male* adolescents. The amazingly short shrift which female subjects and female experience typically get in the general literature is further illustrated by Rosenberg's most recent book, *Conceiving the Self,* published in 1979. This is one of the most cogent works yet to appear on self-esteem, and in it Rosenberg examines the relationship between self-esteem and such factors as social class, race and religion. But whereas Rosenberg devotes entire chapters to these factors, it is only in the closing pages that he discusses the topic of gender, and he dispenses with this topic in a mere five paragraphs. Nowhere does Rosenberg explore the effect of gender on self-esteem, and nowhere else do female subjects warrant mention.

The paucity of work on self-esteem and female experience leaves us in a peculiar bind. On the one hand, there's a certain excitement in venturing into largely unexplored territory. On the other hand, there's a definite risk, for to venture into unexplored territory is usually to end up treading on shaky ground. We refer to the existing research, including research done on male subjects, where it seems applicable. But in many cases there is no applicable research, and so we've relied on clinical observations and testimony from women. Our hope is that research scientists will pursue study of self-esteem issues among a large and representative sample of women. The time for women and self-esteem to get the scientific attention the subject deserves is long overdue.

Women and Self-Esteem

PART ONE

*

Making the Connections

* 1 *

Making the Connections, Defining the Terms

Women and self-esteem? You mean there's a connection between the two?

—Forty-eight-year-old woman upon hearing about this book, 1980

Self-esteem is something probably everyone wants and which everyone definitely needs. We want self-esteem because it increases our chance of finding happiness in life and makes it possible to cope with life's disappointments and changes. We need self-esteem because nothing is as important to psychological well-being. Our level of self-esteem affects virtually everything we think, say and do. It affects how we see the world and our place in it. It affects how others in the world see and treat us. It affects the choices we make—choices about what we will do with our lives and with whom we will be involved. It affects our ability to both give and receive love. And it affects our ability to take action to change things that need to be changed. If a woman has an insufficient amount of self-esteem, she will not be able to act in her own best interest. And if a woman has no self-esteem at all, she will become overwhelmed, immobile and eventually will "give up."[1]

Many women unfortunately have gone through life with a minimum of self-esteem—just enough to enable their survival, but not enough to enable them to live as fully and to be as happy as they might have been. Although everyone needs it, in our culture women's need of self-esteem has traditionally been seen as less great and less urgent than men's need. According to an age-old double standard, high self-esteem is an exclusively male prerogative. In men it is seen as a moral good, and a man who likes and values himself and lets the world know it is considered normal and is said to be demonstrating a healthy self-interest. But a woman who likes and values herself and lets the world know it is condemned for being vain, arrogant and conceited.[2]

This double standard has been around for centuries, and it has colored most of the literature on the subject. When Jean Jacques Rousseau, for example, asserted more than two hundred years ago that *amour de soi*—by which he meant self-love—is "the only natural passion of man," he literally meant man and *only* man. Man, Rousseau said, is driven by the need of self-esteem and cannot love others or even survive unless he loves himself. But when it came to woman, Rousseau did not care much about what drives her or what she may need in order to love and survive. Rousseau saw women as existing solely to be ruled by and to serve men, to bolster men's self-esteem, never to build our own.[3]

More than two hundred years after Rousseau, Pulitzer Prize winner Ernest Becker, too, seems to have meant man and literally man when he said that "self-esteem is the dominant motive of man." In the second edition of *The Birth and Death of Meaning*, published in 1971, Becker throughout uses the terms "man," "he" and "the individual" as he explains the importance of self-esteem, and he uses these terms in such a way as to suggest that by them he means everyone, male and female. But when he starts discussing "the peculiar symbols" that "the individual" keeps running through "his" mind in order to maintain "a warm feeling about himself," the reader comes to understand that the ostensibly genderless individual Becker has in mind is, in fact, very much male. For these "peculiar symbols," Becker tells us, include not only "the money he [the individual] made, the picture he directed, the book he published," but also *"the girl he seduced."* Nowhere does Becker once stop to consider what might be going through the mind of this "girl" or how her self-esteem might have been affected by the seduction. From Becker's point of view, what she feels is apparently not important; she is simply "a peculiar symbol" who exists in the man's mind in order to give him "a warm feeling about himself."[4]

Today, the struggle for self-esteem that women have been undertaking for centuries seems to have a special urgency. When contemporary public figures like Joan Kennedy and Billie Jean King make major decisions in their lives, they announce to the world that their need of self-esteem is the motivating factor, and other women nod knowingly. When women get together to talk about work experiences, such issues as low pay, discriminatory treatment and sexual harassment inevitably come up. But fast on their heels is often one more subject: self-esteem. Bring up the topic in the company of women, as we have often done, and eyes will inevitably light up and someone will likely say, "Self-esteem? You want to hear about a woman with low self-esteem and a lousy self-image? Boy, have I got a story for you."

But then a problem arises, or it often has for us. When we asked women to actually tell their stories for inclusion in this book, many quickly withdrew with the comment, "Oh, you really don't want to bother with me. I'm really not worth it." According to Alfred Adler, "the supreme law" of life should be that "the sense of worth of the self shall not be allowed to be diminished."[5] For women, however, it seems that the sense of worth of the self has not been allowed to develop, or has been allowed to develop only inadequately. Though many women, spurred by the revival of the feminist movement, are presenting themselves more proudly and confidently in public, in the privacy of their own minds too few seem to have favorable images of themselves and hold themselves in high regard, consider themselves truly valuable. Even today in this era of so-called raised consciousness, many of the women we've met habitually downgrade their own worth and when asked to name *one thing* they like about themselves had difficulty coming up with an answer:

> What do I like about myself? God, that's a hard one. I guess I could say my teeth. I have nice teeth. That's the best thing I can say about myself. I have nice teeth.

> I guess I like myself because I'm nice to waitresses and salespeople. I'm not rude to them like lots of people are, and that's good. I suppose that's not a very good answer to your question, but honestly I can't think of anything else.

> You know, I don't go around thinking about this all the time; it's kind of a weird thing to be asked. But if you really want an answer, if I absolutely have to do this, I'll say my disposition. I'm the sort of person who's always easygoing, who never complains. Sometimes I think this is more of a fault than a virtue, but sometimes I like myself for it. No, I can't give you another example. Overall I don't like myself much.

Other women we spoke to couldn't think of anything they like about themselves. Pressed to explain how they typically feel toward themselves, many women described what can only be called self-hatred:

> I guess the feeling I most often have toward myself is this nagging loathing, a kind of disgust. Sometimes everything about me, especially my body,

seems disgusting. Then I get even more disgusted with myself for being so filled with this self-disgust.

There are times when I look in the mirror and want to smash it. Lots of times I feel I'm not worth walking out the door. I see myself as a really useless, small and pathetic person, basically a piece of dirt.

All the women interviewed for this book are functional members of society. Some we met in our Self-esteem Enhancement Groups; others we met at social gatherings, in stores, libraries, hospitals, workplaces and locker rooms; still others we met at demonstrations and workshops, and on planes and buses. They are workers, students, mothers, lovers, wives, friends, all are daughters, and the vast majority lead lives that to an outsider would appear more or less "full." Inside, however, many of these women have gnawing doubts about their own abilities and talents, and are plagued and haunted by the sense that they are without much inherent worth. Not all lack self-esteem to the extent of the women quoted, but few are without self-esteem problems entirely.

Many women accept their low self-esteem as a seemingly unalterable fact of life. Many, taught as most of us were that a good woman is humble and self-effacing, go so far as to maintain that there is something noble and virtuous, something appealing and feminine about self-hatred and self-denigration. What is more, many believe that it really doesn't much matter that they don't love and value themselves. "So what that I have low self-esteem," many interviewees said in essence. "At least I'm not one of those angry women. It's only myself I don't like."

It's only myself I don't like. Consider for a moment how this sentence would sound were just one word changed: It's only Jews I don't like. . . . It's only blacks I don't like. . . . It's only homosexuals I don't like. . . . It's only Chicanos I don't like. . . . It's only children I don't like. . . . It's only foreigners I don't like. . . . It's only old people I don't like. . . . It's only whites I don't like. . . . Consider the shock, the disapproval, the winces such statements would typically be met with. Then consider for a moment whether there isn't a connection between disliking oneself and disliking, for example, blacks, Jews and homosexuals. As Rollo May has phrased it, "The steps are not big from the feeling of worthlessness of one's self to self-hatred to hatred for others."[6]

It's only myself I don't like. Having considered some of the external implications of these words, now consider the internal sadness, the draining away of aspiration, of hope, of energy, of dreams to which they are sorry testimony. Consider, in short, the heartbreak caused by the feeling that one is of little worth. Although some women will remain unconvinced that their own unhappiness is of great consequence, we believe this unhappiness is in itself sufficient evidence of the need to devote attention to the issue of women and self-esteem.

Another reason self-esteem is an especially important issue for women is that our individual levels of self-esteem also have political implications, affecting our actions and status as a group. Women in a male-dominated world face many formidable obstacles men do not face. These obstacles aren't going to magically disappear. Women must bring them down by standing up against them. Every gain women have made in obtaining greater equality in the workplace, in the eyes of the law, in religious institutions, in the media, in the professions and in the inter-personal sphere has been at the cost of enormous struggle on the part of individual women working together. Sustaining that sort of struggle, and mounting new struggles, requires that we women value ourselves. When one woman suffers the unhappiness of feeling that she is not worth much, nor capable of much either, it's easy to say hers is an individual problem. But when thousands of us suffer from lack of self-worth and have limited views of our capabilities, then what we are talking about is a group problem of enormous political implications. Only by raising ourselves in our own estimation can we bring all women up.

But what exactly do we mean when we use the term self-esteem? In everyday conversation and in the professional literature the term is often thrown about loosely, used interchangeably with self-respect, self-love and a sense of self-worth, and also with the term "self-concept." In fact, though, these terms are not all interchangeable. The self-concept or self-image is the set of beliefs and images we all have and hold to be true of ourselves. By contrast, our level of self-esteem (or self-respect, self-love or self-worth) is the measure of how much we like and approve of our self-concept.[7] Or, as we've heard it put, "self-esteem is the reputation you have with yourself."[8]

A person's self-concept will usually contain a wide variety of images and beliefs. Some of these are simply statements of facts whose accuracy is easily verifiable: I am a woman; I am tall; I am black; I am a mother; I am a student; I am a lesbian; I am a secretary; I am poor. Others refer to less tangible aspects of the self, and their accuracy is not so easy to verify: I am smart; I am ugly; I am incompetent; I am sexy; I am unlovable; I am no good; I am worthless.

All the various beliefs and images that go into our self-concepts have one thing in common: None was with us at birth. To be sure, everyone is born with concrete physical characteristics and undiscovered capacities. But no one is born knowing she is male or female, black or white; nor does anyone come into the world already thinking she is stupid or smart, pretty or ugly, shy or outgoing, strong or weak, lovable or unlovable, generally inadequate or basically okay. As far as ideas and impressions of herself are concerned, the newborn can be said to begin life with a "blank slate." Just as she later learns that she is a girl, that her hair is black, that her name is Susie Brown and that she is the daughter of John and Mary Brown, so, too, she learns to think of herself as stupid or smart, pretty or ugly, shy or outgoing, strong or weak, lovable or unlovable, generally inadequate or basically okay.

Many of the basic ideas we have about ourselves were acquired prior to adulthood, and from two main sources: how others treated us and what they told us about ourselves. In early infancy, nonverbal communication played the most crucial role: Depending on how much affection, food, touching and physical warmth was received, for example, we as infants obtained general impressions about whether we were loved and worthy. Then with the development of language capacity we began to translate these general impressions into specific words within our minds, and what others told us about ourselves started to have as much impact on our developing self-concepts as how they treated us. As Morris Rosenberg puts it, "People, as social animals, are deeply influenced by the attitudes of others toward the self" and over the course of time, we come to view ourselves essentially as we are viewed by others.[9]

As we grew up and learned basic ideas about who we are and what we're about, each of us also learned strong ideas about who we should be and what we should be like. Whereas our ideas about who we actually are make up the self-concept or perceived or "as is" self, our ideas about who we should be form our ideal self. Typically, we constantly compare our perceived self to our ideal self, and the wider the gap between the two the lower our level of self-esteem.

None of the ideal standards by which we judge ourselves was with us at birth. Just as no one comes into the world already thinking of herself as a girl, no one comes into the world with any idea whatsoever of what it means to be a good girl. We had to be taught to believe we should be a certain way, and the specific ideals and standards by which we judge ourselves will vary from culture to culture, and even from individual to individual within the same culture.

Taken one by one, each image and belief that goes into a woman's self-concept has bearing on her self-esteem. But the self-concept is not simply a sum of its parts, for when we put the various images and beliefs we have of ourselves together in our minds, we don't give each one equal weight and prominence. Rather, we put the various components together so that the self-concept resembles a collage. Those beliefs and images that are most important to our identity and sense of self-worth (for example, I am a woman; I am a mother; I am incompetent/competent; I am pretty/ugly) will be placed in the center and foreground of the collage, and constitute the core self-concept. Those beliefs and images that are less important to our identity and sense of self-worth (for example, I am a good cook; I am left-handed; I am unathletic) will be placed toward the periphery of the collage, outside the core of the self-concept.

Because of the way we structure our self-concepts, it's possible to have a self-concept containing mostly positive beliefs—a positive self-concept—and still lack self-esteem. No matter how many positive images and beliefs a woman has of herself, if she puts them off to the side of her self-concept, downplaying their importance, low self-esteem will result.

There are actually two types of self-esteem—global and specific. Global self-esteem is the measure of how much we like and approve of our perceived self as a whole. Specific self-esteem is the measure of how much we like and approve of a certain part of ourself. If a woman places a high value on a certain aspect of herself (her looks or intelligence, for example) her global self-esteem will be greatly affected by her specific self-esteem in that one area. But if a woman doesn't value a certain aspect (her cooking skills, for example) her specific self-esteem in that area won't have much impact on her overall or global self-esteem.

Many people confuse global self-esteem and self-confidence. They look at a professionally competent woman, say they wish they had her confidence, and automatically assume she likes and values herself overall. This is not necessarily the case. She may have high specific self-esteem based on her knowledge that she is a good leader and decision maker. But at this point in her life she may not value her work as much as she does sexual relationships, and since she has been without a lover for more than a year, her global self-esteem may be low. Although self-confidence often accompanies high global self-esteem, one can have one without the other.

Some women fear that having high global self-esteem means being arrogant, vain, conceited, egotistical, selfish, and feeling superior and insensitive to others. But this is not the case. Such traits are most common among people with *low* self-esteem. A person who has high self-esteem does not vainly consider herself the center of the universe or see herself as better than others. But she also doesn't see herself as a valueless, inconsequential creature who is worse than others. She simply knows many aspects of herself, has respect for herself, is aware and appreciative of her own worth. She knows she has good qualities, but she doesn't delude herself into believing she is perfect. On the contrary, she is probably very much aware that she has flaws and makes mistakes. Rather than seeing her flaws and mistakes as representative of her worthlessness as a human being, however, she sees them as representative of the fact that she is human.

Some women are also afraid that having high global self-esteem means being narcissistic. Again, however, people whose self-esteem is *low* are the ones most likely to be narcissistic. Moreover, although there are women who display some of the traits associated with narcissism, we believe it could be argued that true narcissism is much more common among men than women—that narcissism is, in fact, a predominantly male problem. As properly defined, narcissism is characterized by a grandiose sense of self-importance; recurrent fantasies of unlimited success, power, brilliance, beauty or ideal love; a craving for constant attention and admiration; feelings of rage, humiliation, or haughty indifference when criticized or defeated; and at least two of the following —a sense of entitlement; exploitiveness, the tendency to take advantage of others and to disregard their rights; oscillation between extreme over-idealization and devaluation of others; and lack of empathy, meaning not just an inability to recognize how others feel, but often an inability to see that others have feelings at all.[10] While not all men display these traits, it nonetheless remains true that the traits that characterize narcissism are precisely the traits that white men in Western culture have been displaying for centuries. Traditionally, among white men these traits have been considered beyond criticism, even admirable, as John Russell points out:

> Men were big in ancient Egypt, big in Greece and Rome, big in the Middle Ages, big in the Renaissance. You only have to look at the history of art to see that men were once the measure of all things. Their physical proportions were ideal . . . Our notions of wisdom, justice, regularity, and endurance were man-based, man-oriented, man-regulated . . . "Man-sized" was a compliment. "Manliness" was a digest of all the virtues. God had made man in his own image, and he'd done a great job.
>
> High art propagated all this wherever it could, and popular art was glad

to take it up. There was no limit to what people would believe about men. If a head of state was spoken as Stupor Mundi—Wonder of the World—no one laughed. If the young Albrecht Dürer painted himself as the most beautiful human being who ever trod the earth, no one reached for the word "narcissist."[11]

Finally, some women confuse high global self-esteem and total self-assurance. But having high global self-esteem does not mean being free of all self-doubts. It's probably impossible for anyone, no matter how high her global self-esteem, to go through life without ever doubting her worth. Feeling occasionally inadequate and uncertain about one's own value and the value of one's life may simply be part and parcel of the human condition, an inevitable and natural consequence of consciousness; and it may be healthy. Yet there's a difference between occasionally doubting and always being uncertain, and there's nothing healthy about a woman chronically feeling she isn't "worth it." High self-esteem doesn't protect us from self-doubts, but it does enable us to entertain self-doubt without being devastated.

* 2 *

Women and Self-Esteem:
Six Common Problems

Among the women we interviewed we found six self-esteem problems to be most common:

There's not much of a self there: Some women lack self-esteem because they lack sufficient knowledge of who they are, and thus feel they have no true self to like and value. Although in an ideal world everyone would reach mid-life with a pretty clear idea of who she is and what she's about, in our world women traditionally have not been encouraged to "know thyself" as men have been admonished to do, and women historically have been denied the opportunities for self-discovery that many men take for granted. As a result, many women we interviewed had great difficulty describing themselves at all. "Shot full of holes," "full of gaps," "a big blank"—these are phrases with which women described themselves to us. In her interviews with 160 mid-life women, Lillian Rubin came across the same sort of responses. Asked to briefly describe themselves "in some way that would give a good sense of 'who and what you are,' " most of the women Rubin interviewed had trouble coming up with an answer, and nearly one quarter could not answer the question at all. "In embarrassment," Rubin recalls, "they finally said one version or another of:

> *I'm blank. Maybe there just isn't much of a self there."*[1]

A woman who sees herself as a blank has virtually no chance of experiencing self-esteem.

I'm a good woman—so what?: Some women have well-defined self-concepts yet suffer low self-esteem because their sense of who they are is greatly constricted. We see this problem particularly among women who have defined themselves in conformity with our culture's traditional feminine stereotypes. Women in this situation commonly describe themselves as wives, mothers, and kind, caring and unselfish people. In short, they see themselves as everything our society says a good woman should be. Yet they often don't feel good about themselves, because kindness, caring and nurturing and the other qualities associated with being a good woman are not highly valued in our culture. Or as one woman put it, "When you're a good woman in this society, it's looked on as no big deal."

The unhappiness felt by women suffering from the "I'm a good woman—so what?" syndrome underscores the crucial role that cultural conditioning plays in determining how we see and judge ourselves. Just as none of us came into this world already thinking of ourselves in a certain way, none of us learned to see and judge ourselves as we do in a vacuum. Rather, we learned to see ourselves and judge ourselves within the context of a culture that has always held females to be inherently one way (emotional, illogical, unmechanical, physically weak, etc.) and males to be inherently another way (tough, logical, mechanical, physically strong, etc.). Existing evidence indicates that perhaps as early as age one but no later than age three, children come to think of themselves not as persons but as males or females, and that from then on gender identity is *the* cornerstone of the self-concept.[2] Once a child has become aware that "I am male" or "I am female," she quickly learns the culture's definitions of what it means to be male or female, and the rest of her beliefs about herself fall into line—or out of line—accordingly. As Fay Fransella and Kay Frost note:

> Our ideas of ourselves do not simply reflect self-observation. We organize, interpret and reinterpret what we find ourselves doing on the basis of notions we already have of what we are about. . . . These basic notions are not constructed from thin air. All societies have systems of belief, more or less shared, about the nature and appropriate behavior of men and women. . . .[3]

The belief that there is one set of behavior and characteristics appropriate for and germane to males, and another for females, has a limiting effect on members of both sexes; in assembling their self-concepts, neither girls nor boys have freedom to pick and choose from the complete pool of human behavior and characteristics. Overall, however, sex-role stereotypes are far more limiting and debilitating to women than to men, for the realm of human experience and behavior that has been designated female is much more narrowly defined than the range that has been labeled male. Consider as an example the widely known Broverman study, in which seventy-nine mental health professionals were asked to describe the characteristics of a healthy adult, a healthy male, and a healthy female. In their compilation they came up with thirty-seven healthy male attributes but only eleven healthy female attributes, and what was considered healthy in one sex was not considered healthy in the other.[4] Here is a sample:

Healthy Male Attributes	Healthy Female Attributes
Very independent	Very strong need for security
Not at all emotional	Very aware of feelings of others
Likes math and science very much	Enjoys art and literature very much
Very worldly	Very interested in own appearance
Almost always acts as a leader	Easily expresses tender feelings

To make matters worse, men and women in our culture are not just seen as inherently different; men are seen as inherently superior to women, and the traits commonly associated with males (e.g., rationality, independence, leadership ability) are the ones this culture values most; whereas the traits commonly associated with females (e.g., emotionality, sensitivity, cooperativeness) are those this culture values least. Not surprisingly, then, in the Broverman study the descriptions of the healthy adult and the healthy male were much the same, while the healthy female was described in direct contrast to the healthy adult. This demonstrates the no-win situation of women in our culture: Either limit your concept of yourself to eleven passive attributes and be a healthy woman, or betray your womanhood by going beyond these attributes and run the risk of being branded as unfeminine and maladjusted.

Given this situation, it is inevitable that many women have come to have low self-esteem. Many of the women we have spoken to have worked hard to live up to our culture's expectations of them. Yet in the process many of these women have learned to devalue the very traits they have aspired to, and consequently have come to look down upon themselves, painting even their positive attributes in a negative light. Only rarely in our interviews did we hear women say, "I'm a good mother and housewife; it's too bad this culture doesn't value that." Instead, women were far more likely to say in self-deprecation, "I'm *only* a mother and a housewife." Similarly, we heard very few women say, "I'm a terrific secretary; it's really unfair that secretarial work is considered so unimportant." Instead, we heard many women say, "I'm *just* a secretary. Big deal."

Compounding the problems created by sex-role stereotypes are the additional barriers to self-development imposed on women because of racism, ageism, classism, homophobia, religious prejudice, and our society's structural and attitudinal inaccessability to people with disabilities. Many women take great pride, for example, in being women of color, in being lesbians, in being Jewish, or in being working-class. But such women still often find their opportunities for self-definition constricted because of cultural stereotypes about their particular groups.

But let me tell you what I'm not . . . . : Unlike those women who at least see themselves as good in some area, some women see themselves as failures in every area. Asked to describe themselves, such women do not hesitate. Instead, they immediately launch into a string of negatives. "Well," a woman with this problem would say, "I'm not all that attractive, not all that smart, not very good at sports, not as capable as the other women who work in my office, not as well-informed as my husband, not as much fun to be around as my friend Anne, not as caring as I should be, not as involved in community activities or as well-read as I should be. . . ."

Women with the "but let me tell you what I'm not" syndrome tend to have extremely high standards for themselves, standards so high as to be virtually impossible to live up to. Moreover, they often have impossibly high standards in a number of different and conflicting areas; they not only want to be perfect, they want to be perfect at everything they do. For them, self-assessment is an all-or-nothing game: either I am perfect or a total mess; either I am stick-thin or I am a fat slob; either I am extremely competent and well-informed or I am totally incompetent and a complete ignoramus; either I am always measuring up or I am always failing.

Because their way of thinking allows for no middle ground between complete failure and complete success, women with the "but let me tell you what I'm not" syndrome greatly exaggerate the severity of their flaws. Time and again, women who are moderately or only slightly overweight have told us they see themselves as grossly obese; women who have large noses have told us they have the world's ugliest, largest noses; women who have muscular legs have told us they envision themselves as having "elephant" legs; women who have sometimes short tempers have told us they view themselves as incredible bitches; women who are mildly moody have told us they see themselves as manic-depressives; women who are lackluster cooks have told us they consider themselves horrible cooks; women who are sometimes late have told us they consider themselves always unpunctual; women who are occasionally slow to catch on to certain ideas and things have told us they see themselves as consistently "out of it" and stupid . . . the list could go on.

If I'm good at that, then it really can't matter: Some women don't see themselves in an entirely or even predominantly negative light—yet they still lack self-esteem. Many women are well aware that they "measure up" in a variety of respects. The problem for them is that they have trouble convincing themselves that their good qualities matter as much as their flaws and failings. "Oh, I know I've got a nice face, that I'm pretty bright, a good teacher, a kind person and all that," a woman might say. "But," she is quick to add, "I should lose ten pounds." In this woman's self-concept collage, those ten pounds occupy the most prominent position, and they loom so large as to make all the positive images and beliefs she has of herself pale by comparison.

The trouble for women such as this is that their self-concepts lack structural balance. Women with this problem usually are accurate in perceiving that they have both flaws and positive attributes. But they cannot put their flaws and positive traits in proper perspective, seeing their flaws as relatively minor parts of themselves. Instead, they shove their positive attributes off to the side of their self-concepts and focus on their flaws, no matter how small, as if their flaws were the most significant things about them.

Preoccupation with flaws, whether they be real, exaggerated or entirely imagined, was quite common among the women we interviewed. Some women go so far as to focus on their flaws to the point where they feel a total identification with them. Or as one woman explained:

> I never gain weight, get a pimple, or make a dumb remark. That weight, that pimple, that remark—I feel they become me.

The woman who feels she is a pimple when she has one happens to be an extremely attractive, vivacious and funny professional with a Ph.D. She does not have a self-concept in which negative images and beliefs outnumber the positive ones. In fact, her self-concept contains many more positives than negatives. Still, she lacks self-esteem because the structure of her self-concept is grossly distorted. She sees herself as if through warped lenses.

Considerable research has been done on the "self-enhancing tendency," meaning the tendency to place the highest value on those areas in which one rates oneself highest. When men have been studied, the self-enhancing tendency has been shown to be particularly strong. That is, if a man excels in a certain area—athletics, say—he is likely to value that area highly and to give his athletic self a prominent position in his overall self-concept, thereby enhancing his self-esteem. Among women, however, the opposite tends to be the case. "If I'm good at that," many women say, "then it really can't matter." What matters, and matters most of all, to many women is precisely the one area—or few areas—in which they rate themselves the lowest, and the low grade they give themselves on one or two specific points becomes the gauge by which they measure their entire worth.[5]

I'm not the person I used to be: Some women have low self-esteem because of something we call self-concept dislocation. Self-concept dislocation occurs when a major event in a person's life forces her to change the way she looks at and thinks about herself, sometimes radically. A woman who has recently had a mastectomy or gotten divorced, for example, will probably go through self-concept dislocation.

Self-concept dislocation can be problematic for two reasons. First, it often takes a while to integrate a new set of beliefs about the self into the self-concept. Second, even when the new beliefs have been integrated, it can take a long time to convince oneself that the new self is okay.

If a woman's global self-esteem has been high, the low self-esteem brought on by self-concept dislocation will probably be temporary. But a woman with a history of low self-esteem will have greater difficulty adjusting to change. Moreover, some types of change in our views of who we are can be unusually difficult to adjust to, regardless of how high our previous level of self-esteem. For example, if a woman has a permanently disabling injury or accident, or is stricken with terminal cancer, multiple sclerosis, rheumatoid arthritis or another disease whose effects are long-term and cumulative, her self-concept dislocation may be severe, and the low self-esteem it ushers in may be long-lasting.

We have found that women are particularly likely to suffer self-concept dislocation and consequently low self-esteem in the wake of the loss of a loved one, whether through death or the dissolution of a relationship. Any loss is bound to bring up feelings of sadness and despondency, and since most of us do not like to think of ourselves as sad and despondent, we might berate ourselves for not feeling better during our times of grief:

I always thought of myself as someone who was pretty resilient and coped well. But when my mother died, I felt so bad for so long. I couldn't bounce back so fast, and I felt terrible for being so gloomy and tired and such a drag for other people to be around. I kept wanting to return to my cheery, resilient, energetic old self, and berating myself for not returning to it. Then it occurred to me that maybe I'd never return to my old self—that maybe this experience was of the magnitude that it would change me permanently. Now I have bounced back in a lot of ways. But in the deepest part of me there's an edge of sadness and vulnerability that wasn't there before, and I don't think I'll ever be quite the same old self I was.

Exhaustion can also bring about self-concept dislocation and with it low self-esteem. Most of us do not like to think of ourselves as lacking in energy, and so just feeling tired and listless (whether because of illness, lack of sleep, overwork, or improper diet) can be enough to cause us to condemn ourselves. Moreover, when we are tired, we are most vulnerable to feelings of insecurity, anxiety and self-dissatisfaction.

Self-concept dislocation is not only triggered by unhappy experiences. Anytime a woman makes a major change in her life—whether by getting married, going back to school, having a baby or changing jobs—her concept of herself will be forced to change, and she may have difficulty adjusting to the new image she has of herself. A woman's level of global self-esteem may shift as she goes through different stages of life, and, aging in itself is bound to bring about a certain amount of self-concept dislocation in a culture that so dreads getting old.

The discovery of new information about the self, even welcome information, can bring about self-concept dislocation, too. For example, a woman who was raised, as most of us were, to think of herself as a heterosexual but who later discovers she is not a heterosexual can suffer severe self-concept dislocation, even though she is glad of the discovery. This woman explains:

The problem for me isn't coming out of the closet so much as it is coming to terms with all the consequences of realizing I'm a lesbian. I lived my life as a heterosexual for thirty-three years, got married, had three kids, did the whole trip. All the while I knew something wasn't quite right and then I slowly realized, "Wow, I'm a lesbian—that's it!" It was a relief to finally be able to admit that. I mean, I had been ignoring the truth about me for all those years. But dealing with all the implications has still been pretty hard. I mean, I grew up in a God-fearing, churchgoing family in the South, and I never thought of myself as different or as an outcast. Then here I am a minority-group member.

I'm not so sure who I should be anymore: As a self-esteem crisis can be triggered by the necessity for readjusting our concept of who we are, one can also be precipitated by a shift in our image of who we want to be. Consider, for example, a woman who was raised with the rigid expectation that she prove her worth by getting married and having children. At first she rejects this ideal, choosing instead to remain single and to pursue a career in advertising, something she goes on to do with success. Going through her twenties and early thirties, she is happy with her choices, and because she's lived up to her ideal self—successful, independent career woman—she is happy with herself.

As she nears her late thirties, however, this woman feels less happy with herself. She begins questioning the value of the advertising profession, and more and more often she thinks that maybe she should put her energy into a line of work that would contribute more to society—maybe teaching the disabled or lobbying for racial and sexual equality—she can't decide. At the same time, as she approaches the end of her prime childbearing years, she has begun to wonder whether she might not want to have a baby after all. To exacerbate her confusion, her father died two years ago, now her mother is seriously ill, needing considerable care, and she is wondering if she shouldn't go back to her hometown to nurse her mother. Doing so would complicate her life; she is well aware of that. But a part of her feels she should care for her mother, just as a part of her feels she should change careers and another part feels she should have a baby while she still has time.

The woman we have described is a woman whose ideal self is in transition. When she compares her image of herself to her old ideal self—independent, successful career woman—she feels good about herself. But when she starts comparing her image of herself to all the other ideal images she's now running through her mind—the ideal of herself as a worker in a helping profession, the ideal of herself as a political activist, the ideal of herself as a mother, the ideal of herself as a good and nurturing daughter—she feels rotten about herself. Until she's able to decide what new ideals she wants to pursue, and until she starts taking action that will bring her closer to those goals, she will probably continue to experience low global self-esteem.

Regardless of what we do with our lives, we are all bound to go through periods when our ideals are in question and in transition, and our self-esteem will plummet or be shaky as a result. The woman who has devoted herself to her husband and children, the woman who has devoted herself to her career, the woman who has devoted herself to her parents, the woman who has devoted herself to religious work or political change—all may seem very different, but all will probably wake up one day asking, "Is this all there is?" And all of us, as we change, grow and mature, are destined to sometimes stop and ask, "What is the meaning of life? Have I spent my life well, or are there other things I should have done with it?" Such questions are normal and healthy. But during the often prolonged and arduous process of searching for some answers that we can live with over the long run, we in the meantime may have great difficulty living with, accepting and valuing ourselves.

BLUEPRINTS FOR CHANGE

I. SEEING OURSELVES AS FRIENDS

This is an exercise adapted from Dorothy Corkille Briggs's *Celebrate Yourself.*[6] We use it at the first meeting of each self-esteem group.

Get very comfortable in a chair. Close your eyes. Picture someone you love or like very much sitting across from you. Tell that person a few things you like about him or her. Say at least three things. Go on if you can. Stop when you feel ready.

Was that difficult for you? Could you see him or her clearly? How many things did you have to say?

Now try to visualize yourself sitting across from you. Tell yourself at least three things you like about yourself. Go on if you can. Stop when you feel ready. Remember, at least three things.

Was that more or less difficult for you than the first exercise? Could you see yourself as clearly? Did you have as many things to say about yourself?

Nearly all the women in our groups had an easier time visualizing and complimenting their imaginary friend than themselves. Don't think ill of yourself if this is the case with you too.

II. SELF-CONCEPT COLLAGE

Often it is helpful to create an actual collage to delineate what your self-concept contains. Take a sheet of paper and place on it symbols (words, drawings, images from magazines) which represent your beliefs about yourself. Place in the middle of the sheet those beliefs about yourself which you consider most important to your identity and self-worth; this is the core self-concept. Away from the core toward the periphery, place those other beliefs about yourself that are less important to your identity and self-worth. The collage might include straight-forward facts (I am a woman, I am black, I am tall, I have acne), roles (I am a daughter, I am a mother, I am a teacher, I am a lover), interests (I play tennis, I am a political activist, I love cats, I study Spanish) and attributes (I am smart, I am ugly, I am ill-tempered, I am funny). Whatever you feel is important about you—no matter if you believe it is negative or positive or neutral—should have a place on the collage.

You might want to use this collage as a point of reference as you learn more about how your self-concept was formed. As you identify inaccurate, negative beliefs about yourself, you might consider symbolically replacing them with more accurate, positive beliefs. Or perhaps you will want to shift images from your periphery into the core or vice versa.

III. THE IDEAL SELF-CONCEPT

It can also be helpful to make a collage representing your ideal self—the self you feel you want to be and/or should be. Compare this with the collage of who you believe you really are. Is the gap between them insurmountable? If so, can you revise your notions of who you should be so that they are more reasonable?

IV. PUTTING OURSELVES IN PERSPECTIVE

This meditation can help us to see ourselves in perspective, not in the distorted way we often see ourselves.[7] Of each role, attribute, self-description, etc., you place in your self-concept collage, try saying the following:

My _____ is a part of me; I am not my _____ .

This helps us see that no aspect of ourselves, no matter how much we like it or dislike it, alone represents us. A woman who tried this elaborates:

> I have no problem saying "My bad temper is a part of me; I am not my bad temper," or "My fragility is a part of me; I am not my fragility." But when it came to things like my intelligence or accomplishments or emotional strength, I thought, "Wait a minute, *I am too* these wonderful things." I really resented the notion that those parts weren't the whole story. But then I saw that it's the type of thinking that keeps me from accepting myself. When my bad temper or fragility was revealed, I used to think "Oh, God, this is all of me." If I continue to boost my ego by sometimes thinking my achievements or intelligence are all of me, I'll still be vulnera-

ble to those times when I think I'm totally defined by the other real but not so wonderful parts of me.

When you focus on one or a few negative aspects of yourself and begin to feel worthless as a result, we encourage you to try this meditation. Seeing that aspect realistically as one part but not the whole of you will help you to accept that aspect. It will also free you to change it if that's what you chose to do.

V. EXAMINING ILLUSION

Dorothy Corkille Briggs has outlined some illusions that we people with low self-esteem need to discard if we are going to feel better about ourselves. Says Briggs:

> You give up the *illusion* that the pain of the past is known and therefore preferable.
>
> You give up the *illusion* that those who rejected you originally were omniscient . . . that they saw you accurately.
>
> You let go of the *illusion* that you put together the package called "Me" accurately.
>
> You give up the *illusions* created by false programmings—untruths you've based your life on.
>
> You give up the *illusion* that you have no other choice.[8]

Do you have any of these illusions? Can you add any to the list?

VI. SETTING PRIORITIES

Sometimes the task of improving self-esteem seems overwhelming because a woman believes she has to make her entire self over into a more worthy being. But building self-esteem more often means learning to accept who you already are rather than creating a new you. To do this, we need to establish a set of priorities. Accepting yourself totally won't come overnight, so it's helpful to decide which areas you want to deal with first, and leave others on the back burner. One of our group members explained how she tackles one problem at a time:

> I look at the areas I need to gain self-acceptance in as slides in one of those carousel slide projectors that can keep going around and around and never stop. I'll press the button, and the slide that will come up will say WEIGHT. I think "no, can't deal with my weight today—on to the next one." The next slide will say MOM and I might think, "no, I'm not ready to deal with my relationship with my mother either." Maybe the next one says MONEY

and I might think "Oh, now there's something I can deal with—the time is right for me to start coming to terms with all the anxiety and problems I have around the money issue." So, I go about doing whatever I need to do about it and I know that MOM and WEIGHT and lots of others are just going to have to wait and that's OK.

VII. I LIKE MYSELF BECAUSE

In our Self-esteem Enhancement Groups, each member each of the seven weeks made three note cards, each beginning "I like myself because . . ." The reasons they gave did not need to be profound; little things count, too. At the last session of the group, each woman made a note card for every other group member stating "I like you because . . ." Each woman thus ended up with twenty-eight note cards that could remind her of reasons to like herself. Such reminders can only help a woman's self-esteem; they surely can't hurt.

Although it might sound silly, we suggest you at least try making "I like myself because" cards, and perhaps share cards with your friends as well. Remember, little things count. At first, most women have a difficult time with this and don't want to commit themselves to any positive statement that is far-reaching in its implications. But as long as it is accurate and specific and positive, any reason for liking yourself is appropriate.

VIII. VISUALIZING OUR LOW SELF-ESTEEM

Can you visualize your self-esteem as an object or living being? For instance, one woman we know visualizes her low self-esteem as a warm, fuzzy bear she clings to tightly when she is afraid to take a risk. Her "fuzzy bear" protects her from taking the risk. Another woman we know says she "reaches" for her low self-esteem in the morning in the same way other people grope around for their eyeglasses when they first wake up. She says she wakes up thinking, "Now, what am I going to hate about myself today?" and does not come fully awake until she finds what it is. How would you visualize any low self-esteem you have? What does it do for you? How would you visualize any high self-esteem you have? What does that do for you?

PART TWO

*

*Close to Home,
Close to the Heart:
Intimate Relationships
and the Shaping of
Self-Attitudes*

* 1 *

Introduction

We have learned to see and think of ourselves as we do primarily on the basis of how others have treated us and what they have told us about ourselves. But not all others count equally. The people who have the most impact on our self-perceptions and attitudes are those we are or were most intimately involved with; usually the more we care about a person, the more we will care about his or her opinion of us, whether expressed through words or actions.

When we were children, the people closest to our hearts were members of our families, particularly our parents or surrogate parents. They had the greatest influence on our developing self-concepts and sense of worth. Yet even while we were still young children, most of us had friendships with people outside the family, and especially as we grew older, these extrafamilial relationships with friends, lovers and spouses also had an impact on our self-concepts and self-esteem. Finally, our self-images and sense of worth are further affected by our experiences of having—or not having—children ourselves. Precisely *how* various relationships with those we hold close to the heart affect the way we see and judge ourselves is the subject of this section.

* 2 *

Different Families, Different Fates

The actuarial conditions that might have influenced her fate include such factors as what sex the child turns out to be, her place in the birth order of siblings (and how it relates to the parents' places in their own early families), the stage of the marriage at which she was born, the family's economic situation and so on. Her destiny did not have anything to do with what sort of child she really was.

—Sheldon B. Kopp
If You Meet the Buddha on the Road, Kill Him!

Most of us first experienced life as members of a family. Our parents and siblings were the first people we came to know. Our first experiences with both love and conflict most likely happened within our family. And our first ideas about ourselves were learned from our family.

Many women believe there must be some inherent justice to which family they were born into. If a woman's family was nurturing and helpful, that must be what she deserved. If, on the other hand, a woman's family was destructive and uncaring and taught her that she was unlovable, that must be what she deserved. But there is nothing rational or just about which family we happened to end up in; the assignment was random, part of the crap shoot of life.

Our early family experiences greatly influenced our self-concepts, too often in negative ways.

Stanley Coopersmith examined Karen Horney's work on self-demeaning feelings,[1] and concluded that parents undermine their children's self-esteem and create "basic anxiety" in their children "through domination, indifference, lack of respect, disparagement, lack of admiration, lack of warmth, isolation and discrimination." The cause of this treatment, he holds, is

> parental egocentricity, which means the parents' wants, needs, beliefs are always more important than the children's and the children are not recognized as *learning* beings. The parent has little sense that their active or passive disregard for the child is teaching the child that she is not worth much. Such treatment results in either outright self-hatred, or an idealized, defensive sense of self which insures frustration, failure and unhappiness for the child.[2]

Coopersmith's conclusions are essentially on target, but they unfortunately seem to attribute sinister motives to the parents. Low self-esteem is *not* usually inculcated in children through conscious or deliberate efforts on the part of the parents. Very few of our parents, if any, brought their infants home, leaned over the crib and said, "If I play my cards right, you'll really hate yourself when you grow up." Typically, the parents of a child with low self-esteem had low self-esteem themselves. Our parents might not have recognized the tremendous power they had in shaping their child's sense of self. Or perhaps they were unable to use their power wisely and well. Raising healthy children is a difficult task, and unfortunately, many through history have found themselves faced with this task at a time when they were not yet equipped for it—emotionally, physically or financially.

To understand what happened to us—and why—after we were born, we need to know about things that happened before we were born. For those of us who had two parents involved in our lives, or one parent and another significant adult (a grandmother, say), the family existed before us. Coming into a family is much like walking in on a party that has been going full blast for some time. There is no guarantee that we will be welcomed, that we will "fit in" with what is already going on, or that we will even understand what is going on. The quality of our parents' relationship with one another, our place in the birth order, their reasons for wanting (or not wanting) us, economic conditions, pre-existing family problems (e.g., illness), the number of children overall—these and other factors all had a bearing on the receptions we received. Yet it's important to realize that we were not responsible for any of these conditions.

Our family's economic situation at the time of our birth and in childhood may have had a huge impact on determining how we eventually came to see and rate ourselves. If there was not enough money to go around, we may have been seen as just an additional mouth to feed.

Coopersmith found that parents' uncertainty about a living wage, underemployment and unemployment correlated with low self-esteem in the children. When daily survival dominated the parents' time and energy, there probably wasn't much left over to devote to a child, and she may have gotten the message that she was a burden.

It has not been substantiated that there is a necessary and causal link between low socioeconomic standing and low self-esteem in children. There is no guarantee that if one was raised in a financially well-off family she will have developed high self-esteem, or that if one is raised in a poor family she will have developed low self-esteem. The crucial factor in terms of self-esteem development is the quality of the parent-child relationship. We have spoken to numerous women who grew up in extremely well-off families yet whose parents were inattentive, abusive, alcoholic and/or disturbed; these women may have been born with the proverbial silver spoon in their mouths, but they still grew up without high self-worth. Conversely, several women we interviewed grew up in poverty or near poverty, yet their parents made up for what they could not give their children materially by spending much loving time with them. These women grew up knowing they are lovable and worthy. By working early and being treated as responsible, some also developed a sense of competence and autonomy that many more financially privileged women failed to attain.

Although money does not automatically bring a child self-esteem and lack of money does not automatically preclude self-esteem, lack of financial security can have a disruptive effect on the quality of the relationships within a family, and this in turn can adversely affect children's self-esteem. Perhaps money problems helped to spark arguments or even bring on an eventual rift between a woman's parents. Perhaps the father, unable to find work, felt compelled to leave his wife and children so that they could be eligible for welfare. Perhaps lack of money prevented the family from taking care of health and dental problems among the children. . . . We could go on with a long list of possibilities here, but the main point is this: While there is no guarantee that money will give children an edge in self-esteem development, a child who grows up in a family where there is not enough money to insure a basic standard of living faces obstacles to self-esteem that children in financially secure families do not face. Moreover, particularly among the urban poor, and now increasingly among the rural poor, the child will definitely suffer the pain of social stigma. Perhaps Kenneth Keniston and the Carnegie Council on Children describe the plight of poor children best:

Poor children live in a particularly dangerous world. . . . Whether in city or country, there is a world where cavities go unfilled and ear infections threatening permanent deafness go untreated. It is a world where even a small child learns to be ashamed of the way he or she lives. And it is frequently a world of intense social dangers, where many adults, driven by poverty and desperation, seem untrustworthy and unpredictable. Children who learn the skills for survival in that world, suppressing curiosity and cultivating a defensive guardedness toward novelty or a constant readiness to attack, may not be able to acquire the basic skills and values that are needed, for better or worse, to thrive in mainstream society.

In some ways we might even say that such children are systematically trained to fail. The covert lessons their environment teaches them about themselves are astonishingly consistent. Such children are smart enough to sense from an early age that the world of mainstream America defined them and their parents as no-good, inadequate, dirty, incompetent and stupid. This sense of self, constantly reinforced, in fact is an accurate perception of the messages our society gives these children.[3]

There have been better and worse times to be poor, of course. Growing up poor during the Great Depression of the 1930s, for example, a child might have felt less stigma than had she grown up poor in the 1960s.

A mother's employment outside the home can be both a reflection of the family's economic circumstances and a source of concern for the child's self-esteem. If our mothers had jobs, did their absence communicate to us the message that we were unlovable? All the evidence answers with a resounding *no* if our mothers were happy to be working, people important to her supported her in working, and quality child care was available. Even today when the majority of mothers of young children work, these can be rather large ifs. Yet studies show that children of mothers who were content to work benefited from the role model of a woman competent at something outside the home as well as within. Girl children gain particularly in estimation of their own sex. The children with problems were children of women who were clearly unhappy with working or unhappy staying at home. Children of women who stayed home and liked it were as well-adjusted as the children of happy working mothers.

Probably the most important factor in determining our level of self-esteem were our parents' motives for having us. Were we wanted children? If so, why were we wanted? What did our parents expect of us? These questions need to be asked if we are to understand how we came to see ourselves as we do.

To be a wanted child does not necessarily mean to be a planned child.

Though it is most common today to speak of the decision to have a child, most of the children born into the world were not decided on or planned ahead of time. Sometimes the discovery of a pregnancy was met with joy, other times with despair. But whatever the reaction, there was little most of our mothers could do once the fact of conception was established.

In most cases, between the time our conception was established and the moment our birth occurred, our parents came up with a variety of reasons to rationalize our impending existence. These reasons shaped their expectations of us, which then helped to shape our self-concepts. To what extent we were able to fulfill our parents' preconceived expectations of us influenced their assessments of our lovableness and worth. Children have an uncanny way of sensing their parents' judgments, even if parents don't express those judgments aloud, and once children have sensed parental judgments, they internalize them as if they were facts.

Researchers Martin and Lois Wladis Hoffman investigated why people want children. Although the 1,569 married women and the 456 of their husbands they interviewed were people planning children, their desires were probably shared by some of our parents. People commonly want a child because:

Becoming a parent marks the official passage into adulthood.

A child is seen as an extension of the self, and having a child is a way to give birth to the unborn self.

A child is seen as an heir apparent, someone to carry on the family line and traditions, and to insure social status.

A child can realize the parents' dreams, and also can have a childhood full of the opportunities and love that the parents feel they have been deprived of during their own childhoods. Women especially may look upon having a child as a way of showing up their own mothers in the job of mothering: "I'm sure not going to raise my children the way my mother raised me."

Having children is the morally and socially correct thing to do, and pressure from friends, family and the larger culture cause parents to feel they must procreate to be accepted.

Becoming parents may provide people with the illusion of having control over their own lives. They may feel powerful in comparison to the helpless child who is so dependent upon them. Or they may believe that the child will save their faltering marital relationship.

Economic utility: Children can help out with the family business, and also can be counted on to take care of the parents in old age.

Having a child is seen as a way for the parents to celebrate their love, and raising children is seen as one of life's major challenges. Child rearing is yet another area in which success-oriented parents can excel and prove their worth.[4]

In listing these various reasons why people want children, we don't mean to imply that all parents are needy, calculating people who desired children for any but altruistic motives, and that their children are in for a rough life trying to meet their parents' needs and expectations. The Hoffman study did find people who had very healthy reasons for having children. And, as Ellen Gallinsky discusses at length in *Between Generations: The Stages of Parenthood,* parents often revise and totally change their expectations during the long haul of parenting.[5]

Nevertheless, it remains a fact that parents are human, and humans often are motivated by personal needs that can be very complex. Although our parents' expectations differed for each of us, it's highly improbable that our parents made it through the nine months of awaiting our arrivals without devising *any* expectations and wishes. In adulthood it is necessary for some of us to consider those expectations and unlearn our views of ourselves as failures, disappointments or as inadequate. Those views are reflections of our parents' expectations, not of us.

Some parents, of course, never devised any reason to want the child they conceived. If the child of such parents was adopted, she might luckily have landed in a loving family but still may have grown up wondering about her identity and lovability:

I grew up in a wonderful home, and my adopted parents gave me everything I could have wanted. Everything except one thing: information about who I really am. I grew up wondering a lot if I hadn't really come from another planet. I was often afraid I had been given away because of something being wrong with me.

Even when kept by the biological mother, and even when raised in a family that to outsiders might seem normal and "happy," an unwanted child grows up under a terrible burden. No matter how much her parents might have tried to hide from her the fact that she was unwanted, a child likely will have picked up the message anyway. Children are extremely attuned to whether they were wanted or not wanted. Sometimes it does not take specially sensitive radar to figure out that one wasn't wanted:

> My mother often told me right to my face that she never wanted me and how horrible my birth was for her. Often she'd be drunk when she'd tell me this, and so she wouldn't remember. But I sure did! I used to pray every night that God would kill me. "Why, why," I used to ask him, "did you put me here?"

In some cases, it may have been that one parent wanted the child and the other did not. In such instances, the child could have come to perceive herself (correctly) as the source of conflict.

In still other cases, it may have been that both parents wanted a baby but were very specific about just what *kind* of baby they wanted. As study after study has shown, most parents historically have preferred boy babies over girl babies. There used to be an economic explanation for this: Boys could help to increase the family fortune, whereas girls (who needed dowries) would pose a drain on it; hence, the greater frequency of infanticide of females. While this explanation no longer holds much sway, the fact of the preference for boys over girls remains. Demographer Nancy Williamson, for example, surveyed 1,500 married women and 375 of their husbands, finding that while many said they would like one child of each sex, twice as many women preferred boys to girls, and their husbands preferred boys to girls by four to one.[6]

Maxine Hong Kingston remembers the valuing of boys over girls as an integral part of her family's Chinese heritage. As a child, she would hear her parents or other grown-ups say, "Feeding girls is feeding cowbirds," and she "would thrash on the floor and scream so hard I couldn't talk." She also heard such statements as these:

> There's no profit in raising girls. Better to raise geese than the girls.

> I would hit her if she were mine. But then there's no use wasting all that discipline on a girl. "When you raise girls, you're raising children for strangers!"[7]

A child who turned out to be a girl when she was supposed to be a boy may immediately have been seen by her parents as something of a disappointment. Or she might even have been despised:

> Early on, my father took me aside and clued me in on the "Bowdin Women's Motto" (Bowdin is my mother's maiden name): "We adore our sons, tolerate our husbands and hate our daughters."

Health is another factor that has a large influence on how children are received. Virtually all our parents dreamed of a healthy baby. When their expectations were not met, problems might have ensued:

I was very ill during infancy. My mother couldn't take me home—I stayed in the hospital another two months. My parents visited every day, but the hospital staff bullied them, made them feel like they didn't know what they were doing and that I might die if I was left without their expertise. That's what my aunts tell me anyway. I think it made my mother skittish about me. She's always been more tentative with me than with my siblings. I was totally fine by school age, but I think the whole experience made her think of me as "too much to handle" and it made her distant from me. I thought she didn't like me.

If the childbirth itself was difficult, it could have influenced a mother's attitude toward her child:

I was raised with horror stories of labor for days, the near death of my mother, all because I was a difficult delivery. She brought it up when she was really mad. But then she would tease me about it, too. She'd say I already almost killed her once, wasn't that enough? It made me feel terrible.

Postpartum depression also might have interfered with the parent-child relationship. Margaret Mead's younger sister by eight years, Elizabeth Mead Steig, had such an experience:

After I was born, mother had a postpartum neurosis, and the doctors in those days sent you to the country. So, the first six months of my life, more than six months, there was a nurse looking after me. My grandmother was there and Margaret was there. I don't have any memories of lack of tenderness. But I have memories that sound like doves cooing, "She's coming, she's coming." But she didn't come. And finally, at Christmas, they let my mother come home.[8]

Elizabeth Mead also feels that she did not have the same parents that Margaret had, because Margaret was "a first child, a wanted child." The death of another sister before Elizabeth's birth further contributed to a change in her parents, and had an impact on Elizabeth:

I never saw her because she died two years before I was born, but I didn't know it was two years before I was born until a couple of years ago, because I telescope time, and my feeling was that she had died and then they didn't want the next baby because they were so sorry for the last.[9]

Elizabeth was in her late sixties when she finally learned of the facts of her sister's death. It is likely that the sister's death contributed to their mother's postpartum depression. Of course, Elizabeth had absolutely no control over when she came along. But had she been born before her sister's death and before her mother's depression, or long after, when everyone had recovered, the way she saw herself would have been different, and perhaps she would have felt wanted by her parents.

Our place in the birth order also seems to influence our personality and self-esteem. Studies tend to contradict each other, but a sampling of findings can illuminate our individual development in relation to our place in the birth order. Clinical psychologist Lucille Forer is one of the foremost researchers in this field. She states:

> . . . firstborns (both male and female) followed by other children have more need for approval than later borns or other children. Therefore, firstborns, in general, have lower self-esteem than later children do.
>
> Second place in a family of three is often considered the most difficult of all birth positions. The second of two children generally is not openly competitive, but the second of three is wedged in a situation which stimulates maximum competitive potential.
>
> Depending on the family situation [the youngest child] grows up either spoiled, in the sense of always demanding more, or deprived, in that everything [she] gets was used by [her] predecessors.[10]

Other research correlating birth order with personality characteristics found:

> Firstborns are more responsible, aggressive, competitive and less susceptible to influence from others.
>
> Only children tend to be high achievers (which does not necessarily correlate with high self-esteem).
>
> Middle children often have lower aspirations than their older siblings.
>
> Last-born children identify more with peers and less with the family than older children.
>
> Athletes are more likely to be later born.[11]

Although, again, the exact impact of birth order has not been measured, it is clear that if we had been born at a different point in our family history, our ideas about ourselves would have been different, too.

At the outset of this chapter we used terms like "accident" and "the crap shoot of life." Life does begin essentially as a game of craps. We had no control over what kind of family we were born into, whether or not we were wanted, where in the birth order we happened to have popped up, how financially secure our families were. . . . The assignment was random. Had we been born into a different family, or into our own family at a different time, it is very likely that we would see ourselves differently than we do. Only by recognizing how myriad factors over which we had no control shaped our perceptions—perceptions of specific others, the world at large and our individual selves—can we attain some control of our lives. Although life may be a crap shoot, in adulthood the dice sometimes do end up in our own hands.

BLUEPRINTS FOR CHANGE

What were the circumstances of your family's life at the time you were born and when you were very young? Perhaps you can answer these questions by remembering what they have said over the years, or perhaps you will have to ask another family member. It is best if you can gather two or three perspectives.

> What were your parents' economic circumstances at the time of your birth? How did this affect you? Did the circumstances get better or worse or stay the same throughout your childhood? If they changed, how did this affect you?

> Why did your parents have children? Why did they have you specifically? How has that influenced their attitude toward you and your ideas about yourself?

> What were their expectations of you, based on their reasons for having you?

> How was your parents' health in your early childhood? If it was poor, how did this affect you?

> Where are you in the birth order? Can you see differences between you and your siblings (if you have them) which reflect your respective places?

> Did your parents want a boy or a girl? Were they happy with the sex you turned out to be?

Once you have gathered this information, you can begin to sort out the "false learnings" that can be attributed to these inevitable circumstances from what you know to be *true about yourself*. One last important question: Is there anything you could have done about any of the important circumstances listed above? Obviously, the answer is no; thus, ideas about ourselves which reflect these circumstances should be replaced with more accurate ideas.

* 3 *

The Early Years:
Essentials of Self-Esteem

> The process of building self-image goes this way: A new reflection, a
> new experience, or a bit of new growth leads to a new success or
> failure, which in turn leads to a new or revised statement about the
> *self.* In this fashion, each person's self-concept usually evolves
> throughout his lifetime.
>
> —Dorothy Corkille
> Briggs
> *Your Child's Self-esteem*

As our self-concepts evolve throughout our lifetime, so our levels of
self-esteem can change over time. However, we will have a solid foundation of self-esteem if, in our early years, we acquired a sense of significance, a sense of competence, a sense of connectedness to others balanced by a sense of separateness from them, a sense of realism about
ourselves and the world, and a coherent set of ethics and values.[1]

Significance

As children, we needed to feel that we were significant. From our
parents we sensed how much we mattered. If we believed we did not
matter much, that we were not important in our own right, then our
self-esteem got off to a poor start. A person who never acquired a sense
of her own inherent significance may suffer guilt about being alive, or
may go through life feeling she is nothing but a victim of fate, totally
incapable of making a difference in the world.

Adults communicate the "rightness" of a child's existence to the child long before any language is spoken. The softness of the adult's touch and manner of holding the child is the infant's first clue to her significance. The child learns whether she is pleasurable to hold, or a source of worry, tension or unhappiness. Without the warmth that comes from physical affection and the nourishment of food, a child will become overwhelmed by anxiety. Even before she learns to structure her perceptions and senses into patterns of thought and speech, a child can begin to wonder in her own hazy yet crucial way whether she is okay, and what she has to do to be okay.

Many believe that in the earliest stages of infancy, the newborn cannot distinguish between herself, others and the external environment at large. She is aware of no boundaries, and experiences her mother and other caretakers as extensions of herself rather than as separate entities. Hence, the newborn is often said, and correctly so, to be entirely egocentric, for she has not yet become aware that her needs are only *her* needs, and that others (e.g., her mother, whose breast the infant experiences as part of herself) have needs of their own, needs which might not be compatible with hers. Eventually, however, the newborn does become aware that she is a separate being, that the world and others exist apart from her, and when she does become aware of this unsettling fact it can strike her as truly terrifying. For it is then that she switches from her (inaccurate) perception of herself as all-powerful to her (accurate) perception of herself as entirely powerless, completely dependent upon someone else (in our culture, usually the mother) to fulfill her pressing physical and psychological needs. Unless someone else does fulfill those needs, the child's first, most basic feelings will be those of anxiety, insignificance, worthlessness and perhaps even terror.

With an understanding of language, the child's sense of self-esteem takes on a symbolic form; what was previously only experienced is now expressed symbolically, through words. Non-verbal communication remains important, but as she grows older, language plays a more and more important role in establishing her sense of significance. Through language a child can have it spelled out for her beyond doubt that she is significant and "special," as this woman recalls:

> Our family is very big on horsing around and teasing but also on telling each other what we like about each other. On our birthdays we would be told one thing every other person in the family liked about us—it was great, worth waiting all year for.

A child will be most certain of her own significance if she believes she is loved unconditionally. Unconditional love is communicated through both word and action. It means that the parents fully understand that their child is a learning being, someone who does not yet have the knowledge and skills she needs to survive on her own in the world. As she grows up, she will learn by trial and error, and her parents realize that she inevitably will behave in ways which they do not like. She may hurt their feelings, do foolish things or be a brat at times. When parents love a child unconditionally, they still love her in the face of her misbehavior. They dislike the behavior, and point this out, but that does not change their feelings toward their child; they do not communicate to her that she is bad because she has done something bad.

If the parents' love is conditional, the child learns that if she behaves well she is a good person and if she behaves differently from what her parents expect she is a bad person; it's not just her behavior that is bad. As a result, she learns that her worth is determined by other people's judgments. Moreover, she learns that others' opinions of her can change radically in response to different behavior, and thus that her worth can fluctuate wildly, too.

Women who in childhood did enjoy unconditional love to some degree (we have found very few women who enjoyed it all the time) tend to be more sure of themselves and less devastated by other people's criticism, because they believe in their own inherent, inviolate worth. If they truly have something to learn from criticism and failures, they will. But they do not take criticism and failure to mean that they are unworthy or insignificant. They feel less compelled to prove their worth through behavior and are less nervous about people changing their opinions of them. They were convinced of their significance when they were children.

Research on how parents handle boy and girl infants indicate that parents might nonverbally communicate to them very different messages about their significance. As yet the results are inconclusive. But it is an undisputable *fact* that once a girl develops an understanding of language, it is definitely communicated to her that she is less significant than boys. A girl may have learned of this simply by the absence of strong, autonomous, competent female figures in the male-dominated world of culture and society that she gradually discovers during her unfolding childhood. Within her family she may have learned she was insignificant by the way her family listened more attentively during dinner conversation to males than females, or the way her brothers were encouraged to take their ideas and career plans seriously while the girls were told it didn't really matter what they did. Perhaps it was even the case that her insignificance was clearly spelled out for her in no uncertain terms. Time and again, women in our self-esteem groups recalled being told outright that males are simply more important than girls. This woman recalls:

> My father always did a lot of boasting about my brother and did a lot of comparing of the two of us, too. I hated this because, of course, I came out on the bottom in the comparisons and felt like garbage. But what really killed me, and I mean it really made me feel like I had been squashed, snuffed out, was when I found out that my father had taken out a life insurance policy for my brother but not for me. I was curious, so I asked my father how come he insured my brother's life and not mine. You know what he said? He said, "Your brother's life is more valuable. He's a boy, and you're a girl." To this day, my father doesn't seem to understand what he said to me, but that's been one of the biggest events in my life.

Competence

In order to have a sense of self-esteem, we as children needed to learn that we have control over our own behavior and that our behavior has an impact—both good and bad—on others and the world. Having a sense of competence simply means believing we can make things happen for ourselves in the world, that we can master our environment. But acquiring a sense of competence is no simple task when one happened to have been born female.

Children learn that they are competent mainly from coming up against their parents' limits and expectations and surpassing them. For instance, parents tell their daughter that she is not yet ready to ride her bike without training wheels. She convinces them that she is. They remove the extra wheels and she rides away—shaky at first—but successful. Not only has she surpassed the limits her parents placed on her, she has also learned that she is a competent human being. She thought she could ride the bike, she tried it and did it!

The little girl who had to convince her parents that she was ready to ride her bike was, fortunately, already confident that she could do it. Yet she would have felt much more confident had her parents had confidence in her, too. By not expecting much of her, her parents put in her path a formidable obstacle that a less confident child would not have been able to overcome. The biggest help to a child in terms of developing competence are adults who believe in her abilities before she has demonstrated or proven them, as Don Hamachek explains:

> When set at reasonable levels, expectations represent the strongest vote of confidence possible. Self-esteem grows out of successfully doing those

things we weren't too sure of being able to do in the first place, and if we have someone who believes in us, "expects that we can," then taking that first step is at least a bit easier.[2]

The problem with expectations in a girl's case is that parents often have far too few. Boys and girls grow up in "different climates of expectation," as Tillie Olsen has phrased it.[3] Traditionally, in white families particularly, the climates have been carefully delineated: Boys are expected to be adept in math, to be mechanical and physically strong; girls are expected to be adept in language skills, to learn to cook, and to primp and preen and be pretty. The expectations parents and our culture traditionally have had for boys are those which lead to a far greater sense of competence than the traditional expectations of girls. Being competent at cooking and putting on makeup, for example, doesn't really give one a sense of power and control the way competence in athletics does.

To make matters worse for a girl, the areas in which she is expected to be competent usually change as she grows older. Again, this is especially true in white families. Many of the women we interviewed recall that it was expected that they do well in school until their adolescence. In high school they were no longer expected to do well. On the contrary, many were encouraged to do less well, for the new expectation of them was that they start preparing for marriage and motherhood by dating. And, of course, they were told that boys didn't like to date smart girls: "Boys don't make passes at girls who wear glasses."

Limits, too, have often interfered with little girls' learning in the area of competence. One traditional mistake stems from the "sugar and spice" view of girls, which promotes overprotection (too many limits and too much isolation). This is based on the premise that girls aren't competent anyway, that girls need to be protected and "done for" rather than learning to do for themselves. A child treated in this way experiences her *parents'* competence, but never her own. Coopersmith found that

> the conditions of indulgence do not provide an opportunity for the child to test his abilities and he must therefore remain uncertain of his adequacy and effectiveness in the world at large. The uncertainty of worthiness thereby produced is resolved by attending to the appraisals advanced by the indulgent parent. Indulgence, in effect, produces illusions of grandeur and omnipotence but does not permit these illusions to be tested in the broader and more objective arenas of performance. The protective, encompassing parent assumes the role of cocoon and maintains the indulged object on a selective and supportive diet that is nowhere else available.[4]

As a girl who has been coddled in this way becomes a woman, she remains unable to experience her own competence; she cannot seem to make anything "happen" for herself.

If a child was disabled or ill, chances are particularly good that parents and society alike undermined her sense of competence by encouraging her to be more limited than she was capable of being:

> Both from my family and the school I was sent to, I got the message that I shouldn't try too hard or I would just be disappointed. Because I was in a wheelchair, have multiple handicaps, they stressed that there weren't too many places in the world I could gain access to. I was totally discouraged from going to college, when in fact I had the ability and started college later in life. I can see their side of it—they thought they were preparing me —but they weren't that realistic. I'm not that helpless. I know there is a lot I can do for myself, but it took me a long time to get over the idea that I am useless to this world just because I'm disabled.

The other traditional mistake in limit setting is providing too few. If a child took on too much, too soon, without guidance from her parents, she will have consistently failed and her self-esteem will have been diminished. With no boundaries to test herself against, she may have felt out of control and anything but competent. Theodore Isaac Rubin describes the link between the parents' style of limit setting and the child's sense of self:

> He automatically, without conscious awareness, applies how they feel about him to how he feels about himself. If they are grossly overpermissive and don't seem to care about him, then he feels he is a person not worth caring about. If they are overbearing and stifling, he sees himself as a fragile, vulnerable fragment of a person rather than a separate, whole, capable human being. If they are excessively punitive or worse—sadistic, he sees himself as a monstrous person who must not trust ordinary human characteristics and impulses, let alone individual differences and his own judgment.[5]

Thus, tenacious patterns of low self-esteem are established.

Children with high self-esteem do tend to have more boundaries than children with low self-esteem, but with one important qualification. High-self-esteem children participate, to some degree based on their age and ability, in deciding what those limits will be and what level they will be set at. As they learn the process of setting fair and empowering limits, they will internalize the process and treat themselves with the same respect. Coopersmith asked parents to react to the statement "Children should not question the thinking of the parents." Eighty percent of the parents of the high-self-esteem children disagreed while only 50 percent of the low-self-esteem children's parents disagreed. Constructive arguments can foster children's sense of competence, and disagreement seems to be an important experience found in families that produce children with high self-esteem, as Coopersmith states:

> Rather than being a paradigm of tranquility, harmony and open-minded-ness, we find that the self-esteem family is notable for the high level of activity of its individual members, strong-minded parents dealing with in-dependent, assertive children, stricter enforcement of more stringent de-mands and greater possibilities for open dissent and disagreement. This picture brings to mind firm convictions, frequent and possibly strong ex-changes and people who are capable and ready to assume leadership and who will not be treated casually or disrespectfully.[6]

In contrast to Coopersmith's model, we see many girls and women who are treated disrespectfully with great regularity and who seem in-competent to do anything about it. Life seems to just happen to these women. Of course, that is not solely attributable to her family training. Evidence of the belief in the alleged incompetence of women is found throughout our culture, and most of us were made aware of it in school. In their widely acclaimed study of elementary school textbooks, re-searchers Jacklin and Mischel found:

> When good things happened to a male character in a story, they were presented as resulting from his own actions. Good things happening to a female character (of which there were considerably fewer) were at the initiative of others or simply grew out of the situation in which the girl found herself.[7]

A child who grew up believing everything just happened to her, who had no opportunity to test herself against reasonable limits (or any limits), would not come to adulthood believing she had any power to shape her own life.

Still, she has to survive somehow. Most likely her competence will be sublimated. Instead of exercising her power in direct ways, she will have learned indirect, manipulative means to get what she wants:

> In my family it was "unladylike" to say out loud what you wanted. I was admonished time and time again that if someone wanted to give me some-thing—candy, take me somewhere, read me a story, whatever—they would offer it on their own accord or just know that I wanted it. I got very good at hinting, pouting and whining to get people to offer what I wanted with-out saying it straight out. Today, as an adult, I've been snapped at so many times, "Why can't you just say what you mean?"

Throughout our childhood, our parents not only set the limits against which we tested ourselves, they also helped us to interpret our experiences. In developing our competence, a helpful message would have been, "It doesn't matter so much whether you win or lose, it is the effort that's important." As children, many of us were robbed of a sense of competence because the outcome of our effort was emphasized as more important than the process of learning about our abilities.

Consider a third-grade girl who is having difficulty finishing her very first major report for class. Her parents encourage her to try to finish it as best she can, but it is still an arduous task for her. All they ask is that she give it her best effort. Even though she is an A student (with occasional B's), she gets a C+ on the report. Her parents emphasize that she learned she can do a report and that next time, with less anxiety about her ability to finish a big project, her grade may go up. What is important is that she honestly tried.

Compare this attitude to that of parents who believe the grade is the actual measure of mastery. Their daughter, also in the third grade, is a mostly A student, but she had trouble with her first report. As a result, she receives a C+. Because of her parents' emphasis on the grade, the girl loses confidence and learns that at that given moment her value is C+.

The second case is also an example of a degree of conditional love. Sometimes we were told we were incompetent when, really, the fact that we tried demonstrated a drive toward competence. As discussed before, our parent's expectations of us color their interpretation of our efforts. As adults, we sometimes have to go back and rethink some of our early endeavors. Maybe we weren't such stumblebums after all. Perhaps the error was not in us, but in too-restrictive limits or our parents' assumptions (e.g., girls can't make a difference even if they want to) about us.

Try as some of our parents might have to set sane and constructive limits and to guide us toward the conclusion that we are able to take care of ourselves, we may have had experiences we had no idea how to handle, and our sense of competence was threatened. Still, in the face of something absolutely beyond our control, we may have acted, seemingly instinctively, in our own best interest and felt our competence increase:

> We were the only Jewish family in our town. My parents went to the neighboring town to temple and were involved in organizing a Jewish community center there. Once someone burned a cross on our lawn, and I was constantly taunted in school, especially by this one girl, Pam. She and her

gang would wait for me on a corner—every day—and knock me around. One day she really jumped me and had me on the ground, and my books were everywhere. Suddenly, I was aware of this crowd of kids around me yelling "Kill the Jew, kill the Jew!" Something in me snapped and I got a surge of strength. I rolled over on Pam and started to bang her head against the ground. I was crazed and didn't hear anything until her sister finally got through to me: "Frances, please stop, she has a heart condition, please stop." I did and the kids backed away.

My house was just a few doors away, and I dragged myself there crying, my clothes torn. I saw my father standing on the porch—he had watched the whole thing. I started crying harder than ever. "Why didn't you help me? How could you just stand there and watch that? Why didn't you help?" He held me in his arms and said, "You had to do that yourself—you'll never have to fight again." He kept on saying that, "You'll never have to fight again." The amazing thing is, he was right. They left me alone after that—they didn't bother me again.

This woman, whom we both happen to know well, has very high global self-esteem and is a model of competence. Her father's response to this situation helped her to realize her own ability to take care of herself, even under the most threatening circumstances. He did not treat her like a victim of the children, as if that was all she could ever expect of life. Nor did he teach her to be as bigoted and hateful as the children who harassed her. His message was simple: "Life can be very unfair, but you can cope with what happens." Unfortunately, many more girls got only the first part of this message.

One area in which many women did not develop adequate competence as children is the area of self-defense. Although females run the far higher risk of being physically violated in our society, boys, not girls, are the ones most encouraged to develop the skills with which to "fight back." Moreover, in boys parents typically have inculcated the *will* to fight back, whereas in girls this will to resist violations of the physical self often has either not been sufficiently nurtured or has actually been stamped out:

> My family was involved in this church group that had lots of proper-type dances, and when I was about eight they started dragging me with them. I hated to dance, but all these men would ask the little girl to dance and everyone thought it was real cute. . . . One time this man I really thought was weird—like he'd hold me in a funny way, a little too close, you know —asked me to dance, and since I had danced with him before and felt uncomfortable I said no. My mother was appalled. She dragged me into the bathroom and told me: "You never, never refuse a man to dance. If you're asked, you dance."

This may seem like a trivial episode, but what was communicated to this daughter was a larger and dangerous rule: As a female you have no right to say no to a man. Experiences such as this tend to have a lasting effect. Working with victims of sexual violence, we have found that even when women have equipped themselves with self-defense skills (by taking karate or a rape-prevention course) it's still difficult for many to put those skills to use when a threatening situation is encountered. Why? First, because while they have belatedly acquired the skills, they still lack the deep-seated confidence in their ability to use those skills, a confidence that really needs to be developed from earliest childhood. Second, many women lack the gut conviction that it's okay for them to be self-protective, that they have the right to stand up for themselves. This seems particularly true of white, middle-class women, as this Hispanic woman observes:

> I didn't particularly like growing up in Harlem, but the one thing it did is teach me survival skills and I see that as a big advantage. I teach self-defense now and there is a world of difference between the urban Hispanic kids I teach and my classes that have some middle-class white women in them. I try to get them to make a fist and hit the punching bag, pretending it's an attacker, and most of them say, "Oh, I could never do that."

Connectedness Balanced by Separation

The third thing we needed to develop in childhood if we were to start off life with a solid foundation of self-esteem is a sense of connectedness to others, balanced by a sense of our separateness from them.

None of us can feel truly of worth if we experience ourselves as cut off and alienated from others. To have self-esteem, we need to feel connected to other individuals, and part of the larger community as well. At the same time, however, none of us can feel truly of worth if our sense of self is totally subsumed by another's identity and we cannot clearly distinguish the ways in which we are different and apart from others. A sense that while connected to others, each of us is a separate and in many ways unique being is essential to self-esteem.

The work of Carol Gilligan and Nancy Chodorow suggests that girls and boys are raised to have markedly different senses of themselves in relation to others.[8] Because girls are the same gender as the primary parent—the mother—they do not develop a full sense of their difference and separateness from her, and this "lack of individuation" that marks the first and most powerful relationship in girls' lives stays with them, extending to other relationships. Conversely, because boys are the opposite sex from the primary parent—the mother—they develop a strong sense of themselves as separate individuals who are very different from others, but a weak sense of their connectedness and similarities to others. These different ways of seeing the self are further reinforced by cultural conditioning. The end result is, as Gilligan has shown, that as adults we women tend to see ourselves as connected selves embedded in a complex web of bonds to others, whereas males are more likely to see themselves as separate individuals cut off from others, or at least independent of them.

The female way of seeing the self in connection to others has traditionally been viewed in our culture as evidence of a deficiency. According to psychoanalytic theory, women have an insufficient sense of separation from others, and we'd be better off if we saw ourselves more as men see themselves. We agree that women's feeling of connectedness can be problematic. In intimate relationships, for example, many women have trouble keeping a clearly defined boundary between themselves and their loved ones, and this results in the woman being so closely attuned to her loved ones' feelings that she doesn't fully experience her own feelings. But we also believe that women's sense of connectedness is in many ways a strength, not a weakness, and that overall it might be more advantageous to feel too connected to others than to feel too separate. In adulthood, a woman who learned in youth to overempathize with others can learn to pull away and more clearly distinguish her own self from another's. A man who has spent a lifetime seeing himself as a lone individual completely apart from others might find it much harder to learn in adulthood how to empathize or bond with others.

Still, it is true that for many women an insufficient sense of their own individuality and separateness does stand in the way of high self-esteem. There are numerous ways in which parents often encourage daughters to play down their individuality and become too dependent upon others for their identity. Sisters might have been forced to dress alike, or a girl might have been forced to dress in a junior version of her mother's outfit. A girl in a large family might have been forced to share all her belongings, told that wanting her own doll is "selfish," and she might also have been told that any desire for privacy was "selfish," too. In some families, there might even have been a prohibition against speaking in the first person:

> In my family, we were told that it's rude to talk about yourself—that if you used the word "I" or said things like "my opinion is . . ." it was a sign of

pride and vanity. When we were little, all us kids—my brothers as well as us girls—were told not to talk about ourselves. But as we got older, my parents were a lot more lenient with the boys. The boys could be real braggarts and real bossy about asserting their opinions and rights, and my parents wouldn't say anything. But if one of us girls talked about ourselves it was instant put-down time. If you'd dare to say something like "I think such-and-such about that," they'd react with a "how dare you call attention to yourself" or "how dare you have an opinion" type of reaction.

If we learned to suppress our sense of individuality in our childhood homes, we might have had difficulty learning to develop it later in life, even long after we left our childhood homes behind:

In my family, my mother never expressed any wishes or opinions different from my father's—and she didn't pursue any interests apart from him either. That's the way they both thought a woman should be, and that's how they expected me to be, too. So, from as early as I can remember, I was taught to always defer to everyone else's wishes. If my brother—there were only the two of us—wanted to watch a certain TV show and I didn't, I was supposed to shut up and go along with him. Or if my father or mother wanted me to do something I really didn't want to do—like staying overnight at my grandmother's house even though I got scared there and my grandmother was mean to me—I wasn't allowed to protest. I had to always go along with what other people wanted because I was taught that you should always put other people's happiness first, yours last . . . . It got to the point where I became so focused on what other people want that I stopped ever asking myself what I want. I mean, I just stopped forming my own desires and ideas because I figured I'll always have to suppress them anyway. Now, if a friend asks me what movie I want to go to or where I want to have dinner, my response is automatically, "I don't know. Where would you like to go? Whatever you want is fine with me."

Knowledge of who we are, independent of other people, is crucial to self-esteem. But the sort of self-knowledge that enables a person to develop a sufficient sense of her unique individuality was difficult for many of us to obtain while growing up. Females are not only often denied opportunities to develop self-knowledge, we have been denied cultural support for the very idea of obtaining self-knowledge. Especially as we came into adolescence, we learned that we'd pay a price if we developed a strong personal identity and sense of self. Bernice Lott explains:

The traditional goal of the adolescent boy is to identify and sharpen his skills, set his sights on the future, make important choices, and clarify his interests and objectives. This is not what adolescent girls are typically urged to do. The contrary message, often subtle but nevertheless insistent, is to be flexible, not to define oneself too sharply because a woman's ultimate identity will be defined by the man with whom she becomes associated.[9]

Because many women in our culture have been taught to focus their attention on getting a man, and because many women in our male-dominated society have had to be dependent upon men for survival, it often turns out that women know far more about men than men know about men. More important, women often know more about men than we know about ourselves. As Jean Baker Miller observes, women have been raised not to ask "What is it I desire?" but rather to ask, "Am I desirable?" Similarly, women are not supposed to ask, "What are my needs and how can I fulfill them?" Instead, women are supposed to focus on asking, "What are men's needs and how can I accommodate them?" Referring to men as "dominants" and women as "subordinates," Baker Miller elaborates:

> If a large part of your fate depends on accommodating to and pleasing the dominants, you concentrate on them. Indeed, there is little purpose in knowing yourself. Why should you when your knowledge of the dominants determines your life? This tendency is reinforced by many other restrictions. One can know oneself only through action and interaction. To the extent that their range of action or interaction is limited, subordinates will lack a realistic evaluation of their capacities and problems.[10]

Realism

To start off life with a solid foundation of self-esteem we also needed a sense of realism about ourselves and the world. Whether she was taught to see herself in an unrealistically idealized way (as the most brilliant creature on earth) or an unrealistically negative way (as a big dummy), a woman will find it very hard to maintain self-esteem without the ability to see herself in realistic terms. In addition, we needed as children to develop a realistic view of the world and our relation to it. It was of no help to us if we got the impression that the world is a fairyland where prince charmings abound, nor was it a help to get the idea that the world is a snakepit where girls and women are destined for misery.

Having a sense of realism means being aware that no one is perfect; we all have flaws. Unfortunately, however, many of us grew up in homes where it was difficult to find a balance between seeing our good qualities and seeing our problems. Some of us were damaged by our parents' refusal to acknowledge our problems. Perhaps we had learning disabilities, but they claimed "there's nothing wrong with my kid." Still others of us were hurt by parents' failure to pay sufficient attention to successes and positive attributes. It was early on that most of us began learning that our flaws and failures are what matter most:

> As a kid, I was warned about being conceited, told that if I ever seemed pleased with myself, the wrath of God would come down on me. But if I felt crummy about myself and said to my mother, "I'm fat, I'm ugly, I'm stupid" then I'd have her undivided attention. She never argued with me— it was just an opportunity for her to tell me that she and God loved me in spite of all that. I don't know how fat and ugly and stupid I really was, but I do know that I got attention and support for running myself down.

Especially if as children we had only our failures and behavior problems affirmed by parents, we were bound to run into trouble. For along with a realistic view of ourselves, what we needed as children was adults' constructive suggestions on how to do better. Without guidance, we weren't likely to learn from their pointing out of what we, sadly, already know:

> I used to lose my temper a lot. As a kid, I got in fights with friends and would pull their hair and scream at them. The kids' parents would complain to mine and my parents would get furious with me. Most of the time my parents hit me, but it was years later before I made the connection between my behavior and theirs. Anyway, I felt terrible about not having friends—I was a real lonely kid. Instead of teaching me how to control my temper, my parents just rubbed it in and told me how nobody was ever going to like me. I already *knew* that.

Concrete information about how the world works also was needed if we were to develop a sense of realism about ourselves and our possibilities. Unfortunately, many of us were given very little useful information about the world—information about how to go about building a career or how to use the legal system, for example. On the contrary, many were encouraged by their families to entertain wholly unrealistic fantasies about their lives:

> As a kid, I really wanted to become an actress. I asked my parents how you went about becoming an actress, and instead of telling me about schools or anything, they told me that famous story about Lana Turner working in Schwab's drugstore and getting discovered out of the blue. So I grew up thinking that one day some talent scout was just going to materialize out of nowhere and—*voilá!*—I'd be transformed into a screen star.

Concrete, realistic information about how the world works and how to function successfully in it is also necessary for our sense of competence. The more we know about the world, the better able we'll be to exercise control over our fate.

Ethics and Values

The fifth essential of self-esteem is a coherent set of ethics and values, a clear sense of what's right and what's wrong, what's good and what's bad. Of course, the child's early notions of right and wrong, good and bad, will be mirrors of the parents'. Jerome Kagan points this out:

> Raising children . . . offers parents an opportunity to validate the value system they brought to adulthood. Sometimes it is similar to the one they took from their families two decades earlier, sometimes it is a radical transformation, struck from intense childhood pain and carried to adulthood in a vow not to visit upon the next generation the destructive practices and philosophies that scarred their lives. Each parent has a chance to promote a hard-won set of ethics and to test the utility of standards that took many years to create. In a sense, each parent is a scientist testing a personal theory of human development with each child.[11]

Ethics are needed because they act as guides for the child's behavior as she makes her way through life, often encountering confusing situations, disorienting dilemmas. A child who has been taught to hold the golden rule dear can decide quickly and without doubt not to gossip about another child because she would not like that to be done to her. As a large group of children maliciously tease a developmentally disabled child, one refuses to participate and goes for help because she has been taught that it is wrong to be cruel to anyone. She does not have to consider her action long nor does she think less of herself for not bowing to peer pressure; she *knows* what is right. A coherent set of ethics protect and guide the child during times when the parent is not available for protection and guidance. And, most important, ethics connect children to beliefs and ideas much larger than themselves. If the ethics are spelled out for her, the child can feel good about her competence in upholding her convictions. There is something, after all, in the phrase, "the courage of her convictions." This also connects her to others who have the same convictions/values, and she is affirmed in this way.

Unfortunately, though, moral codes are often not clearly spelled out for a child, at least not in a way that seems to have relevance to her own life. From the Ten Commandments, a child learns that it is clearly wrong to murder and to commit adultery, but for most children murder and adultery are not commonplace considerations. It is in seemingly small areas that the child's concern—and confusion—usually comes up:

> When I was little, my grandfather would tell me to sneak up behind my aunt's chair at the dinner table, and tip it over. I did this, she fell flat on the floor backward, my grandfather thought it was a scream, and my parents dragged me into the kitchen and gave it to me. I was really confused. They just yelled at me, but I never figured out what I had done wrong. I did what my grandfather told me to do, and since I was always told to obey grown-ups in the family, I thought I had done right.

This girl knew she was in trouble, but she didn't know precisely why. Her ethics were not coherently communicated to her. She knew she was supposed to honor thy grandfather, but she did not know that she was not supposed to do this when it came to tipping over thy aunt. Children often have great difficulty, understandably so, figuring out the difference between right and wrong, because for every rule there typically is an exception, yet parents often do not explain such contradictions well. "Why," a child will ask, "is it wrong when criminals kill but right when criminals get electrocuted?" Common parental response: "Because."

An especially damaging situation is when children live in a vacuum, without any parental direction of what is right or wrong. Then children are burdened with moral and ethical decisions far beyond their capabilities, and their self-esteem usually falters as a result:

> My mother had this one friend, Helen, and her kids were monsters. I was eight, in the third grade, and I saw one of these kids breaking windows in these elderly ladies' houses near the school. I think I was the only one who saw him. That afternoon the principal came around to each class and asked if anyone knew who did it. I figured I was a fink if I told, but I felt sorry for the old ladies. After he left, I quietly told my teacher. Still not sure I did the right thing, I told my mother about it when I went home. She flew into a rage. I told her it was "on my conscience" and I felt I had to tell. She hit me really hard, said "Damn your conscience, what am I going to do about Helen?" and left the room. I never understood what I should have done. Helen remained friends with her—it wasn't until I was an adult that I figured out she probably never knew who told anyway. Now it seems that what her son was doing was serious enough to tell on him, but it took me forever to decide that.

This girl lacked the clarity of conviction that would have assured her that the neighbors' safety was more important than loyalty to her mother's friend. It is not unusual to be vague about these issues at eight years of age. But it is possible, and desirable, for children to have some ideas about priorities, about which issue is more important.

Often the ethics we were taught as children leave us confused because they in themselves are illogical, or just plain contradictory:

> My parents always told us that it didn't matter if you had pimples or you were ugly and fat or you had some big physical defect. It's what's inside a person that counts, they said. The exterior stuff doesn't matter. But while they were telling us that it's what's inside that counts, they were also telling us we should hate black people and Hispanics and Asians because they had the wrong skin color. As children, it was very confusing to us.

Probably the most damaging situation of all is one in which a child acquires a coherent set of ethics that are backward, or upside down. If a child is given transposed notions of right and wrong, notions that are at great variance with what the rest of the world believes, she may end up extremely confused:

> My father raised us with this saying—"Do unto others *before* they do unto you." The world was really a jungle to him and he believed you have to get the first jump on everyone. So as a kid, I was anything but generous. If I thought someone might even be considering being mean to me, I'd be mean first. Most of the time, kids didn't understand—they thought I was coming out of left field. I didn't have all that many friends, and if by chance I did make one, I usually lashed out at them sooner or later in defense. It took me a while to understand that all that wasn't necessary.

Our beliefs about what's right and what's wrong have their basis in our values. Values are often not expressed just in terms of good and bad; they're often expressed just in terms of better and worse. Some children, for example, were taught that while it isn't bad to be black, it sure is better to be white. Similarly, while many of us who were born female were not told it was bad to be a girl, we sure were taught that boys, overall, were better. With this sort of handicap, it is very difficult for a girl child to develop a high level of self-esteem.

A Lifetime Process

Virtually all of us, to some degree, had problems with one or more of the childhood essentials of self-esteem. As adults, however, it is possible to overcome these problems. If we lack a sense of our significance, we can seek affection from those around us and come to be aware and appreciative of how much we matter and the ways we make a difference in others' lives. If we lack competence, we can increase our skills in the areas of our choice and take pride in our efforts. If we lack a sense of community and connectedness, we can reach out to others; and if we lack a strong sense of our individuality and uniqueness, we can seek ways to find out more about the individuals we are. If we are confused and feel out of touch with reality at times or our reality is inordinately dismal, we can turn to those around us for affirmation of our perceptions and affirmation of our inherent worth. If we feel lacking in values or a sense of ethics, we can sort out what is important to us, regardless of what our parents taught us, and evolve our own consistent and compassionate values as people have for centuries.

All of this is easier said than done, of course, but the point is that self-esteem development is a lifetime process. A deficiency in any of the childhood essentials is not irreversible. As we gain in each of these areas as adults, our self-concept is expanded and our potential for self-esteem greatly increased.

BLUEPRINTS FOR CHANGE

I. ESSENTIALS OF SELF-ESTEEM

Can you recall a childhood experience you had that pertained to each of the five areas we discussed? When did you feel significant? When did you experience your power? When were your skills at mastering the environment noticed and applauded? When did you feel connected to a larger community? When did you realize and appreciate your own uniqueness? When did you have an experience that helped you see yourself more realistically? When did you act on your moral code and feel good about that?

Are there any of these five ingredients that you feel deficient in today? How can you go about structuring some experiences to help you make up for that deficiency?

When you were little, how did important adults help you to interpret your experiences? Negatively? Positively? Didn't say much? Realistically? Unrealistically? Judged only by outcome? What is your pattern like today? How do you interpret your experiences? Are there any similarities between past and present? Remember, we can have a lot of *new* experiences, but if they are still interpreted in the old self-defeating way, they will not enhance our self-esteem.

II. PAST EXPERIENCES

Think of one negative experience which occurred more than five years ago and still lives within you, one which you think about from time to time. There are countless ways to interpret any one experience. Share your troublesome experience with a close friend or helping professional. Are there other ways of looking at it? Do you need to be so hard on yourself because of this experience? Can you put it to rest now and use your energy for more productive endeavors?

* 4 *

The Power of Words

Words are the only things that last forever.

—William Hazlitt

Long before a child says "I am . . . (strong, lazy, good at math, especially pretty, funny, good with animals, etc.)," chances are she has heard her parents, teachers, siblings and other important people say "You are . . . (any of the above)" many, many times. A child is not born with preconceived ideas about who she is; she learns them from other people during the process of growing up. As she develops her own sensitivity and judgment, she will find her own words to describe herself. Without a doubt, her choice of words to describe herself will be greatly influenced, for better or worse, by the words she has heard others use in reference to her in the past.

It is inevitable that people who spend large amounts of time with a child will come to some conclusions about the child's behavior (and subsequently about the child herself) based on their observations and reactions. Once spoken, such conclusions often become labels, and labels, more often than not, carry evaluative connotations. In terms of adjectives alone, the English language offers us nearly eighteen thousand to choose from, and most of these contain inherent judgments, as Morris Rosenberg points out:

> Even a superficial glance at any list of adjectives shows that the vast majority are not simply value-free descriptions but imply negative or positive judgments. To call a person "kind" is not a description; it's an accolade. To call him "cruel" is not to describe him, but to condemn him. If we say someone is "ugly," we are providing a much better description of *our*

feelings than of his features . . . In most respects humans appear scarcely capable of seeing someone without at once passing judgment on what they perceive; and this propensity is entrenched in their language. The words we use to describe something express not simply what we perceive but also how we feel about it.[1]

If our parents labeled us with compassion and accuracy, their labels taught us about who we are in a way that enhanced our self-esteem and our realism about ourselves. If labels were applied without sensitivity to their importance, however, they might have turned out to be inaccurate, maybe even destructive.

As children, we could not distinguish unfair expectations (which had nothing to do with us) from realistic assessments of who we were. And because we were absolutely dependent on our parents for our survival, we looked up to them. Hence, when they said we are "plain," "stupid," or "lazy," we did not question their credentials, much less the fairness of their expectations. Their judgments became reality to us. We were not likely to pick and choose among the labels they applied to us. We integrated them all, to some degree, even when they were overwhelmingly negative. As Rosenberg observed in his study of the self-esteem of children:

> . . . even children who believe their mothers think ill of them rarely deny that their mothers' opinions are important to them; the mother-child role relationship is so powerful that it is not easily overcome by selective valuation.[2]

Because we were powerless as young children, we did not have much opportunity to fight against our parents' labels. Moreover, because as children we had not yet developed much mastery of language, we could not fight back with words of our own. Particularly in those families in which it was held that "children should be seen and not heard," children had neither permission nor occasion to challenge parental judgments and labels. To be sure, in the rebellious years of adolescence, many of us consciously and adamantly rejected our parents' opinions of us. Others, however, did not question their early parental labels, and even among those who did, the labels may have stuck all the same, regardless of efforts to discard them. In most cases parents' perceptions became the child's self-conceptions.

Most likely, our parents communicated their ideas about us through both praise and criticism. In many cases, however, the criticism had more of an impact than did the praise because criticism carried the threat of losing the love of those on whom we were so dependent. Since so much seemed to be at stake, we as children became especially attuned to criticism, often to the point of tuning out praise:

> My parents said a lot of things about me to me when I was a kid, and overall they probably praised me as much as they criticized or yelled at me. But the nasty things they said—like that I was a slut and a slob—are the ones I remember most vividly and took most seriously, because they were usually followed up with action, like punishment. I mean, I never got rewarded for doing well in school—that was expected of me, it was no big deal. But when I did things they thought were wrong, that was a very big deal. I remember having to stay in my room for whole weekends on end for pretty minor infractions—like coming home late from school—and being confined like that gave me plenty of opportunity to stew about how rotten a kid I was.

Obviously, it's not just what was said to us that counted, it was how it was said, too. And often critical remarks had more impact because they were shouted in anger or spit out in a "scene," whereas praise may have been offered in an offhand way or a casual tone of voice.

A second reason that criticism may have had more of an effect on the child's developing sense of self is that in many families there was an overemphasis on criticism. Many parents believed (and still believe) that to praise a child is to spoil her or make her conceited:

> Recently I went to visit my parents, and they told me that they've always been real proud of me. This really shocked me because, growing up, they never never said they were proud of me. In fact, all they ever did was point out my flaws and mistakes. "Why," I asked them, "didn't you ever tell me then that you were proud of me? Why didn't you tell me when I had done well in your eyes?" Their answer was that I was *supposed* to do well, and that if they had made a point of telling me they were glad I did well, I'd get a fat head. But they had to tell me when I screwed up, because if they didn't then someone else would, and that would be embarrassing.

Growing up, this woman's "doing well" was as much a real part of her experience as her mistakes. Quite unintentionally, however, her parents fostered low self-esteem in her by failing to balance their criticism of her with praise. As she told us, this eventually had an effect on her behavior, inculcating in her the erroneous and unfortunate belief that since her parents would never be proud of her there was little point in trying to make them proud.

As children we also needed praise and criticism that was accurate and specific if we were to develop a healthy sense of self-esteem:

When I was little, I would draw pictures for hours. When I showed them to my parents, they always took a few minutes to really look at them (although then it seemed I had their undivided attention for hours). Instead of just saying "Oh, what a nice picture, dear," they would say what they liked about it, ask me how I mixed that color, and if they didn't know what the picture was, they asked me. Every time, I felt great and went on to another drawing and then another. It is still a hobby for me.

If this woman had, instead, inaccurately been told she would be the next Georgia O'Keeffe, she might have lost interest in art eventually because of the pressure to perform brilliantly or because in her self-delusion she believed that art held no challenge for her. As it was, though, she received accurate and specific praise for an activity she enjoyed. She learned something positive and realistic about herself.

The criticism we received needed to be specific and accurate too; otherwise it would not help us. Unfortunately, for many of us the criticism we received in childhood was neither. Too often our general worth was attacked rather than our behavior criticized. A child can correct her behavior, but she is helpless to correct her worthlessness. The contrast is illustrated by this woman's memory:

There was a construction site in the neighborhood where I grew up, and we were all warned to stay away because it was dangerous. One Sunday when I was nine, I couldn't stand my curiosity anymore. I took my friend there, and we played in the gravel and sand piles for the afternoon. Our parents noticed we were missing and when they found us, they reacted very differently. My friend's parents were upset. They asked her if she understood that she wasn't to go there and that she had broken their trust. They grounded her for two weeks and she really understood why, even though she didn't like it. My parents, on the other hand, called me a liar and a dirty sneak and hit me. It was as if it was the worst thing I could have done in the world.

The children's behavior did not differ in the least, but the information each child received about herself differed radically.

Some parents offered neither praise nor criticism. They were basically incommunicative, perhaps because they were afraid of saying the wrong thing. This left their small child in a vacuum:

I used to come home absolutely furious when I was a kid. I didn't get along with other kids, and I told my mother about all the terrible things that happened, and she would just nod and say "hm-hm" to everything I said. I wanted her to say, "Oh, those are horrible people" or "Why don't you try it this way next time," anything, but she never ventured an opinion. She had so little interest that I thought she just didn't care about me much at all.

A problem for most of the women we interviewed is that when they were growing up, they received decidedly mixed messages about who they were and what was possible for them and expected of them. When asked to list spontaneously the primary messages gotten in childhood, women often came up with statements that were either incompatible or outright contradictory:

"Tina does everything well."
"Tina can always do better."

"Susan is much better than other people."
"Susan can't get along with anyone."

"Eleanor is the perfect little lady."
"I wish Eleanor had been a boy."

"You can be anything you want when you grow up."
"When you grow up you'll get married and be a mother; that's what girls do."

"Don't ever leave me or I'll die."
"Don't come too close or I'll punish you."

"If you keep on getting good grades, you'll go far."
"You don't need to go to college; your brother does, and because we can only afford to send one of you, we'll send him."

"Helen has an inquiring mind."
"Helen is a busybody."

Which message was the child to take most seriously, to believe as the truth? Most parents were probably not even conscious of the confusing nature of the messages they gave their daughters, but the daughters reported great confusion indeed.

To add to the confusion, many women reported getting one message from one parent, another entirely different one from the other parent:

"Janet is perfect." (From mother.)
"Janet is selfish." (From father.)

"I expect nothing of you—you're only a girl." (From mother.)
"I expect everything of you—you're my daughter." (From father.)

"Sandy is outspoken and articulate." (From mother.)
"Sandy is too loud and opinionated." (From father.)

"Ann is very popular with the boys." (From mother.)
"Ann is a slut." (From father.)
"Ann with her social life is a big bother." (From foster parent.)

"Connie does everything I ask her." (From mother.)
"Connie can't do anything right." (From father.)
"Connie is too fragile—don't expect much from her." (From step-parent.)

"You're just like your father." (From mother.)
"You're just like your mother." (From father.)

Contradictory messages were not intentionally transmitted to the child as a way of making her feel anxious and confused, nor were they probably true to the extent they were stressed. Nonetheless, the confusion caused by such contradictory messages and expectations was real and may have remained so into adulthood. In bouncing back and forth between two conflicting sets of opinions and/or expectations, the child had little opportunity to learn which pole was more representative of the real her.

Looking at single labels, we found that many women were given labels that at first glance seem positive but which later contributed to self-esteem problems. For instance, many women were told they were "lucky"—lucky not to be sick, lucky to have inherited such good genes from their parents, lucky to be white and upper middle class, for example. When they took pride in some aspect of their selves, they were admonished not to be so conceited because, after all, they were "lucky." Their being pretty, smart, having friends, etc., had nothing to do with them, it was just a reflection of their luck. Hence, they were robbed of any chance to feel good about themselves.

Being called "different" also may have been problematic because of the way that differences in this culture are automatically rank-ordered as evidence that we are superior or inferior. If a child was disabled, she might not have been perceived as a person with a different body, but as being handicapped or crippled:

I became my disability in other people's opinions and it bothered me a lot. Any other thing they noticed about me was connected to my disability— and my parents did this especially. It was always "She does so well in school considering she's blind," or "Even though her eyes are cloudy, she's so pretty," or "She's really overcome her blindness and makes friends easily." I think they were trying to compliment me, but it would have been so much better if they had just said, "She's smart, she's pretty, she gets along with people well," because in those ways I was just like any other kid.

Some labels were not subject to various interpretations; they were negative from any point of view. Among the negative labels women received as children, we heard about such ones as "good for nothing," "rotten kid," "lazy bum," "pig," "slob," "parasite," "ungrateful," "selfish," "difficult," "troublemaker," "tramp," "wild," and just plain "bad."

One specific label having extremely damaging effects is "unlovable." This is the ultimate in self-esteem–destroying childhood labels:

> My mother often told me that she and my family didn't love me. She said people in my family *have to* love me, but they didn't, so I couldn't expect anyone outside my family, who didn't have to, to ever love me. Intellectually, I can see now that she was sick and trying to be controlling. And in fact, my father and brothers did love me, but I still struggle with people outside the family caring about me. Why would they when they don't have to?

A question more to the point is, "Why *wouldn't* they?" It is inaccurate to say that someone is unappealing to absolutely everyone in the world. As we discussed previously, there is no justice in which family we happened to be born into. If circumstances or family problems cast us into the "unlovable" category, it need not always be that way. Yet, among the women we interviewed, this label of "unlovableness" was rarely questioned. Their belief in their unlovableness seemed as natural to them as observing that they have blond hair or brown eyes. After much discussion and further reflection, the majority of these women recognized that their parents feared that they themselves were unlovable. Perhaps they were afraid of being rejected by their growing child, and so rejected first in order to prevent discovery of their own perceived unlovableness.

The labeling process we have been discussing here does not occur only in childhood, and our parents are not the only people to participate in it. Throughout life, myriad others will apply labels to us, some of them favorable labels, some of them unfavorable. We have concentrated on the role parents played in early labeling because when we were children our parents had a power over us that is unlike any other power experienced in later life, and that power gave their words an especially great weight. As children we were dependent upon our parents for both our physical survival and our sense of psychic well-being. As adults, however, we are no longer dependent on our parents for either. In the broader scheme of things, William Hazlitt may have been correct in saying that "words are the only things that last forever." In terms of our own lives, however, no words need be immutable, and our parents' words, powerful as they may have been to us as children, need not be the last words.

BLUEPRINTS FOR CHANGE

I. CHILDHOOD LABELS

Although we all have different childhood labels, usually one came through loud and clear and stuck more than the rest. This is probably the label that is the cornerstone of our self-concept today. Without thinking, finish a sentence beginning "I am . . ." as you would when you were ten years old. What adjective came to mind? Did it have a positive or negative meaning? Either way, is it one you still agree with today? Do you have any doubts about it? Do you still need it with you today for any reason? What impact do you think it's had on how you relate to other people today? How does it effect your choices? How does it effect how you feel about yourself? Think of between five and ten other childhood labels and ask yourself the same questions.

II. REPLACING NEGATIVE AND INACCURATE LABELS

As an adult you can reinterpret negative labels which might not be totally accurate. For instance, in our Vermont Law School group, the majority of the women had been labeled "argumentative," "difficult," or "disagreeable" when they were children. Later in life they turned this into at least a value-neutral—if not positive—label of being "good debaters," and used it to help them develop skills needed for their work. Think of the five to ten labels from the above exercise. Is there a more positive and accurate way of looking at them?

III. THE WRONG LABEL OF "UNLOVABLE"

If the unfortunate label of "unlovable" has been placed on you, try to obtain some of your baby pictures. Look carefully at this picture of a sleeping, cuddling or playful infant. Does she look inherently unlovable? What could she have done, what mistake could she have made, that is so extraordinary as to earn her this label? Are there other family members who found you lovable at the same time your parent(s) found you unlovable? What would these more favorably inclined folks say about you then? To remind yourself of your inherent lovableness, you might want to keep the baby picture close at hand.

* 5 *

The Power of Role Models:
Like Parent, Like Child

Do as I say, not as I do.

—Often heard parental command

We learn not only by listening, but also by watching. As children we were probably extremely attuned to the behavior of others, particularly our parents or surrogate parents. We watched them closely, intensely, carefully because they were so frequently around, because they had tremendous power over us, and because by pleasing them we secured our place within their hearts and insured our survival. We also watched them because we hoped they could provide us with an inkling of what it meant to be a "big person," something we someday would be. And in the process of observing our parents' or surrogate parents' clothing, manner, speech and general behavior, we learned how to behave ourselves. Don Hamachek explains:

> Whether parents are aware of it or not, through their daily lifestyles and the *consistency* of their behavior they teach their children how to blend, for better or worse, the basic ingredients for living—how to deal with anxiety, failure, how to handle money, make friends, *be* a friend, how to resolve conflicts and make decisions, how to love and be loved.[1]

The process by which we learned through observation of our parents' behavior is called role modeling. Sometimes role modeling was conscious and intentional. Since imitation is said to be the highest form of flattery, it may have been in our best interest to try to be just like Mommy or Daddy. The little girl who attempted to curry favor with her parents by dressing up in Mommy's clothes or mimicking Daddy's facial expressions was indulging in conscious role modeling. She wanted her parents' approval and knew what she had to do to get it.

But role modeling is often unconscious; more often than not it occurs almost as if by osmosis. As adults we might dress very differently from our mothers and make no attempt to actively mimic our fathers' facial expressions. Yet with frequency most of us catch ourselves acting, speaking or reacting just like one of our parents (or parent substitutes). "Ohmygod," we often hear women say, "I sound exactly like my mother," or "I did that just like my father would have done."

While we learn our behavior, manners of speech and general sense of "place" in society from a variety of adults, most of us had one *primary* role model. When we asked women we interviewed who their primary role model was, many times we were told, "Anybody but my mother." One study reported that 63 percent of the women interviewed said they consciously avoided patterning themselves after their mothers.[2] Many of the women we interviewed said their primary model was another female figure—such as a grandmother or older sister—or their father. Yet when the subject was pursued further, nearly everyone revealed that their mother's impact was probably the greatest of all. Time and again, we heard comments like, "My mother is probably the most important figure in my life," whether important in a positive or negative sense.

Why did our mothers so greatly influence us? Why were they more often than not our primary role models? Some contend that it's only "natural" that girls would model themselves after their mothers, simply on the basis of our sex similarity. We think, however, the reasons are more complicated than that. Mothers stand as the primary role models for young female and male children alike, and they do so because of three factors: availability, warmth, and power, especially *power.*[3]

Let's take availability first. How much time did an adult spend with us in our earliest years? What was the quality of that time, how intimately did that adult relate to us? How emotionally accessible were they?

For girls and boys the availability factor brings Mother most readily to mind. Because of our social arrangements, Mother rather than Father traditionally has been the one to spend the most time with infants (regardless of gender) during the earliest years. When we were infants, it was Mother who most often fed us, nursed us, changed us and cuddled us, and in many cases she was home with us most of the time, whereas Father was absent. Even mothers who worked outside the home probably spent more time with us than did our fathers.

The availability factor often brings criticism of Mother to mind. Hardly anyone accuses men of doing damage to their children by going off to work, but today working mothers are often accused of failing to spend sufficient time with their children. Yet women have also been cruelly castigated for spending *too much time* with their children. The authors of *Beyond Sugar and Spice* aptly point out the no-win situation of mothers in modern times:

> Today, some child development authorities say that "alienation" in young people is caused by the fact that their mothers were not available enough. Twenty years ago, the women who expended all their energies on their children suddenly found themselves attacked as "overprotective" moms. In the fifties, the author Philip Wylie said "momism" was destroying the sons of America. Studies done on American prisoners of war who were brainwashed in Korea suggest that they hadn't resisted because they were sons of overprotective mothers. So the woman who followed the experts' advice when her children were young found herself being attacked by other "experts" when her children got older.[4]

Warmth, the second factor, is as important as availability in determining who our primary role model was, for it was through warmth and affection that our behavior was reinforced. If our role model smiled at us, cuddled us, talked to us and generally made us feel good when we were around her or him, we would have been more eager to be like her or him.

The warmth factor, too, typically brings Mother to mind. Although fathers can be, and sometimes were, especially affectionate toward their children, men have been socialized to be more emotionally reserved and are thus often far less expressive than women—even with their own children. This woman recalls:

> My father was a real nice guy, but he seemed really stiff with us kids. I remember when I was twelve and my little sister was born that he'd often have this funny look on his face when he held her, like he wasn't too comfortable. But the thing I remember most vividly was that as soon as my sister either wet or dirtied her diapers, he'd *immediately* hand her to my mother or me. The same thing happened once when she threw up on him —he handed her to my mother so quickly that I thought he might have hurt the baby in his rush.

The lesson learned here is clear: Father may love baby, but he can't contend with mess; when baby makes a mess, it's Mother's or sister's job to clean it up.

Power, the third element influencing who our primary role model would be, is perhaps most important of all. If the person had a great deal of power over us, then our attempts to please him or her would have seemed to us a matter of survival.

Power most quickly and vividly brings the father to mind, for typically in our society he has power over the mother and the child. But in infancy, a child often does not perceive the father's power. As children, it took us several years to learn that the family name was Father's name, that Father was more highly esteemed and valued in the world than Mother, that Father existed as the "head" of the family. In fact, since Father may not have been around all that much, many of us in our infancy may not have been very aware of him at all.

By contrast, as infants we experienced Mother's power in the most direct, gut-level way. Mother was the one who carried us for nine months and delivered us into this world. She was the one from whose breast (or in whose arms, if we were bottle-fed) we derived the nourishment that kept us alive, Mother was the one who dispelled our discomfort by changing our dirty diapers, Mother was the one who washed us, and she was the one who cared for us when we were sick. From our perspective as infants and young children, no power appeared more formidable than the power of Mother; it was nothing less than the power of life and death. Dorothy Dinnerstein describes this power with eloquence, suggesting that its memory will always live within us but that we will never comprehend it fully:

> Mother had powers more absolute than any that can possibly be encountered later, powers too strong to defy and too awesome to emulate. Her impact, moreover, was felt in that emotionally crucial period when feelings are formed entirely without words, feelings which then survive without ever being touched by words, so that they never fall under sway of more mature rational processes: The child's superstitious reaction to the [mother's] power continues to live a subterranean life of its own, unmodified by that limited part of human sensibility which we call intelligence.[5]

Some contend a fourth factor that influences our choice of role models is gender identity. According to social-learning theory, and some psychoanalysts, boys automatically and naturally identify with men, girls with women. But, as Carol Tavris and Carole Offir point out:

> . . . research has not confirmed this key assumption. When children in an experiment have a chance to copy adults, they show no consistent tendency to mimic one sex more than the other. Researchers who have tried to correlate more global personality traits of parent and child (rather than

concentrating on a particular action) do not find that children resemble the same-sex parent more than the opposite-sex parent. . . .[6]

As a "plausible explanation" for the fact that girls often end up modeling women and boys modeling men, Tavris and Offir suggest that the older a child gets, the more likely he or she is to be rewarded for imitating same-sex behavior and punished for imitating the behavior of the opposite sex. Most of us know that this is so from our own experience. When we were little girls, for example, we may have been considered cute for being "tomboys." But by the time we reached puberty, most of us had discovered that our "masculine" behavior—climbing trees, spitting, getting dirty—would no longer be tolerated. We looked to our mothers as our primary role models as we grew older, because a society which presumes radical differences between the sexes and permits little deviation from the norms left us no other choice.

Of course, many of us wanted another choice, and we looked for it in our fathers. And for many of us what a glamorous choice Father seemed to represent! In our interviews a consistent theme came up: fathers had appeared to their young children as exciting, dynamic, mysterious. They got to leave the house to do interesting things, and no one ever seemed to push our fathers around. Even when they came home tired at the end of the day and rebuffed our plaintive, pathetic cries for attention, we didn't mind. If our fathers failed to satisfy our craving for attention, or even belted us, it was because they were so important in the outside world, and so terribly pressured. ("Hush, dear, or you'll disturb your father.") We could become important, too, in our own small way, by helping him feel good and not making too many demands on him. It was crystal clear: Daddy was dynamic, and he had the most fun.

Mothers, on the other hand, were frequently described to us as "boring," "warm, fluffy pillows," "mousy," and often mentally ill, or at least anxious, tired, depressed and unhappy. Given these two perceived choices, combined with a daughter's growing awareness that society would really not give her much choice, confusion and tension often resulted. Her same-sex parent was the one she was actively encouraged to imitate, but her father was so much more attractive a model. Particularly if a daughter grew up in a conventional male-dominated nuclear family where the mother was isolated from other adults and prevented from full participation in the world outside the home, she might have come to see her mother as representing "regression, passivity, dependence, and lack of orientation to reality"—traits that psychoanalysts long have said mothers represent to both sons and daughters.[7]

On a cognitive level, Chodorow's points are indisputable. But the cognitive level is not the whole story. Yet even though while growing up women may eventually have come to see and thus consciously recall Mother as "mousy" and ineffectual, in our deepest unconscious we still remember that as infants we directly experienced Mother as all-powerful. In our eyes today Mother may represent "regression, passivity, dependence, and lack of orientation to reality," but in our hearts we once felt her—and still may feel her—to represent the magical power of life and death, and of reality itself. This dialectic is crucial to understanding our relationships to our mothers and ourselves.

Part of growing up for both boys and girls is said to be rejecting the mother, who represented the primal power to children of both sexes. But this rejection of the mother is often far less difficult for a son than a daughter. Boys, after all, were never supposed to identify with the mother, although they did, and our culture gives them permission to reject the mother by painting her (in their minds) as despised creatures. Our culture, of course, gives girls permission to view the mother as despised also. However, in seeing the mother this way, the girl, because she is supposed to identify with her mother, is forced to include in her own self-concept a "despised feminine self."

Moreover, it's rarely the case that the daughter's rejection is total. Even as we struggled to separate ourselves from her, most of us continued to love Mother very deeply. As much as many of us might fear the power Mother represented, we still might long to return to that time when we were under its sway. Thus, the process of rejecting Mother and turning toward Father that daughters often go through in adolescence is, in many cases, more apparent than real. Although daughters in adolescence might go through the motions of trying hard to reject Mother, in fact most remain strongly ambivalent. And, as Nancy Chodorow observes:

> A girl's father [often] does not serve as a sufficiently important object to break her maternal attachment, given his physical and emotional distance in conjunction with a girl's desperate need to separate from her mother but simultaneous love for her.[8]

Even if Mother was away much of the time, or ill, she still left her mark; her power still imprinted itself in our minds' most primitive recesses. Mary Lou Shields, in *Sea Run: Surviving My Mother's Madness,* tells of her mother's institutionalization for mental illness during Mary

Lou's childhood. Although she was raised by a grandmother and an aunt, a strong bond of identification existed between mother and daughter. As an adult, she was terrified that she, like her mother, would be crazy and be put away. In many ways, her often absent mother was a stronger model than her surrogate mothers.[9]

Many of the women in our self-esteem groups who remember their mothers as unhappy women, or even emotionally disturbed women like Shields's mother, fear that they will become like their mothers. Fortunately, however, other women in our groups had pleasant memories:

> My mother was one of the most interesting people I've ever known. I used to think she knew everything. Now I realize that she knew a little bit about everything. She used to wow my friends and me with her explanations of astrology, botany, gravity—all that college stuff. I think it encouraged me to be a real learner—one of the things I like best about myself—because she was *so* giving and fun in her knowledge.

Whether or not we enjoyed it, and whether or not our mothers were "fun and giving," it is undeniable that most of those of us who were raised by our mothers turned out to be, as this woman put it, "real learners" at their knees. And, unfortunately, many of the lessons of our mothers were ones that have proven to be constricting to our self-concepts and destructive to our self-esteem. But it's important to remember that no matter how damaging our mothers' lessons may have been, they were not so by design. Popular as it is, the practice of blaming mothers for everything that goes wrong with children is both destructive to the collective self-esteem of women and unfair to our own mothers. Our mothers most likely did not sit down and consciously decide what they would teach us through example. They were probably far too busy and beleaguered to do that. Moreover, our mothers were once little girls, too, and our maternal grandmothers were their models. If our mothers taught us to see ourselves in limited ways and modeled for us examples of women who didn't much like themselves, that was because both they and their mothers knew no other way. All grew up and had to live within a society and culture in which women had few options and which has always held women in very low esteem.

Another problem with blaming mothers is that it lets fathers off the hook entirely. Women get stuck with the kids, and then get stuck with the blame when the kids don't turn out well. But men get to leave the mother and kids behind, and then escape the blame; since they weren't around to do damage, they therefore couldn't have done any. Confronted with a rude, spoiled, obnoxious child, no one asks, "Didn't your father teach you any manners? What's wrong with him?" No, it's always, "Didn't your *mother* teach you? What's wrong with her?"

One of the more important things we gleaned from observing mother was our notion of what it meant to grow up, an inevitability most of us were somewhat anxious about. Even those who now consciously recognize that to be an adult is not necessarily to be just like Mommy still may feel the influence of Mother's model in their self-perceptions:

> I travel all over the country, take my vacations alone or with a lover. I sometimes have more than one lover at a time. I have an advanced degree and own my home. Yet I have this gnawing feeling that someday somebody is going to tap me on the shoulder and tell me that "dress-up" is over and I should go clean up my room. That's it—I feel like a little kid in adult clothes.

Time and again, we heard women proudly recount the detailed differences between their lives and their mothers', then express the fear that because of these differences they had not yet become real adults. We found this to be especially prevalent among childless women. Nancy Friday, too, in her interviews found mother's model consistently in women's minds:

> We try for autonomy, try for sexuality, but the unconscious, deepest feelings we have picked up from her will not rest: we will only feel at peace, sure of ourselves, when we have fulfilled the glorified "instinct" we have trained, *through the image of her life,* to repeat: you are not a full woman until you are a mother. (Emphasis added.)

> First the superficial, outward differences had to be worked through. Mother lived in a house, the women I was talking to lived in an apartment. Mother never worked a day in her life, the daughter held down a job. We cling to these "facts" as proof that we have created our own lives, different from hers. We overlook the basic truth that we have taken on her anxieties, fears, angers; the way we weave the web of emotion between ourselves and others is patterned on what we had with her.[10]

It is helpful to recall here Dinnerstein's observation that the total, primal power Mother first represented to us seemed in our hazy infant view "too awesome to emulate." It is easier for a male to feel himself an adult than it is for a female to feel herself an adult, Dinnerstein argues, because a father's more obvious, concrete power is easier to emulate than is a mother's more subtle, discrete power. "Unable to locate in herself the full magic power which as a baby she felt in her mother," a woman, according to Dinnerstein, may in adulthood still feel in part "a timid child." Dinnerstein continues:

The man can seem to her to fit her childhood ideal of a male adult far better than she herself fits her childhood ideal of a female adult. This flaw in her sense of inner authority deepens from within a feeling of hers which society at the same time abundantly encourages from the outside: that she is unqualified for full world adult status; that she has no right to a voice in consequential public decisions; and therefore that she has no connection with the mainstream of human affairs except vicariously, through a man, so that without some personal alliance with him she can claim no formal place in human life.[11]

We have said that we found this fear of not yet having become a real adult to be most acute among women without children. But there are two kinds of women without children: heterosexual women and homosexual women. For the latter, the fear that one has not become an adult may have a double edge. After all, the real female adult most of our mothers modeled for us was not just a woman with children but a heterosexual woman with children. This lesbian explains:

My image of what it means to be a grown-up woman comes from my mother, whose life pretty much is the straight—yeah, I mean that both ways—stereotype of middle-class surburbia. . . . Me, I've conformed to that image in a lot of ways. Basically, I've been living in a "model" lesbian nuclear family—me, my lover and her two kids. So except for the fact that my "spouse" is the wrong sex, I'm pretty much in line with my image of adulthood. I still feel like I haven't completely grown up, but being in a nuclear family—even a lesbian one— has made me feel less like a child. My lover doesn't have this problem—she's gay, but she came out only after she had been married and became a mother, so she's fulfilled the requirements for adulthood. But I haven't gone through any of those passages, and I don't see them looming on the horizon, so I get scared that I'm gonna end up as a ninety-year-old dyke who still feels like a little kid.

In addition to showing us that being a grown-up woman means being both a mother and a heterosexual, our mothers showed us how to actually conduct heterosexual relationships and other relationships—relationships with women, with neighbors, acquaintances. If our mothers liked themselves and were confident that they had things to offer others, they probably showed us how to initiate and maintain a wide variety of relationships. If, however, our mothers lacked self-esteem, it was probably the case that they were anxious and insecure about their relationships with others, and may have taught us to be suspicious, withdrawn, and also not to initiate. Philip Zimbardo found that 70 percent of the time, shy parents had shy children who had difficulty initiating any kind of relationship. Not coincidentally, both parent and child had low self-esteem as well.[12]

Through watching our mothers we also learned what educational and job possibilities were open to us. Sadly, many of our mothers modeled for us very limited options. But, again, mothers are not to blame for this. Our mothers taught us what they knew, what they had been taught. They could not possibly have taught us about roles and experiences and opportunities they didn't know existed. That would have been a rather unmotherly thing to do—to set us up, to teach us to expect something that they didn't think could really happen for us. Most likely, our mothers were afraid to teach us about the way they would like things to be. They felt it was their duty to teach us the way things are.

But not all mothers conveyed a sense of stifling limits:

> We lived in a very stable black neighborhood, and year after year my mother's friends would come over to talk, and as long as I sat quietly, I could listen. They sometimes talked about sex and orgasms and how you had to ask for what you wanted sexually. They also talked about their work when I grew up, too—not because I would *have to* but because it was a good experience. And moreover, it was wonderful to have your own money. My white, upper-class women friends told me they had a totally different experience. Although it was always assumed they would go to college, it wasn't assumed that they would work. Instead, their security was in getting a man to support them—even though they had skills to do it for themselves. I can't imagine being raised like that—so unsure of my future, putting time and energy into being prepared for something I wasn't expected to do.

Another thing we learned from our mothers was our attitude toward risk. Men tend to perceive calculated risk as an opportunity for some type of growth or expansion where the benefit is highly desired and the experience of failure can be survived. Some women, on the other hand, have modeled risk as something to be avoided or even feared. Hennig and Jardim (authors of *The Managerial Woman)* found that the women executives they studied had learned from their fathers the attitudes that contributed to their success in male-dominated corporations:

> Where her mother saw risk in typically negative terms, terms which made the very act itself a negative ("You will fail"), her father was moving her beyond fear as a first emotional reaction, to an early attempt at evaluation of possible outcomes. He was asking her very simply to use her mind.[13]

Again, this negative view of risk is a lesson that has been passed down:
Our mothers were taught no different, as this old rhyme indicates:

> Mother, may I go out to swim?
> Yes, my darling daughter.
> Hang your clothes on a hickory limb,
> And don't go near the water.

The benefits of calculated risk, (growth, learning and expansion) are crucial to the enhancement of self-esteem, so some risk is necessary for a sense of self-worth. We might have to risk the negative reactions of people close to us when we try to become more assertive. We risk increased responsibility when we begin to perceive ourselves as competent. We risk our children's displeasure with us when we insist on privacy and time alone. We risk failure when we aim for accomplishment. In each case the possible negative outcome is not life-threatening and the potential benefit is great. Yet some of us have been taught to limit ourselves for "safety's sake."

In *My Mother, My Self* Nancy Friday contends that no matter what we do, where we go, what we learn or how we grow, we are doomed to be as miserable as our mothers presumably were; there is no escape. This is inaccurate, unfair to our mothers, and it undermines our sense of control over our lives. Moreover, it ignores the fact that not all our mothers were miserable and unfulfilled. And not all women feel they have cause to blame their mothers. A black woman told us:

> I think this hating-your-mother trip is something for white girls who have a lot of time on their hands. I don't feel it, and my women friends who are women of color say they don't get it either. We tend to respect our mothers for the struggles they went through. We know if it weren't for her, we wouldn't have survived. Sure, we have problems and disagreements, but there isn't all this blaming her for not giving us enough. She gave all she had.

Focusing blame on our mothers is problematic also because it allows us to overlook the role of our fathers or the surrogate fathers in our lives. Men benefit from their lack of availability because their lack of participation in child rearing seems to free them from blame when children don't turn out well. But men benefit from their lack of availability in another way too: When Father is not around much, we tend to make him up, to imagine him. And when we do make Father up, we often do so to his great glory and advantage.

A case in point is Eleanor Roosevelt's distorted view of her father. Throughout her life Eleanor's father ignored and disappointed her.

Once he left her and three of his dogs with the doorman at the Knicker-bocker Club in New York City. It seems he forgot them; the doorman took them home six hours later. He often made dates and stood her up as alcoholism steadily debilitated him. Yet forty years after his death Eleanor wrote that her mostly absent and far-from-ideal father

> was the one great love of my life as a child, and in fact, like many children I have lived a dream life with him. So his memory is still a vivid, living thing to me.[14]

Why would we create romantic and almost delusionary images of our absent, unavailable or destructive fathers? There is no folklore of father-daughter hatred or father-in-law jokes in reaction to imperfect fathers, yet there are volumes in reaction to our imperfect mothers. Why do fathers rate such benevolent "rewriting" in our minds?

It is simple: By the time we have entered school, most of us were at least unconsciously aware that we live in a man's world. If only in our imaginations, our fathers seemed to hold out the promise of access to that vast, exciting, foreign world. By contrast, Mother's world seemed to us small, dull and commonplace. We were all too familiar with Mother's narrow little world. It was more fun to spend time day-dreaming about far-off father than focusing on close-at-hand mother.

And then the issue of power once again enters in, too. Although in our earliest years our mothers had great and primal power over us, as we grew older we came to see that our fathers had a definite if different kind of power over our mothers. Moreover, the kind of power we saw in our fathers was more comprehensible to us now that we didn't just feel, but also had the capacity for language and rational thought. In discussing why girls as they grow up have a harder time identifying with mother's power than boys have identifying with father's power, Dinnerstein explains:

> . . . the transition from the child's own world of thought and feeling to the inconceivable inner world of the same-sex adult . . . is crucially harder to achieve in the girl's case than in the boy's: the inner world [of the mother] that she must come to embrace belongs, on an inarticulate level of awareness, to the magically powerful goddess mother of infancy. In comparison to this mysterious realm, the father's world, encountered later in childhood, is relatively accessible to rational delineation and realistically oriented fantasy.[15]

Not only does Father's power have the advantage of seeming to promise access to a wide, wide world, Father's power is more fathomable to the rational mind.

By charging that fathers have often been so unavailable that daughters have had to make them up, we don't mean to place undue blame on fathers in the same way it has been placed on mothers. Some fathers have been extremely available and warm as well. In the lives of women who have attained worldly success, in fact, a decisive factor that has shown up time and again is that their fathers spent considerable time with them and were extremely affectionate as well. As Hennig and Jardim comment:

> The father-daughter relationship provided an added dimension to these women's childhoods. From it they draw attention, approval, reward and confirmation. It was an added source of early learning, a very early means of expanding their experience, and through it they gained a role model with which they could begin to identify.[16]

That is the good news. The bad news is that when our fathers were around, many (perhaps unconsciously) promoted passivity and helplessness in their daughters by making it abundantly clear that as girls we were not only different, but limited. The one lesson fathers in this culture are expected to transmit to their daughters is how to be a desirable heterosexual woman. Frequently, other lessons are inculcated along with the instruction on how to be desirable to men. Barbara Grizzuti Harrison remembers:

> When I was a little girl I was obligated, by ritual, to tease and cajole my father for my weekly allowance. My brother had to do chores to get his. The clear message was that while I could always wheedle what I wanted with charm, my brother would have to work for what he got. Given the fact that most women find, at one time or another, that they have to work for survival, I think my brother got a realistic message and I got a fairy tale.[17]

But fathers can teach us much more than seductive behavior, and some—to their credit—have tried to. Some of the women we interviewed were told by their fathers that "you can be anything you want to be." This was well intended, to be sure. And as they watched their fathers venture into the world and take risks more or less freely, they might have believed it was true. Later, however, these women discovered that this, too, was a fairy tale and encountered problems with their self-esteem:

> My dad told me I could be anything I set my mind to. All you have to do is work hard, he said. He was a doctor, and I wanted to be a doctor, too. This

was back in the late fifties, when I was in high school, and my father said, "Good, be a doctor. All it takes is hard work." He didn't tell me how hard the world would make it for me to be a doctor. He didn't tell me about sex discrimination, or about how males monopolized the medical profession, or about how when I got to college I would be encouraged by nearly all my science professors—all men, of course—to give up the idea of medicine. I was really torn up. I was sure that what I was going through was *my* fault.

Mothers usually knew better than to tell daughters without qualification, "You can be anything you want to be." Again, this was not because they didn't wish it were so. Rather, they knew all too well that it isn't true. Fathers seem to either impart all the limitations placed on women or they act as if we can be like them and face no restrictions because of gender.

Even as children, we knew there is more to the world than just our parents. And so it is true for the process of role modeling as well. If someone other than our biological parents raised us, had daily authority over us, then probably most of what we have stated above about primary models would apply. However, there are secondary models as well, and they are important. For example, in Hispanic families, where bonds with the extended family are highly valued, the grandmother-granddaughter bond can be as strong as the mother-daughter bond.[18]

Siblings, too, are sometimes secondary role models. Older siblings sometimes become "surrogate mothers," either because of force of circumstance or in order to regain some of the power they lost when they were displaced by the young sibling's arrival:

> I shared my room with my sister, who is seven years older. She always pushed me around and did mean things to me. For instance, when I came into our room, I had to "pay a toll" which usually consisted of her hitting me over the head with a book. It's amazing I didn't have brain damage. She had her side of the room roped off—she even asked my parents to buy her barbed wire—and of course the one door to the room was on her side. Still, I copied her. Our biggest battles were over my getting into her makeup. I wanted to look like her.

As our horizons expanded beyond the family, we may have found role models in teachers, scout leaders, our parents' friends:

> When I was nine, I got real interested in sewing doll clothes. I tried to teach myself, but it was frustrating and not very stylish for my dolls. I kept on asking my mother for help, but she literally couldn't thread a needle. So she arranged for a friend of hers to teach me, since Home Ec in school was

years away. Every week I went to her friend's house for three hours and worked on a project. I did this for years and I loved it.

In addition to being able to teach us things our primary role model couldn't, secondary models also may have validated our primary model. Validation would have been extremely important if our primary role model was unconventional. Financial expert and author Paula Nelson had strong role models of women in finance in both her mother and the family banker:

> Some of my early memories are of sitting with my parents across the desk from Donna Swink, head of the escrow department at the Santa Monica Bank. I remember listening to the discussions, watching everyone go through and sign the papers, seeing the checks exchanged. Occasionally I went along with my parents to talk to real estate people. I saw houses bought and sold and once when I was nine and my parents were out I showed a house to some interested buyers. I simply mimicked all the things I'd heard my mother say, even discussing the terms of the payment: I've always felt that I was lucky to have this kind of early exposure. It's probably the reason it's been easier for me to be free of much of the fear of the financial world that has gripped so many women.[19]

Our parents' own levels of self-acceptance influenced our self-percep-tions. From the time of pregnancy, many parents secretly hope that some of their traits or their mate's will be passed on to the child. A mother might hope for a child with a sense of humor like her own or for a child who has her husband's gentleness. But when less-than-desirable traits are passed on as well, role modeling can become a negative force rather than a positive force:

> My mother was constantly concerned about her weight when I was a kid, and when I reached puberty, she decided I looked "porky." She dragged me to the gym with her, which I hated, and we both went on the same diets, although I ate tremendous volumes at school. I spent my allowance on hot lunches, in addition to eating the rabbit food she sent along with me. She was always on me about how I looked, until I gave up and with-drew. I stopped eating around her. This concerned her right away and she took me to the doctor who told her I was the correct weight and that all my bulges were just normal. After that, she left me alone.

Again, self-esteem was an important variable here. If the mother had had a more positive self-concept and was not so concerned with "fat," she might have recognized that her daughter did not have a weight problem. Or if the daughter really was overweight, she might have demonstrated some reasonable and safe ways to control weight. Better yet, she might have taught her daughter that self-esteem should not rest on a few problem areas. She was not a bad mother, just a mother with low self-esteem.

The process of role modeling is not always a mandate from parent to child to "be like me." When we mirrored a parent's flaws, we were sometimes rejected or even punished. In the parent's mind this was done in the name of love, because they did not want to see us as unhappy as they were and they attributed much of their unhappiness to their unwanted characteristics. As the child becomes physically bigger and *looks* more like an adult in the teenage years, the "mirror" can be much more vivid and unsettling to the parent. Ellen Galinsky makes this point:

> Occasionally . . . parents recognize that their intense response to a teenager's behavior has a ring of familiarity. For instance, a mother who had a hard time talking to her own parents as a teenager and who hoped it would be different in the family she formed is driven almost crazy by her teenager's refusal to talk to her. It was crying that bothered another mother. She had always cried easily, and when she saw her fifteen-year-old daughter doing the same, it irritated her. Another mother had always been overly sensitive, almost raw, easily rebuffed by things that didn't seem to bother others. She was distressed that her son was equally vulnerable.[20]

It makes little difference whether our parents recognized that their child's behavior was probably learned from their own example or believed that the trait was inherited. A parent's adverse reaction can diminish the child's self-esteem, especially if it was dramatic enough and/ or repeated often.

Competition with our role models also may have confused our self-concepts. We may have wanted to be like them and wanted to win their approval, but they may not have wanted us to be like them. Perhaps they didn't much like themselves. Or perhaps they were too insecure to share what they did like:

> My mother's hobby was art. She would paint when she was home with us. I liked art, too, and I would try to paint with her, but she never let me. When I brought things home from my school art class, she was always really critical of them—under the guise of trying to "teach me technique," most of which was way over my head. Finally I gave up and got into animals, especially horses, instead. But I always thought she must be right —she was the artist, not me. Even though I wanted to paint, I was convinced I was talentless at it. Today I'm not even interested in going to a museum to look at art.

This woman can probably overcome her early learning about her artistic ability and pursue it as an interest now that she is out from under her mother's shadow.

As with the power of words, the power of example is often more marked when it has a negative tone. Our parents' rejection in us of the traits we have in common with them probably was expressed more dramatically, perhaps in the form of an insult or a fight. Memories of painful competition may remain vivid especially because, due to our powerlessness, we probably lost most of the time. As a result, it is easier to focus on what our parents didn't teach us rather than what they did. Moreover, we may be tempted to overlook the positive things our mothers modeled because those were probably more subtle, more part of our daily routine:

> One thing that has worked well for me is my ability to really listen to people. I enjoy it. It has helped a lot with my jobs and it's something my friends compliment me on. Once in a while, when I'm really concentrating on what someone is telling me, I think to myself, this is like déjà vu. Where does this familiarity come from? Then I realize—my mother. Every day she took fifteen minutes to a half hour out and really listened to me. She taught me how to do this.

When we look at what our role models taught us and what they didn't teach us, inevitably we return to the issue of self-esteem. The most important things our parents could have modeled for us are self-acceptance and self-love. Adrienne Rich reminds us:

> The nurture of daughters in patriarchy calls for a strong sense of *self*-nurture in the mother. The psychic interplay between mother and daughter can be destructive, but there is no reason why it is doomed to be. A woman who has respect and affection for her own body, who does not view it as unclean or as a sex-object, will wordlessly transmit to her daughter that a woman's body is a good and healthy place to live. A woman who feels pride in being female will not visit self-deprecation upon her female child. A woman who has used her anger creatively will not seek to suppress anger in her daughter in fear that it could become, merely, suicidal.[21]

Although mothers have often said, "Don't be like me—I want you to do better," daughters will benefit much more when mothers can actually be what they themselves truly want to be.

BLUEPRINTS FOR CHANGE

I. ROLE MODELS IN CHILDHOOD

Think back to your childhood. Who was the most available person in your life? Who was the warmest? Who was the most powerful? Considering your answers to these questions, who was your primary role model?

If it was someone other than one of your parents, think of three helpful traits, behaviors or interests this person modeled for you. Think of three unhelpful traits, behaviors or interests this person modeled for you.

If your primary model was a parent, then do the same for both your model and your other parent.

How has each of the above, good and bad, contributed to your self-concept? How have they affected your self-esteem?

II. COMPETITION

Was your primary model competitive with you in any aspect of your life? What happened when he or she felt threatened? How did this make you feel? How has this experience influenced you as an adult?

III. TO BE AN ADULT

Think about how your mother, and other significant female models, shaped your perception of your options for you. What was her (their) attitude toward your taking risks? What was her (their) interpersonal style? Again, think about how this has influenced you as an adult.

What is your image of an adult woman? How closely do you come to this? How closely aligned is your image of the adult woman with your ideal self? Can you think of changes you have to make to lessen the gap between your concept of an adult woman and your own self-concept? There are many alternative images of what it is to be an adult woman.

IV. PERSONAL HISTORY

Try to gather information on at least the last three generations of women in your family. Where did they live? What was their marital status? Did they have children? What were their occupations, hobbies, interests and special talents? Are there any patterns that you see carrying over into your life?

* 6 *
The Legacies
of Troubled Families

> In the storm of our childhoods, we struggled to integrate, synthesize
> and create our personalities and our views of the world. We needed
> our parents' help. But, consumed by their own battles, they enlisted
> ours instead.
>
> —Deidre Laiken, *Daughters of Divorce*

It is a myth that families are always "havens in a heartless world."
Ideally buffers between a helpless child and the "cold, cruel world,"
some families are so troubled as to be devastating to a child's sense of
well-being and self-esteem. Trouble within families comes in a variety of
forms, and while the specific problem Deidre Laiken speaks of is divorce, her observations apply as well to such problems as alcoholism,
physical abuse and neglect, sexual abuse, abandonment, mental illness,
suicide, chronic physical illness, and death within the family. Troubles
like these can greatly disrupt family life and, at least for some period of
time, prevent a child from receiving the love and guidance she needs.
Generally speaking, a child who grew up in a troubled family is less
likely to have received the essentials of self-esteem, more likely to have
been labeled in negative and inaccurate terms, and more likely to have
been influenced by negative role models. Troubled families are not intentionally bad families, but rather families overwhelmed and thus distracted from children's needs and incapable of meeting them. Few troubled families are completely unloving; more often than not there was
just not enough love to go around.

There is probably a large difference between the childhood experience
of a woman who grew up in a family where the mother committed

suicide and the experience of one who grew up in a family where the father was constantly drunk and abusive. And there probably is a larger difference still between these sorts of experiences and the experience of the woman whose childhood home life was disrupted by the long illness of a sibling. But for all these differences we have found that women from troubled families learned certain consistent lessons about themselves and the world. We can break down the general legacies of troubled families into five lessons.

Lesson One: I Am To Blame for My Family's Problems. Everything Would Be Much Better if I Hadn't Been Born.

When something goes wrong, the first impulse of many people is to assign blame. In troubled families the impulse to assign blame is often activated around the clock because so much goes wrong so often. And who in the troubled family is the blame most likely to get pinned on? On the weakest, smallest, least powerful members, of course:

> In our family, my mother was called "Our Lady of Perpetual Blame." I guess you can tell we were Catholic. Of course, we never said this to her face. It was our humorous way, as we got older, of dealing with her crazy rages. Nothing we ever did was right—there was always criticism and ridicule but never any suggestion of how to do it better next time and avoid the lashing out. My parents assumed we were born knowing everything we needed to know, and so if we screwed up, it was intentional, to make them miserable. With that kind of attitude, they felt justified in terrible retaliations against us.

It is easy to see how a child raised in an environment where she was explicitly blamed for a variety of problems naturally would come to conclude "everything would be much better if I hadn't been born." However, a child may have come to this conclusion even if others did not explicitly make her the focus of blame. Seeking a logical explanation for the unhappiness around her, a child may have had an easier time with the idea that she is the cause of the unhappiness than with the idea that there is no one cause, no simple explanation, because life is unfair:

> My father never said his drinking was *my* fault, but he never said it was *his* fault either. I seemed so unimportant to him—I worried about that all the time. I think I unconsciously decided one day that his drinking was my fault. If I couldn't be important for who I was, then I'd be important as the cause of his problem. It was better than nothing.

Particularly if she was caught between parents who were always in conflict, a child may have embraced an illusion of negative power because it seemed better than no power at all. Perhaps one of the parents told the child, "I stay because of you—your father (mother) is a terrible husband (wife) but a good father (mother) to you." This easily could have been heard by the child as, "Because of you, I stay in this rotten situation." The child then may have concluded that she has power over how other people choose to live their lives. And if the parent who complained to the child ends up leaving the other parent anyway, the child may conclude, "I guess I wasn't worth staying for after all."

The same sense of responsibility and inherent evilness may trouble a child after a death in her family:

> When my brother died I was only four, and it was all very confusing. My mother told me that he died because God wanted him, but I didn't really understand what that meant. I tried to get her to explain more clearly why he died, but she didn't have much time for me—she was consumed with her own grief and the exhaustion of taking care of him while he was sick and dying. As time went on, my parents never recovered from the death, and they started taking out a lot of anger on each other and on us kids. As they got more and more out of control with their anger, I knew I must have done something really horrible to bring it on, and the most horrible thing I could think of was killing my brother.

This child developed a bad case of "survivors' guilt." She grew up thinking that things would have been better if she had died—either instead of the deceased family member or in addition to him.

A negative illusion of power does not necessarily follow from all troubled childhoods. Among the women we've interviewed, we've found that they took on blame only in two situations: when blame was explicitly pinned on them, or when they were given no other explanations for the problems. If parents or other trusted adults took the time to explain precisely what was happening and why it was happening, and did this over and over again, a child would not have blamed herself:

> My mother told us *repeatedly* that she didn't know why my father disappeared so much, she didn't know why he said some of the mean things he said to us, but she did know that he loved us. She said it was the drinking that made him do those things—not us kids—and while he had a big problem, it didn't change the fact that he loved us.

Lesson Two: No One Else Has the Problems We Have in My Family. I Am Totally Alone.

A child, along with feeling that she is to blame for her family's unhappiness, often believes she is totally alone in her unhappiness. Sometimes the feelings of isolation are directly linked with feelings of self-blame. This is the case when a child reasons, "This is happening to me, and only to me, because somehow I uniquely deserve this unhappiness."

When we look at the statistics on problem families, the isolation felt by children who grew up and continue to grow up in them appears particularly ironic and tragic. For example, one million cases of physical abuse or neglect of children are reported in the United States each year; one out of every four girls born in the United States today will have been the victim of sexual abuse by the time she turns eighteen; and an estimated twenty-eight million American children are now living with alcoholics. Some family problems—such as divorce, which now affects more than two million children—have been rising over the years, but other problems, such as alcoholism and physical and sexual abuse of children, are not new to the current generation of children—they were commonplace when today's adults were growing up, too. Of course, when it comes to family problems, there is no safety in numbers. But the isolation felt by so many children could be substantially mitigated by public acknowledgment of just how prevalent certain family problems are. Unfortunately, few children today, and even fewer in previous generations, have been informed that they are far from alone in their plight.

A girl or woman who believes her family's problems are unique will be reluctant to confide in others outside the family because of her fear that they won't understand. There are plenty of reasons for such a fear, for many people simply refuse to understand, especially when the source of information is young and female:

> I tried for years to get someone to help me deal with my parents' alcoholism and their sick "Who's Afraid of Virginia Woolf?"-type relationship. . . . But whoever I turned to—the family doctor, the guidance counselor at school, friends of my parents who seemed like they might be sympathetic—they either didn't believe me at all, or if they did believe me, they accused me of exaggerating the situation wildly. "Oh, it can't be all *that* bad," they'd say—if they'd admit there was anything bad about the situation at all.

Many children grew up with parents who explicitly forbade them to take family problems beyond the walls of the home. Sometimes the prohibition was enforced with threats of punishment, or disaster:

> When my dad first started the incest, I was five. He said to trust him, that he was my daddy, he wouldn't hurt me, and this was just what people who loved each other do. Later, when I had it figured out, he told me that if I told, it would kill my mother. My mother was already in the hospital a lot, either pregnant or with bleeding ulcers, so I believed him and kept quiet to save her life.

Prohibitions against talking with outsiders about family problems just added to the shame many children felt along with their isolation. Often the shame about being from such a messed-up family can last for years, preventing a woman from breaking her silence even years after she has left her parents' home:

> I was afraid that if I ever told anyone, they wouldn't want to be friends with me anymore. I'd become perceived as a burden, as somebody who had all these awful problems she drags around everywhere, ruining everyone's fun and bending everyone's ears. . . . I guess I'm ashamed, too—ashamed of coming from that kind of background, and ashamed of not ever being able to stop my mother from being beaten. Especially with my lover, I was afraid that if I told him, he'd think I was contaminated and then he'd leave me, or else he'd think I was weak for not stopping it and then he'd leave me for that too. . . .

Lesson Three: This Really Isn't Happening to Me—It Must All Be in My Head.

Sometimes a child may have been so overwhelmed by a sense of isolation and unreality that she became convinced that her family's problems existed only in her head. It's not a big step from thinking "No one *else* has these problems" to thinking "No one *at all* has these problems, not even me—I must be making them all up." Numerous times in our interviews women would describe an incident of abuse or some psychological assault on their self-esteem and end the description with, "It's so unreal," "I've tried to forget it ever happened," or "Can you believe that really happened?"

> I used to think about having part of my brain removed. I was just a little kid and I knew nothing about lobotomies, but I just knew all these memories of screaming and hitting and choking were in one place in my brain and I was saving up for an operation that would take it all out.

Many children's confusion was exacerbated when they were told to accept the illusions of other family members:

"Mommy's not in the hospital, she's just away on a vacation."

"Daddy's not drunk—he's just happy (or sick)."

"Our fighting is none of your business—it doesn't affect you. . . ." even though the child was kept awake and terrified by the sounds of physical violence.

"When I punish you, it is like giving you medicine to make you better. . . ." even though the punishment was brutal and the child feared for her life.

"This (in the case of incest) is what all daddies do to show their love for their little girls."

Girls told such lies learned to distrust their own perceptions of reality, even in adulthood. Often they end up completely denying or disowning powerful parts of their childhood experience, pretending that the bad things never happened and that they grew up in "perfect" families.

Since they were usually isolated from other families, a number of women from troubled families reported that they got their ideas of what families should be like from books, radio or TV, and that their image of their ideal family seemed far more real to them than did their real families. Often they tried to make their own unsettling, sometimes horrific, family over into an ideal image:

My father took off when we were real young, and I imagined that he was an important businessman, a globe-trotter, and that's why he couldn't come visit. Well, it was up to this wunderkind to put me through college, except that he had gone bankrupt and was in jail for bad checks when it was time for me to go to college.

Lesson Four: I Am So Insignificant and Worthless that I Have To Really Justify My Existence.

A child who grew up in a troubled family had great reason to be insecure, because her survival was dependent upon parents who were anywhere from distracted to completely overwhelmed by problems. Aware that she could not make her way in the world on her own, a child in a troubled family was acutely aware of her neediness and vulnerability. At the same time, though, she was acutely aware that because her parents were so consumed by problems, they could not be relied upon to meet all her needs, and in fact may even have decided or been forced to abandon her. In this situation a child would have felt tremendous pressure to justify her existence, to prove she was worth keeping around. Such a child would have tried to be a source of help to her parents.

In many troubled families, parents were more than willing to enlist their small child's help. Confused and feeling worthless and ignored or abused, the child inevitably began asking herself, "Why am I here? Why was I born? Why do they keep me?" To these sorts of questions the parents of women we interviewed implicitly replied with a number of different answers:

"You are here because I thought having you would fix my marriage."

"You are here to mediate our battles, to cheer me up when I am down."

"You are here to meet my sexual needs."

"You are here to be a target for my rage."

"You are here to take care of the rest of the family while I take care of your father (mother, sibling, etc.)."

No child could have successfully fulfilled any of these roles. But a child on whom such demands were made probably did not see them as unreasonable. Instead, she saw herself as a failure, at the very least a "bad daughter," and might continue to see herself as such throughout her life.

In families where strife between the parents was a problem, the child might have been forced to side with one parent against the other. Thus, the answer to "Why am I here?" was "You are here to be my ally and to be your other parent's enemy." A child put in this position would have been forced to despise any aspect of herself resembling the "enemy" parent. She also would be forced to see the "enemy" parent in an unrealistic, entirely negative light. Most likely, that parent wasn't *all* bad.

Lesson Five: I Have No Control Over My Life—
Once a Victim, Always a Victim.
Life Is Just One Bad Thing After Another.

Very often people whose childhood home life was unhappy fear they will end up re-enacting in their adult lives the very situations that made them miserable as children. They may have sworn, "It'll never happen to me," and may deny any similarity between themselves and the troubled parent(s) they tried to reject. But deep below the defensiveness and denial often lurks the belief that history will inevitably repeat itself. This is not unreasonable on a child's part, as statistics show that children of alcoholics have an increased risk of becoming alcoholics themselves, children who were beaten or who witnessed violence have an increased risk of becoming child and/or spouse batterers, children of divorced parents have a higher chance of getting divorced themselves, and children of a parent who attempted or committed suicide are more likely to be suicidal at some time in their lives. These statistics, however, don't tell the whole story: There is nothing inevitable about the repetition of the past. On the contrary, the course of history can be changed if the child learns there are alternatives to her parents' ways and if she is capable of believing in them.

In troubled families, creative solutions to problems are usually neither pursued nor encouraged. Children learn that their parents' inadequate ways of coping with life's stresses are the only ways of coping. Since "normal" behavior means what most people do, not what is best or most healthy to do, children can grow up thinking their parent's ways—no matter how destructive or unhealthy—are normal. Before long, with no alternatives to compare to, they come to believe that "normal" must be "good" and they grow up with beliefs such as:

> Divorce is a normal answer to problems in relationships; they can't be worked out so it is better to leave.

> Getting drunk every night is normal—it can even be fun and it's a good way to release tension.

> Suicide is the normal thing to do when everything seems hopeless.

> Violence is normal—it's okay to hit or be hit, especially in the name of love.

> It's normal to molest children; they can better meet a person's sexual needs because they are safer, less demanding and less powerful than adults.

Some children who grow up with these beliefs never question the values and coping skills they were taught. Worse, they sometimes become ardent defenders of their parent's attitudes in a backhanded attempt to gain self-esteem. The justification goes something like this: "My parents life-style could not have been so bad or else I would have turned out bad too; if it was good enough for me growing up, it is good enough for me now, and for my spouse and children too."

At the other extreme, sometimes the adult raised in a troubled family tries so hard and fiercely to run away from her unhappy childhood situation that she fails to realize she has run full circle, back to the place where she started. The adult child of an alcoholic may eventually need the assistance of alcohol to suppress any memories, feelings or dreaded similarities between herself and her parent. The adult child of a chronically mentally ill parent can erode her own mental health with worry that she will be just like her parent. The adult child of child-abusers can become crazed at her own children for putting her in a position where she could be like her own parents, and if the rage is not recognized and safely channeled she may well do to her children what was done to her.

For many women who grew up in unhappy homes, the problem wasn't that they learned unhealthy and destructive methods of coping with problems, it's that they learned no methods at all. Boys are encouraged to fight back when others try to violate them, and as a result many males unfortunately see violence as the normal way to try to resolve a variety of problems. Girls, however, are encouraged to do nothing, and the helplessness a girl learned in childhood often carries over into adulthood, where passivity seems the only way to handle problems:

> From being sexually abused, I have a hard time believing I have any control over my body, so when I took a self-defense class, after already being raped—because it was offered as part of a Victim's Compensation Program —it blew me away when the instructor said that if you didn't act submissive, it might discourage the attacker. Since I was a little kid, I've done what men told me to do, even if I didn't like it.

With later experiences to confirm the girl's sense of helplessness and no skills to prevent future victimization, she may well have grown to womanhood concluding, "Once a victim, always a victim."

But girls and women can learn this stance in other ways, too. If, for example, a girl was raised in a home where her mother was beaten by her spouse or boyfriend, she may conclude that being a victim is synonymous with being a woman. As Evelyn Reed explains:

> A mother's victimization does not merely humiliate her, it mutilates the daughter who watches her for clues as to what it means to be a woman. Like the traditional footbound Chinese woman, she passes on her affliction. The mother's self-hatred and low expectations are the binding rags for the psyche of the daughter.[1]

The belief that life is one bad thing after another can become well entrenched in a child's mind, because in troubled families potential happy times were rare and fleeting, always overshadowed by the unhappiness. How to allow and enjoy pleasant feelings is learned just as how to cope with "bad things" is a learned skill. Not only was there little room for good feelings in troubled families, but with everyone competing for the little bit of available nurturing, the child may have learned that it was dangerous to be more competent or happier than her parents:

> When I was thirteen, my dad bought me tickets to a Broadway show for my birthday and was going to take me out to lunch. My mom was real jealous. I was ready to leave when the class bully called. She said I had to do this assignment for her or she would beat me up. I did the only thing I knew to do—I hung up on her. My mother saw or heard me do this and flew into a rage about how cruel and vicious I was. She beat on my head and her ring gashed my cheek. My father did nothing, just took me from the house, told me to go into the service station bathroom and wash the blood off. I did and we went to the play. He never said anything about it, but we all knew she had been building up to it for days.

No one can live without any kind of joy or feelings of competence. Many of the women we interviewed had been labeled as "survivors" or "mature beyond their years" as children living in troubled families, and they liked these labels. Unfortunately, though, as adults they need continuing adversity to keep proving their worth and strengths, and life thus becomes a series of ordeals which must be survived and obstacles which must be overcome.

Still other women learned to live in anticipation of the final bad thing that will happen to them. Many of the women we interviewed who had been sexually or physically abused told us they grew up not expecting to live very long:

> Only the girls were hit in my family, but we were hit a lot. Many times I saw my life flash before my eyes. I was sure that this was it. I was also sure that this was happening to me because I was a girl and that families try to murder their girls and save their boys. Even though I know that's childhood nonsense, I've never been able to picture myself living beyond thirty or so. I was convinced I would either be murdered or executed because I had murdered someone else.

Most people do not experience the full force of the phenomenon called "death terror" until they are adults. Often it is triggered by the death of a parent, an event which brings closer to home the mortality of the following generation. Dealing with the fact of mortality is difficult for mature adults. For children, it is overwhelming.

Many grown children of troubled families look back with some shame at the scared little girls they once were. They wish they had reacted to the troubles in their families differently and will now describe their past fears and behavior as "silly." But the little girls they once were had ample reason to be scared, and their past behavior is nothing to be ashamed of. They did the best they could under circumstances not of their choosing and not of their making.

Today a woman who grew up in a troubled family can help herself greatly by seeking to accept, understand and befriend the little girl she once was. Giving that little girl the love she was deprived of in the past is necessary if the grown-up woman is to learn to love herself.

BLUEPRINTS FOR CHANGE

Growing up in a troubled family can have so dramatic an impact on a woman's self-esteem that it would be foolish for us to suggest one or two exercises to repair that damage. We do, however, have some thoughts on ways to begin to change your self-concept and build self-esteem.

One of the first steps to feeling better about yourself is to recognize the self-esteem–destroying legacies of childhood for what they were: reflections of your parents' problems which have no bearing on your inherent worth. The second step is to believe that you deserve compassion and understanding for the troubled home life you experienced as a child:

> As a kid I was slapped and called all kinds of names and often told I was no good. I have a hard time believing anyone thinks I am any good now. But I read in the papers about kids who get burned by cigarettes and scalded and their bones broken. None of these things ever happened to me, so sometimes I get down on myself and think I shouldn't feel so sorry for myself and I'm just a big baby.

This woman's self-esteem is low enough; she does not need to diminish it further because she is not a "bona fide" battered child. But women who grew up in troubled families often make erroneous comparisons between themselves and others, always coming out less worthy of sympathy themselves. A victim of brother-sister incest believes she has no right to complain compared to a victim of father-daughter incest, even though to her the abuse was devastating. The daughter of a manipulative, withdrawing alcoholic believes she deserves no sympathy compared to the daughter of violent alcoholics, even though her parents may have been just as psychologically destructive. A woman whose parent died in her teen years believes she is not as bad off as another woman who lost a parent when much younger, even though her grief was great and her family was traumatized by the death. To begin to recover, a woman needs to be able to say, "What happened to me may not have been the worst thing in the world, but it was bad enough, and I have feelings about it that deserve to be worked out."

It took at least one other person to instill your inaccurate ideas about yourself; it might well take another person to help you unlearn those ideas. Talking openly about your background to a trusted, carefully selected friend, joining a self-help group or seeing a psychotherapist are all options that have helped other women from troubled families. Reaching out for help does not mean you're sick or crazy; it just means that you're taking care of yourself as you deserve.

No doubt you came out of your childhood with some strengths. Perhaps part of your effort toward more self-esteem would be to channel in a different direction the strengths that have already helped you survive:

> I was somebody's lover when I was four years old. My father trained me well, and I learned to be very good at taking care of other people. Now I am taking that skill at taking care of others and learning to take care of myself. Sometimes I slip back—I put someone else's needs ahead of mine when that isn't the best thing for me. But I'm discovering that I am pretty competent at making myself happy too. Since no one had done that for me in my life, I decided it must be up to me.

* 7 *

Moving On from Our Childhood Families

> In burying the parents of childhood [she] . . . must make do with
> the rest of the world minus two. Not such a bad trade after all.
>
> —Sheldon Kopp
> *If You Meet the Buddha on the Road, Kill Him!*

A common way we rob ourselves of self-esteem is by dwelling on the poor parenting we received. Because our parents raised us all wrong, we came out all wrong, and there's no way we can be all right, let alone worthy. To acknowledge that our parents did something right in spite of their own limitations would result in our saying, "Well, maybe I didn't turn out so bad after all." Then, lo and behold, the next step might be liking and valuing ourselves.

Blaming parents serves other purposes as well. It keeps us bound to our parents, perhaps after our parents no longer want to be connected to us. And it gives us an excuse to wallow in inertia and self-pity. By blaming our parents, we avoid taking responsibility for our own lives and never direct energy toward needed changes. That energy is already used up in lamenting the "irreversible" damage our parents have done.

A woman who wishes she could go into business for herself expresses much anger that her mother drilled into her that if she did not stay home where she belonged, she would have only three choices: to become a secretary, a nurse or a teacher. By myopically focusing her anger on her mother, she fails to see the socioeconomic forces behind her mother's lessons. She overlooks the fact that even had her mother been more positive about her choices, she would still find her options restricted because of sexism and economic "ghettoizing" by gender.

Furthermore, by concentrating only on her anger, she blinds herself to the possibility of change, ignoring that there are scores of business-women around who could be role models for her.

Another woman experienced very real panic as a child when her mother would leave her alone with no idea of where she could be reached or when she was coming back. Never having resolved the fear and anger from that time, she worries that each time her lover leaves, he will not come back. She either clings to him or lashes out, and eventually he does leave and never comes back.

Another woman searches in her adult relationships for the unconditional love she missed as a child. She does not know the term "unconditional love," but she knows what she wants and isn't getting. Her friends and lovers must pass so many tests and meet so many demands to prove to her that they will accept her in spite of her bad behavior. But the proof never materializes. On the contrary, people grow weary of her histronics and end up actually disliking her.

All of these women do not realize that their needs have changed since childhood. The first woman no longer needs to have her mother tell her what to do, or to rely on her mother as her main role model. The second does not realize that, as an adult, she must learn to live with a degree of uncertainty and without constant reassurance of her lover's intention to stay with her. The third does not understand that there is no unconditional love in adulthood, that there are just reciprocal friendships based on the give-and-take between two people who are voluntarily involved with each other. Each woman is motivated by needs that are decades old. No wonder their lives don't seem to be working out.

Many women believe that if their parents taught them that they aren't worth much, then it must be so. But an important task of adulthood is sorting out the negative and inaccurate self-perceptions we were taught and replacing them with something more accurate and positive. After all, we are adults now and have power and the potential for insight, judgment and personal change that we never had before. We are no longer dependent on our parents for our survival and no longer have to rely on them to define who we are and what we're worth.

If we refuse to alter the belief that our worth was determined by bad childhood experiences, then our adult self-concept will be a reflection of then, not now. Nathaniel Branden observes:

> Many a person faces life with an attitude that, if translated into explicit speech, which it almost never is, would amount to the declaration, *"When I was five years old, important needs of mine were not met—and until they*

are, I'm not moving on to six!" On a basic level these people are very passive, even though, on more superficial levels, they may sometimes appear active and "aggressive." At bottom, they are waiting, waiting to be rescued, waiting to be told they are good boys or good girls, waiting to be validated or confirmed by some outside source. (Emphasis added.)[1]

Such waiting diminishes our self-esteem. Beyond recognizing that our needs are different than they were when we were children, we must move on toward the adult task of defining ourselves.

If we feel trapped by unfulfilled needs that arose out of childhood experiences, we first need to understand them as best we can. In terms of the self-concept, it is helpful to understand how much of any belief about ourselves is an accurate reflection of us and how much is the product of circumstance or other people's misperceptions.

Although our parents cannot, and should not, be expected to fulfill our anachronistic needs, they can, if willing, help us to sort out our past in a constructive way by answering our questions and providing information to clarify our memories. Accurate information is important, as Adrienne Rich reminds us:

> Every journey into the past is complicated by delusions, false memories, false naming of real events.[2]

The more of these inevitable false namings we can rid ourselves of, the more we will know about ourselves and the better we can feel about ourselves:

> When I was ten years old, my parents sat me down and told me I was adopted. It was never discussed again and I was told not to tell anyone outside our family. I always felt there was something unacceptable about me in my parents' eyes because of this. Finally, when I was twenty-eight, I built up the courage to ask my mother about the circumstances of my adoption. How old was I? Why did they adopt? Had they had other children who died? Had they tried to conceive for a long time? I was terrified, but when I asked my mother about it, she acted as if she had just been waiting for me to ask. She told me they had wanted children for a long time, but she was infertile. They wanted a baby so much. It turned out she didn't want me to talk about it when I was a kid because of her embarrassment over her infertility—it had nothing to do with me.

Many women who are angry with their mothers have difficulty remembering, or even recognizing in the first place, that it is not the mother they know today with whom they are angry, but the mother of ten or twenty or sixty years ago. Moreover, some fail to recognize that the mother of ten or twenty or sixty years ago was the mother as perceived through the distorting eyes of a small child—and perhaps further distorted in memory. Just as we grow and change, so do our parents, and both our powers of perception and theirs have probably changed over time as well. As children we could not possibly understand the complexity of our parents' lives, but with our adult powers of insight and judgment perhaps we can make headway toward understanding now:

> The last time I was home, for some reason, my mother and I were discussing her denture problems. I had known about them as a child growing up and I always believed her teeth went bad when she was nineteen. As it turned out, they started to go bad then, but they didn't get infected and pulled out until she was pregnant with me, many years later. The oral surgery was really botched, and she had to have several more operations. I was a sickly infant, and she was so sick and not getting proper treatment. It helped me to understand how we got off to such a bad start.

A simple piece of information enabled this woman to let go of some of the pain and confusion she felt about her relationship with her mother.

Before we approach our parents with our questions, we need to ask ourselves, "Do I really want to know what they think?" There can be payoffs in blaming our parents, and sometimes the benefits outweigh the perceived benefits of clearing up the falsehoods Adrienne Rich spoke of. One woman explains this dynamic in her own life:

> My parents taught me a lot of things. Some of them, like my explosive temper and my greediness, I still have and I can blame that on them. It's real clear. Yet they also taught me not to drink or swear or to have sex before I am married or to date black men. Those were strong lessons, too, but I overcame them or ignored them or whatever. So how much of the other stuff can I blame on them?

This woman poses a good question. We don't mean to contradict what we have said about how our childhood experiences shape our self-concepts. But the point that cannot be overemphasized is that as adults we are no longer powerless in relation to our parents. We have considerable freedom to define ourselves. Sometimes we selectively choose our parents' legacies to explain shortcomings of ours that we have absolutely no intention of overcoming.

Some women still feel powerless in the company of their parents and are afraid to engage in an adult dialogue with them. They fear they could be destroyed for asking. Often our stance as children carries over into adulthood and prevents us from relating differently to our parents:

The dependency position of children makes it almost impossible for them to perceive their parents objectively. Even as a grownup, a person may have delusions of his parents' omnipotence and place them in roles of supernatural beings, not seeing them as mortals who have frailties. He may even feel disloyal if he has negative thoughts about them and try to suppress any feelings of anger, hurt or grief toward them.[3]

Still other women compensate for their feelings of fear and dependency by imagining that *they,* not their parents, are omnipotent, and that therefore any questioning on their part would destroy their parents. For some of us, "moving on" means trading in the illusion of negative power for the risk of recognizing the potential of the positive power we have *in our own lives.* As Sheldon Kopp writes:

My sense of power over others will limit my freedom to live out my wishes for myself.[4]

If we decide we really do want to know how our parents think and feel about something in the past, and we are willing to hear their answer, our chances of finding out what we want will be greatest if we keep our request as specific as possible. What is a parent to say to the sweeping accusation, "Why didn't you ever love me?" Sometimes we simply need too much at once without realizing it:

I was in a psychodrama workshop and this woman presented her problem: Her needy and demanding father was coming for a visit and already she was feeling angry and resentful. The leader had her pick someone to be her father, then told her to pick up boots, parkas, purses and the like and to identify each as a need her father had of her and put it in his arms: "You need to be in control, you need to put people down, you need to have all your jokes laughed at, you need to always be right" and on and on and on it went. . . . It wasn't long before this guy was buried in snow gear. Then she was told to pick up objects and identify them as her needs of her father. Her tone of voice changed. Rather merrily she said, "Well, I need to be loved, and to be understood, and respected, and to be left alone," etcetera. When she was through, they tried to make eye contact but couldn't—their "needs" were piled so high neither could see over them. So they were both asked to let a few go. The father let most of them go, except the need to have his jokes laughed at.

The woman in this story would have to let some of her needs go before she could learn about herself as well as being able to "see" her father. It is not as simple as throwing snow gear on the floor; needs may have to be let go one at a time, with considerable help and encouragement from people outside the family.

Even if we ask a reasonable and specific question, we must be aware that our parents may not want to answer. Sociologist Jesse Bernard reminds us:

> Children have always had the option to call on mother for help and support until they were fifty. Mother must have the right to say, "OK, I've done my share. I'm finished."[5]

Fathers have the same right. Circumstances may prevent our parents from giving us what we ask for. It may not be that they don't want to be helpful; it's that they may have complicated lives too:

> I'm sixty-three now and I really wonder when it's going to be over. When my mother was my age, her mother was long since dead, but with people living so much longer, I will probably be really elderly before my mother dies. She calls me a lot and needs a lot from me. At the same time, my daughter is in her thirties and is in therapy, and she demands a lot of support from me too. I thought my old age would be for myself, childless, no longer having to take care of everybody.

Our self-exploratory questions to our parents need to be presented when the time is right for them and in a way that does not intrude on them. It will be helpful to reassure them that we are no longer asking them to define us; we are only asking for some more understanding of how some of our sense of self came to be. However, parents still can and will react defensively at times:

> When I was ten, I got molested by an old man on my way home from school. I told my mother about it, and she told me never to tell anyone and to forget about it. I was only ten, so I did what she told me. Except, of course, for the forgetting about it part. How could I forget it? It was a horrible experience. When I grew up and had a daughter of my own, the molestation really started coming up in my mind a lot, and so one time when my mother was visiting, I asked her why she didn't call the police and why she swore me to secrecy. She got angry at me and refused to talk about it. I kept pressing her, and what she finally told me is that the molestation really wasn't a big deal, that I took it much more seriously than I should have. The guy was really harmless, she said. We've never discussed the subject again.

When we ask about something, we take the chance that our parents' and our own perceptions of an event or issue will be irreconcilably different:

> In my job I've had to deal with child abuse legislation—it's my first contact with any of this. I was telling my father about this, and he said he couldn't

understand how parents could do that. He went on to say he had hit my sister only once, when she had stolen something. I was flabbergasted—I could remember a dozen times he had beaten her. Later, she brought it up with him and he remembered it exactly the same way. In his mind, he only hit her once.

Whom are we to believe? Another integral part of moving on is learning to trust our own judgments as much or more than our parents'.

Some past events and experiences can never be explained by our parents. Obviously, if our parents are deceased, we cannot benefit from their clarification of something important to us. If our parents were not healthy in some critical way, then we must let go without their help:

> My mother was real crazy when I grew up and she still is. She's been in and out of institutions. I used to feel real inferior because I had this crazy mother. I needed her to be a "good" mother and felt terrible that she wasn't. There weren't any real good relationships in our family, so when I was in my thirties and still without a solid relationship, it was easy to blame her. Finally, I realized she was never going to change. I could keep on beating myself up mentally about *her* problem and never get what I wanted, or I could realize that my relationships were pretty much up to me, no matter what she contributed to my outlook. I put more energy into how I was with the men I was dating and less into worrying why she was sick and what it meant about me. She really can't prevent me from having my own family. I would have to do that all by myself.

This woman managed to overcome being defined by having a disturbed mother. Sometimes parents just don't have what we need, or think we need. We can't change the experiences of our past, but we can often change how we feel about them today, (as opposed to how we felt about them when we were children), and we can avoid wasting our time and energy by reliving them. They were bad enough the first time, when we had no choice. Why choose to still actively live with them?

Often we can gain understanding without the direct participation of our parents. Particularly the older we get, the better our chances of being able to see our parents not as all-powerful giants, but as vulnerable humans who've had their own problems and pain. Mitsuye Yamada writes:

> Through the women's movement, I have come to truly appreciate the meaning of my mother's life and the lives of immigrant women like her. My mother, at nineteen years of age, uprooted from her large extended family, was brought to this country to bear and raise four children alone. Once here, she found that her new husband who had been here as a student

for several years prior to their marriage was a bachelor-at-heart and had no intention of changing his lifestyle. Stripped of the protection and support of her family, she found the responsibilities of raising us alone in a strange country almost intolerable during those early years. I thought for many years that my mother did not love us because she spoke of suicide as an easy way out of her miseries. I know now that for her to have survived "just for the sake" of her children took great strength and determination.[6]

Sometimes in our search, in our effort to let go, we risk finding answers that will sadden us:

I go home every year and try to feel like I'm part of my family, but I feel like I'm banging my head up against the wall. The last time I was there, I looked around the dinner table and not only was everyone boring and limited, they also weren't very nice. They were all complaining or gossiping about who wasn't there. I realized that if I weren't related to these people, I wouldn't even be having dinner with them.

Nowhere is it written that members of a family must or will like each other. We tend to discount the opinions of people we don't like or respect. Sometimes we need to adopt the same attitudes toward our family's opinion of us.

Out of even the most defective parenting probably came some good, and so it's always helpful to hold onto the good as we reject the bad. Perhaps the generally cold parent had moments of tenderness and warmth, or the hypercritical parent had talents that were passed on to us. By refusing to be defined by our parents, holding on to the good we got from them and becoming close to people of our choice, we can take the power away from the little girl who could not understand what was happening in her family and give it to the adult who can take care of herself, learn about herself and like herself.

BLUEPRINTS FOR CHANGE

I. REHEARSING

Before you ask your parents any specific questions about the past, have a fantasy conversation with them in your head, or write it out. Prepare yourself for all possibilities: anger, refusal to answer, misunderstanding, defensiveness, not knowing the answer, differing perceptions, etc. Perhaps it would be helpful to rehearse with a trusted friend who could give you feedback about the effectiveness of your approach. Any rehearsal—solo or with a friend—will help alleviate anxiety and prepare you for potentially disorienting responses.

II. Unmet Childhood Needs

What are your unmet childhood needs? Are they needs a person twenty or thirty or sixty years old can realistically expect to have met? Are your needs the kind that you can meet yourself or that you can reasonably ask another person to meet? Or do you still have an intense "life or death" dependency on others that is more typical of a young child? If you are still motivated by unmet childhood needs, can you either let them go or update them?

We have found it useful to remember that between equals it is not fair to ask for something that we are not ourselves willing to give. Unconditional love is an example: If now as adults we are not willing to love our parents unconditionally, then it is not fair for us to demand that they love us unconditionally.

III. Life Decisions

For women who have a particularly negative relationship with their parents and still feel defined by them, we sometimes ask the following questions:

> If you were going to make a major purchase, like a car or a house, would you ask your parents for advice?
>
> If you were seriously ill, perhaps hospitalized, would you want your parents to come and take care of you?
>
> If you had a difficult life decision to make—whether to have an abortion or move out of the country for an extended period of time—would you ask your parents' advice?

Many women who feel bad about themselves because their parents taught them they were worthless will respond without hesitation: "No, I wouldn't involve them in those decisions. They don't understand or know me, they aren't able to be nurturing, they are hypercritical of me, etc." Yet when it comes to the most important decision of their lives, if they are worthless or not, these same women take their parents' word as fact. The next step is to consider why a woman who rejects her parents' opinions in other areas still would embrace her parents' assessment of her worth. Is this the only way she can remain connected to them? Does she fear that if she let the feelings of worthlessness go, she would have to let her parents go and that would be too painful? If so, does she imagine that would bring more pain than she is currently feeling by living with the feelings of worthlessness? Could it be she doesn't want to be fully involved in life and needs the excuse of her parents' negativity? Although we are not responsible for the roots of our low self-esteem, it is often helpful to consider what we gain by perpetuating it in adulthood.

* 8 *

Friends, Lovers and Spouses:
The Power of Chosen Intimates

> Fresh air. To move from family to friends is like throwing the window open on the first true day of spring. The word "bond" comes to take on a different meaning, one that emphasizes its positive side, the connectedness, and submerges the negative, the bondage. Choice breezes in. One can take and leave a friend with more ease than one can embrace mother, sister, sister-in-law, aunt, niece, grandmother. At the same time, the anchor lifts, for one begins to move in a world of friends with greater risk, less assurance.
>
> —Louise Bernikow, *Among Women*

Powerful as they were, our parents and siblings were not the only ones to have influenced how we see and judge ourselves. As we grew older and our sphere of relationships widened, others outside the family had an increasing impact. Of these, perhaps the most influential were and are our friends, lovers and spouses. As opposed to our blood relatives, whom we did not choose, friends, lovers and spouses are people we have chosen to be involved with. And they are often people we have chosen to be more intimately involved with than with family members. In a recent survey, for example, the vast majority of people said that in a crisis they would turn to a friend before they would turn to a family member.[1]

Many past writers on psychology have overlooked the links between chosen intimates and personality development, focusing exclusively on the childhood family. But personality development is an ongoing process that continues through life, and our chosen intimates throughout life label us, treat us in certain ways and model for us certain behaviors just as our parents did. Like our family members, our chosen intimates can effect self-esteem in both negative and positive ways. Although it may be a challenge to find, nothing can enhance self-esteem as much as a truly loving and close relationship with another human being: what a boon and a blessing it is to be able to reveal to another all parts of ourselves, even those parts we think are unacceptable:

> Its always a rush to me when people outside my family genuinely love me, as an adult. They didn't have the advantage of knowing me when I was an infant and lovable. And they don't *have to* like me, let alone love me. So when someone chooses to love me, or I choose to love someone, I feel very special.

On the other hand, perhaps nothing can damage self-esteem as much as an intimate relationship which turns sour. If we are insulted, mistreated, snubbed or rejected outright by someone to whom we have chosen to give our love or affection, we can feel as if struck by a blow, and our self-esteem may be the worse for it—at least for a while. In our heads, we may know that being mistreated or rejected by a loved one does not make us worthless, but in our guts worthless is how we feel.

For women especially, the impact of relationships with chosen intimates is great. Raised to be nurturers and believing in the importance of nurturing, most women place a high value on interpersonal relationships, and our sense of self-worth is tied up with whether we are successes or failures in those relationships. While men can value intimacy, most have been raised to place more stock in worldly achievement and success than in relationships, and so for men the question "Am I worthy?" often translates into "Am I accomplished? Am I a success in the eyes of other men?" Women, however, tend to be more centrally concerned with such questions as "Am I a caring, kind and nurturing person? Am I capable of giving and receiving love? Am I a good friend, lover and/or spouse? Have I lived up to my responsibility to other people in my life?" These sorts of questions are frequently pivotal to a woman's sense of self and self-worth. This holds true, we have found, even for those women who are concerned with achieving worldly success and accomplishment. Such women might derive a significant amount of self-esteem from what they have achieved in the world of work, but still remain fundamentally concerned with their relationships and responsibilities to others.

The Importance of Female-Female Bonds

Past authorities on female psychology tended to acknowledge the importance of women's relationships with males alone. Given extremely short shrift in the literature on female psychology is the role of female-female relationships. And where the existence of such relationships is acknowledged, they are often dismissed as unimportant or depicted in negative terms.

Writers like Lionel Tiger and others have tried to convince us that only men know how to bond and that women are incapable of befriending other women. This and similar notions are not only misogynist, they are entirely out of touch with present and past reality. History teaches us that women have been to one another the best of friends.

Women's ability to bond with women is well demonstrated by the work of historian Carroll Smith-Rosenberg. Researching the experience of women in America in the 1700s through the mid1800s, Smith-Rosenberg found that intense friendships between women were the norm, and women were so involved with each other that men hardly figured in their emotional lives at all. Women, excluded from the domain of men, created a nurturing world of their own that was beneficial to their self-esteem, as Smith-Rosenberg explains:

> . . . an abundance of manuscript evidence suggests that eighteenth- and nineteenth-century women routinely formed [deep] emotional ties with other women. Such deeply felt, same-sex friendships were casually accepted in American society . . . [and] a female world of varied yet highly structured relationships appears to have been an essential aspect of American society. These relationships ranged from the supportive love of sisters, through the enthusiasms of adolescent girls, to sensual avowals of love by mature women. It was a world in which men made a shadowy appearance . . . [and] was, as well, a female world in which hostility and criticism of other women were discouraged, and thus a milieu in which women could develop a sense of inner security and self-esteem. . . . They valued each other. Women, who had little status and power in the larger world of male concerns, possessed status and power in the lives and worlds of other women.[2]

As the research of historians like Smith-Rosenberg and Lillian Faderman illustrate, women in the past placed a high value on intimate relationships, just as many women today do.[3] The crucial difference, though, is that today we are expected to make a primary and intimate attachment to a man, and women in Colonial and nineteenth-century

America established their primary emotional bonds with other women. Although close, loving relationships did exist between some men and women, most women, even if married, turned to women rather than men for emotional sustenance. Moreover, many turned to members of their own sex for physical affection, and marriage in no way meant an end or even an interruption in female friendships. When a woman married, she and her husband were frequently accompanied on their wedding trip by the woman's sisters, cousins, and friends; and as the years went by, women routinely left husbands behind to vacation with their women friends. Moreover, women visited one another in their respective homes as much as possible, sometimes "even dislodging husbands from their beds and bedrooms so that dear friends might spend every hour of every day together." Among Quakers, when a women was dying, "women relatives and friends slept with the dying woman, nursed her and prepared her body for burial."[4]

An important point to be made about the romantic friendships many women in the nineteenth century had is that while they were often passionate, long-lasting, and involved considerable physical contact, they were not necessarily sexual in the sense of involving genital contact. In our supposedly liberated age we tend to make extremely rigid distinctions: relationships are seen as either sexual or platonic, and people are labeled either heterosexual, homosexual or bisexual. But it would be inappropriate to label the women who had romantic friendships as lesbians, heterosexuals or bisexuals, because they lived in a time when female sexuality was suppressed and people did not think of themselves and their relationships as sexual or nonsexual.[5]

The trivialization of women's emotional attachments to one another had already begun by the early part of this century, and by the 1920s a new popular definition of normalcy for women had emerged. According to this definition, "normal" women were those whose primary emotional attachments were to men and who identified themselves first and foremost as wives with principal obligations to husbands rather than as women with principal obligations to their own sex. A generation or so earlier, women had had many life-style options: a woman could remain single all her life, as increasingly many did over the course of the nineteenth century; a woman could remain single until mid-life or later, again as increasingly many did; or a woman could live with another woman in a "Boston marriage," the popular phrase for long-term monogamous relationships many women, especially educated ones, in the nineteenth century had. By the 1920s, however, women's options had narrowed; by then, marriage to a man was seen as the only acceptable course, and the sooner the better.[6]

The reasons the married, male-identified woman emerged as the new model of womanhood in the first decade of our century are many and complex. The loss of many lives and other devastating effects of the First World War may have affected women's attitudes toward men and everyone's feelings about families. The passage—finally—of the Nineteenth Amendment, giving women the vote, may have given some women the illusion that equality was theirs, and it certainly helped to bring to a head hostility to women's increasing independence; and the events and excesses of the Russian Revolution helped trigger a conservative movement in many countries, including the United States. Perhaps most important was the advent of psychoanalytic theories, which held that humans' basic drive is sexual, and that women's correct emotional and sexual preference is for men. Lillian Faderman elaborates:

> Regardless of studies conducted in the first third of the century which showed that love between women was normal even statistically . . . the sexologists maintained that women afflicted with love for other women were abnormal. Freud's disciples encouraged them to get medical help in order to be cured of their condition. What had been recognized as natural now became widely viewed as neurotic . . . a problem that necessitated help by a professional trained in dealing with mental diseases.[7]

Friendships Between Women Today

Despite the present-day cultural imperative to make a primary emotional bond with a member of the opposite sex, we heard repeated testimony from women about the primary importance of female friends in their lives. Sometimes the testimony came in the form of straightforward declarations; feminists, for example, would expressly state that their most highly valued relationships were with other women. In many cases, however, women we interviewed would not label themselves feminists, and their testimony as to the importance of female friendships in their lives came out in a more roundabout way as they discussed their lives and problems in general. Even though many of these women were married or living with men, and many happily so, they often revealed that it was to women that they turned for nurturance and advice, for help in times of crisis, for sharing their deepest thoughts and feelings, and for laughter as well.

Louise Bernikow maintains that this is a culture which strives to keep women "prone in the marriage bed and the childbed, prone on the invalid's couch," and that women's friendships with each other "help [us] to remain perpendicular in the face of cultures that attempt to knock [us] over with the hurricane forces of ideology of what a woman should be . . ."[8] Strength can be gained by sharing common life experiences. Without much or any previous interaction, two women can jump into a conversation together, sharing both the feelings of loneliness and the freedom of being single, or perhaps the dreariness and joys of motherhood, or the feelings of competence and sacrifice engendered in a career. Women affirm each other by virtue of their similarities and empower each other by sharing their different views of the world and ways of coping. Paule Marshall writes of this in a memoir of her mother, an immigrant from Barbados, who spent her days as a day maid and her late afternoons in her own kitchen talking with her women friends:

> There was no way for me to understand it at the time, but the talk that filled the kitchen those afternoons was highly functional. It served as therapy, the cheapest kind available to my mother and her friends . . . it restored them to a sense of themselves and reaffirmed their self-worth.
>   . . . It served another purpose also, I suspect. My mother and her friends were after all the female counterparts of Ralph Ellison's invisible man. Indeed, you might say they suffered a triple invisibility, being black, female, and foreigners. They really didn't count in American society except as a source of cheap labor. But given the type of women they were, they couldn't tolerate the fact of their invisibility, their powerlessness. And [together] they fought back, using the only weapon at their command: the spoken word.[9]

For many of us, our first bonds with females were established when we were young girls. Girlhood friendships are not glorified in our culture the way the relationships of boyhood pals are, but they are tolerated and encouraged all the same. Girls even have an edge over boys in establishing intimate ties with one another, as certain modes of behavior are accepted that would not be tolerated between male friends. Females, for example, are allowed to be demonstrative of affection, as males are not. Girls can buy each other little presents or write each other flowery notes, whereas boys would be ridiculed for doing the same. Long phone sessions, sharing of "secret thoughts" and other intimacies, trading clothes, hours spent giggling and gossiping—all these are standard and accepted features in female friendships and none are standard in male friendships. Boys are more likely to have just a group of buddies, whereas girls are more likely to have a group plus a "best friend," and the intense, often consuming best-friend relationships allow the two parties great opportunity to test and develop their capacities for sharing, intimacy, trust, self-disclosure, nurturing, listening and keeping secrets. Toni Morrison wrote of such a rich and complex girlhood friendship in *Sula:*

> . . . each had discovered years before that they were neither white nor male, and that all freedom and triumph was forbidden to them, they had set about creating something else to be. Their meeting was fortunate, for it let them use each other to grow on.

> . . . They never quarreled, those two, the way some girlfriends did over boys, or competed against each other for them. In those days a compliment to one was a compliment to the other, and cruelty to one was a challenge to the other.[10]

Simone de Beauvoir wrote of her childhood friend, Zaza, "I was dazzled by her originality . . . I loved Zaza so much that she seemed to be more real than myself."[11] And one Puerto Rican woman told us:

> We were told all the time, "If I catch you playing with the boys, you'll get hit." From the time I was a little kid, I was told my safety lay in playing with the girls, that boys get you in trouble and you can't depend on men for shit. So we were segregated very young, and strong bonds with girl friends stuck. Even when I was in gangs, my loyalty was to other girls.

Even though the problems that impede female-female bonding have been vastly exaggerated, problems that drive females apart do exist, and they're likely to start cropping up in adolescence. For many of us, adolescence brought a fundamental shift in the way we looked at both ourselves and our female friends. Prior to puberty, we may have been forced to play with dolls and our activities may have been restricted in a variety of other ways, but overall we probably enjoyed some degree of freedom to ignore our gender and get around the constraints attached to it. As puberty transformed our physical selves so that we were now obviously, unmistakably female beings, however, we could no longer escape the consequences of our gender. Somehow we discovered that as our bodies filled out, our options narrowed, and whatever thoughts we once had about being independent agents and important and worthy in our own right now had to be suppressed: Now we were to see ourselves only in relation to males, and our entire worth and happiness were to be determined by whether or not we were able to land one of those alien but admirable creatures of the opposite sex. Whatever feelings of devotion, passion and admiration we once had for our girl friends now had to be suppressed as well. Now many of us learned to regard girl friends not as valuable in themselves but only insofar as they could be relied on for certain activities: talking about boys; helping you get boys; accompanying you to places where boys will be; never looking better than you so as to not steal boys away; leaving with you if the boys don't show up or prove to be uninterested in you; listening to your problems with your boyfriend once you've gotten one; helping you put the pieces back together when he loses interest, or helping you find a way to let him down easy if you lose interest first. Although in adolescence girls may have had a life mission in common with each other, the common mission of catching a male encouraged competition rather than bonding. And to make matters worse, as we reached early adulthood, our relationships with women were increasingly trivialized in the eyes of others:

> In college I was in a bar with my girl friends, and this guy comes up to us and asks, "Are you girls alone?" My friend had the best comeback: "No, we're together."

The heterosexual imperative and its limiting of options is detrimental to the development of the full potential of all girls, but for those whose sexual preference is for other females, it is especially damaging:

> I have terrific memories of friendships with girls in my childhood, but around junior high I slowly but surely became aware that I was terribly different from them. I had feelings for other girls that were the same as what my girl friends were describing about boys, but I couldn't tell anyone. I didn't know what was wrong with me and I didn't know anybody else like me.

For heterosexual women, the pressure to devalue women friends tends to increase rather than decrease in the early adult years. If a woman is heavily involved in a relationship with a man, or in the pursuit of an education or career, she might find she has little time for her female friends. As the pressure to marry mounts, a woman who is intent on finding a male to mate with may increasingly look upon her relationships with women as second-best.

> In high school and college I always put a high priority on spending time with my girl friends. I was never the type who'd stand up my girl friends if a guy called and asked me out at the last minute. But I found that commitment harder to keep as I approached thirty and was still unhitched. My family never would look at me and say, "Isn't it great that she has so many friends." They say, "She's thirty years old and still not married—she's a failure." I figured my girl friends would always be there, I would always have them. But I felt time was running out when it came to men, that I'd better hurry up and find out before it was too late. So even though I felt

bad about it, I started putting my girl friends on the back burner whenever a man came along.

Our culture's negative stereotypes about female friendships add to the pressures to devalue women friends. Some women reported having been taught views similar to the following, found in a survey on friendship:

To attach too much importance to friendships with women is adolescent.

It will be viewed as latent lesbianism.

If you're single, other women regard a close female bond as evidence of not having made the grade in the competition for men.

Interesting women choose the company of men; they do not seek out or open up to other women.[12]

The most common of these negative ideas is that women can't get along with one another. No one looks at the infantile conflict between Norman Mailer and Gore Vidal, or between the male leaders of the United States and the U.S.S.R., and says, "Oh, those men—everyone knows men can't get along with one another." But women in conflict are seen as engaging in a "cat fight," and when two women such as Eleanor Smeal and Phyllis Schlafly debate the ERA it's taken as further proof that women are always at one another's throats.

Friendships Between Men and Women Today

Our sense of connectedness to the human community, our self-knowledge and our sense of being successful in human relationships can be increased by friendships with men as well as with women:

I was raped by a date not too long after I had moved from the West to the East Coast. The only real friendship I had established was with a male colleague. Thank God I had him. He held me while I cried, talked to me in the middle of the night, sat through all my rage, supported me through all the legal mess. He was everything a woman friend would have been to me. I know his friendship helped me heal faster too. One man I had trusted a totally betrayed and injured me. And then there was this man who was there for me. I came to trust him a lot.

Some women we interviewed had little interest in being friends with men—either they wanted men only as lovers, or they wanted nothing to do with men at all. But there are many women who would like to be friends with men, yet their attempts to establish friendships with men have been unsuccessful.

When women attempt to establish friendships with men and the attempts meet with failure and frustration, the tendency of many of us is to blame ourselves. "If only I had tried harder," many women think, "I would have been able to salvage that friendship." But there are many reasons women and men often have difficulty establishing friendships women find satisfying and beneficial to their self-esteem.

One reason women often are frustrated in the attempt to establish friendships with men is that they can't find men who are at all interested in being friends with women:

> I would like to have more male friends, but it's more trouble than it's worth. If I'm interested in a man as a friend, he often automatically misinterprets this as sexual interest, and I have to go through this ordeal of convincing him it's not sexual. Then he feels rejected when really I was seeking him out to begin with. Many times I've been told being friends with me would be a waste of time when they could be spending their time with some other woman who would be their lover too.

Another impediment to friendships between men and women is the fact that women and men often have entirely different ideas about what friendship is. Studies show that men define a friend as someone to do things with, while women define a friend as someone to talk with and share feelings with.[13] If a man expects friendship to center around playing pool and a woman expects friendship to center around long discussions about the meaning of life, there is little chance of the two developing a friendship that would be satisfying to either one.

Women and men also tend to have different ideas about the amount of emotional expression a friendship should involve. Women often want and expect friends to be physically and verbally demonstrative of their affections. Most men have been taught that the only permissible way to express caring and to seek warmth is through sexual activity. Hence, a man may feel extremely uncomfortable about hugging, kissing, and otherwise touching a female friend, because he has learned that such expressions are permissible only in a sexual relationship.

Other men, however, don't seem to feel uncomfortable enough with the idea of touching a woman friend. Time and again women told us they had tried to establish friendships with men only to find out later that the men were intent on sexualizing the relationship regardless of the women's intentions. A woman who enters a relationship with a man expecting that they will be friends can feel betrayed and used when she finds out later that his main intent all along was sexual.

Much of the world still can't accept the idea of a friendship between a man and a woman, and this acts as a further impediment. Since many believe that the basic drive in humans is the sex drive, they presume that whenever a man and a woman are close there must be sexual tension between them. And if there is no sexual link between a man and a woman who are friends, others might pretend there is, or presume that there is something terribly wrong with the relationship:

> At work I am very close to a male colleague. There's nothing sexual about our friendship, but it wasn't long after we started to become friends that the whole office was all atitter with the rumor that we're sleeping together. I tried to quash the rumors, but gave up after a while because hardly anybody would believe it—and those few who did believe there was nothing sexual going on assumed that the only reason that could be is if one of us is gay or has herpes.

The power imbalance that exists between men and women in our male-dominated society also diminishes the chances of a woman establishing a satisfying friendship with a man. Friendships ideally should be formed by equals, but equality is often difficult when men enjoy so many advantages women don't have. A case in point is money:

> Whether it's a date, a friend, or a lover, I find it very awkward that many men I know make so much more money than I do. If I want to pay my own way, sometimes it's a hardship and I end up resenting it. I don't like the sense of obligation nor the one-up position it puts him in if he pays. I've tried sliding scale arrangements—we both contribute to the evening's expense according to our earning power—and that seems to work best. But still, that frustration about money puts a strain on the relationship and has led to more misunderstandings than I care to remember.

The life experiences of males and females tend to be extremely different from the moment of birth; a lack of common experience alone can be enough to impede the formation of successful female-male friendships. Yet as we see it, the principal problem isn't so much that men and women have different life experiences, it's that men often do not respect and take seriously women's life experiences:

> Guys I've known have always shown this real insensitivity to what women go through and how women feel. Like the other day I asked this male friend of mine to stop calling young women "girls." He thought I was being silly and told me I shouldn't be bothered by that. But I have a right

to be called what I want to be called. I don't think he'd like it if people called him "boy" all the time.

Women can be disrespectful of men's experiences too. Overall, however, women tend to show far more respect for men and what men have to say than men show for women and what women have to say. We see this demonstrated in the research on conversational styles of men and women. Good communication is the basis of all good relationships, but communication between men and women is often impeded by men's interruptions. In one study, for example, a large number of male-female conversations were observed, and men were found to have made 96 percent of all the interruptions.[14] No matter how satisfying a woman's relationship with a man is in other ways, if he is constantly cutting her off in mid-sentence and she is always struggling to be heard, she will get the message that she isn't worth listening to.

Many men also show disrespect for women's privacy and time. Some seem unable to fathom that a woman might value privacy over spending time with men. Virginia Woolf was often irked by the egocentric disrespect for her time and privacy that was displayed by the men she knew. She wrote:

> And the egotism of men surprises and shocks me, even now. Is there a woman of my acquaintance who could sit in my armchair from 3 to 6:30 without the semblance of a suspicion that I may be busy, or tired or bored; and so sitting could talk, grumbling and grudging, of her difficulties, worries, then eat chocolates, then read a book, and go at last, apparently self-complacent and wrapped in a kind of blubber of misty self-salutation?[15]

Lovers and Spouses

For many women, the intimates who have the greatest impact on self-esteem are those with whom the relationship is sexual. "Can you imagine," asks Karen Lindsey, "someone saying we're 'just lovers' the same way people say we're 'just friends'?"[16] Today most of us can't. In the past hundred years sex has become the point of reference for all relationships: those involving genital contact are seen as the most important relationships of all. As the Teri Garr character in *Tootsie* said, many women take shit from lovers that they would never tolerate from friends. And for many women, sexual relationships are pivotal to self-esteem as relationships with friends are not. Although a woman's self-esteem can and often does go up and down depending upon how her friendships are going, we found that the self-esteem fluctuations caused by the ups and downs in a sexual relationship were often much more dramatic:

> A lover is someone I have really bared myself to in the most intimate way. So if I get involved with someone sexually, I feel that much more elated than I do when I first meet a friend. And when a lover is angry with me or leaves me, it seems much more devastating and threatening to my self-worth than it would be with a friend. A lover is someone who has been inside me, and I feel they have the power to take something from inside me if they go.

As sexual relationships have the potential to devastate self-esteem, some women find that they can enhance self-esteem as no other relationships can either. A black woman explains:

> I think the fact that I have a good relationship with my husband has helped me to get a lot of good work done, to really advance in my career. Because my basic human needs are met within my family, I have felt energized and can devote the rest of my energy to my work, which is very important. When I am feeling down or fragile, my husband will hold me, talk to me soothingly, and I feel in touch with the child within me that still needs love and nurturing. I don't think we ever outgrow those needs—I don't think we ever should. There are lots of places to get that—I just happen to get it from my husband. When I do the same for him, hold him and listen and comfort, I feel very motherly and feel very strong and powerful doing so. I like both of these sides of myself. And it's a two-way street between us—both of us give and both of us get. Also, I feel this loving relationship helps me to keep the racism we live with from hurting us more than it could.

Unfortunately, not everyone is able to find that one ideal sexual relationship. In adolescence, for example, many girls found that the boyfriends they were supposed to have just never materialized. With so much emphasis placed on the importance of having a romantic relationship, those who were left out of the dating game could not help but suffer injuries to their self-esteem, particularly so since many lost their close girl friends at the same time that they were failing to attract boyfriends:

> That Janis Ian song "Seventeen" about being left alone Saturday nights and never getting asked out on a date was the story of my high school and college years. I never had a date all throughout my teenage years. I tried to do everything I could to make myself more attractive to boys, but the fact was that I was chunky, had kinky hair, bad skin, and the boys just weren't interested. I really felt worthless, especially because my parents and grand-

mother would always say things like, "What's wrong with her that she can't get a boyfriend?" But the worst thing about it was that not having a boyfriend meant not having girl friends either. My old friends from grade school weren't much interested in hanging out with me once we got to high school, because they wanted to be around popular girls—girls the boys wanted to be with.

The wounds to self-esteem caused by being left out of the adolescent dating game can last well into adulthood. This is especially the case if in adulthood a woman remains out of the running. Most of the women we spoke to who were unpopular with the boys in high school did eventually have lovers, either male or female ones, later in adulthood. But a few had never had a lover even at the age when it seemed everyone else had had many lovers. A woman with physical disabilities explains the effect of this on self-esteem:

> Not having dates in high school was hurtful, but at least then there were other girls in the same boat. But when you're in your twenties like I am and you still have never even so much as kissed someone sexually, it's very lonely. I am the only person I know who has never had a romantic relationship, and I sometimes feel like I'm not a member of the human race because of it.

For women who want a long-term sexual relationship but have not yet found it, being temporarily without a lover can mean being temporarily without a solid sense of self-worth:

> My feelings of self-worth are definitely linked to whether I'm in a relationship or not. When I am involved, I feel much better about myself than when I'm not. Whenever I don't have a lover, I feel that I'm the only one who doesn't have one. Everyone else seems to have a lover except me, and I start thinking that since "all the good ones are taken," the fact that I'm not taken must mean I'm not a good one.

Many women enter heterosexual relationships partly or primarily for financial security. The glamorization of romantic love between men and women that has occurred over the course of this century serves the purpose of masking women's enforced economic dependence on men and making it more palatable. Most women are taught they cannot survive in the cold, cruel world without the support of a man, and our social structure makes financial survival without men very difficult. Women's money worries add to the pressure to merge with a man.

Yet merging with a man, although it can bring greater financial security than a woman alone is able to obtain, often means more problems for woman, not fewer. Marriage particularly can mean radical changes in a woman's life, and a woman who marries is bound to go through self-concept dislocation that might be disruptive to her self-esteem. Although it probably does not apply to many marriage bonds being formed today, Jesse Bernard's observation about the impact of marriage on a woman do hold true for the experience of many women who married in the forties, fifties and sixties:

> Increasingly, the shock implicit in the wife's change in occupation has been recognized. From being a secretary, sales girl, teacher or nurse in her own right, she becomes a housekeeper, an occupation that is classified in the labor market and in her own mind as menial and of low status. The apologetic "I'm just a housewife" that she tenders in reply to what she does illustrates how low her self-evaluation of her occupation is, no matter how loudly and defensively she proclaims her pleasure in it. Although the young wife feels secure among her peers because she has succeeded in a goal—marriage—common to all of them, in other relationships she finds herself ciphered out as an individual. She is no longer the young woman who was an individual in her own right, entitled to ideas, opinions, preferences of her own, but only a shadow; it is assumed that her husband represents her. Employers now see her as bound to another and hence not to be taken seriously.[17]

Today marriage is less likely to entail such a drastic change in a woman's life-style. Today most women with jobs keep them upon marriage. Even so, a woman today is still likely to find that others view and treat her differently after marriage—and this can have an impact on her self-concept:

> After living together for seven years, I figured we were already so settled that marriage couldn't change anything. But it really does. I didn't change my name or my job or anything, but people immediately started calling me Mrs.-somebody-else. It was instant invisibility for me in some people's eyes. Then there's the assumption that while I might continue to work now, sooner or later I'll give it up to have kids, and as a result, some of my work colleagues see me differently, too. At home we also play at a lot more of the traditional roles. I don't know exactly why this is happening— maybe it's the outside pressure and all the childhood conditioning—but more and more since we've gotten married, I've been acting like a wife and he's been acting like a husband. Before, we were two people who switched in and out of roles a lot more easily.

Marriage can affect friendships too. Although it is commonly believed that the elderly are the loneliest group in America, in fact, in one study four out of five people who identified themselves as lonely were housewives.[18] Even if they don't marry, two people can literally "forsake all others" when they fall in love. But, as Philip Slater reminds us:

> . . . what real person could satisfy all our contradictory needs and desires simultaneously? Human beings weren't designed to live in isolated conditions on desert islands. There's no perfect food that would render all others unnecessary, and there's no perfect person either.[19]

Isolation in a relationship can cause us to derive too much of our self-esteem from one person, and it puts us in a position where if that person should reject us, the entire foundation of our self-esteem could be demolished. Women who are most successfully involved with lovers and spouses tend to see the relationship as only one of many ways in which they are connected to other people.

Within any love relationship that a woman highly values—whether it is a relationship between husband and wife, lesbian lovers or heterosexual unmarried couple—there can be problems that undercut a woman's self-esteem. The use of "you are" statements is one. Afraid to tell an intimate that "I am angry" or "I feel closed in" many people say instead, "You are so annoying," or "You are suffocating me." By using "you are" statements rather than "I" statements, the speaker shifts all responsibility for her/his problematic feelings onto the other person, and she becomes the one with the problem. The more a particular "you are" statement is repeated by a woman's loved one, the more she might be tempted to believe it:

> Whenever my husband and I get into an argument, he starts telling me, "You are so unreasonable, such a bitch, a crazy woman, domineering, witchy, and impossible to live with." His latest thing is to tell me I'm a Nazi—that's been the label for about a year now. Whenever I yell at the kids, he tells me I'm a Nazi. I think the problem is that he can't handle the idea of a woman being angry. But even though I know that his calling me names is just a defense for him against his own feelings, the names sometimes can really get me doubting myself. If you get called something enough times, you end up believing it—it's hard not to.

In sexual relationships one of the most difficult issues to deal with is infidelity. Although many people continue in a relationship after an episode of infidelity, and many couples end up strengthening their bonds after one has strayed, a woman can feel devastated to find that her lover or husband has cheated on her. Many women take the fact that a sexual partner has strayed as a direct affront to their own sexual desirability; moreover, for many, cheating is a violation of the most basic trust. And to compound these feelings of worthlessness many women feel guilty about feeling upset, jealous and possessive:

> When I found out my husband had been having affairs, I was devastated. I went around feeling like my insides had been ripped out. My whole universe had been turned upside down. I didn't know how to handle those feelings. I felt so ashamed for having them. Having them meant I was dependent, weak, jealous and possessive. There's that whole image of the scorned woman having the fury of hell. It's such an ugly image, and those feelings made me feel so ugly. I felt so ugly that after a while I figured of course my husband would cheat—with such an ugly, jealous wife, who could blame him?

A particularly irksome problem in intimate relationships is one partner's emotional inaccessibility. Many women complained that the men in their lives are less emotionally expressive than even the most emotionally reserved women they know. Many men will not open up their emotions at all, yet the women who are involved with them keep trying to break through. Often the man keeps his defenses up by telling the woman that her request for even the most minimal amount of emotional expression and nurturing is unreasonable, and she—exhausted by the effort to get some show of emotion from him—eventually comes to believe it. In the end they both agree that "he's not to blame for not meeting her needs, she's to blame for having them,"[20] and she condemns herself for being so emotionally demanding rather than condemning him for being so emotionally unresponsive.

Battery and rape can do great harm to a woman's self-esteem as well, and unfortunately many women suffer such violence at the hands of men with whom they are intimately involved. While the myth is that rape is most often committed by a stranger, recent research reveals that the most common type of rape is marital rape,[21] and the second most common type of rape is rape by a friend, date or acquaintance.[22] Eleven to 15 percent of married women have been raped by their husbands;[23] one out of two women will be battered by an intimate in her lifetime;[24] and one in eight college students has been raped by a male friend or date.[25] Any kind of violence can have a devastating effect on a woman's self-esteem, but violence at the hands of a chosen intimate is particularly shattering. When a spouse or friend abuses his power and rapes or batters a woman he ostensibly cares about, he not only violates her body, he betrays her trust and can cause her to doubt her ability to make sound judgments about other people.

Rejection may not shatter self-esteem the way battery does, but it deals a blow that can come close. If someone whose opinion we value—whether friend or lover—rejects us, it can threaten our concept of ourself and threaten our self-esteem, at least temporarily. Being rejected by a lover especially can conjure up the label "unlovable." To make matters worse, there is always the social stigma of being looked upon as a reject.

Women often—and wisely—end relationships when over the long haul those relationships hurt their self-esteem more than help it. However, even when a woman gets out of a relationship and does so for a good reason, she still might be stigmatized as a failure and a reject in others' eyes:

> After each affair breaks up, I feel like you just ought to write a big "I blew it AGAIN" across my chest. And people do wonder—no matter how supportive they are. You're supposed to go to therapy and get fixed, get cured of this infection or disease you have so you won't blow it again. Did anyone ever stop to think there are good reasons, healthy reasons to get out of a relationship—that doing so might mean success? No, instead it's always failure—failure because you couldn't make it work or failure because you chose the schmuck to begin with.

In the wake of a breakup, women often ask, "What's wrong with me? What did I do wrong? How could I have saved this relationship?" There may be other, often more important questions to be asked at the time: "What were the other person's issues? Were my expectations out of line? Is there a way I can spare myself this pain next time and still risk intimacy with another?" The anger, pain, sadness or grief at the end of a relationship need not be complicated by self-recriminations.

Divorce can be particularly hard on self-esteem, especially if the marriage is a long one. For these women, quoted in an article on divorce after age sixty, marriage had meant everything for thirty and forty years, so divorce was especially traumatic:

> For younger couples, divorce is a fact of life, but for me it was a shameful humiliating event which will leave me tarnished for the rest of my life.

> Whatever he wanted I did it. He wanted cheese blintzes, I made cheese blintzes. He wanted help in the store, I helped in the store. You name it, I did it. Now does he say "thank you"? He lies, he cheats, and for an encore, he defects.

> You go through life's zigs and zags, his coronary, your cancer scare, the kids' stormy teens. And after all that, how are you supposed to say goodbye? And why on earth should you have to?

After half a lifetime, what made him do this to me? He gave me nothing to fix, no hope of change.[26]

No matter when a marriage breaks up, divorce can be devastating because of the feeling of failure it typically calls up. Many people look upon marriage as the single most important relationship of their lives, and when that relationship breaks up, they feel like complete and utter failures. Usually, in the wake of divorce the loss of self-esteem is only temporary, but that still doesn't make it easy to handle.

Widowhood can also engender a loss of self-esteem. Most women who marry and don't get divorced will eventually be widowed instead. To experience the death of a loved one is in itself traumatic and often is accompanied by self-concept dislocation and loss of self-esteem. Not only is a widow defined in the eyes of society by a relationship that no longer exists, she also might feel a part of herself is gone now. And after the loss of any loved one with whom a woman has lived—whether it is a husband or a lover—there will be a vacuum. For some women the space is filled with new connections and self-expansion. For others the emptiness remains for a long time.

Barriers to Intimacy

Nearly all the women we interviewed wanted to have successful intimate relationships but were often prevented from establishing as many successful relationships as they wanted. We've identified some of the specific barriers to intimacy that arise in female-female friendships, female-male friendships, and in sexual relationships. Beyond these specific barriers, however, there are more general barriers that can reduce our chances of finding intimacy in any relationship. Because the failure to have successful relationships often translates directly into low self-esteem, we think it would be helpful to look at some of the obstacles that prevent successful bonding.

Perhaps the greatest barrier to bonding is low self-esteem itself. A woman with low self-esteem may choose to live without much intimacy. She might be terrified of letting someone get too close lest they discover the real her and reject her.

Some women with high global self-esteem lack confidence in the specific area of chosen intimates. Although a woman might believe she is a good worker, a good athlete and a creative person, she might be unsure of her ability to be a friend or lover. She will have a reduced chance of successfully bonding and subsequently having higher self-esteem.

Another barrier to successful bonding can be the unfinished business of childhood. If a woman is searching for monolithic parent substitutes to fulfill needs left over from childhood, her relationships are bound to constantly disappoint her. Surrogate parenting is an unfair request: Who would want the time-consuming responsibility of raising another adult? Among chosen intimates, Sheldon Kopp reminds us, ideally "no one is bigger than anyone else. There are no mothers or fathers for grown-ups, only sisters and brothers."[27] If a woman enters a relationship feeling she is in the position of a needy child waiting for salvation, her chances of a successful relationship will be slim.

Displaced anger from childhood is yet another problem that can interfere with intimacy. Louise Bernikow points out how displaced anger can be especially problematic in relationships between two women:

> Because we are seen by each other as well as by men as nurturers, we ask much of one another. Conflict between myself and another woman often reduces to mother conflict, to issues of engulfment and abandonment. She asked too much of me. I asked too much of her. One of us was a mother, drained by other people's demands, unable to respond to the ordinary needs of friendship. A woman expresses need to another woman with a culturally sanctioned feeling of entitlement that she does not have in relation to a man. Conflict comes from unconscious playing out of mother and daughter, too close, too far away, too desirous of the other's approval, too tied, too suffocated.[28]

Relationships with men can also be damaged by displaced anger from childhood. For example, a woman who never came to believe she could survive on her own might become disappointed or enraged with a man who is not the protector or provider she believes she needs.

Beyond personal history, the structure of our society can also reduce our chances of having happy relationships by narrowing the possibilities. Barriers of race, class, ethnicity, age, religious and sexual preference all reduce the number of possible intimates and make it difficult for us to bond with those "not our kind":

> When I was in junior high, I had this really close friend, Nadine, who was Jewish. The school we attended was pretty much divided along race lines, but somehow Nadine and I became friends. We learned a lot about one another's cultures, and I was real happy that we seemed to be able to get beyond the race barriers. . . . Then one day we were walking together and saw a group of black kids, older than us, who were wearing wild dashikis and afros and combs—this was in the first days of the black-power movement—and I looked at them and thought, "Wow, don't they look terrific." But before I could say anything to Nadine, she grabbed my arm

real nervously and said in a real confidential tone of voice, "You know, what I really like about you is that you don't look like a black person. . . ." I stopped straightening my hair and trying to be inoffensive to whites after that, and I stopped being friends with Nadine. I thought she had loved me, but it turned out she never even really saw me.

Unfortunately, our learned intolerance tends to get worse as we grow older. Living as we do in a culture where our differences are focused on more than our similarities, we find ourselves organized in psychological camps whose boundaries can be difficult to cross. This can sorely limit the number of those we see as possible intimates:

> If I had a choice of spending time with a physically disabled man or an able-bodied woman, I would choose to spend the time with the man. I'm defined first and foremost in this society as a disabled person first, a woman second, so he's going to understand a lot more about what my life is like than she is.

Marital status differences can preclude the possibility of bonding too. Block found that only two out of ten women had friends whose marital status was different from their own.[29] Both single and married women complained they had little in common with each other. Couples tend to bond with other couples, making intimacy more difficult by virtue of the matrix relationship where multiple compatibilities have to exist for the relationship to work.

The extremely competitive nature of our society can be another impediment to bonding. Although some women feel competitive with men, the structure of our society usually places us in situations where we are only allowed to compete *with each other.* Some women still compete for the attention of a relatively few available men. Some women in the workplace compete with each other for the relatively few rewards given women. Some mothers compete for recognition as "good mothers" at the expense of another woman who is comparatively a "bad mother." Some feminists compete with each other to prove who is "more radical than thou." The divide and conquer nature of competition prevents us from seeing ourselves as part of the larger picture, as individuals who could be engaged in constructive and collective struggle from which we all could benefit.

Change can also be a barrier to intimacy in this society. Many of us still hold dear the ideal of a childhood friend who remains a soul mate forever, and when we find our actual relationships not measuring up to this ideal—in quality or durability—we wonder what is wrong with us. Given the number of times people geographically relocate in their lives, life-long continuity in a relationship can be difficult. We live in a "throwaway society" and too often the mentality extends to relationships: "This person is not meeting my needs so I'll turn in him or her for the deposit and get a replacement through another relationship." For some, ending relationships is a perverse source of self-esteem: They deem they no longer "need" the other, have evolved beyond the other and now discard their friend, lover or spouse as if throwing out old shoes that clutter the closet.

Many people prefer the initial rush of new relationships to the often less than exciting reality of long-term relationships. Although an attraction to each other may be spontaneous, a satisfying, self-esteem–enhancing relationship must require risk taking, hard work and acceptance of other people's flaws, and many people are not willing to do that kind of work. Joel Block writes here of friendships; we believe his point has bearing on all types of relationships:

> In the dance of friendship, so much of what you see depends on where you are standing when you look. In newly formed friendships we see only the other's virtues. At some latter point, perhaps when inflated expectations have left open wounds, there is a tendency to see only faults. If a relationship survives this critical moment there is the possibility of capturing the other's complexity and becoming true friends.[30]

A friend of ours calls the first stages of a relationship A.R.P. (Acute Romantic Phase).[31] There is such a person as an A.R.P. junkie who deserts at that "critical moment." A classic example of this is the man who automatically loses interest in a woman after he sleeps with her.

Unfortunately, A.R.P. junkies don't wear signs identifying them as such, and this brings us to a final reason why attempts at intimacy can fail. When two people meet, the decision to pursue a relationship is based largely on guesswork. Choices are often made on the basis of incomplete or erroneous information. We can get hard data on a car's repair record, talk with other people who have owned the car, even take it out for a test drive, but there is no *Consumer Guide* for chosen intimates. Even if we do detect a destructive pattern in the person's history with intimates, we sometimes hope that with us, it will turn out differently. Although women often ask themselves, "How could I have been so stupid (insane or masochistic) as to get involved with that person?" we must remember that not all choices are reflections of ourselves. We made our choices on the basis of the information we had at the time.

BLUEPRINTS FOR CHANGE

I. EXERCISING YOUR CHOICES

Stop and think for a moment about your circle of friends. Do any of them differ from you significantly in:

age   sexual preference
ethnicity   social class
race   able-bodiedness
religion   marital status

We are not suggesting that you collect token friends in each category. But when you think about it, do you find that you rule out entire groups of people as friends or lovers? Do you feel isolated from them? Is their friendship something you might enjoy?

II. STANDARDS OF FRIENDSHIPS

Girls are often taught that it's not okay to have standards for friendship. The clearer we are about what we want in a friendship, the more likely we will be to have successful friendships. Having standards is your right. List what qualities you look for in a friend.

Now list what qualities you look for in a lover. Are they entirely different than what you look for in a friend? Or are they extensions of your first list? If not, does this mean that your lovers are usually not friends?

Are there any qualities you want to reconsider on either list? Any that you recognize that get you into trouble? For instance, the requirement that "he has to have a lot of money" or "she has to be depressed like me" might not be the best criteria for forming self-esteem–enhancing relationships. Just as you might want to choose your friends and lovers carefully, choose your criteria carefully too.

III. MANY KINDS OF INTIMACY

Our culture is extremely limited in its definition of intimacy: "Real" intimacy is a sexual relationship between a man and a woman—even if the man and woman do not know or like each other very much. This is a myopic definition; there are many kinds of intimacy. For instance, traditional Eastern cultures value love between teacher and student above all others, while we scarcely consider this intimacy at all. Bonds with animals can be important, too. Researchers tell us that people ill or incarcerated feel better physically and emotionally when caring for an animal. If we expanded our definitions of intimacy, we might find it is not so elusive, that we have it all around us:

> After my last affair busted up, a friend of mine was consoling me. She asked me why this was all so important to me—it was a good question, since the guy was sort of a jerk. I said I wanted the sharing, the continuity, companionship, warmth, etc. She asked how that was any different than what I had with her or a couple of other friends in my life. She was right; I already had those things—all of them—but not in a sexual context. Given how hard it is for some of that to exist in a sexual relationship, I really started to reconsider what I thought I was so desperate for. I already had most of it. What it really came down to was that I didn't feel "good enough" without being in a sexual relationship.

Do you consider intimacy of a sexual nature the *only* intimacy that really *counts?* Are there other ways that you feel connected to other people or that perhaps you undervalue? Intimacy, in and of itself, wherever we find it, is important.

IV. GROWTH OF FRIENDSHIPS

Joel Block states that there are three conditions necessary to healthy relationships. First, both people must be authentic. They must dare to be themselves, for better or worse. If they present a mask, they can never know if they are liked for themselves. Second, both people must be accepting of the inevitable differences between them. Finally, both people must be direct about their thoughts, feelings, wants or needs. We cannot communicate in innuendo, subtleties or lament—"If you really cared, you'd *know* what I need"—if we expect the relationship to thrive or our sense of self to be expanded or enhanced through this connection with another person.

At the same time, Block identified two toxins in friendships, both stemming from unmet childhood needs: blame and overdependency. There is probably no quicker way to stagnate or eventually destroy a relationship than to blame another person for our historic unhappiness or to expect them to make it all better.

V. CELEBRATION OF INTIMACY

Through Valentine's Day and such events as wedding celebrations and wedding anniversary celebrations, people who are romantically involved have the opportunity to commemorate their relationships. But there is no formal mechanism in our culture to celebrate our relationships with other intimates.

Some women celebrate the anniversary of their closest friendship, and people who are not lovers still express their love for each other on Valentine's Day (and many other days as well). What ways can you celebrate the intimacy of your life?

* 9 *

Daughters and Motherhood

> To have borne and reared a child is to have done that thing that
> patriarchy joins with physiology to render into the definition of
> femaleness. But also, it can mean the experiencing of one's own body
> and emotions in a powerful way. We experience not only physical,
> fleshly changes but the feeling of a change in character. We learn,
> often through painful self-cauterization, those qualities which are sup-
> posed to be "innate" in us: patience, self-sacrifice, the willingness to
> repeat endlessly the small, routine chores of socializing a human be-
> ing. We are also, often to our amazement, flooded with feelings both of
> love and violence intenser and fiercer than any we have ever known.
> —Adrienne Rich, *Of Woman Born*

All women are daughters, and it is difficult for a daughter to grow to
maturity without becoming aware of her own potential to become a
mother, without having to integrate into her self-concept the formidable
knowledge that "I, too, could be a mother." To inhabit a female body is
to be constantly reminded of one's connectedness to the mysterious
processes of birth, growth and death. As our breasts each day provide
evidence of our ability to sustain life once it has begun, so the myriad
changes brought each month by the menstrual cycle bring a deep, often
unarticulated awareness of our ability to begin and carry life within.

The ability to bear and breast-feed children has the potential to enhance women's self-esteem. Many consider giving birth to be the ultimate creative act, and the process of mothering the ultimate female
experience. Despite this, it would be erroneous to claim that women's
reproductive capabilities are always a boon to self-esteem. Having a
baby—or being able to have one—cannot be said to be inherently bene-

ficial to self-esteem, or inherently detrimental either. Factors such as a given culture's attitudes toward fertility, the amount of control a woman is able to exercise over her fertility, the way a woman experiences pregnancy, the way that the experiences of pregnancy and birth are handled in her culture, the culture's definitions of motherhood and nonmotherhood, and the ways societies arrange for child care, all come into play to determine how a woman's experience of having children— or not having children—will affect her self-esteem. Also playing important roles are such factors as a woman's age, class status, economic situation, health, and marital status within a specific society. Becoming a mother in preindustrial African society is qualitatively different from becoming a mother in industrialized America or Britain. And within America today, there's a world of difference as well between the experience of a poor, unmarried woman who becomes a mother at age sixteen without having finished high school and the experience of an affluent married woman who becomes a mother at age thirty-five, after completing college and establishing herself in a career.

Fertility: Attitudes and the Issue of Control

A woman has the greatest chance of experiencing her reproductive abilities in a positive, self-esteem-enhancing way if she lives in a culture that respects the female ability to give birth, and gives women control of their own bodies. If the culture holds that childbirth renders women into nothing but "breeders," a woman is not as likely to look upon her reproductive capabilities with reverence and pride, and she's not as likely to feel empowered because of them. And if a woman cannot exercise control over whether or when she will have children, she is likely to have mixed emotions at best about her fertility.

In most preindustrial societies past and present, women's ability to have children was and is seen as awesome and wondrous, and in many such societies it has been the source of women's esteemed social status and ritual potency. Prior to the time when the male role in reproduction was understood, conceiving a child was seen as a magical act women did all on their own, and accordingly women were considered to possess powers of creation men had no access to. Even after the connection between coitus and conception was made and the male role in reproduction was recognized, women in many preindustrial societies were still revered for the ability to conceive and bear children. Because children were so necessary for the parent's survival, and for the survival of the society as a whole, fertility was emphasized and worshiped.[1]

Women's fertility has been so universally revered through most of human history that it has also been the source of considerable male envy. To ameliorate the male envy of woman's womb, as well as of her breasts and her monthly issue of that sacred substance, blood, various preindustrial societies devised numerous ways by which men could feel more a part of the process of creation. Male bloodletting rites such as circumcision, for example, were invented in imitation of menstruation, and male deities were invented and given the powers of creation that in real life were associated with females. To further enable men to feel that they, too, possessed the procreative powers so apparent in women, men in many cultures were given parts to play in the birth process. Among the Tiwi, for example, men make up for their lesser role in making babies by asserting that in order for a woman to conceive, a man must first "dream" the child's spirit into being. And common in numerous cultures is the practice of couvade, by which men try to share the experience of childbirth by going to bed and dramatically feigning labor as their mates go through the real thing.[2] Many believe that male womb envy that is behind such practices is also what led to the eventual development of male dominance; and a case certainly could be built that it is the male desire to take over the process of procreation that, at least in part, has led to the modern day concern with "test tube babies," and the creation of human life in the laboratory.

According to the common Western stereotype, women in preindustrial societies were helpless to control their fertility; hence they were always burdened by pregnancy after pregnancy and the endless tasks of child rearing, and this rendered them weak, powerless, dependent and confined in relation to men. In fact, this was not the case. In virtually all preindustrial societies, women had numerous methods for controlling their fertility, often very effectively. Contraceptive pastes, intrauterine devices, tampons soaked in solutions with spermicidal properties, cervical caps made out of such items as hollowed-out halves of oranges, pessaries, condoms made from animal skins, withdrawal, extended breast-feeding (which usually prevents ovulation), abortion and, finally, infanticide are all among the myriad methods women in preindustrial societies have used to control their fertility and to space their children.[3] Contrary to popular myth, male dominance did not follow from women's inability to control their fertility. On the contrary, it was *after* their dominance was established that men used their new power to deny women the right and ability to control their fertility as women had previously done. As male-dominated Western civilization developed, birth control was outlawed, the women who possessed the secrets of contraception were designated evil, the very idea of tampering with fertility was condemned as sinful by the Church, and women were legally denied the right to say no when their husbands wanted intercourse.[4] By taking away women's right and ability to control their fertility in these ways, men were thus able to keep women "barefoot and pregnant" against their will, and this served as an effective way of controlling women.

The denial of reproductive freedom rendered women unable to exert much control over their lives. Women were left at the mercy of biology and of men. The physical suffering alone endured by women as a result of (often unwanted) pregnancy after pregnancy was great, as many women lost not just control over their lives but their lives themselves. This woman was so angry at her son-in-law for causing her daughter to become repeatedly pregnant that she begged him by letter to let up on his demand for sex lest he end up killing his wife. The letter was written in 1671:

> . . . listen, I have a piece of news for you which is that if, after this son, you do not let her rest a while, I shall believe you don't love her, and that you don't love me either . . . and I was forgetting this: I shall take your wife from you. Do you imagine I gave her to you so that you might kill her, so that you might destroy her health, her beauty, and her youth? This is no laughing matter. At the right time and place I shall ask you this favor on my knees . . . providing I don't come (to your house) to find a woman who is pregnant and again pregnant and all the time pregnant. . . .[5]

This powerlessness to control their fertility and thus their fate was also felt by some of the women we interviewed:

> It was illegal to get birth control in the states we lived in when I was first married (in the 1950s), and my husband and our doctor—his good friend —were against birth control for religious reasons anyway. I had four children in not quite four years, and after the fourth I lived in dread of getting pregnant again. I felt so completely powerless. I had no say over what was happening to me, what was happening *within* me. . . . I hated the idea of not being able to have any control, I started to hate my husband and I hated having sex with him. Then I hated myself for having all these bad feelings.

In more recent years the laws have been changed so that birth control and abortion are no longer illegal. To be sure, of the types of birth control available today, none is foolproof, many have side effects that could damage a woman's health, and most are designed on the presumption that contraception is a woman's responsibility. Moreover, because of age, economics, language barriers and individual circumstances, not all women have access to the available technologies. Nonetheless, the majority of American women today have greater access to the means to control fertility, and to do so effectively, than did women a generation ago. This has made a world of difference in the amount of control many individual women have been able to exert over their lives.

Our greater freedom to choose is not without its drawbacks, however. For with the freedom to choose comes the necessity to choose. By the very nature of choice, when we decide on one option, we give up others. With that comes self-doubt: "Am I making the right choices?" A woman in her mid-thirties explains:

> I think you can have a situation where there are too many choices, and that's definitely how I feel. . . . I think in some ways it was easier when you didn't have that much choice—you just went ahead and got married and had a bunch of kids and you didn't do a lot of agonizing about it. Today it's like women are faced with all these hard decisions about whether to have kids, when to have them, how many to have, under what conditions to have them. . . . When you're faced with that many decisions, there's a high risk that one of them you make will be the wrong one. But you want to make the right ones, because if you decide to have kids, then you've got innocent babies involved in your decision, and if you decide not to have them, there will come a point when you can't go back on the decision—time will have run out.

The question "Am I making the right decision?" and its attendant self-doubts become particularly pressing when a woman is faced with the decision whether or not to abort a pregnancy. Foes of women's right to choose often portray women as having abortions for fun or, at the very least, with little forethought and little concern for the magnitude and moral dimensions of what they are doing. But anyone who has ever visited an abortion clinic and talked to women about abortion knows differently. Many women pay a high price in self-doubt, guilt and emotional pain for an abortion, and often suffer diminished self-esteem for a long while after as a result:

> There was no way I could have had a baby and have supported it and cared for it the way a baby needs and deserves. But having an abortion wasn't easy. I believe that what was inside me was a living thing, and I feel I am responsible for killing that life. . . . I still feel terrible about what I did, and about myself for doing it. But I felt I had no other choice. My abortion was the best thing I could do, the worst thing I could do, and the only thing I could do.

Historically, an attitude of reverence for women's fertility has prevailed in America as in other cultures, and this has helped women's self-esteem. Women in colonial America, for example, might have felt trapped against their wills in an endless series of pregnancies and births, and they lived in fear of dying while giving birth. But a woman who survived and had raised several children into adulthood would have been proud of her accomplishment—and a genuine accomplishment it would have been in a time when infant and child mortality was so high. In her study of white tenant farm women in the South in the 1930s, Margaret Jarman Hagood found this attitude of maternal pride to still be the norm, although—and this is telling—women who were proud of having had children typically wanted no more:

> There is pride in having borne the number they have, yet almost never is there expressed desire for more. The most common example of the first is the ever present suggestion of self-esteem in both words and intonation of answers to the question of how many children the mother of a large family has—"Eleven. I done my share, didn't I?" or "Ten and all a-living." The pride becomes even more exaggerated when the larger sized families of the previous generation are being reported—"My mammy raised and married thirteen," "I was one of seventeen." . . . The bearing, 'raising' and 'marrying off' of children are everywhere recognized as being a positive achievement, a contribution to the world as well as to the immediate family.[6]

In addition to serving patriarchal interests, our culture's attitudes toward women's reproductive capabilities have been tied to and shaped by economics. When farm life was the norm in America, big families were necessary, and so a married woman's ability to bear her husband children—sons particularly—was especially emphasized and revered. In the increasingly industrialized nineteenth century, however, large families were no longer an economic asset for many, particularly the growing white, urban middle class. For many other groups, particularly the increasing immigrant population, large families still were an economic asset; among the urban immigrant poor who worked in the nation's factories, for example, survival was possible only when a number of children and other relatives were supporting a single household. Yet because the white Protestant middle class generated the culture's dominant values, the smaller family became to be seen as the cultural ideal, and the immigrant population was condemned for not conforming to it. When a Yankee farm wife in the early nineteenth century produced a brood of children to insure family survival, that was all well and good. But later, when immigrant women from Italy, Ireland, or Spanish-speaking countries produced large families for the very same reason, this was viewed by many in the Protestant middle and upper classes as a sign of the ignorant immigrants' inferiority, slovenly sexual habits and superstitious Catholic morality.

Although motherhood—under certain conditions, of course—would remain largely revered in our century, there have been large shifts in the extent to which it has been revered and emphasized. In popular culture in the 1920s, for example, the dominant image of women was as boyish flappers with breasts flattened, not woman as fecund and maternal. In the 1930s the hardships of the Depression meant that many could not afford large families, and the birth rate accordingly dropped to its lowest point ever. In the early 1940s, motherhood was further downplayed as images of strong career women dominated the movie screens, and millions of women entered the domestic workforce to keep the wartime economy running in the absence of men shipped overseas.

It wasn't until the end of World War II that a full-blown mystique developed around motherhood. As never before, a woman's worth became linked to her ability to produce children for her husband. During the war women proved they could keep the country going as well as men could, and they could do any jobs men could do—including shipbuilding, ironwork, machine tool and die making, etc.—at least as well, too. But once the war was over, men wanted their jobs back, and so women were forced out of their wartime posts. To facilitate the process of shoving women out of their jobs, the U.S. Government mounted a huge propaganda campaign whose message, in a nutshell, was that woman's proper place was in the maternity ward having babies or at home taking care of them. With womanhood now seen as synonymous with motherhood, and motherhood alone, women were branded as unfeminine and maladjusted if they were not completely fulfilled by tending children and cleaning house. Magazines like *Look* began to sing the praises of the woman who gave up the more emancipated ways of the past and fulfilled her duty to procreate:

> The wondrous creature marries younger than ever, bears more babies and looks and acts far more feminine than the "emancipated" girl of the twenties or thirties. If she makes an old-fashioned choice and lovingly tends a garden and a bumper crop of children, she rates louder Hosannas than ever before.[7]

The campaign to get women back in their "proper place" worked. The 1950s and 1960s had the highest marriage rates and birthrates in this country's history. A woman now in her sixties recalls:

I don't remember anybody in my immediate family ever telling me I should stay home and have babies, but that's what I wanted to do, and as soon as (my husband) got out of the service I couldn't wait to have them. . . . I always thought that all my feelings about wanting to have children were just my personal feelings, but I now realize they were part of the culture, tied in with a larger social development. There was a big "have babies" industry going, and I was playing my part.

The pronatalism of the post-war era meant that women who did not have children would be greatly penalized. A woman who has no children is still seen in our culture as pathetic, pitiable, empty, barren, unfulfilled and not a real woman. In *Of Woman Born,* Adrienne Rich writes of our culture's prejudice against women without children and how difficult it is to speak of such women without using terminology that carries some connotation of condemnation:

In the interstices of language lie powerful secrets of the culture. Throughout this book I have been thrown back on terms like "unchilded," "childless," or "childfree;" we have no familiar, ready-made name for a woman who defines herself, by choice, neither in relation to children nor to men, who is self-identified, who has chosen herself. "Unchilded," "childless," simply define her in terms of a lack; even "child-free" suggests only that she has refused motherhood, not what she is about *in and of herself.*[8]

Yet even women who did what was expected and became mothers did not necessarily develop high self-esteem as a result. In part, this is because of the superficial nature of our culture's pro-natalism. The fact is, at the same time that motherhood (under certain narrow conditions) has been held up as woman's greatest and most fulfilling accomplishment, women's greatest and most fulfilling accomplishment has been trivialized as far less important and valuable than men's accomplishments. To women, the message of our male-dominated culture has been, "Having a baby is a worthwhile thing for a woman to do. But the things men do are what really count."

Unfortunately, some feminists in the early stage of the women's liberation movement that developed in the early 1970s added to the denigration of motherhood. Some feminists put other women down for "just" having babies and raising children, and many women with children, already trivialized by the male-dominated culture, felt further demeaned by feminists. The feminist trivialization of motherhood not only did damage to the self-esteem of large numbers of women, it presented to women a new definition of womanhood that stands at odds with the reality of most women's lives and feelings. In *Mothering,* Elaine Heffner elaborates:

> Women were for a time told that the only way to be a real woman was through motherhood. In order to be whole they would have to sacrifice those parts of themselves that longed for expression in other ways. Now women are being told that in order to be whole they must sacrifice the impulse to mother. In order to be free they must fight the trap of motherhood. Neither view addresses the full range of women's feelings. . . .[9]

Since Heffner's observations were published in 1978, there has been a renewed appreciation within the women's movement for the capacity and role of mothering. Still, among women and among the larger American culture, contradictory attitudes toward women's ability to become mothers continue to exist.

Experiences of Pregnancy

Becoming a biological mother means spending nine months pregnant, and the experience of pregnancy brings with it significant changes in physiology—and often large changes in how a woman feels about herself, too. Some women report an increased sense of well-being and empowerment when pregnant, while others experience pregnancy as unpleasant and debilitating. These two women, for example, experienced pregnancy in completely different ways, and their experiences had the opposite impact on their self-esteem:

> I just loved being pregnant. I felt really at peace with the world, that all was well with it—not intellectually, because intellectually I knew that wasn't the case, but in some way deep inside. . . . And I loved the sense of being ripe, the bigness of it.

> My two pregnancies were the worst time of my life. I had morning sickness all the time, not just in the morning. I kept getting sinus infections and headaches, my veins got all varicose, and I got so fat I was really grossed out by myself. I just had this heavy, bloated, bulging feeling all the time. And when you feel that way and are puking half the time, too, it's really hard to feel good about yourself.

Still other women experience pregnancy as a mixture of feelings and sensations, some good, some bad, but none standing out later as definitive:

> I had a miserable pregnancy and then a few fairly trouble-free ones, but even during the trouble-free ones I had some negative feelings. Overall,

though, I look upon my pregnancies as not being all that significant in the long run of my life or in terms of how I feel about myself. I'm glad I had the experience of becoming a biological mother, but basically my pregnancies were just mildly interesting experiences that I passed through on the way to the larger life-consuming task of being a mother.

There is probably a good chance that a woman will have a more positive attitude toward mothering and toward herself as a mother if her pregnancy has been an experience more positive than negative. Unfortunately, having a positive experience of pregnancy can be difficult in our culture because of contradictory attitudes toward pregnancy and the often demeaning ways pregnant women are viewed and treated. On the one hand, pregnancy is often seen as a debilitating illness, and the pregnant woman is seen as handicapped and even a bit obscene. On the other hand, there is a strong myth in our culture that pregnancy is the most wonderful experience of a woman's life, the time when a woman should feel her best. Consider the dictatorial "you should feel great and if you don't you're a failure" tone of this passage from *For the Young Mother To Be*, a pamphlet for presumably unwed teenage mothers published in 1974 by Mead Johnson labs:

> Pregnancy, *under any conditions,* is one of the most significant and wonderful experiences a woman can have. *You must not let your experience be marred by the problems that surround it.* During the next nine months you will be your healthiest, and with just a little care you can look prettier than you have ever been in spite of your changing figure. Your skill will be clear and radiant, and your eyes will sparkle with anticipation and excitement. [Emphasis added.]

Our culture's attitudes toward pregnancy and the pregnant woman are contradictory in other ways, too. Pregnancy is said to be the experience that, more than any other, signifies female maturity transforming one into a fully grown woman. At the same time, though, the pregnant woman is frequently infantilized in our culture. We see this most notably in the area of fashion: For many years the predominant motif in maternity fashions was the "baby doll" look, and it was difficult for pregnant women to find sophisticated clothes—or even plain maternity clothes without puffy sleeves, little bows at the collar or frills of some sort. And the infantilization of pregnant women occurs in other ways too:

> I had been working in a hospital lab as a technician for nearly three years when I got pregnant, and I never had any problems being given credit for competence. I always felt respected there, and when I was first carrying

that didn't change. But when I really began to show, the head of the lab kept asking me if I was sure I could run the tests okay each time work came in, and he also started reviewing all the procedures with me—as if I was new and just starting training. I had heard that pregnant women often weren't taken seriously, but I hadn't really known what that meant. Then there I was being treated as if being pregnant was like having a lobotomy.

Experiences of Birth

For a woman who wants to have a child, the experience of giving birth has the potential of being one of life's most positive and empowering. For most of history, however, most women have not been able to realize this potential because the risk of infant and maternal death during birth were high. As a result, women's experiences of birth were often shaped and shaded by fear of losing their lives in the process of attempting to give life to another.

In our century most American women's birth experiences have been far less positive and empowering than they could be, not because of the fear of death but because of the medical establishment's take-over of the birth process. To be sure, as medicine has grown in power and influence in our century it has done much to decrease infant and maternal mortality rates, thus making birth in some ways safer. Yet increasing medical control and intervention in the birth process has also brought with it new dangers, and also has meant new risks and humiliations for mothers.

In our century birth, which once took place at home in the company of women, has been transformed by medicine into something that happens in hospitals under the control of male doctors. The male medical profession has arrogated more and more responsibility for bringing life into the world, and has rendered the mother's role as passive, uninvolved and depersonalized as possible. When allowed to give birth as they see fit, most women prefer to move around during labor, and to stand or squat during delivery. In American hospitals, however, women have been forced to lie down—a position that maximizes both the difficulty and pain of birth. Medicine's way of alleviating this increased difficulty and pain is by giving women drugs that either kill their feelings below the waist, render them unconscious or create amnesia so that all memory of the birth experience is erased. This tranformed the birth process, giving the doctor a more active role than the woman. Suzanne Arms describes the process succinctly:

The history of childbirth can be viewed as a gradual attempt by man to extricate the process of birth from woman and call it his own. . . . Man placed woman on her back in labour, then devised metal tools to pull her baby out, then knocked her senseless with anaesthesia. And it was man who, throughout history, did it all in the name of "saving woman from her own body." . . .[10]

Physician Michelle Harrison gives a more detailed description of the dehumanizing way doctors treat women who are giving birth:

When I was in medical school, the ward patients in labor received little or no pain relief, while the private patients were given scopolamine, a drug that wiped out the memory of the labor and birth. Many women loved it and would say, "My doctor was wonderful. He gave me a shot to put me out as soon as I came to the hospital. I never felt a thing." Those women weren't put out, but they didn't remember what had happened to them, at least not consciously. When these women thought they were "out," they were awake and screaming. Made crazy from the drug, they fought; they growled like animals. They had to be restrained, tied by hands and feet to the corners of the bed (with straps padded with lamb's wool so there would be no injury, no telltale marks) or they would run screaming down the halls. Screaming obscenities, they wept, behaving in ways that would have produced shame and humiliation had they been aware. Doctors and nurses, looking at such behavior induced by the drug they had administered, felt justified in treating the women as crazy wild animals to be tied, ordered, slapped, yelled at, gagged.[11]

Perhaps the most telling indicator of the medical establishment's take-over of the birth experience is the rise in the incidence of cesarean births. In her account of her obstetrics-gynecology residency at a major American teaching hospital, Harrison recounts episode after episode in which doctors decide to do C-sections when this procedure is not needed and not wanted by the patient. Harrison believes doctors would prefer to cut into the uterus and remove a baby surgically rather than allow the mother to give birth through her vagina because in a vaginal birth "there is not much for a physician to do but watch," while in a C-section the doctor, as the performer of an act of surgery, is able to feel "a sense of excitement and of power and of personal accomplishment" that is not present in a vaginal birth. Harrison allows that some C-sections are necessary to save lives, but she and others also believe the vast majority are not only unnecessary but actually increase the dangers to both mother and child.[12]

The medical profession in our century also increasingly rendered women passive for long periods *after* birth, not just during it. In some societies, women return to their normal activities immediately after giving birth. In America, however, physicians have routinely required long periods of bed rest—and long (and lucrative for the medical establishment) hospital stays. A woman who gave birth several times in the early fifties recalls:

> There was a lot that happened in terms of attitudes and procedures for childbirth between my generation and my mother's. . . . The doctors took more and more control, and they were really against you. Everything was designed to really cripple the woman. My mother when she had children in the twenties had to stay in bed for three weeks—that was the view then. If you had a baby then, you were allowed to sit up on the ninth day, allowed to put your feet over the side of the bed after thirteen days, and allowed to get out of bed for a little walk on the twenty-first day. . . . By the time I had kids, things had changed, but not much. My doctor wouldn't let me out of bed for fourteen days.

Along with the increasing takeover of the birth process by medicine also came the rise of child-care experts. These experts—mostly men, such as Dr. Spock—held that women are equipped with a maternal instinct that makes us naturally suited for child care. Yet these experts also held that women needed the endless advice of men in order to care for their children correctly. The male child-care experts served the purpose of undermining women's confidence in our own abilities to care for children just as effectively as medical practitioners undermined women's self-assurance about our ability to have children without medical intervention. A woman now in her early seventies recalls:

> I was told that my milk wasn't any good, and that it would be best for my babies to bottle-feed them. . . . I felt really bad about that, really guilty, as though I was an unfit mother. . . . After my third child was born I started questioning the doctor's advice and looking into nutrition and new ways of infant care, and the doctors were against me totally. When I went my own ways, I was always in terror that I would do something wrong. . . . There were always people telling me how I should bring up my children. The doctors, the baby books, the nurses and all my family told me how to feed the babies, when to put them to bed, how to put them to bed. No one believed I could do it on my own. I was so tense all the time I had young children, so afraid I'd do something wrong. It really made it so being a mother was in many ways an undermining experience for me.

The Pleasure and Costs of Mothering

Pregnancy lasts nine months, giving birth usually takes just a matter of hours, but nurturing and raising children takes decades. In American society today, the primary responsibility for nurturing and raising children falls on mothers. We are told that this arrangement is natural, but in fact there is no biological necessity for this. Some male primates participate along with the females in caring for the young,[13] and in various preindustrial societies child rearing is shared by the group. Among the African Ibos, for example, the prevailing belief is that "the child of one is the child of all,"[14] and in America when most people still lived on farms and in extended families, child care was similarly shared by others in addition to the mother.

Among the world's wealthy classes in particular, the idea that women who bear children should alone be responsible for raising them has never had many adherents. Historically, the aristocracy in Europe has placed the responsibility for nurturing and raising children on members of the lower classes, with an aristocratic mother turning her child over to servant women immediately after birth and those servant women performing all the duties we today associate with mothering, including breast-feeding. In America, members of the upper classes have likewise placed the responsibility for mothering on members of the lower classes. The child of slaveholders, for example, might have been breast-fed by her biological mother, but beyond that she would have been cared for primarily by slave women—and she would have received more mothering from her "mammy" than from the woman whose body she came from. Even after slavery was ended, it still remained common for white children from wealthy Southern families to be mothered more by black servants than by their biological mothers, just as today the British aristocracy routinely turn their infants over to nannies for mothering and affluent whites in America are increasingly relying on women from Latin America to mother their young.

For the vast majority of working and middle-class American women in the twentieth century, having a child means taking primary responsibility for nurturing and raising it. Some women might be helped by their own mothers, or by their husbands, or by day-care facilities. But overall, the primary responsibility for "mothering" falls on the mother —and the mother alone. It is a huge responsibility, one that many women are not prepared for, or are even fully aware of when they think of becoming mothers, as Judith Arcana points out:

> Women often speak of "wanting a baby." The person being created is only going to be a baby for two years—even in a conservative estimate. She will, however, be dependent on her mother, in this society, for fifteen to twenty years longer. One does not hear women saying, "I'd like to have someone

physically and emotionally dependent on me for most of her needs for fifteen years." But that reality is hidden behind the socialization that makes us want "babies."[15]

Although the job of mothering as our culture defines it is burdensomely huge, it does carry with it many potential pleasures. In talking to women with children about their experiences of mothering and how these have affected their self-esteem, we heard over and over how good it feels to give love to a child—whether the child is biologically a woman's own, adopted, or the child of a friend, relative or employer. Rarely in our achievement-oriented culture is there public discussion of the deeply satisfying and peaceful sensations that come from nurturing another. But many women know this from experience:

> I never thought of myself as a particularly warm or giving or sensitive person until I had kids. In fact, I was afraid to have kids because I didn't think I had the love I thought they'd need in me. But when I had my first baby, I found that love in me. It was really a tremendous feeling, that outpouring of tenderness I felt. Holding my baby, I felt this sense of oneness and contentment I had never felt before, and it really changed how I saw myself. I could say of myself, "I am a person capable of great love," and before I hadn't been able to. It really changed how I see the world and feel about myself.

Mothering can also increase women's sense of connectedness, both to other individuals and to the future. Moreover, children can be fun and fascinating, and involvement with them can add a dimension to life that many would not want to do without. Also, an enormous amount of pride and satisfaction can be obtained from the knowledge that one has raised children well—or that one has at least given the difficult job of child rearing her best shot.

Yet many women find mothering to be less pleasurable than it could be. One reason for this is our culture's impossible standards for maternal behavior and emotions. Thanks to the media and ever present childcare experts, women are constantly bombarded with ideal images of the perfect mother and are constantly admonished to live up to an endless set of unrealistic expectations. A good mother is supposed to be totally devoted to her children; she is not allowed to get tired or bored by child care and housework. Nor is she supposed to feel anything but love for her children. A woman who feels—as most mothers do—moments of boredom, anger, frustration, resentment and other "negative" emotions toward her children is taught not that she is a normal mother but that she is a bad mother.

Another reason many women find mothering less satisfying than it might be is that mothering is sorely undervalued in our society. The important work of nurturing children is, first of all, unpaid labor, and this alone symbolizes its lowly status.

Yet perhaps the most important reason women find mothering less than fulfilling is that even though the potential pleasures of mothering are great, in our society so are the costs. Because our society places the entire responsibility for nurturing and raising children on mothers alone, most mothers pay considerably for their pleasures in lost freedom, leisure time, access to employment and power, friends and mobility. A woman in her late fifties reflects:

> It's hard to sum up my whole experience of being a mother in a few words, but if I had to, I'd say it was good in lots of ways, terrible in lots of ways, and that even in those areas it was good, it could have been better. When you're a mother, you find yourself very grateful for small things—for that one free afternoon every once in a while, for that one word of appreciation, for those stolen moments cuddling with the babies when the heart is like melting. . . . But having had time to reflect on this, I think my regret is that the way this society is set up makes it so hard to have those good things. I don't mind that I gave up things because I had kids. I don't think any mother minds giving things up. It's that we had to give up so much—and for so long—that's what I mind.

An obvious way women "pay" for becoming mothers in our society is by being forced to give up employment outside the home. Some would prefer not to work outside the home when their children are young. However, many others want and have outside employment but find their employment options are sorely limited because they are mothers.

With affordable quality day care made available and work schedules adjusted to better suit the needs of persons with children, a woman with children would not be put in the predicament of having to choose between putting her children first or her job with an outside employer first. With some changes in our society, women would be able to care for children and do wage work in balance—and without ending up totally exhausted as so many employed mothers do. As it is, though, a woman with children is confronted with a society-created conflict between children and employment that, no matter how she resolves it, can cause her to feel torn and that she is failing in some area:

> With my first baby I wanted to be able to work part-time, but the company said no way—it was either work full-time as I had been doing, or leave my job. So I worked full-time—we really needed the money—and I felt guilty

and terrible about it. I had wanted a child for so long, but now that I was finally a mother I felt I was failing at it—neglecting my baby, and for a glorified secretarial job I never much liked. So when I had my second baby a few years later, I wanted to do it differently, and fortunately my husband had gotten a better-paying job, so staying home was something I could do. But that brought problems, too. I felt great about being able to really be there for my baby, but I also felt that I had become a diminished person in some ways. Although I never liked my job that much, once I was without it, I realized how much it had given me a sense of competence and belonging in the world. As a mother I rated myself a success, but as an individual human being I felt like a failure.

The hard economic realities of being a mother typically mean a woman with children must be financially dependent upon someone else —whether a husband or the government. And this forced dependency can be detrimental to a woman's self-esteem too:

> I wanted to be able to give my babies full-time care. My mother had always had to work, and I looked forward to not having to do that. I thought it would be wonderful not to have to go out to a job and leave my babies behind. And in some ways it has been good. But when I gave up my job, I also gave up equality in my relationship with my husband. He brings home the money now, and while we say it's our money we both know it's his. I feel like a child again.

Those women who give up employment to stay home with their young children full-time often find the arrangement brings with it the added cost of isolation. Speaking of the dilemma of middle-class women who do not work outside the home when their children are young, Madonna Kolbenschlag explains:

> Being queen of a small kingdom [the household] is better than being a lackey in a large one—or so it may seem, for a time. . . . [But eventually] the uneasiness will set in. The panic and the rage. The monotony, the trivilization of energy, the social isolation can overwhelm the housewife . . . These apocalyptic feelings [the full-time mother and housewife often has] in her maturity are the tragic result of exclusion from work that might have given her a sense of control over her world, her destiny, her soul.[16]

We should point out here that these observations apply as well to working-class women. In her study of life in working-class families, Lillian Rubin found that while some women expressed the desire to stay home with their children full-time, most in reality did not want to have to give up outside employment. Women who had become full-time mothers and housewives complained of boredom, lack of freedom, isolation and feelings of entrapment; and they looked favorably on jobs because, among other reasons, jobs mean "getting out of the home."[17]

Of all the costs extracted from women who have children today, perhaps the most unfair and most damaging to self-esteem is the cost of selfhood. When women give birth, we are not expected to just give up jobs, nights of sleep, time spent with friends, and yearnings for a life beyond the domestic sphere; we are expected to give up our very selves. According to the dictates of our culture, the only moral and only proper way for a mother to be is self-sacrificing; and if a woman is not entirely self-sacrificing, she is selfish—it's an either/or situation, and there's no room for a middle ground. This rigid dichotomy not only unfairly demands the impossible of women, it has behind it the odd assumption that somehow it is good for a child to be raised to selfhood by someone who has not achieved selfhood herself. Lisa Cronin Wohl elaborates:

> In a book that I read before my own daughter was born, one mother said, "I never gave up anything vital for my child." At the time, that woman sounded selfish to me. Now in the wake of experience, I think I know what she meant. Of course a mother gives up a lot for her child: Blood, sleep, tears, not to mention time, money and peace of mind. But a mother must not feel obliged to give up herself. Not unless she wants to raise a mother-less child.[18]

The Pleasures and Costs of Childlessness

Our society makes being a mother a far more difficult, time-consuming, exhausting and often lonely and isolating experience than it need be. Hence, it was probably inevitable that when Ann Landers asked women about their experiences as mothers, the overwhelming majority said they had been monumentally disappointed by them, and probably wouldn't "do it all over again" if they had the choice.

Yet it's also difficult to not be a mother in our society. As is the case with being a mother, not being a mother carries with it many potential pleasures—pleasures such as freedom, increased economic stability and the ability to have relationships and experiences that raising children often precludes, or at least defers until later in life.

> I have never wanted to be a mother. Even when I was a little girl, I was never fascinated with babies nor did I enjoy playing house as much as I enjoyed reading or drawing or "creating" things with play dough. I like my own mother a lot—I think she did a fine job with us, but I have never wanted to follow in her footsteps. The other day a friend of mine who very

much wants children told me she can't imagine not wanting children, she's wanted them so much and for so long. I can't imagine wanting them; I don't understand why women would want to tie themselves down that way. There are lots of ways to be creative and expressive—I guess mothering just never appealed to me that way.

At the same time, though, not being a mother in our culture brings with it great costs, the principal one being social stigma. Even today women who do not have children are commonly perceived as deficient, aberrant and even pathetic. Those who feel the sting of social stigma most acutely are women who want to become biological mothers but who are unable to do so. A woman who tries to conceive but cannot might find her self-esteem flagging as a result:

All my life I've wanted kids. When I was a little girl and people would ask what I wanted to be when I grew up, I'd always say "a mommy"—and I never wavered from that desire even as I grew older and felt pressure to have a career and be more than a mommy. . . . I had so much invested in this image of myself as this earth mother having a whole brood of kids—it just never occurred to me that I might not be able to conceive. . . . Finding out that I can't have kids has really shaken my basis for self-worth.

Even women who do not want to be biological mothers and are confident that this choice is what's best for them still are often stigmatized as a result, and this can undercut their confidence and self-esteem:

What bothers me most is that I am trivialized because I am not a mother. Even within my own family it's like I haven't graduated to adulthood. They take my sister—who is ten years younger than me—much more seriously than they take me, because she is married and has kids. Her problems with her marriage and her children are seen as real problems, while my problems with relationships, work, money and all the rest are pretend problems. And at the same time, other people glamorize my lifestyle. They don't see that all the choices that come with being an independent woman who is not a mother are ones you get no support or guidance for, and they can be very traumatizing.

Within certain subcultures in America, being a grown woman who is not a mother can be even more difficult:

In Latin culture your wealth is your family, and a woman is supposed to contribute to the family's wealth by producing children. White women have some models for not having children. But there is no Chicana equivalent for Katharine Hepburn. A Chicana is really under incredible pressure to be a mother. If you do not have children, something is considered horribly wrong with you, and you are pitied—even if you don't want children.

It is true that white American culture does provide an occasional positive model of the "childless" woman in the figure of Katharine Hepburn. But such models are not all that positive, for the message they convey is that it's okay to be childless *only if you do something really spectacular with your life.* A woman who does not have children must prove herself exceptional in achievement in order to compensate for her failure to be a "real" woman. If a woman does not have children and lives an ordinary life of no remarkable achievement, she is assumed to be an enigma at best, unfinished at worst:

> I think what bugs me the most is the assumption that until you give birth to a child, you yourself remain a child. With that goes the assumption that you are immature, selfish, unable to give to others. Some women with kids act like I'm missing out on some secret essential wisdom and I'm a lesser person for it. To some degree I guess I feel the same about them. Anyway, I call the care and compassion I give my students mothering. I've fully participated and rejoiced in my nephews' and nieces' Bar Mitzvahs and soccer tournaments, and I've nursed them when they were sick. It's funny —kids clearly see me as an adult and as someone who is loving. It's other adults who judge me because I don't have biological children. I might not be a mother, but because of the way I live my life, I see myself as a sister to the earth.

Women at different points in history have been told variously that the way to fulfillment and self-worth is through motherhood—or through eschewing motherhood. In fact, there is no one true path of fulfillment for all women. Either option—becoming a mother or remaining without children—offers potential for higher self-esteem. Neither guarantees it. And both in our current world entail costs.

BLUEPRINTS FOR CHANGE

I. ATTITUDES TOWARD YOUR REPRODUCTIVE SELF

Whether or not you have made a choice to be a mother, not to be a mother or are still undecided, it can sometimes be helpful to examine your feelings specifically around the different elements of the choice. Do you value or not value your own potential to reproduce? How do you think the culture values this potential? If you are not able to bear children, how has this affected your sense of self? Do you believe you have control over your fertility? If you have been pregnant, what was that experience like and how does it affect your attitude toward mothering?

What was the experience of giving birth like and how has that influenced your attitudes toward mothering? What are the structural constraints determining your options for child care? How large a role does being a mother or not being a mother play in your self-concept? How do cultural attitudes toward either choice translate into judgments about yourself?

II. ATTITUDES TOWARD EACH OTHER

Do you impose hierarchial value judgments when thinking about mothering? For instance, do you disrespect lesbian mothers, welfare mothers, etc., yet still value mothers over women who are not mothers? Do you believe being a mother is synonymous with being an adult? With being worthy and fulfilled?

In general, what are your attitudes toward women who have made a different choice than yours? Do you see yourself as better, or at least better off? Or do you see them as being better, or better off, than you? Is it really necessary to rank-order your experiences? Can you find common ground in your experiences? Do you see how the important work of nurturing others can be carried out regardless of which choice a woman makes?

PART THREE

*

*Far from Home,
Far from at Home:
Women's Experiences
in the Wider World*

* 1 *

Introduction

Our self-attitudes are shaped not just by our relationships with those we hold close to heart, but also by experiences, people and institutions in the world beyond the intimate sphere. From the time we learned to cross the street, we began venturing beyond home, and as we grew older and went to church, school, the movies and a variety of other places, the larger world had an increasing impact on how we saw and judged ourselves. Even when we are not interacting directly with the outside world, it and its various institutions still shape our lives and consciousness in important if often subtle ways. Precisely how experiences and institutions outside the interpersonal sphere affect women's self-esteem is the subject of this section.

The impact of the larger world outside the home demands special attention today because that impact is greater now than ever before. Prior to the twin developments of industrialization and urbanization, women's life experiences were largely privatized with women sticking close to home. The home served as a self-contained economic unit, a school, a health-care facility and a social center, among other things, and so there was little reason to venture beyond. A woman in colonial America would probably go to church, and to friends' and relatives' houses for visits. But she wouldn't have gone to school or the hospital, because such institutions did not exist. Nor would she have gone to a tavern, "publick house," or many other "public" places, because much of the public sphere was essentially off limits to women. Even if a woman had to leave her family and seek work outside her home, she still would have found her experience largely limited to the domestic sphere. In colonial America a woman looking for paid work basically had the choice of being a household servant or a prostitute in a brothel. Women who were slaves were also likely to work in the domestic sphere, and slaves who worked in homes or in fields had no access to the world beyond their masters' territory.

It was in the nineteenth century that women's sphere widened. For women who worked for wages, the industrial age opened up a new place of work, the factory, although many women, including the black women freed from slavery in the latter half of the century, still had the choice of only servitude or prostitution. Later in the century an additional avenue for working women was opened up by the invention of the typewriter, which from its initial manufacture was presented as a machine made expressly for women.[1] The typewriter had a revolutionary impact on women's lives, as did another nineteenth-century development—the establishment of public schools, and the opening of them in the elementary grades to females. As the typewriter brought women into a previously male enclave, the office, so the establishment of public education brought women into the previously all-male world of academia, first as students, then as teachers in the elementary grades. A similarly revolutionizing set of changes would also be brought about by the institutionalization of health care in the nineteenth century. With the establishment of hospitals, women would have a new occupation—nursing—while women also would start to spend time in hospitals as patients.

The experience of women who did not work outside the home was also revolutionized by the changes in the nineteenth century. For women of the middle class, the move from large farms to smaller city houses or apartments meant a shrinking in the size of their traditional sphere. At the same time, these women's responsibilities were further reduced by such innovations as bakery-baked bread, preprepared foods (store-bought butter, jams, and smoked meats, for example), and such newly invented labor-saving devices as vacuum cleaners, washing machines, gas stoves and central heating systems. Although some critics would bemoan the passing of the days when women's time was occupied by baking, canning, sewing and other arduous household tasks, others celebrated technology because of its "potential to make women's lives much less isolated and home-bound." Among the fans of technology was Thomas A. Edison, who said that with ever more sophisticated technology, woman

> will give less attention to the home, because the home will need less; she will be rather a domestic engineer than a domestic laborer, with the great-

est of handmaidens, electricity, at her service. This and other mechanic forces will so revolutionize the woman's world that a large portion of the aggregate of woman's energy will be conserved for use in broader, more constructive fields.[2]

One of the "broader, more constructive fields" women in the middle class found their energy and time freed up for in the nineteenth century was the field of social reform. With middle-class women's actual domestic responsibilities narrowed and the forces of industrialization creating a world in which urban poverty, the exploitation of workers, alcoholism and other social ills were rampant, women increasingly came to look upon the entire world as a large home and took responsibility for cleaning it up and making it safe. Women by the hundreds of thousands in the nineteenth and early twentieth centuries became involved in women's organizations dedicated to such goals as the abolition of slavery, women's suffrage, temperance, improved factory working conditions, better health care for the poor, and even pacifism and socialism. In the process, women founded a new institution—the settlement house —and also found new ways to keep the ties to other women that had done so much to build women's self-esteem in the past. For women in the nineteenth century, the various women's organizations were a way of retaining the bonds between women that the rapid changes in society had threatened to put asunder. The feeling of community that women obtained from the myriad women's organizations is evident in this report from a women's club in Arkansas, written at the end of the 1890s:

> All ages, young and old and middle-aged, gathered in the membership and there is a delightful fraternity of spirit among them. The old bring their ripe experiences, the younger their youth and eager enthusiasm for knowledge. The result is a blending of social and intellectual life as nearly ideal as can be found in this mortal world.[3]

As women in the nineteenth century increasingly took on the role of society's caretakers, another role that fell to women was that of consumer. Where just a generation before, most women were principally producers, by the end of the Civil War women were seen as having a moral duty to consume as much as they could of the rapidly industrializing economy's growing array of consumer goods. To help middle-class women take to this new role with enthusiasm and dedication, merchants in the years soon after the Civil War came up with an entirely new type of commercial institution—the department store. Department stores such as Wanamaker's, Marshall Field and Macy's enticed women out of the home not only by offering under one roof a wide variety of products and services (watch repair, picture framing, etc.), but also by providing lavishly appointed rooms where women could sit and write letters, read the papers (provided free by the stores), and commune with other women. The architecture of the new department stores was "monumental in design," and "almost cathedral-like in character," according to Sheila Rothman. Wanamaker's, for example, had a massive auditorium with a Grand Court complete with marble columns, and a Greek Hall with six hundred seats. The ladies room in Macy's was ornately decorated in Louis XV style and adjoined an art gallery where women could enjoy a taste of high culture.[4]

Although the shrines of the new religion of consumerism, the department stores, were built with middle-class women in mind, the working classes were also encouraged to embrace the values of consumerism. Between 1890 and 1920, more than 23 million people from Eastern Europe and Italy arrived in the United States, taking their places in urban factories. For the consumer economy to really work, it was necessary to get the immigrant population and the relatively recently emancipated black population to spend as much of their meager wages as possible on mass-produced products. As Stuart and Elizabeth Ewen point out, "the promise of the 'melting pot' was inextricably tied to the consumption of American goods."[5] Advertisers told immigrants and blacks that to become truly part of American society they had to buy American. This the working classes did in large numbers, filling their apartments with mass-produced items that symbolized the bounty of America and adorning themselves in American-style finery that would announce to the world that they belonged. Jane Addams, the founder of Hull House, noted that "the working girl" who lived in a tenement spent a disproportionate amount of her income on clothing, and that this made sense in America because here a person is judged by her clothes.[6] In the slum neighborhoods on New Year's Lower East Side, shops sprang up that promised their poor clientele that they could look like "Fifth Avenue peacocks" but for a fraction of the price. And in the part of New York known as "African Broadway" in the 1890s, "conspicuous consumption" was as heartily embraced as it was in white middle-class neighborhoods, as the New York *Tribune* condescendingly reported in 1895:

> Always and invariably on "dress parade" is the new quarter. . . . The younger women, arrayed in gowns that are wonderfully good imitations of the fashions, though heaven knows how they can afford them, walk in pairs and trios up and down Seventh Avenue. . . . The people . . . are poor

with only a dollar or two standing between them and starvation most of the time. . . . [Nonetheless, one sees] daily a promenade of gayly dressed girls and . . . young colored men. Yellow is the prime tint of the young colored girls' clothes. The favorite dress of the young men "in style" is a glossy silk hat, patent leathers, a black suit with a coal sack of remarkable shortness, and a figured waistcoat. Paste diamonds are *de rigueur.* [7]

Another institution that sprang up in the nineteenth century was the funeral parlor. When America was still a rural, agrarian society, death occurred in the home, and women would lay the dead person's body on a plank of wood and wrap it in cloth for a simple burial in a plain coffin. With the appearance and growth of the funeral industry, tending the bodies of the dead became the province of men called funeral directors, and the values of the consumer society dictated that the fancier the funeral, the better. Bodies now were embalmed, made-up in garish cosmetics and dressed in finery, then placed in ornate coffins with satin linings, and perhaps publicly displayed. Women were edged out of their former role in tending to the dead, and attitudes toward death grew increasingly sentimental as the rituals grew more contrived and lavish. [8]

The establishment of new institutions such as the public school, the hospital, the settlement house, the department store and the funeral parlor has had impacts on women's experience and sense of self that we are only beginning to understand today. Our total life experience from birth to death has become institutionalized in a way that would have been unimaginable only a few hundred years ago. Not only do women spend more time today than ever before in the world outside the private sphere of the home, that outside world has been so radically transformed by new institutions as to bear little resemblance to the public world of the not too distant past.

Within the private sphere of the home, our experience has been radically transformed, too. At the same time new institutions were taking women increasingly out of the home, the development of modern communications technology began to bring more and more of the outside world into the home. Because of TV, radio, newspapers, magazines and mass-audience books, the home today functions less and less as a place where it is possible to escape the values and pressures of the larger world.

In looking at how our sense of self and self-esteem are affected by such institutional forces as religion, schools, and the mass media, a term that came to us was "authority figures with no faces." The world we live in is full of authority figures; these are more often males than not, and more often privileged, able-bodied white heterosexual males at that, and some of them have faces with which we are familiar. Our priests, rabbis, ministers, school principals and bosses, for example, are authority figures whose faces we know, as are such persons as our doctors, the judges we meet when we go to court, the President and the TV newscaster who brings us the nightly news. But standing behind these men and giving them much of their authority are invisible authority figures. These "authority figures with no faces" are the men who, though either now dead or just unknown to us, determine what it is that our religious leaders and schoolteachers teach us, how our bosses treat us, how our doctors minister to us, what the judges we encounter will consider fair, and just what it is that the TV newscaster will present to us as news. We never see them, but these authority figures with no faces play a major role in shaping our life experiences.

Of all the invisible authority figures who exert power over us, perhaps the most powerful are the Western world's principal philosophers. Most of us don't spend much time thinking about the works of Western culture's philosophers, and if we do spend any time thinking about them, we're likely to conclude that they don't have much to do with us. In fact, though, the men considered the great thinkers of Western culture do have plenty to do with us. For the ideas of the philosophers have shaped history, and history shapes our culture and institutions, which in turn shape us.

In her study of the works of the major political philosophers, Susan Moller Okin makes a perceptive point that says much about the continuing power these men's ideas have on us. Looking at the ideas about the sexes propounded by philosophers from Aristotle to John Locke, Okin observes that when thinking about men, the principal concern of political philosophy has been with the questions, "what is man? what is man's nature?" and "what will make man happy?" When thinking about women, however, the principal concern of political philosophers has always been with the question "what is woman *for?*"⁹ This functional way of thinking about women has historically shaped all our culture's institutions and continues to shape our experience today. What is woman *for?* has been asked by theologians, by those who determine what we were taught in school, by the men who make our laws, by the men who set economic and workplace policy, by the men who determine what images and messages will be promulgated by the mass media, by the men who run the medical and other helping professions and by men on the streets. And all these men have decided that what woman is *for* is to serve men and meet men's needs, never our own. As we shall see, this presumption that woman is for the service of men surfaces time and again as we move about in the larger world beyond the home.

* 2 *

Religions as Institutions, Spirituality as Experience

> I tell my clients to try to separate the wheat from the chaff. Take what's positive [from religion] and treasure it. If some aspect of religion divides you from yourself and others, then I don't think it's good. I think we all can tolerate a bit of selfishness, and by that I mean, "Love yourself." It's as simple as that.
>
> —Mary Gilligan Wong,
> psychotherapist and former nun[1]

It has become a commonplace to say that religion in America has been declining in influence for several centuries and that our society has become increasingly secular. But the fact remains that most of us were raised according to some form of religion, and religion plays a central role in the lives of many Americans. For those exposed to it, our religious training provided us with answers to a variety of fundamental questions: Who am I? Why was I born? What is the meaning of life? Is there a God and a purpose and order to the universe, or is the universe simply an accident of chemistry where randomness prevails? Is there life after death; if so, is there a heaven and a hell? What is sin? What is goodness? What is my place, as an individual and as a woman, in this world? . . . As our individual religious training shaped our answers to these and other questions, so the religion we were raised with also shaped, and probably continues to shape, the way we see and judge ourselves. For example, the values and ethical principles by which we judge ourselves good or bad, worthy or unworthy, tend to be determined in large part by our religious training.

Many people claim to have outgrown religion entirely. But even if we as adults have rejected our childhood religion, or have made a conscious decision to eliminate religion from our lives entirely, religion probably still affects us deeply. For as theologian Carol P. Christ observes:

> Religion fulfills deep psychic needs by providing symbols and rituals that enable people to cope with [difficult] situations in human life (death, evil, suffering) and to pass through life's important transitions (birth, sexuality, death). Even people who consider themselves completely secularized will often find themselves sitting in a church or synagogue when a friend or relation gets married or . . . has died. The symbols associated with these important rituals cannot fail to affect the deep or unconscious structures of the mind of even a person who has rejected these symbolisms on a conscious level—especially if the person is under stress.[2]

While any religion will influence self-esteem, those that have the largest impact on American women's self-esteem are Protestantism, Roman Catholicism and Judaism. In that order these are the most popular religions in the United States, and if an American woman was brought up according to any religion, she was more than likely brought up as a member of one of them. This is the case even for those women whose families came from parts of the world where Buddhism, Hinduism, Islam or other religions were indigenous and most common, since many people gave up their "old world" religions once they came to America and adopted the seemingly more American Christianity instead. This is also the case for those women who have their ancestral roots in Africa and for those whose families were native to America as well. American blacks lost direct connection to African culture when they were yanked away from their homeland to be made slaves, and once in America they were granted no other option but to turn to Protestant religion when they sought an avenue for spiritual expression, strength and solace. Similarly, as white people of European stock invaded North America, they made it increasingly impossible for the Native Americans to practice their traditional religions, forcing them to attend schools run by Christian missionaries and making conversion to Christianity in many instances a prerequisite for survival. As a result, many Native American children ended up greatly influenced by Protestantism or Catholicism, although in large numbers of cases Native Americans hung on to their own heritage surreptitiously.

Protestantism, Catholicism and Judaism all have the potential to affect women's lives in myriad positive ways. For example, although many intellectuals have scoffed at religions as "the opiate of the masses," many people throughout history have found in Judaism and Christianity important sources of strength, solace and moral integrity that have inspired and enabled them to stand up against oppression and injustice. And despite the notion, again popular among many intellectuals, that religion is only for superstitious and sheeplike types with low levels of intelligence, the fact is that religious faith and intelligence are in no way incompatible. Many highly intelligent people are deeply religious because, in addition to the needs mentioned by Carol Christ, religion fulfills a variety of other important needs many people feel urgently. These include the need for community, the need for rules, limits and a sense of order, the need for a sense of connection to something larger than oneself, the need for acknowledgment and expression of the spiritual aspects of being, the need for the mysteries of the universe and human existence to be acknowledged and explained, the need to come to terms in some way with the fact of mortality, and the need for a sense of purity and goodness. This woman happens to practice Judaism, but women of other faiths expressed to us similar feelings about the needs religion helps meet:

> Faith and spirituality are incredibly personal, and you really can't explain them to people by appealing to the intellect. But there's a lot about being alive that can't be explained or understood by the intellect alone, and the way I see things is that I either pretend whole parts of me don't exist or I try to explore and express those spiritual parts through religion. In my own case religion means Judaism, and there's a lot about Judaism—like the seders, the other rituals, the sense of right and wrong it's given me—that has really enriched me and given value to my life.

The Creation of God in Man's Image

While Protestantism, Catholicism and Judaism can and often do affect women in myriad positive ways, these religions also can and often do cause women great pain, and they often do great damage to women's self-esteem especially. Much of this owes to the unfortunate fact that Protestantism, Catholicism and Judaism all have long histories of being patriarchal in both doctrine (God is a father; woman brought sin into the world; women are less holy than men) and in practice (only men can administer the Catholic sacraments; only men can be priests; only men count to make up a quorum in temples). Today some of this is changing: Women are being ordained as rabbis and Episcopal priests; the liturgical language used by some Protestant sects is being altered to be less male supremacist; and there have been challenges to such blatantly woman-hating practices as the tradition of orthodox Jewish males to begin each day thanking God they are not women. Moreover, there always have been some exceptions to the patriarchal patterns: The Society of Friends (Quakers), for instance, has long articulated and even attempted to uphold the equality of the sexes. Overall, however, patriarchal doctrines and practices are still the general rule today. In fact, some of the fastest-growing religions in the United States today—among them the Church of Jesus Christ of Latter-day Saints, or Mormons, the evangelical Christian churches, and the Christian cults such as Rev. Sun Myung Moon's Unification Church—are precisely those that preach for women near total subordination to men and complete submission to the role of wife and mother.

An important thing for women to know about Judaism and Christianity is that neither originated as patriarchal. Judaism has its roots in the Sumerian religions of Babylonia, and these religions were based on belief in a variety of different gods of both genders. The most well-known and powerful female god worshiped by the Sumerians was Inanna, called, among other things, "the queen of heaven, the goddess of light and love." The early Hebrews worshiped both male and female deities, among them the goddesses Anath and Asherah.

It wasn't until the reign of David that the Hebrew tribes in great numbers began to embrace Yahwism—the belief that there is only one god, and that this "Lord God" is a male—and this happened for largely political reasons. As early proponents of Yahwism such as Moses knew, the various Hebrew tribes would be impossible to unite and control as a single entity as long as they gave their allegiance to a variety of different gods and goddesses. Only when the Hebrews believed that there was one and only one legitimate God would they be firmly united and would men like Moses be able to credibly claim that they were hand-picked by God to lead. To further secure their claim on authority, the male leaders of the Hebrews needed people to accept not just that there is one Lord God, but that this one Lord God is a male god. The end result was that according to Judaic law, it became the highest crime to worship any god or goddess other than the one male God, Yahweh ("Thou shalt worship no other gods; thou shalt not worship false idols"). According to the Old Testament, Yahweh is "a jealous god" whose wrath will strike anyone who dares to continue to go "a-whoring" after other gods and goddesses.

Christianity underwent similar changes in its early stages, too.[3] Jesus during his life had attracted a variety of followers, and after his death a number of different groups claimed that they were his true heirs and their interpretations of his teachings were the correct interpretations. One such group was the Gnostics. The Gnostics saw Christianity very differently from the way it was seen by the twelve men who called themselves Jesus' sole official apostles, and who eventually won out and established themselves as the only "orthodox" Christians.[4] Whereas those who called themselves orthodox believed in one God and depicted Him in masculine terms, the Gnostics believed that there may have been two or many gods, and they frequently spoke of god or gods in feminine terms—as the "Mother of Creation" and "the Womb that gives shape to the All."[5] Moreover, as they rejected the idea of one male and authoritarian god, they also refused to believe in the legitimacy and authority of the male church hierarchy of pope, bishops and priests that the orthodox Christians said represented God's will. Believing in the equality of everyone in Christ's eyes, the antihierarchal Gnostics took turns playing the roles of priest, bishop and prophet (preacher) when they worshiped, and they assigned these roles by drawing lots each time they gathered for services. Members of both sexes participated equally in the drawings, and church women had full opportunity to offer Mass, perform the sacraments, and give sermons.[6]

Over time, the orthodox church hierarchy started by the twelve apostles became more and more powerful. The Gnostics were persecuted as heretics and their teachings and writings were suppressed. And as the orthodox church became increasingly powerful, it became more and more male supremacist. Whereas Jesus' own teachings and actions clearly affirm the equality of the sexes, as men like Paul rose to power, Christianity came to have less in common with Christ's teachings than with sexist traditions taken from patriarchal Judaism. No longer would God be spoken of as both a mother and a father; God was now a he. No longer were males and females seen as equal in God's eyes and as having equal access to salvation; males were clearly superior, and males were closer to God and heaven. Although Genesis 1:27 states quite clearly that "so God created man in his own image, in the image of God he created him; male and female he created them," St. Paul declared that women should remain silent in church, and only man was created in God's image:

. . . a man . . . is the image and glory of God; but woman is the glory of man. For man was not made from woman, but woman from man. Neither was man created for woman, but woman for man.[7]

Unfortunately, it is this opinion of Paul, not the view given in Genesis 1:27, that has predominated in Christian thinking for nearly two thousand years.

The damage done to women's self-esteem by the belief that only man is created in God's image is incalculable. Every male is instantly, fundamentally affirmed by the belief that God is male, and also by the patriarchal practices that follow from it. By contrast, every female is negated. There seems no doubt that we women would feel much better about ourselves if we had grown up exposed to the images of powerful goddesses that people prior to the establishment of patriarchal religions were surrounded with, as Adrienne Rich points out:

> Let us try to imagine for a moment what sense of herself it gave a woman to be in the presence of such images. If they did nothing else for her, they must have validated her spiritually (as our contemporary images do not), giving her back aspects of herself neither insipid nor trivial, investing her with a sense of participation in essential mysteries. . . . The images of the prepatriarchal goddess-cults did one thing: they told women that power, awesomeness, and centrality were theirs by nature, not by privilege or miracle; the female was primary.[8]

For a woman of color the image of God provided by the patriarchal religions is doubly negating because the God given us by Judaism and Christianity is not only male, he is also white. And as the belief that God is a male has been used to oppress women, so over the years God's name has been invoked time and again to support white supremacy.

Woman as Evil

Next to the idea that God is a white man and only white men are created in God's image, perhaps the belief of patriarchal religions that is most damaging to women's self-esteem is the belief that woman, through Eve the temptress, brought evil into the world and thus is responsible for "the fall of man" and his banishment from the garden of Eden. According to both Judaism and Christianity, woman is the earthly embodiment of evil, as Tertullian, an influential early orthodox Christian thinker, did not want anyone to forget:

> God's sentence hangs still over your sex and His punishment weights down upon you. You are the devil's gateway; you are she who first violated the forbidden tree and broke the law of God. It was you coaxed your way around him whom the devil had not the force to attack. With what ease

you shattered that image of God: man! Because of the death you merited, the Son of God had to die.[9]

For some women, the suffering that has resulted from the belief that woman is "the devil's gateway" has been excruciating indeed. While no fully reliable records exist, scholars estimate that somewhere between thirty thousand and nine million people were executed as witches during the three hundred years beginning in the 1400s and continuing as late as the eighteenth century in the case of Scotland. Most of these so-called witches were women, and old women at that, and they were typically put to death by burning, pressing or—the preferred method because it was cheapest—boiling in oil.[10]

Women have suffered and still suffer because of the belief in woman as evil in more subtle ways, too. As Jean Baker Miller has pointed out, when women experience failure and fully confront our powerlessness in male-dominated culture, some often feel not simply bad in the sense of feeling lousy, but bad in the sense of evil. When things don't turn out well, as we've already observed, women have a great tendency to automatically assume that we are somehow at fault, that we are to blame because we *must* have been in the wrong. This Miller sees not simply as a consequence of low self-esteem, but as a consequence of low self-esteem stemming from women's unconscious internalization of the belief that women are inherently evil.[11]

Original Sin

In addition to shaping our attitudes toward ourselves specifically as women, religions shape our attitudes toward human nature, life and ourselves in more general ways. The Christian notion of original sin, for example, has influenced many women's self-esteem as much as the belief that God is a white male. Although women are singled out by patriarchal theology as especially evil, the doctrine of original sin in essence states that every child at birth is tainted by sin. A corollary of this is the belief that people are by nature sinful and depraved, and that we must spend our lives trying to make up for this. One woman we interviewed reported that when she was a child, the first thing she had to do each morning was get down on her knees and contemplate her inherent sinfulness. Others reported spending many nights during childhood and adolescence crying because of their fear of eternal damnation. And most Catholics also can recall that during Mass they had to repeatedly hit themselves in the breast with the hand and say over and over, "I am not worthy."

Theoretically, the belief that people are naturally depraved, sinful and unworthy does not mean we are all doomed, since with sin is supposed to come the possibility of being forgiven for sin through confession and penance. But that is the theory. For many women the psychological reality was far different, as what affected them most deeply was not the promise of salvation but a sense of impending doom and constant guilt for just being alive:

> I got this very punitive notion of life from religion. Life wasn't something you were to celebrate, it was something you were to be punished for. . . . It was like religion meant not just that a lot of aspects of life—sex, dancing, having fun—were sinful, but that there was something sinful about life itself. The way I felt growing up wasn't that we were born with original sin, it was that being born itself was the original sin—and you were essentially doomed to go down the tubes straight to hell from there.

One of the most unfortunate aspects of the doctrine of original sin is that it allows for no distinction between who one is and what one does: original sin means not that a child has *done* anything bad, it's that she herself *is* bad—and not by her own doing. The end result is that she begins, and may well go through life, with what one writer has called a "deep feeling of sin-stained unworthiness." [12] A woman raised according to the tenets of Judaism, which does not accept the notion of original sin, is at a distinct advantage in this respect.

The Glorification of Suffering

Those raised in Christian religions that emphasize humans' inherent sinfulness also typically were raised to believe that the way to salvation is through suffering. The message inherent in Catholicism and some Protestant religions is that people deserve to suffer and that suffering is good and noble. The Roman Catholic Church is especially gory in its glorification of suffering: graphic and detailed images of Christ's bloody torture and crucifixion constitute a large portion of standard ecclesiastical art, and most Catholics grew up with an intimate knowledge of the horrific ordeals that were suffered by such holy martyrs as Saint Lucy (who responded to a man's admiration of her beautiful eyes by ripping them out and giving them to him on a platter, thus insuring that he would not want to marry her and she could remain a virgin) and Saint Agnes (Christ's "little lamb," tortured and burned at the stake like countless others). According to the ideology of martyrdom, the more you suffer the purer and closer to God you are.

Jews over time have established a special relationship to suffering as well. Jewish theological teachings might not emphasize suffering to the extent that Catholic teachings do, but since Jewish history has been largely a history of pain and persecution many Jews understandably get the idea that to be born a Jew is to be born to suffer—and that suffering is noble. Like many Catholics, some more fortunate Jews go through life with a terrible guilt for not having suffered enough.

Despite the different stance each takes to suffering, one thing the male leaders of Judaism, Catholicism and Protestantism alike have agreed on is that women have been singled out by God to endure special suffering because of our responsibility for bringing evil into the world. According to Genesis, woman is to be punished for causing the fall of man by bearing children in great pain, and according to I Timothy, women can only be saved by enduring the pain of childbirth over and over again. The idea that a certain amount of suffering naturally comes with being female has caused many women to take pain without complaint and has caused many others to see pain as inescapable, something we can't do anything about. Moreover, it has greatly reduced women's chance of self-esteem, for as theologian Dorothee Soelle has observed, "The more a person perceives her suffering as a natural part of life, the lower her self-esteem."[13]

Attitudes Toward Authority

Religions also teach us the "proper" stance to take toward authority. We need to be able to question authority in order to fully experience our potential and to fully respect ourselves, but questioning authority is precisely what the men who run the patriarchal religions have prohibited most strongly. The Hebrew god portrayed in the Old Testament is so bizarrely authoritarian that he cannot tolerate any questioning of his will whatsoever. When Lot's wife shows human concern and compassion for the family she is leaving behind, and thus disobeys God's order not to look back on the home she is departing, God immediately turns her into a pillar of salt—and we are to believe that is only just, because she dared to question God's authority. When Abraham is ordered to kill his son Isaac, he sets out to do so, but at the last minute is prevented from doing so as God reveals that he was only testing Abraham's obedience—and we are to believe that Abraham was right to blindly obey God even if that meant nearly murdering his son.

Christianity ended up endorsing as an ideal blind allegiance to authority, too. In the New Testament, Christ is shown questioning both the will of God and earthly authority, and his example teaches that skepticism toward authority is acceptable, even desirable. But the men who set themselves up as the orthodox representatives of Christ after his death were quick to align themselves with the more traditional Judaic view of authority, and, like the patriarchs of Judaism, they too taught that questioning the will of God was not to be tolerated. And since they set themselves up as God's sole legitimate spokesmen on earth, this meant they would not tolerate any questioning of their authority either.

By teaching that the only proper stance to take toward authority is one of cowering, unquestioning obedience, those in positions of authority within both Judaism and Catholicism have been able to exert an enormous degree of influence over the lives of the faithful. The influence can remain even when the stance of blind allegiance to authority appears to have been rejected in other respects:

> I don't think I can pin this all on Judaism, as I think my own individual upbringing factored in big, too, but I have spent the bulk of my life not questioning authority—not questioning anything. . . . I think this tendency to be in awe of authority is part of why so many Jews are such true believers when it comes to politics. I think socialism was the unquestioned new religion for a lot of secularized Jews, just like neoconservative politics for some Jews now is the new religion today. . . . For me, it was feminism. When I started to question, I adopted feminism, but it took me a long time to start asking some questions about that. Just like all those old lefties who couldn't tolerate questioning socialism as the one true path, I had a hard time taking responsibility for becoming my own authority on what I believed. . . .

Women raised as Roman Catholics often have equally great difficulties becoming their own authorities, learning to rely on their own powers of judgment to decide what is right for them, what is wrong. As Mary Gordon has put it, many women who were raised Catholic are "fighting a life's battle to stop being overawed by authority."[14]

Since Protestantism was founded in protest against the authority of the established Rome-based church, it might be expected that the Protestant churches would encourage a healthy attitude of suspicion toward authority. In some Protestant denominations, among them the Unitarian Universalists, the Congregationalists and the Quakers, such an attitude is encouraged. In other Protestant churches, however, blind allegiance to divine and church authority is encouraged as much as in

Judaism and Roman Catholicism. Here the Mormons are an especially ironic example. The Mormon Church was founded by an adolescent boy who claimed to have had a vision in the woods, and for this claim he was greatly persecuted and finally murdered, facts the Mormon hierarchy makes much of today. Yet if today another adolescent boy came along and said he, too, had had a vision, it's a pretty sure bet that the men in the Mormon hierarchy would excommunicate him, just as they excommunicated Sonia Johnson for supporting the Equal Rights Amendment in defiance of church authority.

God the Omnipotent

Also making it difficult for us to become our own authorities is the belief, advanced by many religions, that God is omnipotent and omniscient. If we are to have self-esteem, we need to believe that we have some control over what happens to us and how we act, and that we can make things happen for ourselves. But if we believe God is up there in the heavens pulling all the levers, controlling all the moves, it will be virtually impossible to get a sense of ourselves as active participants in the shaping of our own destiny. When one believes that God's will controls everything, one has no choice but to surrender to it:

> My mother lived a life of terrible hardship and she never fought back. She was completely unable to distinguish between kinds of hardship, between what was unavoidable and what might be avoided and maybe even fought or prevented. When she lost a baby to illness, it was God's will. When my father beat her up, it was God's will. When her boss was unfair to her, it was God's will. When she got ill and had pain, it was God's will. Everything was God's will, and so her life stance was totally passive. She never said something's wrong here—things don't have to be this way, they could be better. Things were the way they were—that was God's will.

The belief that "it's God's will" is often very helpful when we need to come to terms with and accept a painful and inexplicable event—a death, an illness, a disappointment, a hurricane, for example. But the belief that *everything* that happens can be explained by God's will undermines self-esteem because it undermines our ability to find our own authority. Finding our own authority means not just gaining a sense of control over our lives, it means taking some responsibility for ourselves and our lives too:

> When I was little and asked my mother how babies were made, she told me that women have vaginas and that when God wanted you to have a baby,

he put his seed up there and you got pregnant. She forgot to mention precisely how God got this seed up there, and so I had this image of God sending seeds flying around at random. I felt completely terrified about "catching" one, but I also felt I had no choice—that when God wanted me to get pregnant, pregnant I'd become. . . . Growing up, I know this affected my feelings about birth control. Although I try to be responsible, deep down I have this resigned feeling that it's all beyond my control.

Religion and the Work Ethic

Religions also shape our attitudes toward work, and our attitudes toward work in turn shape our attitudes toward ourselves. Judaism and Protestantism may not glorify suffering the way Roman Catholicism does, but they make up for this by glorifying toil. Over time, this has rubbed off on American Catholics, many of whom now seem to glorify hard work, considering it as noble as suffering.

Regardless of our particular training, most of us probably have been influenced by the Protestant work ethic, which is central to American culture. The Protestant work ethic—which says that those who work hardest and achieve the greatest successes are the worthiest in God's eyes—arose out of the teachings of Martin Luther and John Calvin, Calvin especially, and marked a complete departure from the medieval Roman Catholicism that reformers like Luther and Calvin rebelled against.[15] By and large, the Catholics preached that the best way to earn God's grace was to remove oneself from the world to the greatest extent possible, live in Spartan simplicity and poverty, and spend as much time as possible in contemplation of the divine, self-examination, prayer, penance and meditation. "Good works"—acts of charity, offerings to the church—had an important role in the Catholic conception of life because one could earn grace through them, but work in and of itself was not seen as good. On the contrary, the Catholic view saw work as simply a means to an end—survival—and people did only as much work as meeting their basic needs required.

These attitudes began to change in the sixteenth century, when Luther taught that God wanted people to live not lives of monastic simplicity and poverty in which otherworldly concerns were primary, but lives fully engaged in the everyday world of work and commerce. Although Luther in fact was against practices by which some people in acquiring wealth rendered other people poor, his teachings were taken to mean that the pursuit of worldly wealth and success was morally good in and of itself.

Under Calvin, work and material achievement were glorified as morally good even more. This can be understood only in the context of Calvin's doctrine of predestination. Calvin set forth a world view both extremely cruel and cut-and-dried. Part of humanity, he said, is saved, the rest is damned; who is in which camp is already determined at birth, and there's nothing humans can do either to change their fate or find out ahead of time which group they belong to. While accepting the bulk of Calvin's doctrine, his followers could not quite accept the part about not being able to find out which camp you were in, because to accept that would mean to have no hope and no purpose whatsoever. As a result, they modified Calvin's doctrine to allow that the saved—the *electi*—could be recognized by their actions in the here and now. Yes, they said, everyone's fate is predestined and there's nothing anyone can do to change it. But you can find out your fate by testing yourself in the marketplace, the material world: If you don't have what it takes to succeed, you clearly are not one of the *electi*, but if you do succeed, that's obviously a sign that you count among those chosen to be saved. Hence, it came to pass that the Protestant work ethic endorsed as holy such traits as diligence, perseverance, self-discipline, emotional control, thrift, ambitiousness and covetousness as among the highest virtues (far higher than such Catholic virtues as humility, poverty, compassion and charity) while condemning as immoral sloth, extra sleep, relaxation, emotional expression and any activity that seemed to waste time—including frequent visits to church and extensive praying. Since over time the Protestant work ethic became central to the collective American consciousness, most of us to some extent judge our worth according to how disciplined, diligent and materially successful we are.

Salvaging the Positive

Some women have been so affronted by the misogyny and other negative beliefs that run through Judaism and Christianity that they have rejected the patriarchal religious traditions entirely and recommend that other women follow suit. Theologian, feminist and author Mary Daly has taken this position.[16] So has Sheila Thompson, who is less well known than Daly but equally unrelenting in her rejection of the entire Judeo-Christian tradition.[17] Thompson has had plenty of firsthand exposure to how cruel patriarchal religions can be to those born female. Raised in a strict Christian home, she was taught "to be a slave to please men," and while she played this role "beautifully and expertly," she found it brought her "no happiness and no sense of self-dignity or self-worth." In her early twenties Thompson became pregnant out-of-wedlock and in complete despair wrote to Billy Graham for help. Graham wrote back, Thompson relates, "telling me that if I had lived a few hundred years earlier, I would have been burned at the stake for the sin of becoming pregnant out-of-wedlock." At that point Thompson "became almost angry"—*almost* because "it is still difficult for me to be really angry with anyone"—and she turned to the Bible for guidance and "searched frantically among the passages to find the answers." Instead of finding the answers she was looking for, Thompson "slowly and very painfully" found herself questioning the basis of her faith, the Bible itself. In her words:

> The Bible tells men that women are sex objects, but it would be best if they never touched them at all. It tells men that women are unclean, sin-inciting, cunning, contemptuous, and that men are to be women's masters. . . . I always wondered why my father, the Christian . . . treated my mother like a slave. And I always wondered why she accepted the role willingly. I know now. I have read the Bible. The Christian slate is there for all to read and it cannot be wiped clean, although some clergypersons are trying to do so. If a woman has to believe in a god, I suggest she worship one of the female goddesses, for Christianity is a male religion, written by men, for men, with a male god.[18]

The pain patriarchal religions have caused and continue to cause so many women is palpable and enormous, and it cannot be ignored or discounted. Yet many women do not agree with the conclusions reached by women like Mary Daly and Sheila Thompson. Instead of believing that because misogyny and many other negative beliefs run through the Judeo-Christian tradition women must reject this tradition in its entirety in order to have dignity and self-esteem, many women have long been sifting—and continue to sift—through the sexism and other negative aspects and have found in Judaism and Christianity important sources of strength and solace, and many humane values they can live by. Moreover, many women find that their needs—especially for community and ritual—are best met by Judaism and Christianity because, their misogynist and other potentially problematic strains aside, these are the predominant religions in our culture today. A woman explains:

> For a while I rejected all religions, but I felt I was missing something, so I explored a lot of alternative religions. I went to ashrams, did meditation, and participated in full moon rituals worshiping the goddess. All that was meaningful to me, but for some reason—maybe advancing age—nothing really satisfied me totally. And so, at age thirty-two, I joined the Episcopal

Church again, the church I rejected in my teens. What brought me back to it is that the rituals and symbols there are the ones I know from my childhood, and they have a meaning for me that others don't have. Also, there is a sense of belonging to the real, mainstream world that I get in my church that I didn't get at the ashrams.

Another woman explains how having a "mainstream" religious tradition to fall back on in a time of crisis helped her cope:

I haven't figured out the role of religion in my life—whether I want it, and what I want. But when my father died, I was really glad that I had been raised Catholic, because it provided us with a real clear set of rules about what to do. A lot of people think Catholic wakes and funerals are creepy and overdone, but I think that having those familiar prayers to say, smelling the smell of incense, and going through rituals that everyone was familiar with and had been through before helped me to heal.

In the end, each of us has to decide for ourself whether or not to explore spiritual aspects of experience, and what specific religion we'll adopt if we do want to explore and express our spirituality. But whatever decision we make, it's helpful to keep in mind the belief of the Gnostic Christians that each person should and can rely on her own inner authority to make the decision that's best, and that if we are to look for God and truth we need to start by looking within. It's helpful, too, to keep in mind these words, attributed to Jesus in the Gnostic *Gospels of St. Thomas:*

If you bring forth what is within you, what you bring forth will save you. If you do not bring forth what is within you, what you do not bring forth will destroy you. . . .

For whoever has not known himself has known nothing, but whoever has known himself has simultaneously achieved knowledge about the depth of all things.[19]

BLUEPRINTS FOR CHANGE

I. The Essentials of Self-esteem

If you had some religious training, consider its influence on the essentials of your self-esteem. How did your religious training contribute to or diminish your sense of significance? Your sense of power and competence? Your sense of community? Your sense of individuality? Your sense of reality? Your values and ethics? Did you have any positive role models in your religious training? Negative role models? How were you labeled? How did religious training influence your ideals? Hopefully, you were given some accurate and positive ideas about yourself as a result of religious training. Can you identify what was negative and inaccurate, throw it out and replace it with something more positive, accurate and up-to-date?

II. IMAGES OF GOD(S)

Most of us were raised with an image of God as a white male, and that did little for the self-esteem of girls and people of color. Since faith can be intensely personal, there is nothing to stop us from visualizing God (if you believe in God) in our own way. Perhaps you will visualize God as female, or male *and* female. Or perhaps you will visualize a variety of goddesses and gods to symbolize various aspects of your faith. In Alice Walker's novel *The Color Purple,* Shug explains her image of God to her lover Celie:

> Here's the thing, say Shug. The thing I believe. God is in you and inside everything else. You come into the world with God. But only them that search for it inside find it. . . .
> Don't look like nothing, she say. It ain't a picture show. It ain't something you can look at apart from anything else, including yourself. I believe God is everything, say Shug. Everything that is or ever was or ever will be. . . .
> She say, My first step from the old white man was trees. Then air. Then birds. Then other people. But one day when I was sitting quiet and feeling like a motherless child, which I was, it come to me: That feeling of being a part of everything, not separate at all. I knew that if I cut a tree, my arm would bleed.[20]

III. RECOVERING THE POSITIVE IMAGES

Although the Judeo-Christian tradition is patriarchal, both the Old Testament and the New Testament of the Bible do give us images of strong women. Going back through biblical texts, can you find positive images of women that you consider affirming? Did any of the women in the Bible—Sarah, Ruth, for example, or Martha, Mary and Mary Magdalene in the New Testament—serve as role models for you? If you were raised as a Christian, what do you recall about Christ's relationships with women? Do you think he valued women? Does his behavior toward women suggest he did?

IV. Re-mything the Bible

Although the Bible does offer strong images of women, often the stories in which women appear are told from a male perspective, and the women's experience is overshadowed by the men's experience—or not delved into much at all. What if Genesis had been written differently? What if, for example, it was Adam, not Eve, who played the role of the tempter? And looking at Sarah, Abraham's wife in the Old Testament, consider what her experience and feelings might have been. She was an old woman when she gave birth to Isaac, and she must have been upset when Abraham decided to prove his deference to God by following God's command to kill Isaac. Can you try to imagine what Sarah might have said had she been given a chance to speak out about her husband's attempted murder of their son?

V. The Importance of Rituals

Religions give us rituals to mark birth, death, marriage, the passage of time, and to celebrate and honor life and the divine. Are there rituals from your own religious background that had or have special meaning for you? Can you recall experiences when rituals helped you to cope with life's difficult transitions, or enhanced your celebration of happy events, increased your awareness of the mysteries of the universe, and/or gave you more of a sense of community? If some of the religious rituals from your upbringing seemed to you to be depressing or to have lost their meaning, can you think of ways they might be modified to meet your present-day needs better? Have you ever participated in or observed the rituals of a religion not your own? If not and you would like to, perhaps a friend from another religious background would be willing to introduce you to them. Perhaps you also want to consider creating rituals of your own.

* 3 *

If Only We Had Learned Differently: The Impact of Formal Schooling

Most of us spent a major portion of our time during our formative years in school, and schools today are among the most powerful of influences. The primary purpose of formal schooling is to socialize children, to equip them with the skills needed to function as productive members of society, and to inculcate in them the larger culture's values as well. Schools shaped our most fundamental beliefs about our purpose and possibilities in this world, while at the same time providing us with our basic conceptions of the nature of knowledge, truth, excellence, and history.

When seen in historical context, the impact of formal schooling on our self-attitudes appears remarkably enormous. Today we take it for granted that virtually everyone in our society spends a large chunk of childhood in school; going to school is what children in our society do. But, in fact, the concept of all children receiving at least an elementary education in school is relatively new. For most of Western history, formal schooling was a privilege available only to males (and a very few females) of the upper classes, and until the late Middle Ages schools were run by the Church, and learned discourse was conducted in Latin, a language unintelligible to the vast majority of the populace. Charlemagne sought to increase interest in academic studies with the establishment of schools throughout Europe in the early Middle Ages. Later the interest in education grew greater with such developments as the establishment of secular universities, the use of vernacular languages rather than Latin for official and learned discourse, and the invention of the printing press. But it was only with the Enlightenment and the advancement of the principles of the revolutionary doctrine of democracy that the idea of formal schooling for large percentages of the populace gained widespread acceptance.[1]

Although today public schools are open to both sexes, and the predominance of women in elementary teaching often gives the impression that schools are female-dominated, the fact is that institutions of formal learning originated as male-only enclaves, and recognition of females' right to education came only relatively recently in history. For millennia the claim that women were unfit for rigorous mental exercise was used to keep women out of the academies and universities, and also as an excuse to give inferior training to those relatively few women privileged enough to be formally educated. A well-educated woman during the Renaissance, for example, would not have been instructed in such strenuous topics as philosophy, mathematics, history, Latin and Greek, because they would have contradicted the purpose of a woman's education at that time, which was to make her a more agreeable, submissive and ego-massaging companion to men.[2] Male education encouraged self-reliance and intellectual daring, but female education was designed to equip a woman to run a household, to be able to do needlework, to appreciate (but not create) art and beauty, to keep herself attractive, and to be obedient, religious, cheerful, and always admiring and deferential to men. The idea that knowledge does not become a woman was so widespread for so long that even as late as the Renaissance much "learned opinion" on the subject of women held that women should not be taught to read; and once some women were taught to read during the Renaissance other writers cautioned that women should not be allowed to read much other than pious religious texts.[3]

Even as the ideals of democracy gained increasing popularity during the Enlightenment, the idea of equal education for females remained strongly resisted. In *Émile,* published in 1762, Rousseau set forth a formula for the proper education of women that was widely influential. According to Rousseau, women should be trained to be dependent, passive, self-effacing, self-sacrificing, and should also never be free from a sense of "being reigned in." In his view, proper subjects of study for women were such as sewing, lacemaking and grooming, and the purpose of women's education was to make women able to "lease and be useful to men, as well as to honor them, care for them, console them, and render life sweet and agreeable to them."[4]

Rousseau's ideas about female education reflected a philosophy put into practice abroad and here in America. In the grammar schools set up in colonial Massachusetts, for example, initially "girls were usually admitted only during the times when the boys were not there"; more-over, "they were banned from all learning beyond the elementary level."[5] The predominant view throughout the eighteenth century was that a proper female education was that which would equip women for "religion, morality and housewifery," as Phyllis Stock points out:

> Dame schools, which provided training in female skills, plus moral train-ing, existed here as in England. The common (grammar) schools were attended irregularly by girls, who learned reading and sewing while their brothers learned reading and writing. Most towns were reluctant to pay for school for girls; too much education, as (Massachusetts) Governor John Winthrop remarked, could lead to madness in women. From 1650 to 1776 the male literacy rate in New England rose from 60 percent to 90 percent; that of women, from 30 to 45 percent.[6]

Although much has changed since the time of the American Revolu-tion, and women have caught up with men insofar as literacy is con-cerned, vestiges of old attitudes toward women's education still remain. While women gradually were allowed equal access to elementary schools, secondary schools were slow in opening their doors to females, and colleges, universities and professional schools were slower still. It wasn't until well into the nineteenth century that college educations began to be made available to women. And even then most existing institutions of higher learning did not become coeducational; separate colleges for women were established instead.

It is not only in admissions policies that vestiges of the old attitudes toward women's education have remained in our time. Although this is changing somewhat in some places today, when most of us went to school, our experience there was far different from that of the boys. We may have been in the same elementary school classrooms as boys, but within those classrooms there probably were clearly marked divisions: In kindergarten the girls played with dolls, the boys with trucks; in the higher grades the girls excelled in English, the boys in science. By the time we got to high school, the separations had become more rigid: Boys took shop while girls took home economics (just as Rousseau had recommended); boys took physics, girls typing and shorthand. And for those who went on to college, the segregation became more rigid, with the women students steered into the humanities and predominating in such courses as nursing, early childhood education and art history, and the men flocking toward the sciences, engineering, higher mathematics, medicine, and business management.

Access to educational opportunities is affected not just by gender, but by other factors too. One of the most popular American myths is that no matter what your socioeconomic class, race or ethnic background, if you get a good education, you'll be able to go far. But unless you are white and grew up in a relatively wealthy area, getting a good education is not easy. Schools in inner city ghettos, in impoverished rural areas and on Indian reservations are generally poorly funded, understaffed and offer to their students inferior opportunities compared to those offered students attending much better funded and better staffed suburban schools. Because our educational system is set up in a way that favors affluent students and puts the poor at a great disadvantage, schools in general tend to reinforce the existing class structure.

What We Were—and Weren't—Taught

Most of us began school at the age of five or six. We were in no position to prevent being sent to school (although we might have tried). Nor were we able to challenge what we learned in class once we got there. School was a formidable institution, our teachers and principals were large adults who wielded great authority, and we were small children, powerless, vulnerable, naïve, eager to please. Instead of analyzing what we were taught or questioning its veracity or validity, we more likely just believed it.

Our inability as young children to question what we were taught is particularly unfortunate for those of us born female, because much of what we were taught in school impeded the development of our self-esteem. The standard elementary curricula most of us were exposed to is one that showcases men and male achievements while ignoring women and female achievements—or trivializing those few that do get mentioned.

To be sure, much that we learned in school led to a sense of power and competence. For example, reading is an invaluable skill in that it gives great pleasure and opens up entire universes of possibility while also making it much easier to survive in the world. The problem is, though, that as we began to master the basics of reading we were also being taught that as females we are less important, less capable, less active and less interesting than males. Although the world's population is more than 51 percent female, a very different picture was given by the books most of us learned to read with—and children are still learning to read with today. Looking at 134 elementary readers published by fourteen different publishers and used in suburban schools, one study group found that in a total of 2,760 stories

—boy-centered stories outnumbered girl-centered stories by 5 to 2;

—adult-male main characters outnumbered adult-female main characters by 3 to 1;

—male biographies outnumbered female biographies by 6 to 1;

—stories about male animals outnumbered stories about female animals 2 to 1;

—male folk and fantasy stories outnumbered female folk and fantasy stories 4 to 1.[7]

The fact that females do not receive equal time—far from it—in these books is enough in itself to give girls the unmistakable impression that we are not important. But even worse, where female characters do appear, they typically conform to negative stereotypes. Female characters, child as well as adult, human as well as animal, are portrayed more often than not as weak, dependent, catty, unable to make friends, afraid to take risks, overly concerned with their appearance and emotionally unstable. Boys, by contrast, are more often than not portrayed as strong, independent, solid and reliable friends, brave and enterprising.

Even a field like mathematics, which would seem to have nothing to do with gender, may have been presented to us in a way that communicated the lesson that girls just don't count as much as boys. In reviewing elementary school math books, for example, Marsha Federbush found that when problems were presented, they often did so in a way that reinforced demeaning stereotypes of girls ("Susan could not figure out how to . . .") and ego-boosting images of boys ("Jim showed her how . . ."). When pictured in illustrations, females, Federbush found, were usually shown cooking, sewing, watching male activity, and/or being confused and waiting for male help. Males, by contrast, were depicted sailing, climbing mountains, going to the moon, and always solving problems. And looking at higher math curricula, Federbush also found books written as if mathematics was a field contributed to by men and only men. For example, "not a word is ever mentioned" about Emmy Noether, although Noether was one of the principal creators of modern abstract axiomatic algebra.[8]

We should point out here that no one ever sat down and said, "Let's come up with schoolbooks that will make boys feel good about themselves, and girls feel bad about themselves." The androcentric bias that ran through our grade-school texts is part and parcel of an androcentric bias that shapes virtually the entire curriculum from first grade on, and this bias did not arise as a result of a conscious decision on the part of publishers. The bias we see in readers and the rest of the curriculum developed as an inevitable by-product of the centuries-long tradition of confining formal education to men and only men. The exclusion of women from institutions of formal learning for so long virtually guaranteed that every area of academic inquiry would have men and men's concerns at its center. Men recorded their experiences and called it history; men looked about the world and called their observations science; men wondered about the existence of God and the problem of evil and called their speculations theology; men did handiwork and called it art; men made up stories, wrote them down and called them literature; and men thought about such topics as truth, beauty, justice and the nature of existence and called their opinions philosophy. Not coincidentally, many of the so-called truths men discovered in the process served to keep men at the center of attention—and the top of the heap. Among these are such "truths" as "man is the measure of all things"; "man is unique among the animals"; "man is woman's natural superior"; and "man is the most perfect being in nature." Laugh as we may today at the naked narcissism of these supposed truths, the sad fact is that the self-aggrandizing sentiments behind them still shape considerably the nature of academic enterprise. Most children are still taught according to an academic tradition that effectively eliminates the experiences, contributions and perceptions of more than half the human race.

Not just our early reading books but the very language we were taught to use in school communicated to us the insidious lesson that girls and women just don't count. Before we went to school, we learned that people come in two genders. We learned that our fathers and the fellow who brought the mail are called men, and that our mothers and the lady who lived next door are called women. And, as Casey Miller and Kate Swift point out, if we had seen the lady next door and said "There's a man!" we probably would have been corrected and told very firmly that she is a woman and that a woman is not the same as a man.[9] Once we got to school, however, we were taught that, contrary to what we had been taught before, it is proper to speak of man and men as though these terms included the lady next door. Learning about "prehistoric man," "man the hunter," "man the toolmaker," "man the inventor," "man and science," "man and government," etc., we were supposed to now make a switch from thinking of man as someone male to thinking of man as someone somehow male *and female*.

The use of the supposedly generic "man" went against everything we had been taught previously, and against what we knew to be true. In her study of children, Aileen Pace Nilsen found that a majority of both sexes visualized male people when they heard statements such as "man must work in order to eat."[10] Other researchers working with college students found that they as well associated the supposedly generic "man" used in their school books (as in such headings as "Political Man," "Social Man," and "Industrial Man") with male persons rather than with a mixture of humans of both sexes.[11] Obviously, the mandatory use of the terms *man, men* and *he* as if they were representative of all humans is not only confusing, it is negating to the female sense of self. As Miller and Swift observe, a boy's self-esteem is bolstered considerably but a girl's is not when they open the Britannica Junior Encyclopaedia and read that "man is the highest form of life on earth. His superior intelligence, combined with certain physical characteristics, have enabled man to achieve things that are impossible for other animals."[12]

The language we were taught to use in American schools was doubly negating to those whose roots were in cultures other than Anglo culture. Children from Native American cultures were taught that the languages their ancestors had spoken for centuries were uncouth and inferior, and they were forced to speak English instead; the use of Indian languages in schools was in fact outlawed by the U.S. Government. And children whose families had come to the United States from Europe and Asia were also informed that their own languages are inferior, and that they must speak English. Maxine Hong Kingston was so traumatized by not being able to speak Chinese that she did not speak a word for three years once she started school. Even years later she still feels uncomfortable speaking English:

> When I went to kindergarten and had to speak English for the first time, I became silent. A dumbness—a shame—still cracks my voice in two, even when I want to say "hello" casually, or ask an easy question in front of the checkout counter, or ask directions of a bus driver. I stand frozen, or I hold up the line with the complete, grammatical sentence that comes squeaking out at impossible length. . . . During the first silent year I spoke to no one at school, did not ask before going to the lavatory, and flunked kindergarten.[13]

The literature courses we were taught in school once we had learned to read and write the English language furthered the invisibility of women and people from non-Anglo cultures. In the higher grades, few school literature programs overlook the women writers entirely; Edith Wharton's *Ethan Frome* is standard fare, as are at least mentions of the Brontës, Jane Austen and Harriet Beecher Stowe. And some black writers such as James Baldwin are also often taught in schools. But overall, writers who are both male and white are given the most attention by far. The few women writers whose work is studied are usually white, and the few black writers studied are usually men. The work of black women, Asian women and Chicanas is nowhere to be seen.[14]

Probably the field in which men have been most thoroughly show-cased and women most thoroughly excluded is that of history. Women have been all but entirely wiped off the standard historical record: We learned about Renaissance Man, Man in the Middle Ages, Enlightenment Man, Man in the West, etc., but we learned nothing of woman in these times. This is both a direct consequence of women's subordinate status in a male-dominated world and an effective means of furthering it. Women were not deemed important, so women were not included in history books, and the fact that women do not appear in history books perpetuates the notion that women are not important—never were and never will be.

In itself, the exclusion of women from history has a disastrous effect on our sense of worth. When a boy reads history, he is instantly validated; he finds strong images of male warriors, conquerors, explorers, inventors—images with which he can bond, and which enhance his self-esteem. When a girl reads history, she is instantly invalidated; she, too, finds images of male warriors, conquerors, explorers, inventors. But these are not images with which the girl can readily identify. She looks, in longing, for strong female images, but does not find them. The standard historical record gives her a Joan of Arc (burned at the stake), a Betsy Ross (whose claim to fame was sewing), a Carrie Nation (moralistic battle-ax), a Florence Nightingale (super-nurse), a few queens (all of whom obtained the throne because there were no male heirs). Beyond this smattering of female images, conventional history gives the girl nothing, literally nothing. It is no wonder so many women feel "full of blanks" when the history of our sex is represented by blank spaces.

If women's exclusion from the standard historical record only rendered women invisible, it would be bad enough. But, to add insult to injury, our induced ignorance of women's role and contributions to history has enabled the acceptance of widespread dispersal of a number of misogynist myths that do further damage to women's self-esteem. One of the most damaging of these myths is that women through time have been the passive receptors of culture, never creators of it. "If women really are equal in ability to men," the predictable question goes, "then how come women never accomplished anything of note?" The answer is that women through time have, in fact, accomplished a great deal but men did not consider women's accomplishments worth recording. Worse, men have often appropriated women's accomplishments, presenting them in history as their own. Take, for example, the myth of "Man the Hunter." According to what most of us were taught, hunting males provided the meat that enabled our earliest human ancestors to survive, and it was Man the Hunter who invented the first tools, mastered fire, developed language, and made the other material and conceptual contributions that enabled the human race to progress through time. In fact, though, our earliest human ancestors were vegetarians and fructarians, not carnivores, and it was Woman the Gatherer, not Man the Hunter, who provided the bulk of the nourishment that enabled the species to survive. Moreover, anthropological evidence suggests that it was woman, not man, who played the most active role in the creation of early human culture. It was probably she, not he, who invented the first tools (possibly child- and food-carrying slings fashioned out of long grasses), who mastered fire, who developed such skills as pottery, weaving and building, and who also played the primary role in the development of language, mathematics, and the sciences of horticulture and agriculture.[15]

In addition to damaging our collective self-esteem by obscuring women's important historical contributions, the obliteration of women from the historical record caused us to be taught certain conclusions about history that in fact are wrong. Take, for example, the way we were taught to conceptualize different historical periods. The view of Western history ascribed to by most of our teachers was probably one that sees the democratic period in Greece as the height of civilization, the Middle Ages as a time when civilization deteriorated, the Renaissance as a time when civilization again progressed, and the period following the American Revolution, particularly the Jacksonian era, as one of increasing popular liberty. This is the conventional, androcentric view. But when Western history is viewed from the vantage point of women, the picture that emerges is the exact opposite. For women democracy in Athens meant either concubinage or, in the case of citizens' wives, perpetual confinement indoors and a protein-deficient diet. For women the Middle Ages meant increasing freedom and power in many respects, as well as improvements in diet and health. For women the Renaissance meant a loss of freedom and power, the denigration of the kind of learning women had traditionally developed, and the escalating terrorism of the witchcraft persecutions. For women the period following the American Revolution, particularly the Jacksonian "Age of the Common Man," meant fewer legal rights, not more.[16]

The extent to which women have been omitted from the standard historical record is all the more obvious when we look at the way women in American history have been portrayed. Most of us learned about our nation's history from an entirely male perspective. We did not learn, for example, about the crucial roles women played during the Revolution, nor how this period saw the active politicization of women for the first time, nor, finally, how women fared during and following the war. We learned virtually nothing about the struggle for the vote that spanned more than seventy years; instead, we learned simply that women were "given" the vote in 1918. And we learned nothing about the widespread and radical feminist movement which had obtaining the vote as only one of its goals; instead we learned to think of the early feminists as suffragists, as if their sole concern was with that one issue. By omitting so much important information about our past from the curriculum, those who educated us not only deprived us of knowledge that would enable us to think more highly of ourselves as women—they also deprived us of knowledge that could be of use to us in our own struggles today.

Women of color are particularly hurt by the androcentric standard curriculum. For in addition to being sexist, the view of the world we were given in school was most likely racist as well. A basic assumption underlying much of what we were taught is that white America represents the pinnacle of civilization, and that all other peoples and cultures are backward or somehow deficient by comparison. If we learned anything at all about cultures in, say, Africa or Asia, we most likely learned that they are "primitive" and the people who comprise them are "savages."

As far as our own nation is concerned, we probably learned little about the experience of blacks, or of Hispanics or Asians in the United States either. Similarly, if we learned anything at all about the people who had lived in the Americas long before white settlers claimed the land as their own, we probably learned a lot of vicious lies. Unfortunately, the lies still persist, and many Native American children educated in white-run schools were taught not to prize their heritage, but to hate it—and to hate themselves, too. An Ojibwa woman recalls:

> I went back to school in the fall. Now that I could speak English, I never kept my mouth shut. We read a history book about "the savages." The pictures were in color. There was one of a group of warriors attacking white people—a woman held a baby in her arms. I saw hatchets, blood dripping, feathers flying. I showed the picture to the Sister. She said, "Rose Mary, don't you know you're Indian?" I said, "No, I'm not." She said, "Yes, you are," I said, "No!" And I ran behind a clump of juniper trees,

and cried and cried. I spent a week in the infirmary. I didn't eat. I was really sick.[17]

Beyond the androcentrism and racism, one of the biggest problems with what we were taught in school is how little the bulk of it had to do with the reality of our lives. Time and again in talking to women about their school experiences, we heard the same questions: Why in school were we never taught anything about emotions? Why weren't we taught about our bodies? Why was there never any discussion about what it feels like when a loved one dies, and how we can deal with that crisis? Why, if schools saw fit to equip us with such practical skills as cooking, typing and driving, didn't they also try to equip us with information that could help us take care of ourselves and move in the world more effectively? Or, as one woman put it:

In school you never learn what's really important. They teach you all about this battle and that battle and about how the solar system works, and you don't learn much that's going to help you understand yourself and live your life. I mean, I can name the geological ages backward and forward, but I never learned the names for parts of my own body, and no one ever taught me that feelings are important. They taught me to type in school, and I'm glad for that, but no one taught me about how you stand up for yourself and ask for a raise or how you go about getting help if you're being treated unfairly. . . . I always thought something was wrong with me. It didn't occur to me that you're not born knowing what you need to know to make it through life, and that the problem was that no one equipped me with the basic tools necessary to be an adult.

Who Taught Us and How They Taught Us: The Elementary Years

More likely than not, our first teacher was a woman; indeed, the majority of our teachers were probably women, at least in the early years, because elementary teaching is a profession in which women predominate. As we got into high school, male teachers would become more the norm, and if we went on to college, we would find that virtually all our professors were men. But in those early years when we first went to school, and when we were most impressionable, most eager to please and least likely to question, our teachers were women. It was with women that we came to associate the institution of school, and all the power, authority and knowledge that school represents.

The androcentric nature of much of what we were taught might seem odd considering that women taught us. But women came to constitute the majority of elementary teachers for the simple reason that women could be hired cheaper than men, not because of any concerted female effort to take over the education of the young. The real power in education always has been with men, and this is true today as much as ever. Although women may predominate in elementary teaching, most university and college professors are men, as are most school principals and administrators, most school district superintendents and most state officers of education. By and large, it was men such as these who made the final decisions about what we were taught in school—and who still make those decisions today.[18]

As small children we experienced our female teachers as unshakable pillars of authority. Our teachers may have had little power when dealing with the principal or the men on the school board. But we did not know this. When it came to dealing with us, the power they exercised was formidable—perhaps even absolute.

Depending on whether our teachers criticized or rewarded us, deemed us successes or failures, and felt us worthy or unworthy of special attention, our self-esteem was probably affected accordingly. Moreover, our sense of possibilities for the future was shaped by our teachers, because both their power over us and their presence in our lives many hours a day, five days a week, put them in a prime position to be role models.

Our teachers were probably not especially concerned with building our self-esteem. Their principal job was to get us to do our schoolwork so that we could move on to the next grade according to schedule. Getting us to do our schoolwork meant maintaining order in a classroom, and toward this end our teachers had to create an atmosphere in which their own authority was beyond question. If our teachers told us to open our books to page 23, to line up and march around in a set fashion, or to ask questions in a certain way, we knew there would be severe penalties for noncompliance. We did what we were told because in the hierarchy of school and classroom, we had no other choice.

To keep their young charges in line, the teachers that women we interviewed had when they were young used a variety of techniques that unfortunately could hurt children's self-esteem. One such technique was creating an atmosphere where children are always on the hot seat. School might have been the most stressful environment we were ever in, for nowhere else is a person under such constant scrutiny and subject to such continual judgments as in school. In school our work was always graded; and because of innovations such as surprise quizzes we were always under the pressure of knowing that at any moment we might be called upon to prove ourselves. Moreover, not just our work but all our actions were under scrutiny and judgment. Our teachers had absolute power to judge our conduct, our level of cleanliness, our congeniality and our intelligence, and also were given authority to pronounce judgments on such immeasurables as our amount of motivation. At any time in school we could have been singled out from the rest of the students and demanded by the teacher to account for why we were looking around or doodling, or—worse—to account for our innermost thoughts ("Sally, are you daydreaming?").

Many teachers also used shame and ridicule. If the judgments our teachers pronounced on us were positive or at least constructively critical, perhaps they would not have been so damaging. As it was, though, many of our teachers resorted to verbal shaming and ridicule in order to keep us in line. Many women we interviewed recalled being told by their frustrated teachers that they're stupid, that they'll never learn, that they were bad children. One of the most common ways of shaming students was to say "You're just not trying hard enough." Some shaming techniques involved more than words—e.g., making the child with behavior or severe learning problems stand in the corner. In addition, some teachers ridiculed children for things over which they had no control—how they dressed, what they looked like, the way they talked if they had accents, the way they were built, their family's class status.

Labeling was yet another common feature of classroom life. The teaching profession seems to be in love with labels: "gifted," "learning disabled," "underachiever," "overachiever," and "emotionally disturbed" are just a few of the common ones teachers routinely apply to children. These labels, once applied, usually stick with a child for the rest of her school life and usually determine what classes she's put in, what is expected of her and what directions she is encouraged to go in. The child labeled "gifted" may go through life feeling a pressure to perform. The child labeled a "slow learner" or "poor reader" may continue to perceive herself that way forever. And the woman once labeled an "overachiever" will never be able to be confident in her abilities; she'll always be afraid of being "found out" for not really being as bright as her performance and accomplishments indicate.

Schools are hierarchies, and within individual classrooms learning ladders, tracking and other innovative variations on the hierarchal theme were often used to keep us in line, too. One of the most effective ways for teachers to maintain control in classrooms and to get students to do their work is to threaten them with getting left back a grade. Getting left back is the ultimate disgrace: The child who has gotten left back is exposed to all the world as someone who couldn't make the grade. Teachers often replicated the ritual of going ahead versus getting left back in small ways in class. For example, if a child did her work one week, the next week she could move to a higher level on a learning ladder. For those who were able to keep moving up, learning ladders were no doubt effective; also, they aided self-esteem. But learning ladders at the same time crushed the self-esteem of the child whose progress was slow, or who was unable to make it at all.

Corporal punishment was yet another tool used by some of our teachers. The ultimate violation of a child's sense of self and self-worth that can happen in school is to be struck or beaten by a teacher or principal. Unfortunately, we heard of many instances where a woman as a young child had been hit by her teachers. If school was the first place outside the home that a child spent any significant time, being hit in school can have shaped her entire view of the outside world. As one woman put it:

> I saw the world as a place where you might get hit at any moment, for no comprehensible reason, and where you had no right to hit back. I just assumed because school and my home were that way, every place was like that too.

Many of us were positively influenced by our teachers all the same. Most of the women we interviewed recalled early school experiences as a mixture of both good and bad. While most remembered painful and humiliating experiences, many also held onto the memories of experiences that made them feel good about themselves:

> I wasn't a very good student, and I had a lot of trouble with being picked on by other kids, so school wasn't my favorite place. But in fourth grade I had this teacher who for some reason took to me and built me up. Most of my other teachers in the other grades either just ignored me because I didn't excel or actually made me feel I was mediocre. But this teacher was so nice to me. She really went out of her way to make even the poorer students feel we were worth teaching.

Particularly for children who grew up in troubled families, school could be a haven, and teachers their best allies:

> For me, growing up in foster homes, school was the one place I truly felt I belonged. A lot of teachers really went out of their way for me, to make me feel like I was capable and worth something. Even when I was sent to Catholic schools, this happened. I know there are a lot of people whose memories of Catholic school are horrible, and I knew some nuns who were crazy and beat the kids. But my own experience wasn't like that. Those

nuns gave me love, and in their own way they gave me some confidence in myself.

From our interviews we found that often a single positive experience with a teacher could have had an enormous impact on the entire outlook of a small child from a troubled family. Sometimes one affectionate, encouraging and supportive teacher made the difference between self-hate and the start of self-acceptance for a child.

Women with disabilities also may have been especially helped by school. Although children with disabilities are often treated as inferior at regular public schools, and are encouraged to see themselves as more limited than they are in some special schools, some women with disabilities did have school experiences that were mostly positive:

> My school was excellent although it was called the "Industrial School for Crippled Children." Because my mother was sick most of the time, it took the place of my mother. . . . My teachers approached my father when I needed a bra. When I needed information about menstruation, they told me about it. The school for handicapped kids gave me a sense of security that I didn't have at home. The one thing they stressed was that we accept and support each other as disabled. My only complaint is that they didn't prepare me to compete with my nondisabled peers. My first year of college was so difficult for me—I just didn't understand people's competitive behavior.

Later School Experiences

The further we went in school, the lower our chances of having experiences that would boost our self-esteem. For as we got into the higher grades, and went on to college (for those who did), our teachers were more and more likely to be males rather than females. The fact that men teach in the higher levels of education, and teach important subjects like calculus, physics and philosophy, while women are stuck in the lower grades teaching such elementary subjects as reading, basic writing and arithmetic cannot help but communicate to female students that the higher knowledge is for men and men alone. Women can be affected by this even if male teachers have gone out of their way to attempt to build in their female students a sense of possibilities:

> In my senior year in high school I had a chemistry teacher who got behind me one hundred percent and encouraged me to major in chemistry in college and do it or medicine as a career. But when I got to college, it didn't take long for me to lose my confidence. There wasn't one woman

teaching in the hard sciences, and there weren't any others in the higher
level chemistry courses. I was looked upon as an oddball by my classmates,
and my professors either condescended to me or came right out and discouraged me from pursuing sciences further. That stuff is hard to take at
that age. I chickened out and signed up for the nursing program.

Complicating matters for the female student, particularly the college
or graduate student, can be the sexualization of the student-teacher
relationship that often occurs at the higher levels of education when the
professor is male and the student female. The "fuck or flunk" formula,
so demeaning to women, unfortunately has become something far too
many female students are familiar with. Equally common, some women
have had the experience of being encouraged for their minds only to
find out later that their male professors were only interested in their
bodies all along:

> I had this philosophy professor who kept telling me I had a really creative,
> original, insightful mind, and that I should take myself and my potential
> more seriously. Idiot that I am, I actually believed the guy. It was the first
> time in my life I had felt that kind of confidence in my intellectual abilities.
> Then it turned out that he was just trying to get into my pants, and that
> blew me away, just devastated me. I felt so stupid for having believed him,
> and so humiliated.

We don't mean to suggest that all male professors are spiders, their
female students innocent flies. Many male professors have encouraged
their female students with no intent of seduction. Yet even in such cases,
there may have been cost to the female student's self-esteem. For in
emulating and trying to please her male professors, the female student
must deny her gender and her connectedness to members of her sex, as
Adrienne Rich observes:

> The male teacher may have a genuine "fatherly" relation to his gifted
> student-daughter, and many intellectual women have been encouraged and
> trained by their gifted fathers, or gifted male teachers. But it is the *absence*
> of the brilliant and creative mother, or woman teacher, that is finally of
> more significance than the presence of the brilliant and creative male. Like
> the father's favorite daughter in the patriarchal family, the promising stu-
> dent comes to identify with her male scholar-teacher more strongly than
> with her sisters . . . he confirms her suspicion that she is "exceptional."[19]

Probably worst off of all is the woman who doesn't get any encouragement from her male professors at all. Often it happens that unless a
female student is either extraordinarily gifted or extraordinarily beauti-

ful, she will be ignored or actively dissuaded by her professors. Meanwhile, male students who are less exceptional than she may well be treated like budding geniuses, their banal insights regarded as truly pithy, their mediocre dissertations lauded by their male colleagues as "major contributions" to their field. No wonder that females, who generally do much better academically than males in their early years, tend to fall back in adolescence—and often out of the game entirely—by late high school and college.

Women who are not from the middle and upper classes are especially likely to find the world of higher education particularly alienating. To begin with, women from working-class backgrounds have a diminished chance of getting into colleges and universities because of the costs involved, and also because of the fact that college and university admissions offices tend to show a preference for students from the nation's best-funded schools. And in most instances once a working-class woman does enter the university world, she will be in a minority:

> I was lucky and got a scholarship to a pretty prestigious university. It was a weird experience for me. On the one hand, I was proud to be a scholarship student, and proud to be from working stock, unlike those rich-kid preppies. I really felt superior to them in a way. But on the other hand, I felt sort of ashamed of my background. A part of me wished I could be like the rich preppies—they seemed so carefree and glamorous. I vacillated between feeling proud of my background and feeling ashamed all the years I was in school, and today I still am pained by that split in myself.

As the university world is upper and middle class, so is it largely white. Women of color are apt to feel doubly that they don't belong:

> I was the only Asian on my campus. It was very hard to go day after day and never see another face that looked like mine. I felt I stuck out like a sore thumb and I felt invisible at the same time.

Beyond Equal Access to Education

Early proponents of women's rights such as Mary Wollstonecraft and John Stuart Mill seized on education as the key that would enable women to challenge men's traditional dominance and stand as their equals. They argued that if women's education trains us only to be subservient and dependent and to be skilled only in domestic duties and piety, then of course women will appear and act as men's inferiors. To be able to claim full human rights and be accorded respect as a full human being, they contended, a woman has to be given access to the same education made available to men. As long as women remained without such basic skills as reading and writing, there would be no chance whatsoever for equality of the sexes.[20]

The arguments of feminists like Wollstonecraft and Mill were revolutionary for their time, and they were also basically sound ones. It has become apparent, though, that their arguments did not go quite far enough. Wollstonecraft and Mill did not question the content of what was taught in schools, nor the manner in which lessons were taught; they simply assumed that the education men had designed for men was the education that women should want for themselves. But as we've seen, much of what we learned in school negated and trivialized women, and many of the standard classroom methods commonly employed by teachers are potentially crushing to any young child's sense of worth and personal autonomy. To be sure, in terms of access to education and basic skills women today are much better off than women a hundred or so years ago. But as acquiring basic skills went hand in hand with learning a curriculum that is sexist and racist, our educations have not given us a great advantage over our foresisters in terms of self-esteem. Indeed, it may be that some women's self-esteem is actually lower because of school than it would have been if they had been born centuries earlier and thus weren't exposed to the thoroughly androcentric and racist world view promulgated by the educational establishment.

BLUEPRINTS FOR CHANGE

I. THE ESSENTIALS OF SELF-ESTEEM

How did your schooling contribute to or diminish (in most cases it was a combination of both) your sense of significance? Your sense of power and competence? Your sense of community? Your sense of individuality? Your sense of reality? Your values and ethics? Did you have any positive role models in school? Negative role models? How were you labeled at various times? Did you encounter any troubled adults in the school system? What was their impact on you? Hopefully, you were given some positive and accurate ideas about yourself in school. Can you identify what was negative and inaccurate, then throw it out and replace it with something more positive, accurate and up-to-date?

II. QUESTIONING WHAT WE WERE TAUGHT

Think about specific things you were taught. Are they necessarily true? A good case in point are the lessons we learned about people of color and about women in history. We can't take what we were taught as the last word.

In addition to questioning what we were taught, it is often helpful to our sense of selves to *expand* our knowledge. The American school system gives the impression that once people graduate from high school or college, they cease to learn. But adult education is a viable option in many communities, and it exists for people who want to expand their knowledge. Community colleges, recreation departments, continuing education departments of colleges and universities, some women's organizations and the like offer courses, and sometimes they are inexpensive or offer scholarships. Many women specifically feel they "missed something" in the particular areas of physical education, shop and auto mechanics, math and sciences. Adult education can help us to fill in some of the gaps. For others, continuing education is an extension of interests developed in school. It is also a way to connect with our community. Remember, no one knows everything and no one is ever too old to keep on learning.

III. QUESTIONING HOW WE WERE TAUGHT

Was school an environment where you felt anxious because you felt "on the spot" and therefore did not learn in a relaxed manner? Did your teachers use shame or ridicule? Were you subject to classroom hierarchies which affected your feelings of personal worth? Were you placed in classes that were remedial or advanced? How did these experiences influence your self-concept and your relationships with other children? Was corporal punishment used against you? Do your experiences affect your attitudes toward learning today? Techniques such as ridicule and shame are not generally used in adult education. And in rare cases where they are, you now have the power to stop attending when you please. We encourage you to look at shaming and ridicule as inhumane and to begin to question any sense of inferiority you grew up with as a result of these methods. The problem was with the methods—not with you.

IV. TEACHING CHILDREN TODAY

Not all women choose to be involved in the teaching of children today, but for those who are, there is much we can do. If you are a teacher, we hope you will consider the impact your teaching has on malleable self-concepts as well as being concerned with the knowledge you impart. We have found that many teachers are concerned with both today. If the problematic methods of teaching we've delineated are used in your school, do you have to use them? Can you work to replace them with more humane methods? What can you do within your classroom to ameliorate whatever detrimental effects they might have? How are you a role model for your students?

Many parents with school-age children today understand the importance of being aware of what is taught in their children's schools and how it is being taught. The extra effort it takes to be active in parent-teacher associations, to observe children's classes, to protest teaching styles that diminish our children's self-esteem, to read over their textbooks for demeaning stereotypes of people is often hard to generate, but it can be well worth it.

Those of us who are not directly involved in the education of children today and who do not have children in school can still play an important role. We can offer assistance to the parent groups that are working for better schools. We can take self-esteem-enhancing programs into the schools. We can beware of what we teach young children by our example. We can share with children we know information to counter negative lessons they might learn about women and members of minority groups, or about what their options for life are. For example, it might be helpful for a little girl to know that in fact there are women carpenters and that they can make good money. And it might be helpful for a little boy to know that some of the world's greatest dancers are men, and that they can be held in high esteem. The answer isn't to abandon our schools as they are now or to encourage children to drop out of sexist, racist or otherwise demoralizing schools. Rather, the task at hand is to question and transform those institutions so that the process of learning enhances the self-esteem of us all.

* 4 *

Gaining Power in Some Areas,
Losing It in Others:
The Impact of Government

What impact does government in America have on women's self-esteem? This is a question for which there is no definitive, categorical answer. A poor woman who lives in a ghetto where there is considerable police harassment, where people's private lives are subject to the close scrutiny of government welfare workers, and where government policies have helped to create high unemployment might well experience the government as an oppressive force that engenders in her feelings of powerlessness. Since the sense that one has some power to exert control over her life is essential to self-esteem, this can only undercut her sense of self-worth. A Native American whose people have suffered so greatly at the hands of the U.S. Government might also view it as primarily oppressive, as might an American woman of Japanese descent whose family was wrongly imprisoned in camps by the United States during World War II. By contrast, a financially well-off white woman who has been able to rely on the police for help when her house has been robbed, and who has the good fortune to be able to exercise her right to life, liberty and the pursuit of happiness without government interference, will likely see the government as a protector and liberator, one that enhances her ability to exert power over her life and safeguards her human dignity. Obviously, whether a particular woman's sense of personal power and her dignity are helped or hurt, or both, by government has much to do with such factors as race, socioeconomic class, age and where in the nation a woman resides.

When we asked women if they thought their self-esteem was influenced in one or many ways by government, it became clear to us that many women feel alienated from government, wholly estranged from it and convinced that they are unable to exert any power over it. Although we in the United States supposedly have a government that is of the people and for the people, the fact is that the U.S. Government was founded by men (and white, property-owning men at that) to protect the rights of men (again, white property-owning men).[1] Even today after more than two hundred years, our federal government (as well as most state and local governments) remains a government run primarily by white men who do not have the interests of all the people—women as well as men; poor as well as rich; black, Asian, Native American and Hispanic as well as white—at heart. Most women seem aware of this, whether consciously or only intuitively. One result is that many women express little active interest in government, seeing it essentially as a male arena, like a football field. Other women, although they might be interested, feel there is little they can do to become more involved in or to influence government. "I don't understand it," "It's too big and intimidating," "It's beyond me," and "It's not something I can do anything about" are all phrases we heard often when we asked women how they perceive government and their relationship to it.

The Impact of the Law

In addition to expressing a general feeling of estrangement and powerlessness over the government, women we asked about government's impact on self-esteem expressed four main concerns. First, many are concerned that those in government in the United States are not fully committed to equal rights for women or to taking women's issues seriously. Considering our history, such concern is understandable. After all, it took more than seventy years of struggle for women to finally win the vote, the Equal Rights Amendment still has not been added to the Constitution despite more than fifty years of effort, and thousands of state statutes that discriminate against women remain on the books throughout the nation. To be sure, considerable progress has been made so far in winning equal legal rights for women. But there's still a way to go before women can be assured of equal legal rights in all circumstances in all states. In most states in 1983, for example, a woman who has been raped by her husband still has no legal right to prosecute him for it; marital rape is simply not a crime.[2]

Discriminatory laws do not in and of themselves cause low self-esteem. Rather, self-esteem is influenced by the limitations and restrictions the law ends up placing on women, and the general climate laws help to create. For example, most women who support the ERA probably don't feel personally bad about themselves because of the ERA's defeat; the defeat might make such women angry, but it doesn't make us feel worthless. Yet the fact that the ERA still has not been incorporated into the Constitution does affect the opportunities and liberties available to women and how women are treated in the world, and this in turn does effect our self-esteem. Thus, while it would be foolish to suggest that passage of the ERA would suddenly and automatically lead to higher self-esteem among women, it would be equally foolish to say that the ERA and other changes in the law won't make any difference at all. True, legal remedies such as the ERA won't solve women's self-esteem problems. But the ERA will help to create a climate in which it will be easier for women to develop and maintain high self-esteem, and in that sense it surely can't hurt.

Enforcing the Law

Women often also voiced concern that those charged with enforcing laws (police, judges, government prosecutors, staffers at agencies such as the federal Equal Employment Opportunity Commission, for example) are often as insensitive to and biased against women as the men who have made our nation's laws. Reason for such concern is most evident within the criminal justice system. This is changing somewhat today in some parts of the country, but traditionally the criminal justice system has been quite lax in safeguarding women's rights. Until recently, for instance, a victim of rape could expect that if she reported the crime and tried to prosecute the rapist, she would be the one to be treated more like a criminal than he. Similarly, women who have sought police help when their husbands have battered them often have found that the police don't want to get involved, don't take the women's complaints seriously, or actually side with the abusive husband. Being treated in such ways robs women of power and can greatly hurt women's sense of self-worth. And to make matters worse for poor women and women of color, class and racial prejudice within the criminal justice system further diminishes many women's chances of being treated fairly and respectfully.

In divorce cases where the court orders fathers to pay child support, the government again has done a generally poor job to date in enforcing the law. Although in the early 1980s the government had begun to step up efforts to force absent fathers to make their court-ordered payments, in 1983, according to the *Wall Street Journal,* two million men still weren't paying all or any of what they owe in child support. Just counting the cases where the women and children have ended up on welfare as a result of the men's nonpayment, these fathers owe more than $8 billion.[3] Since it's virtually impossible to feel a sense of personal power and worth when one is without the financial means of survival, the government's failure to go after fathers who are delinquent in their payments has the effect of greatly undercutting many women's self-esteem.

Laws prohibiting discrimination on the basis of sex and race are often poorly enforced, too. In part, this is due to the way the civil rights enforcement system is set up. When a landlord or employer discriminates against a person because of color or gender, it is up to the person suffering the discrimination to initiate and pursue action to redress the problem. In the workplace, for example, no government officer is on hand to spot discrimination and protect women from sexual harassment. If a woman has been discriminated against or harassed, it is up to her to act as the police, going to the proper state and federal agencies and filing a complaint. Whether a woman will be helped by those agencies depends greatly on who is President at the time, because a President can hold back funds from civil rights enforcement agencies, thus making it hard or impossible for them to do their job. This is what Ronald Reagan has done.

Putting the principal responsibility for enforcing civil rights laws on those whose rights have been violated places women in an extremely difficult position. Because many women have been brought up to have so little sense of themselves as persons with rights, they are often incapable of recognizing when their rights are being violated. Obviously, such women are not going to take action to protect their rights. Other women are able to perceive when their rights are being violated, yet still often have difficulty filing complaints because it would mean making trouble and that goes against most women's training. Moreover, some women are hesitant to file complaints about discrimination and harassment because of the risk of being retaliated against. Thus, it's often the case that whether a woman takes action or not, she ends up paying some cost in self-esteem:

> I had a solid case against my employer for sex discrimination and sexual harassment, and a lot of people told me I should pursue it, but I never did. I think I should have taken action. It would have been the brave, principled thing to do, and I would like to think of myself as somebody brave and principled. But filing a complaint against him also would have been a not very nice and a very unladylike thing to do. It would have made me

vulnerable to a lot of criticism from people around town that I'm a trouble-maker, and I know it would be hard for me to get another job unless I moved away . . . . I think I would have had more self-respect if I had done something, but I think I also would have had a lot of bad feelings about myself for being not nice and a complainer, too.

The Welfare System's Impact

When we asked women how they felt government affected their self-esteem, we heard a lot about women's experiences with the welfare system. Our nation's welfare system shapes the day-to-day experience of millions of women, for the population dependent upon welfare is made up mostly of women and their children. Of the 22 million people receiving food stamps in 1982, 85 percent were women and their children. In 1982, women and their children also made up 93 percent of the four million people receiving Aid to Families with Dependent Children, or AFDC.[4]

Most recipients of welfare are women and their children because of what has been labeled "the feminization of poverty." Rising birth rates among unwed women and rising divorce rates mean that the number of women raising children on their own has been skyrocketing in recent years. And the fact that most women's jobs are the lowest-paying in the economy, that most divorced fathers fail to pay child support even when ordered by the courts to do so, and that affordable child care is not available to most women, mean that it is extremely difficult for the growing number of women who head U.S. households to survive financially. Consequently, in recent years the number of poor adult males in the United States has declined, and the number of poor adult women has mushroomed, so that they and their children make up the vast majority of the nation's poor. The National Advisory Council on Economic Opportunity has predicted that if the impoverishment of women continues at the rate it progressed between 1967 and 1978, the entire poor population of the United States will be made up of women and their children by the year 2000.[5]

There is much the U.S. Government could do to help the growing legions of poor women in America. Government-funded day care would make more women able to take employment (as it is now, the costs of child care are so high that women can't afford to take jobs outside the home). Better enforcement of laws designed to give women equal pay for equal work and to insure equal job opportunities for women would enable some women to get better-paying jobs. Affirmative action programs, subsidies to companies that train and hire women, job training, and incentives (such as tax breaks) to companies that institute schedules more suited to women with children all would help, too. So, finally, would going after divorced fathers who fail to pay court-ordered child support. While the government has made some efforts in these areas, overall very little has been done to try to solve the problems behind women's poverty. Instead, the government offers women welfare.

Our nation's welfare system does little to allay a woman's feelings of powerlessness and worthlessness that come from not having enough money to exert some control over her life. As Barbara Ehrenreich and Karin Stallard report, even before the welfare cuts instituted by the Reagan administration, the average AFDC monthly payment for a family of four was $398, and "there was no state where the combined benefits or AFDC and food stamps were enough to bring a family *up to* the poverty level."[6] What is more, our nation's present welfare system does nothing to ameliorate the complex socioeconomic factors that push women into poverty in the first place.

The present-day welfare system undercuts the self-esteem of those women forced to rely on it in several ways. First, welfare forces women into a position of total dependency that many find extremely degrading and which also exacerbates and engenders feelings of helplessness. A woman whose physical disabilities make it impossible for her to get by without government help explains:

> If you are disabled, you have to remain below the poverty level—and that's really poor—to get any help at all. And you have to beg for whatever help you get. It's demeaning. Unless you get lucky and inherit money or something, you never control your life. The people in the agencies are all able-bodied, and they encourage dependency because they feel powerful that way—and they look down at you for being dependent at the same time because that makes them feel powerful, too. There's a part of them that wants to keep us dependent to keep the agency going. They need us to be dependent as much as we need the government's help.

Women who are not physically disabled but who receive welfare are further demeaned by moral condemnation from those who work within the welfare system, from politicians who rail about "welfare cheats" as if all women on welfare were just lazy bums, and from the general public. Another woman explains:

> I think the worst thing about being on welfare is being classed as a poor person. It's like in the eyes of the world you're the scum of the earth. At the welfare office when you first go to apply, they humiliate you. They

make you wait all day without paying any attention to you, and then when you get in to talk to someone, they ask you a lot of degrading questions about your sex life, practically accusing you of sleeping with a whole bunch of men and trying to hide it. . . . If you go to a hospital or you try to get a phone and they know you're on welfare, forget it—you're gonna be treated like dirt. It's the same in the supermarket. The way some of these well-dressed women in the checkout line look at you when you're counting out your food stamps is incredible. They act like you're some kind of slime.

Unfortunately, as poor women are penalized for being on welfare, so they are penalized for trying to break out of their dependent position. The way the welfare system has been set up, women who get jobs automatically lose benefits, often to the point where once a woman has paid for child care and transportation she actually has less money than she would if she did not have a job. A woman who tried several times to make it on her own explains:

I know some women who are on welfare who shouldn't be. There are always a few bad apples giving everyone else a bad name. But most of the women I know really want to work. They hate being on welfare. You feel so hopeless and helpless on welfare. You're the bad girl, and the government is the sugar daddy you have to go begging to for crumbs. It's really degrading. But if you try to go out and make it on your own, they cut back your benefits. If you're making minimum wage or only a little more and you have to pay for baby-sitters and carfare back and forth from work and you also have to get clothes—if you have to do that, working is futile. The way it's set up, by getting a job you deprive your kids of food on the table *and* you deprive them of your presence in the home. It's like you can never win.

Militarism and the Nuclear Arms Race

When we asked women about government's effect on their self-esteem, we also heard a lot about women's fears and anxieties over the nuclear arms race and the ever more dangerous militarism of the men who run the world's governments. In a speech made some months prior to this country's entry into World War II, President Franklin Delano Roosevelt outlined the "four freedoms" a democracy should ideally provide: freedom of speech, freedom of religious expression, freedom from want and freedom from fear. The U.S. Government does admirably well insuring the first two freedoms, perhaps better than any other government in the world. As we've seen, though, the U.S. Government does less well in providing its female citizens with freedom from want.

And where the fourth freedom, freedom from fear, is concerned, many women believe the U.S. Government through its pursuit of the nuclear arms race with the U.S.S.R. is doing more to generate fear than to allay it.

A popular American myth, presented as fact in school history books and reiterated time and again by Presidents and military leaders, is that the U.S. Government has always used its military might for the sole purpose of protecting people from fear rather than for generating it. The truth, however, is more complex. To be sure, the United States has in important instances used its might to keep the world free from fear. This was the case in World War II, which might have ended with the entire world dominated by fascism were it not for the military effort of the United States and its allies. But in many other instances this country has used its military might for far less honorable and defensible purposes. The Native Americans, who lost three fourths of their total population and the lands they had inhabited for thousands of years at the hands of the U.S. military, learned this through firsthand experience.[7] So have the inhabitants of Vietnam, Cambodia, Chile and numerous Central American countries. And so, finally, did the civilians who were in Hiroshima and Nagasaki, Japan, when the United States dropped the atom bombs. Many of us have been taught that the United States had no choice but to use atom bombs against Japan; there was no other way to end the war. In fact, however, the United States Government did have some choice in the matter, as the Japanese were well on their way to defeat when the bombs were dropped. The atom bombs were used not simply to end the war, but to end the war in a particular way—one that would insure that America would enter the postwar world in the most powerful position possible. By using the atom bomb, a weapon no other nation—enemy or ally—had, the United States was able to establish itself as the single mightiest nation in the world.[8]

In the postwar years, the U.S. Government has spent an increasing amount of time, energy and taxpayers' money desperately trying to remain the world's number-one nuclear power. Unfortunately, however, along the way the Soviet Union (and other nations) began to build nuclear weapons, too. With both the United States and the U.S.S.R. trying to keep up with the other for decades, the two governments have now assembled arsenals capable of wiping out the world several times over. In the process, they have introduced to human consciousness an entirely new type of terror—terror of a war that will bring about not just a few hundred thousand or a few million deaths, but possibly the annihilation of every living creature on earth. As one group of activists put it, "the men in government say they are protecting us. But never have we been so afraid."

The fear of nuclear annihilation that many people feel today eats up our energy, destroys our optimism, and makes it difficult to plan for the future. Indeed, it undercuts our conviction and hope that there will be a future, thus causing many to view all human bonds as transient and tenuous, and making many women doubt the wisdom of bringing children into the world. Moreover, in many the nuclear arms race has fostered feelings of complete and paralyzing powerlessness and helplessness. There is a pervasive attitude of "What's the use?" in America today. Neither the fear of nuclear annihilation nor the feelings of helplessness and pointlessness that it calls up are conducive to self-esteem. In an era when life itself is threatened, it's especially difficult for an individual to believe that his or her own particular life has much value.[9]

The ethic of nationalism teaches that we are to see ourselves as inhabitants of a particular country first and foremost, inhabitants of the planet earth second—if at all. And the ethic of patriotism teaches us that we should feel proud that we are citizens of a nation that can boast so much military might. But a lot of women don't feel better about themselves because of our nation's nuclear strength, and as long as the men who run the world's governments continue to have the power to wipe us all out almost instantaneously, women will continue to face a formidable obstacle in the effort to build higher self-esteem. Women have worked hard to gain power in a number of areas. But if the world remains on this course of self-destruction, whatever power women gain in other areas ultimately won't make much difference.

BLUEPRINTS FOR CHANGE

I. VOTING

One of the most important things we can do to take some control over our lives and the government that so effects us is to vote. Generations of women struggled for decades to win our right to vote, and for that reason alone our right to vote should not be taken lightly.

II. INFORMING OURSELVES

The less we know about how our government works and what it is doing, the more powerless we will be. Many women we have spoken to automatically skip over newspaper and newsmagazine stories dealing with either national defense or the economy; told so long that those areas are none of women's business, women are often intimidated by the very terms "national defense" and "economics." But we've also found that once women get over the initial intimidation and do start learning about these areas, they are often surprised to find themselves a lot more capable of understanding than they had anticipated.

Since the government is so huge, most of us don't have enormous amounts of time to keep track of government affairs. But we can select one or two issues and make it our business to stay well-informed. Study groups can also be a help.

III. WRITE AND TELEPHONE

Once we become better informed, we will probably form opinions on a variety of subjects and probably will want to inform our elected officials of how we feel. It is well within our rights to contact our representatives through letters, telegrams and phone calls; and we *can* have an impact by doing this. Some women keep stamped postcards already addressed to their representatives in the Senate and House—and also state officials—close at hand and write a card each day expressing their opinions about some important issue—the ERA, the MX missile, abortion, the nuclear arms race, etc. Although legislators don't read every letter, they *do* have their staffs count the numbers of correspondence on each side of an issue, and this often influences their votes.

IV. ORGANIZE AND DEMONSTRATE

While individual efforts like writing letters are important, we will be most able to exert some power over our government if we band together with others and exert pressure collectively. There are many organizations we could join to influence our government; sometimes just giving these organizations a small amount of money or signing a petition they have sponsored can be a help. Also helpful are demonstrations. Demonstrations such as the civil rights movement's and the anti-Vietnam war movement's marches on Washington, the 1978 ERA march on Washington, and the June 1982 march for disarmament in New York City not only informed those in government of what numbers of the governed believed and felt, they also gave those who participated a sense of solidarity and empowerment.

* 5 *

Never Done:
Women's Work Experiences

> Women's success stories that we read in the nation's media are too often merely token triumphs. They offer little more consolation to the mass of restricted women than the fame of a few black entertainment or sports stars offers to America's largely restricted black population. What really counts is opportunity for millions of human beings, and not occasional headlines for a few.
>
> —Muriel Humphrey,
> *Women in the U.S. Labor Force*

For more than sixteen years, Marie Leuck worked as a skyscraper cleaning woman, going in to make Manhattan's Equitable Life Building spick-and-span in the wee hours of the morning. Then in April 1982 something miraculous happened to Leuck: She and her husband, a bus driver, won a million dollars in the New York State lottery. Suddenly rich, Leuck was able to quit her job and buy both a diamond ring and a four-bedroom house of the sort she had always wanted. Yet for all the benefits of being a millionaire it wasn't too long before Leuck started missing her job. As she explained to a reporter in September 1982:

> I had a system. Get up, take a shower, go into work at four. The Equitable Life Building. I worked there 16 years, I loved it. There was a purpose.[1]

Marie Leuck's story illustrates the key role that work plays in our lives. Not all women love their work; indeed, if one survey is to be believed, a full 73 percent of employed people claim to hate their jobs.[2] Yet whether we love it or hate it, the fact is that most of us do have strong feelings about our work. Our work—meaning both our paid work in the labor market or our unpaid work in the home—occupies a substantial portion of our time. It shapes up, defines us and gives meaning and purpose to our lives. This is particularly the case in our American culture because of the widespread influence of the Protestant work ethic. Here in America, perhaps more than anywhere else, a person's worth is intrinsically connected to her work.

Women in the Paid Labor Market: Myths and Realities

Women have always worked. In fact, women have always done the bulk of the world's work, performing all the necessary but menial and typically unpaid jobs that enable society to keep going. However, in the United States it has been only recently that women have moved into the paid labor force in large enough numbers to warrant media and government attention. From 1960 to 1980, the number of women in the paid work force nearly doubled (from 23 million to nearly 45 million), and by 1980 more than half the adult female population was in the paid labor force.[3]

With the surge of women into the paid work force over the past twenty years, there has arisen a widespread perception that as more women move into the work force, women in general are moving up. This perception is fostered—and perhaps even created by—the mass media, which frequently feature success stories of glamorous career women who have made it. Popular as she may be, however, the glamorous, successful career woman we see on TV and magazine covers is none other than Horatio Alger in drag—the feminine personification of an enticing but misleading myth. For the fact is, as more and more women have moved into the paid labor force, women in general have not moved up. Most women today do not have careers, they have jobs. And the jobs that women have continue to be both the lowest-paying and the lowest in prestige of all jobs in our economy.

To be sure, for some women in some areas the dream of upward mobility has materialized. Although the increase in the number and proportion of women in such previously nearly all-male fields as architecture, medicine and engineering has been small, there has been an increase in these professions all the same; and in one field—law—the rise in the number and proportion of women has been large. Similarly, there has been an increase in the proportion of women who hold managerial jobs. And labor statistics show that black women previously employed as domestics in private households have been able to move in greater numbers into clerical jobs.[4] Yet for all these positive, albeit small, changes, for most women relative wages and opportunities have not grown over the past two decades, they've shrunk. Rose Laub Coser, writing in 1980, points this out:

> On the average, women employed full-time are paid less than 59¢ for every dollar earned by men in comparable jobs—a decline from 20 years ago when that ratio stood at 64¢. Women's occupational segregation has also gotten worse. In 1976, 60% of working women—up from 52% in 1962—were segregated into just four occupations: clerks, saleswomen, waitresses, and hairdressers.[5]

We should point out that since 1976 the general pattern of women's segregation into a small number of traditionally and predominantly female occupations has not changed much. Moreover, a closer look at the statistics indicate that even where women's opportunities have increased, the increases have not been as great as they might seem on the surface. For example, although there are more managers today, women managers are more likely to hold low- or mid-level rather than executive positions, and their upward mobility is far more limited than men's. And while more black women may be moving out of private household jobs into secretarial positions, black secretaries still comprise less than 10 percent of all secretaries—and only a handful of specialty secretaries, e.g., legal and medical secretaries.[6]

The fact that women's job opportunities and earning potential tends to be so limited in itself can injure women's self-esteem. Although higher wages wouldn't guarantee higher self-esteem for women, being paid more certainly wouldn't hurt. Particularly for the millions of women living in poverty or struggling to stay out of poverty today, increased earning power would mean a dramatic difference in the amount of control they could exert over their daily lives. With greater job and earning possibilities, some women might not feel so powerless and discouraged, nor so down on themselves and the future:

> Sometimes I look ahead and wonder, What's the point? I've been a secretary, a waitress, a hospital aide, and an assembly-line worker in a clothing factory—and all those jobs have been lousy-paying and exhausting and not very stimulating. I didn't have the opportunity to go to college, so my options are pretty narrow. And even going to college probably wouldn't have made a difference—I know lots of women with college degrees who are waitresses and secretaries. So anyway, the future looks pretty bleak. I can see myself thirty years from now in my mid-sixties still being a secre-

tary, and it depresses me. That's not who I want to be, but I really don't see lots of ways out.

For the vast majority of the women we interviewed, money is a consistent source of worry, depression, anxiety and unhappiness. Many of the women we spoke to wanted to leave their husbands but could not because of lack of money. Many also felt that they were inadequate mothers because their lack of money prevented them from providing their children with what the women believed to be necessities. Virtually all women said that lack of money had greatly restricted their opportunities for self-fulfillment. "If I'd had the money," we have heard many women say, "I would have gone on to school. But I didn't have any money, and so here I am stuck in this lousy job (or marriage)."

More than twenty thousand respondents participated in a money survey whose findings were published in *Psychology Today* in 1981, and 33 percent said that because of insufficient money they have had to delay changing jobs or careers; 31 percent of the childless married couples reported having had to postpone having children; and 23 percent of the currently separated couples said they have had to postpone divorce. Moreover, due to lack of money, 44 percent reported having had to reduce socializing with friends; 34 percent reported an increase in family tensions; and 28 percent reported having had more arguments with others.[7]

Perhaps the most interesting aspect of the *Psychology Today* money survey was what it illustrated about money's effects on the emotional states of women as compared to men. Asked what feelings they had associated with money over the past year, more women than men associated money with anxiety, depression, anger, helplessness, envy, resentment, fear, guilt, panic, sadness, shame, hatred and spite. Conversely, fewer women than men associated money with happiness, excitement, respect, love and reverence. In some cases, the differences between the men and the women were slight; for example, 22 percent of the women and 20 percent of the men reported feelings of sadness over money. In other instances, however, the differences were marked: 50 percent of the women but only 30 percent of the men had felt helplessness because of money, and 57 percent of the women as opposed to 46 percent of the men said they had felt depression because of money.[8]

While the narrow options women face in the work force are enough in themselves to hurt our self-esteem, we found that women are doubly hurt because of the prevalence of the myth of women's upward mobility. Women often told us that they would have a much easier time coping with limited opportunities and low pay if they did not always have to contend with media images of the successful career woman who has made it. The myth that women today are "making it" in great numbers encourages women who don't make it to hold themselves personally at fault.

The myth of upward mobility also encourages some women to feel ashamed of the work they do:

> It makes me feel good about myself when I say I'm a good worker, when I say I'm someone who has a job and does it well. But if I say I'm a good secretary—that doesn't make me feel good about myself at all. There used to be a time when I felt differently about it. When I was growing up, it was an accepted thing that lots of women who worked were secretaries, and being a secretary wasn't something to be ashamed of. But now all you hear about are women doctors, lawyers, bank executives and even astronauts— and it's like if you're still just a secretary then you've really failed.

Just as damaging to women is the myth of meritocracy, which holds that if a person is hardworking, bright and industrious, she'll ultimately be rewarded with success. Conversely, it says that if a person doesn't succeed, it is because she deserves to fail. This myth is particularly damaging to women because of the extent to which discrimination against women due to race, age, ethnicity and physical disabilities remains rampant in the American work force. Sadly, because of the myth of meritocracy, some women are unable to perceive discrimination. If they are treated unfairly, they simply assume they must be at fault instead:

> At the bank where I used to work as a teller, I trained a whole lot of guys who always came in getting paid more than me and who always ended up being promoted way ahead of me after they had been there awhile. Even though I trained these guys, I always assumed that they got ahead because they were better than me—smarter, more competent. Even after I started reading about sex discrimination and how it's especially widespread in banking—even then I still couldn't connect that with what was happening to me. I thought what was happening to me was happening to me personally because I personally couldn't quite cut it—not because I was a woman in a man's world.

In a report released in late 1982, the U.S. Commission on Civil Rights concluded that sex and race discrimination persist at an "alarming" level in the U.S. job market today. The report found women are discriminated against because of sex "virtually everywhere, at every age level, at every educational level, at every skill level." Not surprisingly, it also found that black and Hispanic women are doubly discriminated against, and consequently black females constitute the largest group of people who work full-time yet earn so little that they remain below the poverty level.[9]

While all women face discrimination because of gender, and women of color face the double burden of sex and race discrimination, perhaps the group most discriminated against of all is women with physical disabilities. A woman who uses a wheelchair explains:

> The two greatest barriers to the handicapped are access and transportation —a job doesn't do you much good if you can't get to it and can't get in the building. But more than that there are the assumptions people make about disabled people. Most likely, if you can get a job placement, it will be in a social service agency, because people assume we are caring and concerned and long-suffering, and that we all want to do nothing else but help people. But that's if you can get a placement—and that's a big if. Save for a few job training programs and social service jobs, the doors are pretty much closed to us, and we are encouraged to do as little as possible. Fields like engineering or business are completely out. People seem to think there's something obscene about a disabled person wanting to work for profit.

Adding to the problem of discrimination are the problems of sexual harassment in the work force. While discrimination makes getting decent jobs difficult for women, sexual harassment makes just surviving in a job difficult. Time and again in our interviews we heard tales like this:

> What bothered me about waitressing was all the hassles from the guys in the kitchen and the come-ons and put-downs you get from customers. When I went to work as a secretary in a stockbroker's office, I thought things would be different. But it's really not that different after all. The men aren't as gross as the cooks in the restaurants could be, but they take all their frustrations out on you and do a lot of verbal abuse anyway. They comment about my boobs, they touch and pinch, and whenever there's a screw-up it's because we women are "dumb broads" and "stupid bitches." Then if you tell them to lay off, they say you're acting like one of those "uppity women's libbers" or else you must be "on the rag."

Sexual harassment is demeaning, humiliating and painful, and it can seriously undercut a woman's self-esteem.

A Love-Hate Relationship

Most women we interviewed could complain at length about their jobs. The hours are too long, the pay is too low. Their bosses don't appreciate them. Their bosses expect the impossible. Their bosses are jerks. Working conditions are oppressive; the work itself is tedious—and/or frustrating, boring, routine, menial, stultifying, deadening—and the list could go on and on.

Yet for all the complaints, we also heard women speak about the satisfactions of having a job. Women typically reported finding satisfaction in their jobs for at least three reasons: because work provides a sense of purpose and a routine; because work provides a sense of community with coworkers and colleagues, and also a sense of belonging in the larger world; and because work provides money and thus some sense of security. Even if a woman does not make a lot of money, she still may feel a sense of satisfaction on payday:

> All week I can feel really bad about my job, but then payday comes and I feel better. My check isn't big, but it's mine, I earned it and I'm worth it. It does give my self-esteem a boost for a while.

Some women find having a job satisfying because they were raised to believe that having a job is what a responsible grown woman is supposed to do. Just as some women were brought up to believe that a grown-up woman is one who is married and has children, others were brought up to believe that they wouldn't become real adults until they were self-supporting. A black woman explains:

> I know white women who thought they never would work, but I was brought up to believe that I never would not be working. As a black *woman* I grew up knowing I could always get a job. Even if it was scrubbing floors in white people's home, I could still get a job, whereas a black man couldn't be so sure. I can't imagine expecting to rely on men for financial support, and I can't imagine not working. Work is like breathing —that's what I learned and that's what I believe today.

Another reason some women find having a job satisfying is that a job can be, and often is, an outlet for the desire to nurture and help others. Some women, even if they had the opportunity to take other kinds of work, still might choose to remain in nursing, teaching or another traditionally female occupation because those occupations involve direct human contact and helping others:

> After my last child got into high school, I started night school to get an M.B.A. My original field was social work—I had worked in corrections and in a school program to help delinquent kids stay in school and out of jail. When I started going for my M.B.A., I thought what I had done before wasn't really important in the larger scheme of things—that the

world of business and high finance was the place to be. But now that I've almost gotten my M.B.A., I feel differently. Stocks, bonds, mergers, high finance deals—all that stuff I don't think is very important anymore. What's important is people and helping people. The more I was exposed to the business world, the more convinced of this I became.

Even waitressing, a job not usually thought of as one of the helping professions, can provide the satisfaction that comes from feeling you've helped someone:

> Waitressing is an explicitly nurturing job. A lot of women who waitress get real protective of their customers. Sure, we all have our bad days and can be real bitches. But a good waitress is one who sees herself as a care giver. If you haven't waitressed, this might seem hard to imagine, but there can be something extremely satisfying about taking good care of your customers. It's a nice thing to make a person's meal pleasurable, and if you do it well, you'll know it and it makes you feel good.

But the types of jobs that provide the most human contact can also be those that provide the most flak. Because it's the job of bank tellers, waitresses, receptionists, secretaries, telephone operators, social workers, etc., to deal with the public, a lot of hostility gets vented at them. A bank teller explains:

> In this line of work you really take a lot of abuse. People come in here and take out their bad moods on you all the time. I think it's especially bad when you're a bank teller, because a lot of people have a lot of anxiety about money, and they're distrustful of banks. They see the banks as out to get them, and since they see me as the bank's representative, there's a lot of spillover of their feelings about the bank onto how they treat me.

Waitresses are similarly likely to get flak. Sometimes it can cut deep, especially if a woman takes great pride in her abilities:

> When you're waitressing, you get grief from the kitchen, grief from the customers—that goes without saying. Some of it can be blown off pretty easy. But it's the grief you're catching that has to do directly with your abilities as a waitress that's often not so easy to blow off, because attacking a waitress's ability to waitress is the same as attacking her ability to nurture—and attacking her ability to nurture is tantamount to attacking her overall worth as a woman.

An additional problem for some women whose jobs involve nurturing and helping is guilt. If someone wants to do good in our culture she or he is automatically seen as suspect. But many people genuinely want to help others and are sincere in their desire to do something that will leave the world a slightly better place. The belief that there's something pathological about anyone who wants to help is so widespread, however, that some women who want to do good end up feeling bad about themselves because of it. A hospital social worker explains:

> I work with people who are dying, and their families. I feel my work is important and that I do make a difference in a small way in helping people deal with the terrible trauma of death. Yet sometimes I feel guilty because in essence I'm drawing a salary because people are dying. If people weren't in so much pain, there wouldn't be a need for a lot of us in the helping professions. Lots of times I feel bad about making a living off death.

Not all women's work, of course, provides an outlet for the urge to help others. Some work doesn't involve others much at all; it involves things. Women who do repetitive work with machines—such as factory sewing, assembly-line work or keypunch operations—may find their work especially unsatisfying and stultifying. Doing the same thing over and over, particularly if it's something that isn't challenging to begin with, can lead to a deadening feeling:

> I don't think the guys who designed jobs ever heard that variety is the spice of life. I'm the type of person who needs a change of pace every so often, otherwise I feel like I'm a zombie. When I worked as a file clerk, I couldn't stand it—always the same thing to do, and always that Xeroxing, over and over. But the worst job I ever had in terms of boredom and frustration was working on the floor of [a store like K-Mart]. I was in ladies' wear, and my job was to keep everything folded. So I'd fold and fold, and fold some more. Then as soon as I was done, some lady would come over and mess up the neat piles I had just folded, and so I'd have to do it over again. It drove me crazy.

But certainly not all women feel oppressed by repetitive work. A keypunch operator explains:

> My job pays me enough money to help my family out, and it's real clear-cut work. I don't expect it to be exciting, so I don't find it boring or dull. If it's not mentally stimulating, that's okay with me, because then when I go home I don't feel mentally exhausted.

Needed: A Recognition of Comparable Worth

Overall, we found that most women were able to find some value and pride in their work, whatever it was:

I feel really put-down when I hear someone talk about being a maid as a demeaning job. I don't find anything at all demeaning about cleaning toilets or washing someone else's floor. It's work that has to be done. It's clean, and it's honest and useful. I think being a maid is a lot more honorable than lots of things people do—like building nuclear weapons. How can anyone be proud of that?

Women's urge to find cause for pride in the work we do brings us to the issue of comparable worth. In the early 1970s, feminists focused much attention on the goal of breaking down sex barriers and getting women into previously nearly all-male occupations. A common view then was that liberating women meant enabling more and more women to do work formerly in the province of men. However, there's more to women's liberation than simply enabling women to do work traditionally assigned to men. To be truly liberated, the work of traditional women's work needs to be publicly recognized, and women need to be remunerated accordingly.

The jobs that women traditionally have done, and large numbers of women will continue to do in the future, are vital to our economy, and those women who take pride in their jobs have ample reason to do so. The problem is, however, that if a certain job is done mostly by women in our economy, it is automatically devalued in prestige, and the women who do it are paid low wages accordingly. Maids are paid and esteemed less than janitors not because the work they do is any dirtier or less valuable, but because maids are women and janitors (or custodians, as they are called to indicate their higher prestige) are men. Librarians are paid and valued less than tax assessors not because their job is less important, involves less complicated tasks or requires less education, but simply because most librarians are women and most tax assessors are men. Secretaries are paid far, far less and are valued far, far less than managers not because they are less vital (often the work of a secretary is the most vital, and many businesses would cease to function if the secretary failed to show up for just a day); secretaries have lower pay and prestige than managers simply because most secretaries are women. The comparable-worth principle means recognizing that women's work has been devalued and underpaid simply because it's work done by women and giving women the wages and respect they deserve for their work. If traditionally female work like nursing, secretarial work, hairdressing, waitressing and elementary teaching were remunerated and respected as "women's work" should be, the collective self-esteem of women would no doubt receive a much-needed boost.

Women and Success

Although most working women employed full-time earn less than fifteen thousand dollars per year and do so in a narrow range of occupations, there are women who have broken out of "the pink collar ghetto" and found success in such traditionally male areas as medicine, business and law. While women who have made it constitute only a tiny percentage of all working women, their experiences still deserve attention. Does "making it" in a man's world according to men's definitions of success lead to higher self-esteem? The answer, we've found, is both yes and no.

The knowledge that we've done any job well can help our self-esteem. And the knowledge that we've done a job we were told we never would be able to do can boost our self-esteem even higher. Hence, a woman who succeeds in a job that historically has been a man's job often feels a great surge of self-esteem as a result:

> Growing up, the only image I had of a person in business was the image of a businessman. That was the only word I ever heard used. Being a businesswoman just wasn't in the realm of possibility. So now that I am a businesswoman, I feel I've done the impossible. I have found out that I can do so much more than I was brought up to believe I could do, and that feels great.

If the knowledge that "I can do it" pushes up a woman's self-esteem, so can the money a successful woman earns. A lawyer explains:

> I am now making more money than I ever dreamed of, and it makes an incredible difference to have money like this. It's true what they say about money being power, and I don't mean power in a negative way but in a positive and personal way. Having money has given me so much more power over my life. I have a sense of control and options that I never had before. It makes me far less anxious, and has also had a big effect on my relationships. I used to feel a lot of insecurity that came up in my relationships with men. I expected lovers to make that insecurity go away. But now that I have financial security, I find I am much more secure in my relationships with men. I think a free-floating anxiety about my ability to control my life was getting transformed into a specific anxiety about my ability to get a man to support me.

Although there are many self-esteem benefits that can come with success, there are some drawbacks, too. Even though the numbers of women in business, law, medicine and other high-prestige, high-pay fields have risen, they have not risen enough to alter the fact that the high-prestige and high-pay professions are still men's domain. Women going into men's domain are in alien territory and are subject to special problems and special pressures as a result.

> There's still so much sexism in the business community, and so you're always on the line. You can try to ignore put-downs, but still you have to prove yourself against unfair standards. Because you're a woman, you do really have to do everything twice as well as a man. The pressure to prove yourself—and prove all women worthy at the same time—is so intense. If a guy has a bad idea or blows a deal, it's written off with the attitude "everyone makes mistakes" and he's not permanently branded as an idiot as a result. But if a woman messes up, she's incompetent—and, even worse, it's taken as proof that all women are incompetent. There's really no room for errors in a bind like that.

Adding to the problem of extra pressure, a woman who makes it in a man's world may experience doubts about her femininity. To be successful and ambitious in our culture traditionally has meant to be unfeminine, or even mannish. Cynthia Fuchs Epstein observes:

> Conflict faces the would-be career woman, for the core of attributes found in most professional and occupational roles is considered to be masculine . . . persistence and drive, personal dedication, aggressiveness, emotional detachment, and a kind of sexless matter-of-factness equated with intellectual performance. . . . Women who work in male-dominated occupations . . . are often thought to be sexless. The woman who takes her work seriously—the career woman—traditionally has been viewed as the antithesis of the feminine woman.[10]

Women who've achieved a degree of success in the work world also are sometimes troubled by torn allegiances. This is particularly true if a successful woman remains aware of how unusual her situation is compared to most women's and she feels a bond and responsibility to women who are less fortunate:

> When employers got the word to give blacks equal opportunity, they heard black *men.* And we black women haven't made the gains in the work world that either white women or black men have made. As a result, the few black women who have achieved some success in the work world are in an extremely difficult position. Many black women know that they are the token black woman in their workplace. They know their employers have no intention of hiring any more. This creates a dilemma—should the token black woman lobby for other women to be hired even though this might mean losing her job, or losing her token position if more black women are actually hired?

"Making it" in the work world necessitates putting our own personal interests and ambitions first. As most women do not want to be selfish, success may come only at some cost to a woman's image of herself as a moral and "good" woman. On the one hand, a woman may like herself more for being successful; but she may like herself less for how she's had to act in order to become successful:

> I have lots of mixed feelings about myself and what I'm doing. I'm real proud of what I've accomplished, and I know I never would have been able to get this far if I hadn't focused on my goals and put reaching them as my first priority. But in doing that I had to say no to my friends and family a lot. I couldn't really be there for people when they needed me because my career and schooling always had to come first. So while I feel real proud of my accomplishments, I don't feel real good about myself as a friend.

Some women experience such a deep conflict between the female values of nurturing and being nice that they were raised with and the male values of personal gain and ambition that success for them turns out to be less satisfying than they expected. A woman in medical school or law school may learn, for example, that she can be just as emotionally detached, logical, ruthless, ambitious and otherwise professional as men in her field have long prided themselves on being. But once she's learned that she *can* do it just like a man, she may find herself asking: "Do I *want* to do it?"

Women's Work at Home

Most women who work outside the home also work within the home, particularly if they are married or single mothers. Despite the dramatic changes for women in the paid work force in recent years, there has been little change in the fact that child care, cleaning, shopping, cooking and all the other household tasks are seen as women's responsibility. The married woman or single mother who works outside the home has typically not one but many jobs. This is obscured by our culture's insistence that housework isn't real work, as Nona Glazer and colleagues point out:

> Married women in the labor force and women heading families must be recognized as multiple jobholders. Multiple jobholding now has a very narrow meaning—"moonlighting"—which refers to holding a second paid job to meet regular expenses. Our failure to recognize housework and childcare as work comes from the archaic view that work only includes activities that bring earnings. If our views of housework were revised to acknowledge that what the homemaker does is work, we (as a society)

would not continue to let employed women carry an undue burden without society's encouragement and aid. The everyday life of the average employed wife and mother is far different from the "ideal" lives of women who are married to men prominent in business, the professions and government; unlike these latter women, 70–80% of employed American women cannot afford to hire regular household and childcare help or to purchase sufficient convenience foods and appliances to lighten the load.[11]

Although some men may "help" their employed wives with housework and child care, all the studies on the subject have shown that even among dual-career couples the primary responsibility for housework and child care (whether doing it or arranging for it to be done by someone else) still is usually with the woman.[12]

For women there is constant overlap between work outside the home and work within the home. A woman with children and home responsibilities does not forget them once she arrives at her paid job. Nor does she forget the responsibilities of her paid job once she returns home to her family and her domestic jobs. The end result is often a feeling of being overwhelmed and of never really being done with work:

> It's very hard if you've got both a family and a job outside to feel you're really measuring up and succeeding. Having to work, I feel I'm in some ways a failure as a mother. I'd like to spend more time with my kids than I'm able to. And having a family, it's hard to feel you're doing your best at work. If my boss wants me to attend a seminar on a weekend or stay late at night, it means depriving my family, falling down as a mother. And then even when I'm concentrating at work it's hard to free myself of my family responsibilities. Like I'll be in the middle of talking to a client, and suddenly it pops into my head that we're low on toilet paper at home, and I'll go off the track trying to remember if there's extra toilet paper in the upstairs bathroom.

Even if a woman is able to resolve the problem of lack of affordable child care that keeps so many women out of the paid work force completely, having the primary responsibility for a family still will hamper her flexibility and chances of upward mobility:

> There are a whole lot of jobs in the Help Wanted ads that attract me but that I'd never even try to apply for because I've got kids. If you've got kids, or at least young kids, certain types of jobs you just don't even consider. The job I'm in now (managing the women's clothing department in a large chain store) is probably the best I'm going to do, and I've gone as far as I can in it. There's still room for advancement, but the next rung on the ladder has been closed to me because I've got two little boys, and top management knows that if one of my little boys is sick, I'm going to stay

home from work, and if one has an accident at school I'm going to get the hell over there as fast as I can. As a mother I can't give them the loyalty— or sometimes the overtime—they want out of me. So while I won't get fired, I'm not going any further either.

There are problems inherent to the homemaker's role that are experienced by women even if they do not have another job outside. As much as a woman may tell herself that her work inside the home is important, the fact that women do not get paid for the myriad jobs they do for their families in itself communicates to women that housework is not important. Moreover, the never ending nature of women's work in the home precludes a woman from ever feeling that she's finally done. As soon as she finishes a task like cleaning or cooking, she has to turn around and do it all over again. A woman who has worked as both a homemaker in her own and a maid in other people's homes explains:

> When I cleaned other people's houses, I got paid for it, and that made a difference in how I looked at the worth of what I was doing. I also had a set number of tasks I would do in a set number of hours, and then I'd wash my hands and be done. So it wasn't a work of art or a scientific breakthrough that I had accomplished, but at least I felt I had accomplished something. In my own home, I never get that feeling. There's always something else to do. You cook one meal, clean up, then two seconds later you're cooking another. You don't feel you're getting anywhere. Especially when my kids were young, I felt completely trapped and paralyzed, like there was always two inches of grape jelly on the floor and my feet were permanently stuck in it.

Unemployment: The Ultimate Insult

As we write this chapter, the United States economy is in the middle of a deep recession, and unemployment rates are the highest they have been since before World War II. The network news shows, national news magazines and newspapers all have given ample attention to the unemployment problem, yet they present it as if it were a problem that affects only men. When we are told about the terrible plight of the unemployed, the focus nearly always is exclusively on unemployed men.

Although the mass media give the impression that unemployment is not a problem for women, this is not the case. Millions of women who want to work have lost their jobs, or are trying to enter the work force for the first time and can't find any openings. Wanting to work but not being able to find it is the ultimate affront to self-esteem. Time and again in our self-esteem groups and interviews we heard women make comments along these lines:

> If you want to know about low self-esteem, try being without a job. You don't have to go very long before you feel utterly worthless. You feel like a reject. And the more you go for job interviews and bang on doors only to get turned down, the more and more like a reject you feel.

Unemployment may be particularly damaging to women's self-esteem because of women's tendency to blame ourselves for misfortune. We saw this demonstrated dramatically on a 1983 network news show in which unemployed people were interviewed. Most of those interviewed were men; one woman was included. The men all discussed how hard it is to be unemployed, but not one of them intimated that he felt it was his fault. The lone woman when interviewed, however, said immediately that "it has occurred to me that it's my fault, that there's something wrong with me."[13] We heard similar comments frequently from unemployed women we spoke to:

> Even though more than half of the plant has been put out of work, I still feel like I am at fault. When I run into men from the plant, they're all angry at Reagan and the economy and the world. But I feel like I'm a bad person and that's why it happened, even though I know in my mind that's not true.

If unemployment that is caused by poor economic conditions hurts women's self-esteem, so does unemployment that is forced upon women because of age. Again, the problems that come with retirement are usually presented in the media as problems affecting only men. Women, too, can suffer the feelings of dislocation, failure and diminished self-esteem that come with being told your time for useful work is over.

In talking to women about retirement, it occurred to us that the "empty-nest syndrome" some women go through when their children leave home needs to be looked at in a different perspective. Usually, the empty-nest syndrome is viewed as a product of a woman's pathological attachment to her role as mother. But men often have a difficult time adjusting when they retire from their work, and this is not considered pathological. We think it would help those women who go through the empty-nest syndrome to see the problem not as one peculiar to motherhood, but as part of a more general problem called retirement:

> A year ago I was a contributing member of society. I had a routine, a place to go, work to do, a purpose. Now I'm seen as a dried up, useless old bag

who is leeching off the Social Security system. It's a swift move from being a person of worth to being a good-for-nothing in need of "handouts."

Women's mixed feelings about work and being out of work reminded us of the saying, "You don't know what you've got until it's gone." We may hate our work, feel oppressed, bored and frustrated by it; and we may complain about it often and vehemently, but when we lose it, we often miss it and want it back. For as Marie Leuck found out, work gives us a purpose—something money can't buy.

BLUEPRINTS FOR CHANGE

I. EXPECTATIONS OF WORK

What attitudes were you raised with in regard to women and work? Was it assumed that you wouldn't have a paying job, or that you would have to in order to survive, or that you would have a job because it was a good thing to do? What specific kinds of jobs did you think were available to you? Did you expect to work inside the home? Were you taught that this was more or less valuable than having outside employment? How does your early training effect your work today? To what degree has your work life turned out as you expected it would? If it turned out differently, has that contributed to or diminished your global self-esteem?

II. MEANING OF WORK IN YOUR LIFE

What does your work—inside or outside the home—contribute to your sense of yourself? Does it offer you a routine? A sense of purpose? A sense of connectedness to other people? Enough money to survive on? Is there anything you need from your work that you aren't getting now? Is there anything you can do about that?

III. WORTH OF WORK

How do you measure the worth of your work? By your paycheck? By ways in which it contributes to the well-being of others? By the degree to which it enables your material survival? By the degree to which it enables you to measure up to your ideal sense of self?

What do you think other people's attitudes are toward your work and its worth? Do you think it is valued as much as it should be? Does this value or lack of value translate into a sense of being valued or not valued as a human being? What stereotypes do you think people have about the work you do? How do these stereotypes affect your sense of self? Do you think other people's attitudes toward your work would change if it were done by a man? What are *your* attitudes toward other people's work? Do you think some work is inherently more worthy than other work? Without compromising your values, can you break down parts of this hierarchy and begin to see that there is worth to many kinds of work?

IV. SUCCESS

How do you measure your success as a worker? If women use traditionally male measures of success (objectively gauged by the size of the paycheck and how high up you go in the organization) then we are bound to feel less than successful. If you don't get a desired job, raise or promotion, do you feel peculiarly at fault? Instead of blaming yourself, consider if there might not have been a form of discrimination (age, sex, racial, just to name a few possibilities) operative. If so, can you find some other ways to use your energy other than blaming yourself? Think carefully about your definition of success and about the standards you measure yourself against at work. This is particularly true of women who work in the home who do not have so many tangible measures to consider. Can you develop a standard for considering yourself worthy and successful in your work that is realistic?

V. FILING COMPLAINTS AGAINST SEXUAL HARASSMENT AND JOB DISCRIMINATION

If you have been sexually harassed by a boss or co-worker, or discriminated against because of sex, race, national origin or age, you have the right to file a complaint to have the injustice redressed and win monetary compensation, if that's appropriate. The federal Equal Employment Opportunity Commission is in charge of handling harassment and discrimination complaints, but first you must file a complaint with the appropriate state agency—either a state human rights agency or equal opportunity agency. Your local women's center, the local National Organization for Women chapter, the local branch of the American Civil Liberties Union, or your local legal aid office should be able to direct you to the appropriate agency in your state. Once you have filed a complaint with the state agency, they are supposed to conduct an investigation within a set time period—usually ninety days. If they find in their investigation that you have adequate grounds to press suit, your case will be turned over to the regional EEOC office, and they will handle it from there. If the state agency does not conduct an investigation within the specified time period, the case automatically comes under EEOC jurisdiction.

The EEOC usually takes a long time—perhaps years—to process and litigate cases, and—depending on who is President of the United States at a given time—the EEOC can take longer, or might not do much at all. To insure your best chances of winning a case, you will need ample documentation. Keep a written record of the exact times, places, and circumstances of all or any instances of harassment or discrimination. Get copies of whatever letters, applications or other written documents will support your case. Also find out if your co-workers will testify on your behalf. Enlist as many witnesses as you can. In cases of discrimination, try to get as many others as possible to join in making the complaint with you. This will strengthen your case, better enabling the EEOC to file a "class action" suit rather than an individual suit. It will also make you less vulnerable to being singled out as a lone troublemaker or complainer.

If you file a complaint, it is illegal for your employers and co-workers to try to retaliate by taking away your job responsibilities, harassing you, ostracizing you or doing anything else that would cause you to feel uncomfortable and to consider withdrawing your complaint and/or leaving your job. However, these illegal practices are common anyway. Again, document any and all types of retaliation, and recruit witnesses to testify on your behalf. Report all kinds of retaliation to the agency with which you filed your original complaint; the retaliation may be grounds for additional complaints. If your work situation becomes so intolerable that you are forced to leave to retain your mental health, you have been in essence fired—or "constructively discharged." This is grounds for suit, and you may seek monetary damages.

Going through the complaint and litigation process is usually very unpleasant. Before taking action, you will have to weigh the possible benefits (justice, knowing you've stood up for yourself) against the possible risks (getting harassed or discriminated against further, losing your job, tying up your time and mental energy). If you do take legal action, remember you are doing what it is right and call on friends to give you emotional support through the long haul. If you decide not to take action, or you file a complaint and then decide not to follow through, remember that this is your right too. You have no reason to berate yourself for not taking action, if that's what you decide is best.

To help you reach the best decision, ask your local women's group or the ACLU to put you in contact with others who have filed complaints already. Their experience can help you better understand the risks and benefits involved. But whatever decision you reach, keep in mind that you are not to blame for whatever harassment or discrimination you have suffered.

* 6 *

Women in a World of Mirrors and Images: The Impact of the Technology of Imagery

In Dickens' *Dombey and Son*, there is a passage in which a character describes what the world looks like from the windows of a train.[1] The railroads were a new technological feat then, and as the passage shows, they altered people's view of the world radically, just as airplane and space travel later would. As one writer has put it, "every new bit of technology, whether experienced directly or vicariously, seems to give one a new eye for things."[2] We see this particularly when the technology is the technology of imagery and the things it gives us a new eye for are ourselves. Just as human perceptions of the world have been changed by the train and airplane, so our perceptions of ourselves have increasingly been shaped over time by the myriad mirrors and images that abound in our modern world. For example, two hundred years ago many American families did not have mirrors in their homes, and a woman might well have gone through her daily routine week after week without inspecting her image in a looking glass.[3] Today, however, most of us begin each morning with a close look in the mirror as we brush our teeth; and as we go through the day we constantly confront images of ourselves reflected back to us via glass. We find mirrors in our cars, in public restrooms, in supermarkets, on vending machines in the subway, in department and other types of stores, and in restaurants and on the exteriors of buildings, too. In fact, it's not uncommon today to go into a restaurant and find entire walls covered with mirrors. Nor is it uncommon to see massive buildings with mirrored surfaces plastered on every side. In America today mirrors are everywhere.

Mass-produced images are everywhere in the world we live in, too.

Only a century and a half ago, the idea of capturing a picture photographically, then mass-producing it, was just an idea. Today that idea has become reality, and thanks to continuing advances in photographic technology, cinematography, printing, and mass communications, we are constantly bombarded by images both visual and auditory. On billboards and book covers, on the exteriors of buses and the interior of subway cars, on TV and in movie houses, in newspapers and magazines we confront image after image. Many of the images we see as we go about our daily routines are of others, but some are bound to be of ourselves, for over the years the living-room lineup of family photos, the driver's license mug shot and the snapshot in the wallet have become commonplace facts of American life. Together with the auditory messages transmitted to us via the radios we listen to in our cars and homes and the sound systems that blare out in stores and elevators, the visual images of self and others that we ingest daily do much to shape our perceptions of the world, ourselves and our place in the world. And as the images that confront us everywhere shape our concepts of who we actually are, so they shape our ideas about who we should be. It's hard to make it through a day without seeing images of the ideal selves our culture admonishes us to try to be. We may laugh at the idealized images we see on TV and in magazines, or we may find them stupid and irritating. Still, they do surround and affect us.

The Rise of Self-consciousness

Of all the images that confront us daily, perhaps none has such a direct impact on our sense of self and self-esteem as do the images of self we see in mirrors and photographs. As a picture is worth a thousand words, so it is that a picture of ourselves in a mirror or photograph can have an immediate and dramatic effect on our sense of self-worth. This is demonstrated quite well in a 1983 television ad for the Ayds Diet Plan. The commercial opens with a woman standing next to a man who is pulling a developing snapshot out of a Polaroid-type camera. When the woman's image has fully developed, he hands the photo to her. As she looks at the photo, an expression of horrified disgust comes over her face. "Oh no," she says, "have I really gained *that* much weight?" The scene then switches to indicate a lapse in time, and we now see the woman sitting down to a dainty, low-cal meal, her appetite apparently having been shrunk to proper proportions by Ayds. Once again enters her friend the photographer, who points his camera in her face and plate, saying approvingly, "You really *are* eating less. I've got to get a picture of this." He snaps the shutter, and—click—freezes forever an image of the shamed fatty eating her way to a higher plane of feminine perfection.

The tale told by the Ayds Diet Plan ad stands in stark contrast to the story in the myth of Narcissus. In the myth a young man named Narcissus sees his image reflected in a pool of water, and overwhelmed by its beauty, he falls in love with it. For centuries women in Western culture have been castigated for being like Narcissus, for being in love with the image of ourselves we see in mirrors—and now photos. Yet the fact is, when confronted with images of our actual selves, women tend to react more like the women in the Ayds ad than like Narcissus. Although not all women dislike what they see in mirrors and photos, the vast majority of the women we interviewed reported that they are more prone to dislike than like what they see of themselves. Describing the experience of a woman friend who agreed to make a half-hour videotape of herself, Anthony Brandt provides a case in point:

> She first took off her clothes—no disguises, all honesty—and used the camera to look at her body, to get to know it. She didn't like that, either. . . . Everything she found herself saying, she told me, was defensive, a farrago of excuses and bravado about her looks, her way of moving, her physical style. . . . She could only conclude that this unpleasant, insecure, phony creature was really who she was. After five minutes or so she burst into tears and cried helplessly for the rest of the half-hour. She *hated* it, hated that image, that self on the monitor. It took her days to recover.[4]

Evidently, the advances in the technology of imagery may do more to damage our self-esteem than to build it. When confronted with reflections of ourselves in mirrors and photographs, many—perhaps most—feel not self-love, but something closer to self-hate.

Today's technology of self-imagery breeds an intense self-consciousness that is difficult to slough off. We might like what we see when we look in a mirror or at a photo of some happy moment in our lives, but in the very act of looking at our image we become distanced from ourself, viewing it as an object apart. Many women we interviewed complained of feelings of being outside themselves, of feeling that as they go through the day they are often watching themselves. Such feelings are probably inevitable today, due to the preponderance of reflected images. And because most of us tend to be nervous or insecure about how we look and how we come across, this sort of self-consciousness often is accompanied by considerable self-doubt. Some of us have become dependent upon the technology of imagery to confirm that we're real and we're okay or even that we exist:

> My mother is one of those types of women who always pulls out a compact when she gets nervous. We would always tell her she looked fine, but she'd have to check it out for herself. It was like she was afraid that if she didn't keep constantly on guard, this ugly self would crawl out and transform her—sort of like Jekyll and Hyde. I used to laugh at her for this, but I basically do the same thing myself. I don't carry a compact, but I cannot go near a mirror or a darkened window without looking in it to check out whether I look okay. I always look the same, and so you'd think that by now I wouldn't have to keep making sure. But I keep checking.

The Proliferation of Stereotypes

The myriad images of others we are exposed to daily can affect our self-esteem also. On a daily basis, most of us are exposed to three types of media: advertising (magazine ads, TV commercials, radio ads, posters, billboards, etc.); entertainment media (TV shows, pop music, magazines like *People* and *True Confessions,* comics in newspapers, novels, magazine fiction, etc.); and the news media (TV newscasts, newspapers, newsmagazines, nonfiction books, periodicals, etc.). Together, these provide us with a vast array of images of women, images often entirely different. As we read the morning paper, for example, we might see a predictable cheesecake photo of a bathing beauty, a story about a legal controversy in which a woman lawyer is quoted, and another story about a "blond divorcee" who was found murdered. Then listening to the radio, we might hear a woman newscaster reporting from Europe, another woman—this one a pop singer—crooning about her man, then hear a male disc jockey tell a cruel mother-in-law joke after the song. Later, flipping through a women's magazine, we may read about a young mother's work organizing her community against the company that dumped toxic wastes in her town, then we might see several pages of ads in which women are either cooking for their families or proclaiming the marvels of the program that helped them lose a hundred pounds, and, flipping on, we might encounter ads in which women are shown modeling revealing underwear from Frederick's of Hollywood. Still later, watching soap operas on TV, we see women doctors and business executives domineering their spouses or fighting with female colleagues over men, ads in which a rather moronic woman is expressing concern about the way her carpet smells, and then, back on the soap, a neurotic woman plotting to murder her sister-in-law. Stopping

at the supermarket before dinner, we might see a rack of "girlie" magazines, all showing abundant female flesh on their covers, a *Life* magazine with a bikini-clad beauty on the cover, a *People* magazine with
another scantily clad beauty on its cover, and a *National Enquirer* with
a big-bosomed film star on its cover and a headline that reads "Scientists Say Most Women's Libbers Have Mental Problems." That night
we might watch TV and see a woman news reporter standing in front of
the White House, a show about a crass and abrasive mother, a police
show in which women are victims and men are rescuers, and a show
such as "Dallas," where all the women are wealthy and glamorous and
stick by their men. Before bed, we might turn again to the paper to read
the comics page, where we see Flo of "Flo and Eb" once again whee-
dling money out of her henpecked husband and Mary Worth meddling
in everyone else's life.

Certain types of images appear far more frequently than others, and
in combination the various media all contribute to the proliferation of
stereotypes. The image of women as catty is a stereotyped image. This
image has been repeated enough times in the various media that it has
taken on the quality of a representative truth about women in general
and thus some people believe all women are catty.

Since the first cave drawings were made, all human cultures have
devised symbols, images, myths and songs that represent reality as the
people within that culture see it. The prehistoric women who invented
pottery drew images of women as potters inside of caves, and painters
like Brueghel the Elder depicted realistic scenes of peasants in the field.
But these images did not become stereotypes, because they were not
mass-reproduced and disseminated into mainstream life. That changed,
however, with the eventual invention of modern means of mass reproduction, and still later with the invention of electronic communications.
Where once human-made visual images and written works were each
unique objects that stood and were seen apart from mainstream life,
modern technology now enables visual images, written works *and* auditory signals (songs, for example) to be reproduced by the millions and
to reach the mass of the population.

The proliferation of stereotypes that modern technology has made
possible has given us a culture in which no group has been spared
stereotyping. Stop people on the street and ask them what the stereotyped image of Southerners is, and one response probably will be
"Southerners are racist." And so it goes with other groups. Asians are
inscrutable. New Englanders are thrifty and taciturn. Californians are
flaky. Black men are either athletes or shiftless bums emasculated by

"their" women. Feminists are ugly man-haters. Telephone operators are rude. New Yorkers are tough. Jews are greedy. Gay men are effeminate. Lesbians are butchy. Easterners are snobs. Hispanics are hot-blooded. Black women are maids or prostitutes or on welfare. WASPs are uptight. Older women are "biddies." All working-class and poor people have totally miserable lives. Blondes are dumb. These are just some of the more common stereotypes that abound in our culture today. The list could go on.

Not all stereotypes are clearly negative, but upon closer examination we can see their limiting nature as they strip away our individuality and render us a "type." Elaine Kanzaki Wong writes specifically of effects of stereotypes on Asian women:

> Occasionally, Asian women meet men who are what I dub "Orientalphiles." These men claim to be enamored of everything Oriental, i.e., the artwork, classic paintings, pottery, enamelware, clothing and various artificial artifacts. In short, they admire everything about the culture and, of course, that includes Oriental women. Because so much is presented as negative in the stereotypes about Asians, the Asian woman finds herself distinctly vulnerable in this positive stereotype situation and might respond positively when she might be better responding negatively. Is she not, after all, being regarded as another Oriental *objet d'art?*[5]

Women are one of the most stereotyped groups in our society. Here's a sampling of the more popular stereotypes of women that abound in American culture today:

Woman as Evil: The image of women as evil temptresses with diabolical plans to do harm to men is a common theme in pop music lyrics ("Witchy Woman," "Evil Woman" and "Maneater"), in television programming today ("Dynasty," "Knots Landing," "Falcon Crest" and every soap opera), and in feature films *(Body Heat, An Officer and a Gentleman, In the Still of the Night).* Women with teeth in their vaginas or who are hiding other deadly weapons with the intent of killing their unsuspecting lovers are prevalent images in pornography as well.

Woman as Sex Object: In every medium, women are depicted as sex-kittenish playthings for men, useful only for men's sexual gratification. Moreover, women's sexuality is used to sell everything from blue jeans to scotch to automobiles to industrial machinery. Given a moment to think or to look around our environs, each of us could come up with scores of examples.

Woman as Victim: Again in every medium, women are frequently portrayed as victims in need of rescue by males (most police programs, with the exception of "Hill Street Blues" and "Cagney and Lacey"), victims who bring on their own victimization through gross stupidity, or victims who are being justifiably punished for evil or sexual behavior *(Looking for Mr. Goodbar, Straw Dogs, Dressed to Kill)*. The helplessness of the female victim is often glorified (songs like "Love Has No Pride," and the "I'm Black and Blue and I Love It" Rolling Stones advertising campaign).

Woman as Madonna: Many of us were raised seeing an endless parade of perfect mothers in the characters of Mrs. Cleaver, Mrs. Nelson, Mrs. "Father Knows Best" and Donna Reed. The all-giving, one-dimensional mother is still alive and well on every soap opera and in commercials (the Italian mother or the mother of a child with a common cold). This image is not only narrow and unrealistic, it has become a tyrannical ideal against which we often unfairly measure our mothers and our performance as mothers.

Woman as Destructive Mother: Media portrayals of violent criminals often make the point that the poor boys had mothers who were so castrating and malevolent that their sons had no other choice than to become antisocial. This is particularly true in dramas about rapists: He is not responsible for his hatred of women, his mother is *(Rage)*. Short of turning men into criminals and psychopaths, mothers make their children miserable *(Portnoy's Complaint, Psycho, Frances, Kramer vs. Kramer, Ordinary People)*. This extends to a preponderance of negative stereotypes about mothers-in-law, stepmothers and foster mothers.

Woman as Mentally Ill: The entertainment media seem most interested in exploring the lives of women who can be portrayed as mentally ill. Rarely do we hear about women who—like most of us—have problems and cope with them without going crazy or becoming bizarre. But we hear plenty about women who are neurotic and incapable of figuring anything out without the help of an expensive psychiatrist *(An Unmarried Woman, Fear of Flying,* the women friends of the star on "Family Tree"), and we hear even more about women who are either suicidal or just plain insane *(Edie,* the myriad articles and books about Sylvia Plath, movies such as *The Three Faces of Eve,* and *Frances,* the women in Tennessee Williams plays). Not only are mentally ill women commonly portrayed, but they are portrayed as if they were their mental illnesses—nothing more. When the life of Billie Holiday is made into a movie *(Lady Sings the Blues)* or the life of Edith Piaf is made into a play *(Piaf),* their problems are emphasized at the expense of a more total understanding of them. And although we do hear and see stories of women alcoholics, mental patients, drug addicts, etc., who overcome their problems and become "good" women, they are still defined by their problems.

Woman as Moron: We see her most often in advertising: She is so obsessed with ridding her environs of dirt that she spends all her time and energy getting "caked-on grime" out of corners, gunning down germs with an arsenal of wonder products, talking to a little man in a little boat in her toilet bowl, and fretting about dirty shirt collars of her slovenly husband who won't wash his neck. On television and in films, working-class and rural women in particular are often portrayed as dolts ("The Beverly Hillbillies," "Petticoat Junction," Edith Bunker, "Laverne and Shirley," the women in "The Honeymooners"). However, this image of women as idiot cuts across class lines. "I Love Lucy," Phyllis Diller and "Gidget" also are examples.

Woman as Obstacle to Other Women's Happiness: This is the stuff of soap operas, pop music ("Nobody"), films *(All About Eve)* and television shows in which women fight with each other over men, money or recognition. We also see it in advertising ("Mother, I'd rather do it myself!" and commercials where women competitively compare their laundry or the well-being of their children).

Woman as Superwoman: This is a standard image in newspaper feature columns about career women. Slick providers of simplistic advice tell us we can "have it all," Enjoli assures us that if we wear their perfume we can be a supermom, high-paid executive, gourmet cook and cosmic lover to our husbands simultaneously, and then Geritol takes the credit for it. The superwoman image is fast becoming an ideal just as prevalent and oppressive as Woman as Sex Object or Woman as Madonna.

Compounding the problem of stereotyping in the mass media is the problem of unequal representation. The number of images of women we see is relatively small compared to the number of men. In prime-time TV, for example, male characters outnumber females by a margin of three to one;[6] and on children's TV only 16 percent of the major characters are female.[7] In the movies a similar situation prevails, with the leading female roles in the last decade being so few in number that all but a handful of female superstars like Jane Fonda and Meryl Streep go for long periods without work.

To further compound the problems of stereotyping, the mass media are not just dominated by men, they're dominated by white men. On prime-time TV, a full 62 percent of the characters were white males in 1980 (compared to 68 percent in 1968);[8] and in network children's TV only 3.7 percent of the characters in 1982 were black, 3.1 percent Hispanic and 0.8 percent Asian. Native Americans were represented solely by Tonto on "The Lone Ranger Adventure Hour."[9] Perhaps the medium where white males dominate the most is film. According to the NAACP, only 12 of the 240 feature films released by American studios in 1981 had black males in leading or supporting roles, and only one black female had a leading role (Cicely Tyson in *Bustin' Loose).*[10] As for

Asians, Native Americans, and Hispanics, almost never do they appear in studio films, and where they do appear, it's only in the most stereotyped roles—as evil Japs and seductive lotus blossoms in World War II movies, scalping savages and stupid squaws in Westerns, and moronic and seedy señors and señoritas in B movies. This insults ethnic group viewers, and also hurts minority group members who have worked in the entertainment industry. Rita Moreno, for years confined by typecasting to play flamenco dancers, Indian maidens, and sexy, dumb and barefoot señoritas, explains:

> I wasn't conscious of the casting stereotypes in those days—not that they've completely changed now. If you were a Latina, you played poor, brown-skinned princesses: Mexican, Spanish, Indian; we all looked alike. Or so they seemed to think. . . . The more I played those dusky innocents, the worse I felt inside. Once I was an Indian maiden in *Jivaro*, with Rhonda Fleming. There she was, in frills, all pink and blonde and big-breasted. Right next to her, I had an ugly wig on, brown-shoe-polish make-up, and wore a tattered leopard skin. I felt ugly and stupid, and every time I looked down at my bare feet I grew more ashamed. . . . A little later I was doing a film with Richard Egan. Near the end, when I got jilted, I asked him, "Why joo no luv Oola no more?" When he told me, I took two steps back and fell over a hundred-foot cliff. I call it the Yonkee Peeg school of acting.[11]

Not all the images of women in the media conform to the stereotyped patterns. Women do appear in the mass media in a variety of roles. In the news media alone there are many white female reporters, some black female reporters, and now several Asian women as anchors. On TV there have been strong female characters like Billie Newman in "Lou Grant," Elaine Nardo in "Taxi" and Mary Tyler Moore to counteract the airheads in the jiggle shows. In the thirties and forties there were numerous films portraying strong women, often played by Katharine Hepburn, Bette Davis and their counterparts. Since the 1970s, a handful of movies such as *Julia, Lianna, Autobiography of Miss Jane Pittman* and *Harold and Maude* have appeared along with those that show women as neurotics and sex objects. And in the print media a variety of women's magazines provide affirming images of women, as do works of fiction ranging from *Little Women* to the Nancy Drew series to the myriad feminist-inspired novels that have appeared in recent years. Yet while these positive images do exist, they exist as exceptions to the rule.

Media stereotypes are especially damaging to children. A child exposed to Saturday morning network TV sees a world where, as Kim

Hayes has remarked, "there is only one Smurfette amid hosts of Smurfs."[12] A child who watched "The Winds of War," which drew the second biggest audiences of any TV special in history, saw an America populated only by whites.

Most grown women are not dummies who are indoctrinated into believing that because women are depicted in the mass media in a certain way then that's what we as individuals must be like. But regardless of how we women perceive ourselves, the way others perceive us and thus treat us is usually shaped to a large extent by media stereotypes. Virtually every woman we interviewed, regardless of color, has had the experience of being seen and treated as an inferior by women and men alike simply because she is female. And women of color, lesbians, older women, and women with disabilities have had the experience of being viewed as doubly inferior because of the stereotypes about both women and their particular group. For example, Anita Neilsen and Linda Jeffers, Wampanoag Indians who give tours to the public at the Wampanoag Indian Program at Plimouth Plantation in Massachusetts, report that many of the people who come to the site believe, first of all, that "all the Indians are dead." Then when they are told that this is not so, they presume that the Indians practiced scalping, that Indian women are all drudges and slaves to men, and that the Indians encroached upon the white settlers' lands rather than the other way around. (Many visitors ask Neilsen and Jeffers sincerely, "How did you happen to move near the Pilgrims?" as if the Pilgrims had been in Massachusetts first.)[13] That stereotypes propounded by the mass media do indeed affect how others see and treat us is further illustrated by a woman who uses a wheelchair:

> I don't consider myself a pitiable person; there's a lot I've done with my life that I'm very proud of. My biggest problem comes from other people and what I call their "emotional inaccessibility." The image of disabled people in this culture is very limiting. Because of the heroic, long-suffering, saintly stereotypes, it's automatically assumed that if you're disabled you're sweet, docile, very religious, asexual, that you're very naïve about the world, and that you'd never smoke, drink or say the work "fuck." People think you're very weird and they use these stereotyped ideas about you as a way of keeping you at a distance.

Advertising and the Rise of Consumerism

Of all the media, the advertising media are probably the most annoying in that ads are so impossible to avoid. If we want to watch TV, we can look at the printed listings in the newspaper and decide what to watch; but we have no way of deciding what commercials we'll watch with that show—we get what we get, no forewarning. We can decide not to buy certain publications, but we can't decide not to see the billboard that is right there in front of us on the highway, or the poster that faces us on the subway. Advertising images intrude everywhere—in the middle of TV and radio shows, in the middle of magazine and newspaper articles. A door-to-door salesman can be told to get lost, but in the case of the advertising media the salesman never knocks—he just waltzes right on in.

The increasing prevalence and power of advertising in our culture goes hand in hand with the growth of consumerism. Over the past 110 years, American society has been dramatically transformed from one where frugality and self-reliance were principal values to one where the emphasis is on "conspicuous consumption" of an ever vaster array of mass-produced goods—and advertising and women have played major parts in this transformation. The first ads appeared in the 1880s, when manufacturers decided to use newspapers and magazines to alert the public of the availability of their products. Initially, ads were simple and straightforward statements about the virtues of the advertised products. By the 1920s, however, advertising had become a $1 billion-a-year industry, using ever more elaborate and sophisticated techniques; and the industry's aim was summed up by one advertising executive as the creation in consumers of a "dissatisfaction with what they now have in favor of something better."[14] Moreover, by the 1920s the advertising industry already was focusing the bulk of its efforts on breeding dissatisfaction in women in particular because women were then, as they are today, the principal purchasers of consumer goods in the United States.

From the beginning, the dissatisfaction that the advertising industry has set out to inculcate in females is not just dissatisfaction with what we have, but more fundamentally dissatisfaction with who we are and what we look like. As Kathryn Weibel notes, the presumption of advertising is that the best results come from manipulating the self-image of the consumer, and since women are the major consumers, "this means an emphasis on manipulating the self-image of females."[15] To insure that women will buy, advertisers must do more than appeal to women's desires, for desires can always be deferred. Advertisers must convince the consumer that she *needs* the advertised product; and since most of what is purchased today has nothing to do with survival, the consumer must be told not that she needs the advertised product to survive, but that she needs it to be personally of worth. While most ads play on the "this product will make you worthier" theme in somewhat subtle ways, one shampoo and hair dye company advertises its wares by having a woman say outright, "It's more expensive, but I'm worth it." The implication here is that if you buy a less expensive brand, it must be because you have low self-esteem, and if you buy the cheap, generic brands, then you're obviously a slob who has no self-esteem at all.

The majority of ads aimed at the female audience today call up in women self-doubts about one of two particular issues: our ability to be sexually attractive to men, and our ability to nurture. Ads for jewelry, fashions, cosmetics, weight-loss plans, toothpaste, and even such items as liquor, automobiles and cigarettes all are designed to raise in women such questions as "Am I pretty? Am I desirable? Is my skin too blotchy? Am I too fat?" And ads for home-care products, food, health-care products, children's toys and clothing, health and life insurance, home furnishings, vitamins and the like are all designed to cause women to ask of ourselves, "Am I nurturing enough? Do I take care of my loved ones well enough?" In both groups of ads, the hope of the advertisers is that women will decide that no, we aren't sufficiently attractive and no, we aren't sufficiently nurturing, and as a result we'll feel guilty and then will try to assuage our guilt by purchasing their products.

The problem for many women today is that thanks to advertising, the distinction between realistic standards and unattainable ideals has been blurred. All cultures have always created ideals of the perfect beauty (the "Mona Lisa") and ideals of the perfect, nurturing woman (the earth mother). But these ideals were *not* seen as standards—or goals— that the average woman was supposed to strive to live up to. Living up to the culture's ideals was seen, correctly so, as impossible.

What's different today is that technology in this age of mass production has created the illusion that yes, it is possible for the average woman to live up to our culture's ideals of perfect beauty and perfect nurturance. The message of advertising is that if we buy this soap, that makeup, and a million other things, we can become the Mona Lisa; and if we purchase Pampers, St. Joseph's Aspirin, Nyquil, Maxwell House, Charmin, Stove Top Stuffing, Johnson's Floor Wax, Prudential Life Insurance, Campbell's Soup, Wonder Bread and endless other things to nourish and nurture our loved ones, then we can become the earth mother. Moreover, with the illusion that it is possible for us to reach the ideal state of beauty and nurturing also has come the belief that those ideal states should become our goals, and that if they are not our goals, then there must be something wrong with us. In our advertising-permeated culture, a woman is morally condemned for being fat or for not being nurturing, but as long as she is trying to get thinner or to be more nurturing (and is buying products to help her reach those goals), she is tolerated. However, a fat woman who rejects the ideal of beauty and doesn't give a damn about losing weight is considered to have something terribly wrong with her, as is a nonnurturing woman who has no interest in becoming more like a Maxwell Housewife.

Most of the women in our self-esteem groups could cite several specific ads they found particularly irksome or demeaning to women, and many could also cite specific ads that upon seeing them had made them feel worse about themselves. For most, it is not specific ads that hurt self-esteem as much as the general climate created by all the thousands of ads we're exposed to in combination. The general climate created by the mass of advertisements is one in which acceptance of ourselves as we are now is made impossible. In this climate we are told time and again that no matter how good we look and how well we take care of our loved ones, we can always do better.

Overload, Powerlessness and Passivity

As the climate created by the advertising media is not conducive to self-esteem, neither is the climate created by the preponderance of violence and horror in the entertainment and news media. A growing number of movies of our time—among them *The Texas Chainsaw Massacre, My Bloody Valentine,* the *Halloween* series, and *Pieces*—serve no other purpose than to titillate the audience by showing scene after scene of human beings hacking other human beings to bits. Even such critically acclaimed serious and supposedly artistic films contain gorily detailed scenes of gratuitous violence. *Raging Bull,* for example, contained scene after scene of people pummeling one another mercilessly, and *Raggedy Man,* ostensibly a sympathetic film about the difficulties faced by a single mother, builds up to a totally unnecessary bloodbath when the heroine is saved from near rape by a mysterious hero who mauls the would-be rapists with an ax. The human race as depicted in prime-time TV is similarly barbaric.

All the horrors brought into our homes via TV newscasts and newspapers and newsmagazines can add to the despair about the state of the human race and the world that so many of us feel today. A good description of the news media's ability to affect how we feel about our world and ourselves comes from Stuart and Elizabeth Ewen's account of a fictitious woman named Beverly Jackson:

Beverly Jackson sits at a metal and tan Formica table and looks through the New York *Post.* She is bombarded by a catalog of horror. Children are mutilated . . . subway riders are attacked. . . . Fanatics are marauding and noble despots lie in bloody heaps. Occasionally someone steps off the crime-infested streets to claim a million dollars in lottery winnings.

Beverly Jackson's skin crawls; she feels a knot encircling her lungs. She is beset by immobility, hopelessness, depression.[16]

Most of the women we interviewed were familiar with this sense of "immobility, hopelessness and depression." The mass media today enable us to feel that, as one cable news show says, we're "in tune with the world." But being in tune with the world can make us feel very out of synch, for as our technology has advanced to bring world events into our living room, our ability to psychologically handle what we hear, see and read about has not advanced accordingly. The technology of mass communications has increased our power to perceive, but the more we perceive the more powerless we as individuals tend to feel. Occasionally, a move like *Gandhi* will remind us that there are other possible ways of living and that single human beings when united together *can* make a difference. But most of what we see, hear and read about does the opposite, encouraging either desperation or an apathetic stance of "What's the point?"

A sense of powerlessness can also be engendered simply by the process of ingesting the media's images and messages—regardless of what those are. Today many of us spend a good deal of time passively sitting back and taking images and messages in rather than creating images and messages of our own. Watching TV for lengths of time can be especially deadening. Television has been called "bubblegum for the eyes," but for many it's more a narcotic than a candy. Women, already rendered politically and economically powerless within our society, are at great risk of being rendered more powerless by the plug-in drug of TV. Television can be entertaining, and to the extent that it can sometimes provide a distraction from the pressures of our own lives, it has the potential to affect us positively. But for many women, particularly those who are isolated and housebound, TV is not a distraction from life, it is a substitute for it. Many women today spend an enormous amount of their time watching life go by—and it's someone else's life, not their own, that they're watching. Compared to the glamorous, exciting lives depicted on TV, particularly in the soaps, most women's lives appear dull and inconsequential. When one feels like a spectator in life rather than a full participant, self-esteem is bound to be low. Unfortunately, this is precisely the feeling the technology of imagery tends to engender.

BLUEPRINTS FOR CHANGE

I. Examining Stereotypes

What stereotypes are typically applied to you? What impact do you think this has had on your self-concept? On your behavior? When an expectation is very strong, people have nothing to lose by living up to it. Can you discern any negative stereotypes that have influenced you in this way? Are there any stereotypes you would consider positive that you spend much time and energy trying to live up to? What stereotypes do you have about other people? As you think or speak, try to identify them specifically, paying special attention to stereotypes you have of members of specific ethnic, religious and racial groups. Question those stereotypes: Do you or can you find evidence that contradicts them? How would you feel if someone inflicted these stereotypes on you? What is the point of holding onto your stereotypes? Do you speak up when another person promotes damaging stereotypes of others and the groups you belong to?

II. Taking Action

When you see an image that offends you, do you choose to do something about it? If you see it in a store (book cover, album cover, advertising for a product, etc.), firmly but politely tell the store manager why you are offended and ask him to remove it. If you feel strongly enough, you might want to inform him that you will withdraw your business if the offensive material isn't removed. For instance, a group of women we know asked a grocery store manager to place pornographic magazines out of the reach of children. When he did not, they saved up their receipts from that store for one month, presented them to him and told him that he could expect to lose that much business if he did not move the pornography. Also, call radio station managers when woman-hating songs and ads are played. Women are often surprised to find that station managers are concerned about how they feel. You can also write manufacturers and inform them you usually buy their products, but due to the offensive nature of their advertising or presentation of their products (as in a record album cover) you refuse to patronize them anymore.

Advertising and packaging are intended to get us to spend money on the product. Our most basic form of power here is *not to buy*.

III. THE POWER OF LAUGHTER

It isn't easy (or always appropriate) to keep a sense of humor about the stereotypes of women we are bombarded with, but often we don't want to spend the time and energy to protest the images to their sources, and so we might want to ridicule them instead. Naming commercials, programs, films, songs, etc., as inaccurate in their portrayal of women can be a first step. It seems more and more that women are talking back or laughing out loud at their TV sets and movie screens when a demeaning image is presented. Not only does this allow for some emotional release for us, it informs others around us (in a movie audience, for example) that the images are untrue and damaging. Moreover, it opens up the possibility that others will agree with us, thus affirming our sense of reality and making it less likely that we will internalize any part of the negative stereotype. Even if those around you think you are being "too sensitive" or "silly" or "rigid," you have the right to your reactions if an image used in the culture offends you.

IV.

Several organizations exist to help women join together to protest damaging images of ourselves in our culture. Here are the names and addresses of three organizations that are concerned with eradicating sexist, violent, racist and other demeaning images:

Women Against Pornography
358 West 47th St
New York, NY 10036

Action for Children's Television
46 Austin Street
Newton, MA 02160

Women Against Violence in Pornography & Media
P.O. Box 14614
San Francisco, CA 94114

Perhaps there is already a chapter in your community and you have the time and inclination to join or to contribute money. If you belong to another kind of group (PTA, neighborhood organization, B'Nai B'Rith, church organization, women's group), you might invite them to give a presentation to your group. If there isn't a chapter in your area, write to the aforementioned addresses and you can receive information on how to form a chapter or do this type of work in your community. Each of these groups has been effective in having negative images of women and minority groups removed from various forms of the media.

* 7 *

The Not So Helpful
Helping Professions

In the United States today more than $360 billion per year is spent on health care, making the health-care industry the second largest industry in the U.S. economy, second only to defense.[1] Much of this money is spent on female health care, for as women are the principal purchasers of consumer goods in the United States, we are also the principal consumers of health care. Women make two thirds of all visits to physicians for medical help,[2] and women also comprise two thirds of the population served by mental health facilities and 84 percent of all private psychotherapy clients.[3] Whether rich or poor, white or of color, urban or rural, no American woman today can avoid being in some way affected by the burgeoning health-care industry. Even if a woman never personally visits a doctor—and this is rare, because most people in twentieth-century America were literally born into the hands of the medical profession—or seeks psychotherapy, she still will be influenced by the medical and psychotherapeutic professions because the language, ideas and assumptions of these professions are constantly disseminated throughout the entire culture. Through ads for a vast array of drugs, TV shows that center on hospitals and glorify doctors, and news stories about miracle cures and the latest breakthroughs in transplant surgery, the average American is made increasingly familiar with the philosophy and practices of modern medicine. And through newspaper advice columns, radio talk shows hosted by psychologists, and magazine articles that ask "Can This Marriage Be Saved?" or report on the latest theories about alcoholism, depression and child care, most people acquire at least a nodding acquaintance with the terminology and methodologies of the psychotherapeutic establishment.

The impact of the medical and psychotherapeutic professions—or the "helping professions," as they are often called—on women is especially great because of the intimate nature of our personal interactions with those professions. A doctor is someone who has access to our most private selves: with his fancy instruments he probes our vaginas and other places we cannot see for ourselves; with his scalpels he can cut through our flesh and remove pieces of us; with his X-ray machines and sonar scanners he can literally see inside us; and with his questions he culls from us information about everything from our sex lives to our sleep and dietary habits. Psychotherapists have similar access to our most private selves, for they are in the business of baring and probing souls as much as medical doctors bare and probe bodies. Moreover, we typically see doctors and therapists when we are ill or troubled—when we are feeling our most vulnerable and defenseless. Our interaction with doctors and psychotherapists, combined with the vulnerable position from which we interact with them, makes it difficult not to feel deeply affected by what they say and do to us.

Not only do doctors and psychotherapists have access to our most private selves, they also wield great power over us. Part of this power derives from the status of physicians and psychotherapists as authoritarian "experts" privy to supposedly superior knowledge and backed up by the weight of "science." And part of it derives from the simple fact that whereas most health-care consumers are women, most physicians, psychiatrists and psychologists are men.* Physicians and psychotherapists speak not simply with scientific authority, but also with male authority. Even if a physician or psychotherapist is female, she most likely has been trained according to male-determined traditions within male-run institutions that teach male-devised theories and male-devised methodologies.

The Rise of Male Medical "Science"

When the creators of "Marcus Welby, M.D." cast Robert Young to play the knowledgeable, kindly and trustworthy physician of the show's title, they made a very smart move. Young was already well known to millions of TV viewers as the knowledgeable, benevolent patriarch in "Father Knows Best," and as the casting director surely knew, the authority Young had established in the first show would automatically carry over to the second. What could be more natural than the progres-

* Because most physicians are men, we will use the pronoun "he" when speaking of a woman's relationship with her doctor.

sion from father to doctor? And what could be more fitting than the implicit suggestion that today doctor knows best, just as father knew best in the past?

The preponderance in the media of heroic white male physicians such as Ben Casey, Marcus Welby, Dr. Kildare, Hawkeye Pierce, and Trapper John, M.D. together with a plethora of soap opera doctors, these convey the impression that men are somehow specially gifted in healing, and that therefore it is only natural and just that medicine today is monopolized by men. Viewed historically, however, this, in fact, is an anomaly. Through most of history, health care was the province of females. Moreover, healing was an art whose theories and methods every woman had free access to, not a science whose secrets were held by an elite few to be dispensed as commodities for fees. In many preindustrial societies, male "witch doctors" and shamans do exist, but these men are usually turned to only as a last resort, and the basic tasks of health care—from dispensing herbal mixtures to midwifery—are women's province.[4] In Europe and America too, healing historically was woman's domain, with male doctors—where they existed—treating only the very rich. Only relatively late in history—within the past few centuries—did men take over health care, and they did so by establishing medicine as a profession from which women were entirely excluded, as Barbara Ehrenreich and Deirdre English explain:

> The conflict between women's traditional wisdom and male expertise centered on the right to heal. For all but the very rich, healing has traditionally been the prerogative of women. The art of healing was linked to the tasks and the spirit of motherhood; it combined wisdom and nurturance, tenderness and skill. All but the most privileged women were expected to be at least literate in the language of herbs and healing techniques; the most learned women traveled widely to share their skills. The women who distinguished themselves as healers were not only midwives caring for other women, but "general practitioners," herbalists and counselors serving men and women alike.
>
> The historical antagonist of the female lay healer was the male medical professional. . . . While the female lay healer operated within a network of information-sharing and mutual support, the male medical professional hoarded up his knowledge as a kind of property, to be dispensed to wealthy patrons or sold on the market as a commodity. His goal was not to spread the skills of healing, but to concentrate them within the elite interest group which the profession came to represent. Thus the triumph of the male medical profession . . . involved the destruction of women's networks of mutual help—leaving women in a position of isolation and dependency—and it established a model of expertise as the prerogative of a social elite.[5]

Medical Care Today

Women today visit physicians more often than men not because women are sicker than men, but because the medical establishment's seizure of control over reproduction necessitates that women be dependent upon doctors. A hundred years ago, most births and gynecological care were handled by midwives. By 1930, however, the male medical profession had seen to it that "midwives were almost totally eliminated from the land—outlawed in many states, harassed by local medical authorities in other places."⁶ Today, the American medical profession has by and large been successful in convincing most women it's wrong and dangerous to go through pregnancy and birth without the intervention of a physician. Moreover, in the United States, most methods of birth control can be obtained legally only through a physician. By maintaining a monopoly on the dispensation of birth control aids in this country, physicians can both control women and insure that they will always have a steady stream of customers coming back for a prescription refill or new diaphragm fittings, each time coughing up another fee.

Modern scientific medicine today is something most of us can't live without, but can't live with either—at least not very comfortably. If we become ill, discover a lump in our breast or fall down and break a leg, most of us have no choice but to turn to the medical profession for help, just as we have no choice when we want birth control. If we are lucky, we will be helped: The doctor's diagnosis will prove correct, his treatment will be effective, and—if we're extremely lucky—the doctor will treat us as if we were human, not as if we were some imbecilic, unfeeling object. If, however, we're not so lucky, we might be misdiagnosed, given treatment or medicine that is not only totally inappropriate but makes us sicker, and/or treated condescendingly, cursorily or even cruelly by the physician.

Unfortunately, the chances are considerable that when we visit a doctor we will encounter maltreatment in some way. Virtually everyone, it seems, has had some sort of experience with doctors who are either incompetent or so arrogant as to be beyond questioning what they do, and virtually everyone knows a litany of medical horror stories. We've all heard about unnecessary surgery performed for no other reason than the physician's profit, patients who are given the wrong anesthesia and die as a result, doctors who confuse patients and perform on one the operation that was supposed to be done on another, doctors who operate drunk, diagnoses that are grossly wrong, doctors who needlessly medicate patients and/or don't warn them about the possible effects of the medication, doctors who withhold from patients and their families important information, doctors who sexually abuse their patients, doctors who insult and condescend to their patients, and doctors who respond to any questioning of their authority, omniscience and treatment from a patient by labeling the patient as crazy, uncooperative, belligerent, ungrateful and obviously unwilling to get well. While there are many competent and compassionate doctors, there unfortunately are enough who are not competent and compassionate to make distrust of the medical profession justifiably widespread.

Women are especially likely to suffer maltreatment at the hands of doctors. Most doctors are men, and as such they are not immune to misogyny. In fact, a doctor is more likely to be sexist than the average man, for a heavy dose of misogyny historically has been a standard component of formal medical training. Doctors traditionally have been taught that women are narcissistic, masochistic morons given to hysteria and hypochondria, and that all our medical problems have their roots in our reproductive organs (seen as diseased by definition), in mental illness ("it's all in your head"), or in a pathological inability to adjust to "the feminine role." Consider this discussion of dysmenorrhea (menstrual cramps) from *Obstetrics and Gynecology,* a leading medical-school textbook:

> It is important to ascertain how crippling the symptom is and how much emotional gain the patient is deriving from it. For example, does the whole household revolve around whether or not the mother is having menstrual cramps? Is the dysmenorrhea the focus for the expression of depression, anger, or a need to be dependent?

> The adult woman who presents this symptom very often is resentful of the feminine role. Each succeeding period reminds her of the unpleasant fact that she is a woman. . . .[7]

Consider as well this description, from the same book, of "the normal woman":

> The (normal) woman gives up her outwardly oriented active and aggressive strivings for the rewards involved in identification with her family . . . and sacrifices her own personality to build up that of her husband.[8]

Also consider these pronouncements on menopause by physician David Reuben in his best-selling *Everything You Always Wanted to Know About Sex but Were Afraid to Ask:*

As the estrogen is shut off, a woman comes as close as she can to being a man. Increased facial hair, deepened voice, obesity, and the decline of breasts and female genitalia . . . all contribute to a masculine appearance. Coarsened features, enlargement of the clitoris, and gradual baldness complete the picture. Not really a man but no longer a functional woman, these individuals live in a world of intersex *[sic]* . . . sex no longer interests them.

To many women the menopause marks the end of their useful life. They see it as the onset of old age, the beginning of the end. They may be right. Having outlived their ovaries, they may have outlived their usefulness as human beings. The remaining years may be just marking time until they follow their glands into oblivion.[9]

Sadly for women, the misogynist theories doctors learn in medical school often translate into misogynist practices. Moreover, the misogyny is often accompanied by racism and class prejudice. For example:

The hysterectomy is now the most common major operation performed on females in the United States, and if doctors continue to perform hysterectomies at present rates, surgeons eventually will have removed the uteruses of one out of every two women in America. The need for many hysterectomies is medically debatable, with more than one third alone performed because of uterine fibroids doctors claim are abnormal and will lead to cancer. In fact, uterine fibroids are quite common, and most are benign.[10]

In welfare hospitals across the United States, it has been common practice for doctors to sterilize poor women after giving birth and to do so without the women's informed consent. The poor women who suffer forced sterilization are most often Native American, black, Hispanic, mentally retarded or physically handicapped.[11]

Doctors take men's reports on illness more seriously than they do women's. In a study conducted by a male physician, fifty-two men and fifty-two women described the same symptoms to male doctors, and the physicians did more extensive medical histories and examination on the men, and ordered more extensive lab tests as well. The doctors were more likely to dismiss the women's symptoms as evidence of hypochondria.[12]

The birth control pill was put on the market and prescribed for millions of American women on the basis of limited and unreliable testing as to its safety and side effects. In one of the shoddy studies, the pill was administered to 132 Puerto Rican women, five of whom died. Although blood clots were indicated in three of the deaths, no autopsies were performed to determine the cause of the deaths.[13]

The Halsted radical mastectomy, the most disfiguring and traumatic method of attempting to cure breast cancer, was until recently the most common method used by American doctors despite the fact that there has never been evidence that it is the most effective method.[14]

In a study at the Southwest Foundation for Research and Education in 1971, Dr. Joseph Goldzieher gave 398 Chicano women what the women believed were birth control pills. But unbeknownst to the women, seventy-six of them were actually given placebos; and ten percent of these women who thought they were on birth control pills became pregnant within four months. When Dr. Goldzieher was questioned about the ethics of tricking the women in this way, he told a reporter from the New York *Post*, "If you think you can explain a placebo to women like these, you never met Mrs. Gomez from the West Side."[15]

As a way of justifying their takeover of the birth experience, doctors routinely claim that the only safe birth is a physician-managed hospital birth. In fact, medical intervention in birth often creates more hazards than it prevents, and the risk of infection or contracted disease for mother and child alike is nowhere as great as in a hospital. While the medical profession has been reluctant to do much research on home versus hospital births, Dr. Lewis E. Mehl of the University of Wisconsin studied two thousand births, nearly half of which were at home. He found that there were thirty birth injuries among babies born in hospitals, none among those born at home; that fifty-two of the babies born in hospitals needed resuscitation but only fourteen born at home did; and that six of the babies born in hospitals suffered neurological damage, compared to one baby born at home.[16]

Doctors routinely prescribe tranquilizers for women more often than they do for men, even when men and women complain of the same symptoms. A federal report in 1979 found that 60 percent of mood-altering drugs, 71 percent of the antidepressants, and 80 percent of the amphetamines prescribed by American physicians were prescribed for female patients.[17]

Writing in the September 1970 issue of the *Journal of Obstetrics and Gynecology,* Dr. George S. Walter, Maternal and Child Health Consultant to the Indian Health Service in Fort Defiance, Arizona, explained his reasons for being opposed to abortion rights as follows: "The pregnant woman symbolizes proof of male potency and if the male loosens his rule over women and grants them the right to dispose of that proof when they want to, the men then feel terribly threatened lest women can, at will, rob them of their potency and masculinity. This flaunting *[sic]* of traditional subservience may . . . function in the frequent professional insistence upon sterilization as a 'package deal' with abortion. In this way, the male physician can maintain control."[18]

Many women have suffered severe trauma because of misogynist and often racist medical practices. The cost to women's collective well-being and self-esteem because of needless radical mastectomies and hysterectomies, and medical intervention before, during and after birth is so enormous as to be beyond estimation. There is also the toll of countless small humiliations that women suffer at the hands of physicians. The standard gynecological exam, for example, can make a woman feel embarrassed, degraded and objectified. Another example is the shaving off of women's pubic hair before giving birth, a humiliating practice that has been routine in hospital births, supposedly for the sake of hygiene, although studies going as far back as the 1930s show shaving actually triples the chance of infection.[19] Also humiliating to women is the all too frequent suggestion by male doctors that whatever ails women can be cured by a good lay:

> I went through this period where I was having blinding headaches, and since I had had cancer several years before, the headaches really worried me. I had recently moved to a new city and hadn't yet found a doctor there, so I went to a clinic near where I worked. The doctor I saw was young and very full of himself, and after asking a few brief questions about my medical history he started asking about my sex life. I tried to be as evasive as possible, but he kept persisting, insinuating that the reason I was having so many headaches was that I wasn't having enough sex. I got really upset because he was so pompous toward me and his insinuations were so degrading—and he hadn't even examined me! When I kept resisting his questions, he—still without examining me—finally said, "Well, I guess we could run some tests, but I don't think we'll find anything." He had already made up his mind what was wrong with me. He knew it *must* be a sexual problem, it could be nothing else.

While the misogynist attitudes that pervade much of the male medical profession cause particular humiliations for women, we should point out that modern medicine is dehumanizing to anyone, regardless of sex. One physician, writing in the New York *Times,* gives a good description of the indignities routinely felt by anyone who must take the role of the patient:

> The feeling has come over almost everyone at one time or another: a sense of deep embarrassment in a doctor's office or in a hospital room. It's a kind of humiliation that seems to grow out of vulnerability, nakedness, of being handled, left exposed to be clinically peered at and examined like a grapefruit in a grocery.
>
> Some of the indignities may be unavoidable. Others are not: the ill-fitting gowns that leave you standing in the hallway or X-ray department showing

more of yourself than any passerby has a right to see; or the almost inde-
scribably mortifying experience of being carried as an invalid from one
treatment area to another by callous and careless hospital workers, moving
your body along as if it were being loaded on a ship by longshoreman; or
being exhibited in a teaching hospital to groups of strangers who discuss
you impersonally in your own presence, using language you don't understand; or revealing intimate details about your life history or finances in a
crowded office where everyone can overhear.[20]

Beyond the embarrassments and indignities modern medicine visits
on the patient, modern scientific medicine has a detrimental effect on
our self-esteem in other important ways. First, modern medicine undercuts our trust in ourselves and our powers of perception. It does this by
requiring that we place our trust in doctors to tell us what's wrong, and
that we further place our ultimate trust in machines or lab tests. Fundamental to the practice of modern medicine today is the assumption that
regardless of what a patient feels, she is only ill if a doctor and his
technological testing tools can verify it. Instead of trusting what our
bodies tell us, we are to trust what doctors and their machines and lab
tests tell us. Since the doctors and their tests tell the truth, it follows
that if we feel pain even when the physician and his tests tell us "nothing's wrong," we must be crazy. The problem with this is that doctors
and their tests are not omniscient diagnosticians. In fact, they often
make mistakes. Before a patient discovers a mistake has been made,
however, her trust in herself is eroded, and she begins to doubt her own
sanity:

I was sick for the longest time with abdominal aches, weakness, and bloat-
ing. I went to the doctor several times, but he couldn't find anything
wrong, so he told me to go home and relax. But my pain kept getting
worse, so I went back to the doctor, and this time he ordered an ultrasound
test to see if I had an ovarian cyst. The test showed no cyst, so I got sent
home again, feeling like I was crazy, like I was imagining it all. After a
couple of days I was really so sick I could hardly walk, so I went back to
the doctor and he ordered an ultrasound again. This time they found a cyst
that the technician said was as big as a grapefruit. It was in danger of
rupturing and I had to have surgery immediately. But all during those
weeks and weeks, I was told nothing was wrong, and I had begun to believe
it instead of believing in what my body was telling me.

As it undercuts our trust in our own powers to perceive our illnesses,
modern scientific medicine also undercuts our ability to believe in our
own powers to heal ourselves. The standard way modern medicine deals
with illness is through pharmaceutical and physician intervention. If

you want to become well again, you are to take medication, go through X-ray treatments or undergo surgery. Although this is changing somewhat today, modern medicine traditionally has placed no stock in people's own ability to heal or at least help ourselves through better nutrition, exercise, visualization techniques, changes in environment and life-style or through spiritual means. Reliance on pills, fancy medical technology and heroic feats by surgeons is simply much more profitable for the medical profession, and it also increases physicians' sense of power. Unfortunately, many of us are all too willing to go along with this system. Taught we have no powers to heal, taught that we need doctors to do it for us, many of us are unwilling or unable to take any responsibility for our health whatsoever. The idea that we might be able to help ourselves is alien to our upbringing; ironically, taking pills or playing the role of the passive patient seems to come more naturally.

Even if a woman has been fortunate enough to receive competent and compassionate care, if she is forced into the role of a patient, this cannot but undercut any sense of personal control and self-reliance she strives to have. A woman who has had to spend a considerable portion of her life in hospitals explains:

> I wouldn't be alive today without the medical profession, and overall my main doctor and the nurses who've cared for me have been wonderful, although I often have had to deal with residents who act like I'm a piece of meat in a butcher shop. Yet even when you get good care, the fact is that when you're in a hospital, you are assigned a subordinate, passive role. It's like a basic part of the bargain is that if you want the medical profession's help, you have to promise to do what they want you to do and not to ask too many questions. You are someone who has things done for and to you, and it's all according to the hospital's schedule and rules, never your own. You eat when they decide it's time for you to be hungry, you get to wash when it's convenient for them, you go for a walk when they want, and you sleep and wake up according to their schedule, too. I need to be in the hospital a lot because I need intravenous drugs and the aid of machines that you can only get in a hospital, but while those things help me physically, psychologically being in a hospital is very bad for you if you're ill.

Women with limited financial resources—and that includes a growing number of women today—are also rendered particularly powerless by modern scientific medicine. A woman with comprehensive medical insurance and/or abundant financial resources is able to exercise some choice in the kind of medical care she receives. She can choose what hospital she stays in, and if she is unhappy with one physician, she can seek out another, and yet another after that. But a woman who is of limited means and not covered by health insurance does not have the luxury of getting a second opinion. She must take whatever medical care is available in government-subsidized clinics and hospitals, and that often means getting second-rate care by interns, residents and medical students, for whom she serves as a teaching tool, and generally being treated like less-than-worthy lower-class trash by the entire staff.

Modern medicine diminishes our self-esteem in another way, too, for it makes it extremely difficult to experience a sense of wholeness. First, scientific medicine has always drawn a strict but arbitrary distinction between the mind and the body, between physical illness and mental illness. Too rarely in the diagnostic and treatment process is the whole person taken into account. Instead, many physicians only treat specific diseases, and many focus on the body to the exclusion of the mind or on the mind to the exclusion of the well-being of the body. For example, when Frances Farmer was committed to a state mental institution in the 1940s, she was badly beaten by orderlies. As she writes in her autobiography, days went by with no attention given to her bruised face or infected, blackened eye:

> I had been with six doctors and not one had offered to tend my wounds. They had chosen to see only a troublemaking, insulting ex-movie star. How could doctors assume to heal the mind while ignoring a wounded body? Or did they too believe the insane could not feel?[21]

Modern medicine also looks upon the body as broken up into separate, specialized parts, and in the process the fact that these separate, specialized parts are interconnected often gets lost. In a hospital, for example, a person is automatically robbed of her identity as a human. Instead, she is identified and referred to as her illness, and as her physician's property—"Dr. Martin's hysterectomy," "Dr. Welby's breast cancer case."

The Psychotherapy Industry

There is probably no single explanation for the fact that women receive psychotherapy more than men do. Instead, a number of different factors are probably involved. First, women in our culture have been socialized to be more open than men about admitting we have problems or are feeling troubled. Second, women have also been socialized to ask for help when we have problems. Third, in a sexist society life is more stressful for women than men, and the added difficulties women face might cause women to feel that we are "going crazy" more often than men.[22] Fourth, once a woman comes into contact with the helping professions, she is more likely to be labeled mentally ill and in need of psychotherapy than a man showing the same behavior and problems. For example, it is likely that a woman who visits the family doctor because of headaches will be encouraged to seek psychiatric help, while a man with headaches will be treated as if his problem were medical, not psychological. Similarly, a male hospital patient who is hostile and uncooperative to the staff probably will be tolerated as normally frustrated and angry about his confinement, while a female hospital patient who acts hostile and uncooperative probably will be labeled mentally ill.

Although many women are psychotherapy providers (this is particularly true of counseling social workers, most of whom are women), those with the most power, authority, and respected status as experts in the field are psychiatrists and psychologists, most of whom are men. By and large, the theories and methods that guide psychotherapists in their analysis, diagnosis and treatment are the theories and methods that originated with men—and this holds true even for female psychotherapists.

From Freud on, most men who have claimed to be experts on human psychology have looked upon the male as the normal and ideal human being and have viewed females as deficient, weak, castrated, deformed and inferior by comparison. The conventional "informed" view of women that long has been taken as an unalterable truth by so-called experts on psychology holds that women by definition are immature, narcissistic, masochistic, incapable of complex moral decisions, selfish yet selfless, given to exaggeration and hysteria, untrustworthy, submissive, incapable of independent thought or action, and plagued by a terrible envy of man's wondrous organ, the penis. Moreover, conventional psychological theory has also held that healthy women are heterosexual, married women, that women enjoy sex only when it is initiated by their husbands, and that women's only possible fulfillment can be found in marriage and motherhood. Thus, the "childless" woman is doomed to a perpetual stage of psychic dissatisfaction.

In the traditional psychotherapeutic relationship the psychotherapist sees his principal task as helping women adjust to the "feminine" role our society requires women to fit into. If a woman cannot or does not want to adapt to this role, or if she finds herself unhappy, angry and frustrated because of it, the psychotherapist labels her as sick and treats her accordingly, sometimes medicating her with tranquilizers that make her more passive and malleable. As the traditional psychotherapist sees things, the problem at hand is not that society has unfair and constricting definitions and expectations of women. No, the problem is that some women are unwilling and unable to conform to those unfair and constricting definitions and expectations. In the view of the traditional psychotherapist, the problem is never with society, it's always with the individual woman.

The "it's all in your head" myth espoused by traditional psychotherapists is based on a view of psychology that entirely ignores the social reality of human experience, and how human experience is affected by gender, race, class, economics, working conditions, etc. Psychotherapist Miriam Greenspan comments on the pernicious consequence of the unfortunately widespread notion that emotional problems are always a person's own individual making, never the result of social forces:

> The most obvious (and therefore most neglected) fact about theories locating [the cause of all emotional problems] within the individual is that such theories end up blaming the victim. If women are depressed or sexually frigid, psychologists tell us, it is because they are "masochistic" personalities. If the working man finds himself feeling like a machine, he is suffering from a "somatic delusion," a symptom of psychosis. The objective oppression that women and working people suffer and which contributes to the formation of such symptoms is thereby rendered invisible.[23]

In the 1960s and 1970s a number of new psychotherapeutic philosophies and approaches became popular as part of the "human potential movement." While different in many respects from the established traditions, the new philosophies and therapies were just as likely to ignore and hide social, political and economic causes of emotional problems, and to blame the victim for her problems. According to one of the more insidious tenets of the human potential movement, we all create our own reality. Taken to its extreme, this school of thought holds that the only things preventing people from total liberation and happiness are our own negative attitudes and unwillingness to be free and happy; since there is no objective reality to racism, sexism, poverty, class oppression, working conditions, etc., these factors can't be said to cause unhappiness or to prevent people from achieving bliss.

The philosophies of the human potential movement are as sexist as the most traditional philosophies, too. On the surface, the human potential movement seems to be liberating for women because where traditional psychotherapy has encouraged women to accept a constricting, socially defined feminine role, the human potential movement has encouraged women to reject that role and become more assertive, independent, aggressive, and self-centered—more, in short, like men. While this might appear to be liberating at first glance, the fact is that the human potential movement's notion that the key to women's happiness lies in becoming more like men rests on the same misogynist premise that the more traditional schools of thought rest on. In both cases males are looked upon as representative of the norm of mental health to which women should be compared, and it is taken for granted that the male way of thinking and acting is the better, indeed the ideal, way.

Within the general practice of psychotherapy, we can find many oppressive standards and treatments. For instance, an impoverished woman who is distressed and overwhelmed by having three small children at home will most likely not be able to afford private psychiatric help and therefore must rely on public mental health centers:

> When you're on welfare, you have no choice, you have to go to a public clinic. Always, they give you some white male student. He always asks me if I'm having trouble sleeping. Of course I do—I live in a ghetto, it's noisy, the kids keep me up. I can't sleep, but that's not what I'm there for. I'm there because I'm afraid I might hurt my kids. But all he cares about is can I sleep or not. So he takes me next door to a shrink who talks to me for all of five minutes, prescribes enough sleep medication for me to kill myself with, and that's that. I suppose I could go back and see that kid some more and answer his questions about my not sleeping, but who needs it?

On the other hand, a middle- or upper-class woman who feels similarly distressed and overwhelmed and has health insurance can afford to shop around for an experienced and sensitive therapist. If she does hurt her children, she is less likely to have them removed from her care by the state's protective service agency, or if they try, she will have more resources to fight them. And if, over time, she feels so distressed and overwhelmed that she needs to be hospitalized, she possibly has the choice of a private facility which resembles a rest home more than an institution. Meanwhile, her less financially well-off sister will be treated for the same problem in an overcrowded public institution where care can be substandard and enforced work is part of her "therapy," and moreover, where she may not be able to leave of her own free will.

The unexamined misogyny that underlies the views of many psychotherapists regardless of what school of thought they represent means that women who receive psychotherapy run a risk of being more hurt than helped by therapy. And to make the risk of being hurt even greater, abuses of power on the part of psychotherapists are unfortunately common. One study documented that 6.1 percent of licensed Ph.D. psychologists had sexual intercourse with clients in therapy and an additional 3 percent became sexually involved with clients within three months after therapy ended.[24] Moreover, the psychiatric community has a long history of using such barbaric practices as psychosurgery, excessive sedation, and forced confinement in institutions to keep those deemed mentally ill powerless and under psychiatric control. Even where such barbaric means are not used and the intentions of those in the helping professions are kind, it is often the case that helping professionals have a stake in keeping those they help dependent and powerless. A woman raised in a state institution for the physically disabled explains:

> I think a lot of what the doctors, psychiatrists and social workers do to people in institutions isn't done maliciously, it's just done unthinkingly. People in the helping professions often need to be surrounded by people they perceive to be weaker than they are. Lots of people who work in institutions really seem to be able to feel good about themselves only by being around people they see themselves as better, stronger, wiser, and more knowledgeable than. I think that a lot of the problems this leads to could be dealt with if the helping professionals who get off on being in charge just had some self-awareness so that they knew what they were doing. But a lot of them don't seem aware of how much they need to feel needed. So they continue to see themselves as these wonderful savior-types who are doing all the helping, when in fact those of us who are receiving their help are actually helping them to feel strong and powerful and good about themselves.

Some who practice psychotherapy are in dire need of psychological help themselves. In *I'm Dancing As Fast As I Can,* Barbara Gordon describes shopping around in Manhattan for a psychotherapist to help her after she came out of a psychiatric hospital where she had been treated for Valium addiction. Since she originally had become addicted to Valium with the help of a prescription-happy psychiatrist, Gordon knew that many psychotherapists were not to be trusted automatically. Still, she was shocked and appalled to find in her search psychotherapist after psychotherapist whose behavior was so weird (one expensive therapist's "help" consisted solely of asking Gordon to "touch the chair," "touch the lampshade," etc.) that Gordon could only conclude that they were far crazier than she.[25]

Yet despite the risks, there are many genuinely helpful and competent psychotherapists around, just as there are helpful and competent medical doctors. Many women have been helped and are today helped by psychotherapy, and the chances that women will be helped even more in the future are increasing because of the growth in the area of feminist psychotherapy. Feminist psychotherapy does not necessarily mean psychotherapy provided by women, as there are male psychotherapists who practice feminist therapy and female ones who don't. Feminist psychotherapy is distinguished by its goal, which is neither to force women to conform to constricting feminine roles nor to encourage women to emulate an equally constricting masculine model of mental health. The goal of feminist therapy, instead, is to help women find out who we are and to value who we are, and to do this without giving up the qualities of kindness, nurturance, empathy and concern for human relationships that our special socialization usually equips us with. Miriam Greenspan elaborates:

> The task of feminist therapy is not to encourage women to develop a male style of ego based on the model of competitive and aggressive individualism. Rather, it is to help women develop their own female style of self without the subservience that it has always entailed. This is a matter of helping women take ourselves seriously as primary persons. . . . To do so is not to abandon our psychic structures in favor of men's. It is to use the positive aspects of our own identity structures on our own behalf and in our own interests—which, I believe, are truly the interests of all human beings.[26]

BLUEPRINTS FOR CHANGE

I. MEDICAL MYTHS VERSUS REALITY

Most of us to some extent have had our views and expectations of the medical profession shaped by the images of the heroic miracle-working doctors seen in the media, especially on TV. When you hear the word "doctor," what is the image that comes most readily to mind? Does this image match up with the real doctors you have had contact with? Do you think the media image of the doctors as all-knowing and all-powerful fosters feelings of nervousness, intimidation and powerlessness on your part when you actually see a doctor? Do you think this image perhaps causes you to expect too much—miracle solutions perhaps—when you see a doctor? If you are intimidated by doctors, remember that they are not gods or heroes like the men on TV.

II. INFORMING YOURSELF

One of the reasons there is such an imbalance of power between physician and patient is that most of us know very little about our bodies and how they work. Books like *Our Bodies, Ourselves* and self-help courses in nutrition and general health care can help you reclaim power and responsibility for your health.

III. PREPARE FOR DOCTOR'S VISITS

If you plan to visit your physician for a specific problem (as opposed to a routine physical), write down beforehand a description of the problem, when it bothers you, what you think might be contributing to it, and any other information that seems pertinent to you. Often when we get into the examining room, we become so nervous and distracted that we forget information that could be important. For example, the words which would precisely describe a pain in the abdomen escape us, and we can't remember if there's any time of day the pain is particularly bad, or if it seems to be affected by a certain activity. Writing down everything beforehand will prevent you from feeling stupid when you can't answer the doctor's questions and from leaving the doctor's office, then suddenly remembering something you should have told him or her.

IV. GETTING INFORMATION

Physicians are sometimes remiss in giving their patients information about what is wrong with them, what the treatment options are and what the pros and cons of each treatment is. Some physicians just refuse to answer questions ("Oh, you don't need to know that," or "I wouldn't worry your pretty little head over that"), evade them with condescension ("My, my, aren't we interested? I didn't know you were planning to go to medical school"), or answer them in impenetrable jargon designed precisely to make understanding impossible. But you have a right to ask your physician questions, and you have a right to have those questions answered to your satisfaction. Again, it's helpful to write down the questions you want answered beforehand; that way you won't forget them if you get flustered when face to face with the doctor. Ask the physician each question, and write down his or her response so that you will be able to look over it again later. If he or she evades your questions, keep persisting ("Doctor, you haven't answered my question. It's information I very much need . . ."). And if he or she uses impenetrable jargon, request—again and again if necessary—that he or she give you an answer in plain language, in a way that you can understand. If your physician refuses to take the time to talk to you straightforwardly or withholds information from you, it might be time to switch doctors.

V. SHOPPING AROUND

If your financial situation is such that you do have a choice of physicians, shop around for one you trust and feel comfortable with. It is entirely appropriate for you to ask a physician questions about his or her education, philosophy of health care, experience, special areas of interest and expertise, etc. If a physician responds to your inquiries about his experience, philosophy and expertise with a "how dare you ask" type of attitude, take your business elsewhere! Also, never undergo surgery without a second opinion; even if you are in a "charity" hospital, a second opinion is your right when surgery is being recommended. If you do decide to have surgery, investigate your surgeon well. How many of this type of operation has he or she performed? With what success? How many of his or her patients have died during surgery? Remember, any surgery that requires total anesthesia is a serious operation; it should not be agreed to lightly.

VI. SELF-HELP GROUPS

Support and self-help groups for people with arthritis, multiple sclerosis, cancer, and various other illnesses can be extremely beneficial for those with such illnesses. Equally helpful are groups like Alcoholics Anonymous, Al Anon and Al-A-Teen (for families of alcoholics), Parents Anonymous (for people who have abused or are afraid of abusing their children), incest survivors groups, etc. Such groups can be a good way of seizing some power in dealing with an illness and/or a problem like your parents' alcoholism or sexual abuse that occurred when you were a child. Beware, however, of groups that are structureless and leaderless. Someone needs to be in the position of leading the group, guiding its direction, and watching out for the well-being of all the group's members while the group is interacting. At the same time, though, beware of groups who have "gurus" or overbearing leaders who seem to have all the answers. You might want to ask beforehand about the turnover in the group. Do people find it helpful and stay with it? If you go to a group once or twice and don't like it, then don't feel that you have to go back. If any other group members pressure you into returning, try not to succumb; trust your own feelings.

VII. CHOOSING A PSYCHOTHERAPIST

If you want to see a psychotherapist individually and you have the option of shopping around, by all means do so. There must be a special fit between client and psychotherapist if the therapy is to be helpful, and you're not likely to find that fit with the first person you visit. Also, psychotherapy costs plenty of money. You wouldn't buy expensive shoes without careful consideration, and you certainly wouldn't buy them if they were the wrong size.

The following suggestions for shopping for a psychotherapist can also be helpful for those who must go to government-subsidized clinics because of lack of financial resources. Within a government clinic, there are usually numerous psychotherapists to choose from, and it is your right to choose:

1. Identify as specifically as possible why you want to see a psychotherapist and what your goals in doing so are. Some women seek out psychotherapy for general problems—feeling depressed, chronically unhappy or anxious, etc. Others, however, have more specific problems and goals—dealing with incest in their past, getting "unstuck" about making a career change, coping with the death of a loved one, resolving marital problems, etc. The psychotherapist who might be best able to help you overcome depression might not be the same one who could best help you come to terms with the incest from your childhood or go through the grieving process after your mother's death.

2. Try to get recommendations from people you know and trust who have seen therapists for reasons similar to yours. Remember, the therapist who was so great at helping your best friend figure out her childhood family situation might not be so great at helping you decide whether to make a major change in your life today. If you cannot get recommendations of therapists from friends, try calling the local Mental Health Association or state licensing board to find out who in your area is qualified to help with problems of the type you want help with.

3. Once you have gotten the names of one or several therapists, interview them. Explain as best you can what it is that you want to deal with in therapy and what your goals for therapy are. Then ask the therapist how he or she can be helpful. Ask about the therapist's training and familiarity with the specific problems you want to deal with. How much experience does the therapist have in this area? Is the therapist up on the reading and research in this area? What kind of supervision from other professionals does this therapist receive? Also, ask about the therapist's general philosophy, attitudes toward women, and such matters as religion and sexual preference if these are important issues for you. If you are deeply religious and a therapist thinks religion is for superstitious dolts, then this is not the therapist for you. Similarly, if you are a lesbian and your therapist has never worked with lesbians before, you might want to consider someone else. In any event, if the therapist is defensive, evasive, or reacts disrespect-

fully to you as you ask questions, then this person is probably not someone you want to work with.

4. Shop around until you find someone you are confident can help you with your specific problems, and with whom you feel comfortable revealing yourself. If you feel at all uncomfortable with someone, don't assume it will go away or that it's your problem. Keep looking. Above all, trust your own feelings.

5. If you feel comfortable with a therapist but he or she is brand-new to the specific issues and problems you want help with, consider the options carefully. Is this what's best for you? Remember, the therapist is not doing you a favor; you will be paying for this time, and it may be the only time in your life that is all for you. You are not there to help the therapist. Think carefully before offering yourself as a learning experience.

6. In an initial interview you might feel comfortable because the therapist offers some personal information to show you he or she has experience with the issue and problems you want to work on. While this can put you at ease, watch out if the therapist talks too much about his or her experiences. If the therapist goes on too long, in therapy you might find yourself listening to the therapist's stories more than relating your experience. It can be very easy for women to slip into the role of taking care of troubled people—and troubled therapists are no exception.

7. If after interviewing a therapist, you decide you want to begin working with him or her, make an agreement that after a certain amount of time —four or six weeks, for example—you and the therapist will discuss and assess whether the relationship seems helpful, and then will decide whether to continue the therapy or not. If you decide to stay in therapy with this person, continue to set up periodic checkpoints to assess the kind of progress you're making. If you reach a point where the therapy no longer seems helpful, discuss this with the therapist and consider stopping the treatment.

8. Be especially cautious if medication is recommended, particularly after the first session. Taking medication is a serious matter; you might want to obtain two opinions. If the therapist does not take the time to explain all the side effects of the medication, or tells you that there are none, be sure to get a second opinion. Never take medication against your better judgment.

9. Beware of therapists who make snap judgments, or offer instant formulas for happiness or oversimplified diagnoses. Of course you came to therapy looking for answers, but they take time. Ideally, a therapist is an objective partner in your search, someone who can tell you what he or she observes in your behavior and what he or she thinks that means in your life today. But the answers must come from you, not from the therapist. Again, trust your own feelings and perceptions.

* 8 *

Where It's Hardest to Feel at Home: Women's Experiences in Public

> It is a violation of my natural external freedom, not to be able to go
> where I please . . . my personality is wounded by such experiences,
> because my most immediate identity rests in my body.
>
> —Hegel

In ancient Athens, women of the upper classes were not allowed to venture outside the home. Today in America most of us, regardless of class background, venture beyond home on a regular basis. Much of our time outside the home is spent within the confines of an institution— school, workplace, hospital or church, for example. However, some of our time, indeed a significant portion, is spent in what we would call "public space." By public space we mean the streets on which we run to catch the bus or walk to work, the local library, and the laundromat, the supermarket and shopping mall, the theater where we go to see movies, the trains, subways and planes we ride, and stations and airports where we depart and arrive, and the restaurants we eat in and the hotels and motels we stay in.

The Shape and Feel of Public Space

Any examination of our experience in public places needs to begin with a look at our physical environment. The way we perceive the world, ourselves and the relationship between the two is greatly influenced by the physical structures that surround us. These structures determine the shape of the space we move in, and in so doing they shape our experience and consciousness within that space too.

The shape and feel of the environment we move in when we go outside have a great influence on our sense of connectedness or nonconnectedness to nature in particular. For millennia the majority of humans lived in harmony with nature. They derived considerable strength from their sense of connectedness to nature and sought to symbolize and enhance that connectedness through the structures they built. This changed, however, with the Greeks. The Greeks saw themselves not as connected to nature but apart from nature and superior to it. And so they developed a man-aggrandizing style of architecture that is in marked contrast to the traditions of most non-Western cultures, particularly Native American cultures, as Jamake Highwater points out:

> The Greek temple is an expression of the man-conceived divinity—and not a response to nature's divinity . . . Greek architecture is a symbol of Western man's attempt to escape from nature. All subsequent Western civilizations have lived with that dubious and dangerous conception of freedom from nature. The architecture of the West makes an exoticism out of place just as animals in zoos and plants in botanical gardens make an alien curiosity of the beings of nature.
>
> The American Indian has an entirely different view of humanity and nature . . . because the landscape itself is sacred it therefore embodies a divinity that it shares with everything that is part of nature, including human beings, animals, plants, rocks . . . everything.[1]

Thanks to the changes first ushered in by the Greeks, and later accelerated by industrialization, the world many of us confront when we go outside is one that has become increasingly overwhelming and artificial. Especially in urban areas, it is often hard to feel connected to nature— or to other humans. To be sure, modern urban life increases the sense of community for those who feel part of a distinct neighborhood or for those who want a sense of being in the middle of the action. But for others urban life means less of a feeling of community, not more. Where it used to be common for people to live in small towns or villages where they knew all their neighbors, today it's not uncommon for urban apartment dwellers not to know who it is that lives above and below them, or next door. Indeed, many find that it's necessary to cut off feelings of connectedness to others just to survive in an urban environment. A Manhattan resident explains:

> When I go out of my apartment, I have to shut off parts of myself, because out there on the streets you see so many bums in gutters and shopping-bag ladies and people who are obviously deranged and in pain and in need of help. But you can't stop and think about all these people, you can't feel

sorry for them or try to do something for them because, really, what *can* you do? Like most people in the city I know, I just try as much as I can to block it all out. I think there's something very terrible about doing this, but I feel I have no other choice.

Suburbia can be similarly unconducive to a sense of community, with each family keeping to itself behind its own patch of lawn. Barbara Cameron, a Lakota Sioux who grew up on an Indian reservation, describes how alienating she found the atmosphere when she visited a white town for the first time:

> During my first memorable visit to a white town, I was appalled that they thought of themselves as superior to my people. Their manner of living appeared devoid of life and bordered on hostility even for one another. They were separated from one another by their perfectly politely fenced square plots of green lawn. . . . After spending a day around white people I was always happy to go back to the reservation where people followed a relaxed yet respectful code of relating with each other.[2]

A sense of belonging in the public world is especially difficult to obtain if one has physical disabilities. Structural barriers that impede the free passage of persons with disabilities make it apparent that the public world is the domain of the able-bodied. Designers and builders long have erroneously assumed that everyone in the world has full use of all the senses and parts of the body, and as a result have created an environment that is downright hostile to the disabled:

> Trying to move about in the world, we are constantly given the message: You can't come here, and we don't want you here. This is what every building that has stairs but no ramps or elevators, every bus you can't get on, every curb you can't negotiate tells you. People don't even realize how they keep you out. Like when it snows, a lot of people don't even bother to shovel the sidewalks in front of their stores and houses anymore. They aren't aware that to a person in a wheelchair or who needs a cane or walker that's a hostile act because a sidewalk that isn't shoveled is impassable to someone who has a wheelchair or cane.

What Happens in Public Space

As the environment we confront when we go out into the public world has become increasingly artificial in its shape and feel and intimidating in scale, so it has become increasingly unsafe. This brings us to the issue of what happens in public—and what happens a lot is violent crime. Today women in theory have greater ability to move about freely in the world than ever before. Hardly anyone says anymore that it's improper for a woman to go to a bar at night or to a movie alone. But while women in theory have greater mobility, for all practical purposes, women's ability to move about the world as we please is as restricted as ever because of the prevalence of crimes of violence. With the United States able to claim the highest rate of violent crime in all the industrialized world, we all know that none of us is without risk of becoming a victim of a mugging, a robbery, or an attack on our lives by yet another murderous maniac out to make the six o'clock news. Such knowledge undercuts our most fundamental sense of control over our lives, and with that our self-esteem.

An increasing sense of danger is something that women today feel acutely. As women we are doubly vulnerable; for while men can get mugged, women not only can get mugged, we also can get raped. And as hundreds of thousands of rape victims know, an act of rape, even though it may take only minutes, is so deep a violation that it can shatter the self-worth a woman has taken a lifetime to build.

For women who are disabled or elderly, the threat of violent crime is especially great. Able-bodied younger women can at least tell themselves, "Well, I could always run." For many, though, that's not an option.

Few of us go around reminding ourselves over and over just how vulnerable we are; we try not to think too much about what might happen to us, because if we didn't put it out of our minds we might find ourselves unable to go out at all. But somewhere within us, most of us do remain acutely aware of the danger we are in, and somewhere within, most of us feel a constant fear.

The fear most women feel when we venture out into the streets to do the laundry or some shopping or to go to work is so much a part of us that we might not even recognize it as fear. Only when we hear footsteps following too closely behind as we walk home, or feel someone pressing his pelvis too tightly against our back in a crowded subway car, or notice with alarm that shadowy figure standing in the doorway across the street—only when these sorts of things happen do we suddenly become fully aware of how watchful, wary and on guard we have become. Many are fearful even at home, and with good reason, since the chances of someone's breaking in are rising, too. Again, our fear at home is not something we're usually aware of—until, that is, we hear that strange noise by the window, or are awakened in the night by a stranger's voice on the phone telling us what he wants to do to us.

Street Hassling

Although it has become increasingly unsafe for anyone, the part of the world considered the public sphere long has been and still is essentially a white man's world. With few exceptions (various inner-city ethnic neighborhoods and ghettos, a handful of women's bars) white men in our society can go virtually anywhere in public and not be made to feel they don't belong and have no right to be there. True, white men run the risk of being mugged. But if they are mugged, they will not be told it was because they went where they shouldn't have gone—that they overstepped the bounds of their proper, circumscribed place.

The right to move about the public world as one pleases is one of the most fundamental measures of freedom, and historically, denial of this right has been a gauge of oppression. When segregation was still the policy in the South, whole sections of the public world were off limits to blacks. And when Hitler was in power in Europe, Jews were barred from going certain places, and also could leave their homes and go into public only if they wore badges signifying their religion. No matter how high a black person's opinion of herself may have been in the segregated South, as soon as she stepped out into the public world, she was reminded of her second-class status. And no matter how proud a Jew may have been of her religion in Hitler's Germany, each time she ventured into public, she was forced to wear a symbol intended to shame her.

In America today there are no municipal, state or federal ordinances restricting the right of any group to move about as they please. There is, however, an unwritten rule that gives men the right to harass and humiliate women on the streets, and through the ugly male pastime of street hassling men make sure that when women venture out in public, we will feel uneasy, unwelcome, and aware of our inferior social status. Cheryl Benard and Edit Schlaffer, political science professors at the University of Vienna, have found male street hassling to be widespread throughout the Western world. Interviewing sixty men they witnessed harassing women on the street to find out what motivates them, Benard and Schlaffer discovered that street hasslers are men of all ages, races, income and classes, and that their behavior's most important attribute is what it symbolizes:

> The genuinely *public* world is the main arena for harassment. The street, as a place where strangers encounter one another, is also the place where societies have always taken care to clearly mark the lines of order and

status. It is on the streets that members of subordinate groups wear special clothing . . . or show symbolic deference to members of the superior group. Harassment is a way of ensuring that women will not feel at ease, that they will remember their role as sexual beings available to men and not consider themselves equal citizens participating in public life. . . . [Moreover,] it blurs the borders of women's right to personal integrity, and . . . [denies] her right to move freely, to choose which interaction to participate in and which people to communicate with.[3]

Street hassling comes in three basic forms. First, there is visual hassling, such as hostile, leering, menacing stares. The second form is verbal hassling. This runs the gamut from "psssst-pssst," whistles and animal sounds to comments such as "Hey, baby, lookin' good" and "Oooh, Mama" to threatening remarks and commands along the lines of "Hey, baby, suck my dick."

Growing up, many of us were told that when men whistle at us on the streets or make comments along the lines of "Oooh, baby, I like what I see," we should feel complimented. But men who whistle and comment do not do so in order to make us feel good; they do it to make themselves feel good by forcing us to see ourselves as they see us, by forcing us to see ourselves as objects in their eyes. Men could get plenty of pleasure just from watching women, just as women can get pleasure watching men—or watching animals running or nature's beauty, for that matter. But there's a difference between watching, and staring to the point where the watched becomes self-conscious, and a bigger difference still between looking and voicing one's impressions aloud. Men stare and make comments aloud not only because they feel they have a right to judge any woman they see, but because they feel they have a right to invade our consciousness and make us acutely aware that we are being judged. They are motivated not by a desire to compliment women, but by a desire to assert their power and to force women to recognize their power.

The third type of street hassling is physical hassling. Again, included in this category is a multitude of sins: pinching, patting, dry humping (a favorite of perverts on the subway), goosing, "accidentally" brushing breast or thigh or crotch with the hand, and outright grabbing. Again, the desire to assert their power over women is what motivates men in this practice.

Street hassling is often thought of as a predominantly urban problem. We found, however, that it is prevalent in rural areas, too. The main difference is that in rural areas, it's more common for verbal harassers to be in cars or trucks when they harass women.

Since the street harassment of women is so widespread and common a practice, we might expect that there would be a vast body of research about it. But until Benard and Schlaffer began their research it was entirely ignored by social scientists and the legal community alike:

> Stamped as trivial, the [street] harassment of women has received no attention from sociology, and cities that regulate almost everything from bicycles to dogs and the use of roller skates in order to keep the traffic moving have no ordinances or rules to guarantee women the right to free passage. Men, yes; the solicitations of prostitutes are carefully restricted in order not to offend them.⁴

Men who practice street hassling seem to use no discretion in picking their victims; they will hassle any woman they please, regardless of her race, age, ethnicity and the way she is dressed and carries herself. Still, some hasslers will pick on some types of women more often than on other types. White men, for example, may feel especially entitled to harass women of color and men of color might feel especially powerful when harassing white women. To be harassed on account of sex plus race can be particularly terrifying. A black woman explains:

> I've been hassled by black and Latin men, but the difference is that I can talk my way through a group of black or Latin men—when I see them on the street corner they really don't scare me. But groups of white guys terrify me. They feel so entitled to make racial and sexual slurs, to grab at me, to stand in my way and jostle me and laugh at me.

Slights and Stereotypes

Our experiences in the public world are also shaped by more subtle interactions that occur between us and the strangers we encounter in public. How shopkeepers, restaurant personnel, fellow subway riders and others perceive us and what they think of us translates into how they treat us, and how they treat us, in turn, can affect how comfortable we feel in the public world.

Unfortunately, as a woman has dealings in the public world, she runs a high risk of not being treated with much respect. At the butcher shop, the man behind the counter is as likely as not to call her "honey" or "doll." If she goes into a restaurant to dine alone, she's likely to get a lousy table, and poor service to boot. If after the meal she asks to see the manager, he's likely to say something like "I'm always pleased to talk to pretty girls (ladies)." Later, if she's driving and has to cut in front of another car, the other driver may well yell "Bitch!" or something defamatory about "lady drivers." If she has to go to the repair garage to see about a part, she'll most likely be visually inspected and then rated by the fellows in the shop; if she doesn't rate highly in their eyes, they'll probably laugh and make fun of her when she turns her back, and if they rate her as hot stuff, they'll probably whistle, snicker and/or make obscene gestures. Or perhaps they'll say, in voices just loud enough to make sure she'll hear, something along the lines of, "I wouldn't kick her out of bed" or worse. If a woman goes into a bar for a drink, she will likely be intruded upon time and again by men looking for pickups or for someone to listen to the maudlin and boring stories of their lives. And if a lone woman checks into a hotel, she has a good chance of getting bad service from the desk clerks; and later, if she dares to go into the hotel lounge alone, she might well end up being suspected of being a prostitute. That happened to one of the authors of this book in a Boston hotel, and it also happened to Gail Brewer, an executive who travels three weeks out of four on business. After flying into New York from Los Angeles late one night, Brewer later told the Washington *Post:*

> I was sitting in the hotel lounge wearing my business suit. It was 11 o'clock, but I was still oriented to West Coast time, so I wasn't tired. I'd checked in and gone to the lounge to relax after the long trip. After a few minutes, a hotel security guard came up and asked me if I was a registered hotel guest. I just stared at him, took a deep breath and said, "Yes I am." The next day I spoke to the hotel manager.[5]

A man in a business suit sitting at 11 P.M. in a hotel bar anywhere in the United States would never be called on to account for his right to be there.

While the sorts of experiences we have described don't happen to all women every day of our lives, they or similar ones have happened to most at some time. And while the men to whom these experiences don't happen often tell us that they are trivial, just "little things" and we shouldn't be upset by them, usually it's precisely the little things that add up to make a difference in our day-to-day lives.

When a woman is with a man in public, others are less likely to treat her with outright disrespect. Instead, the disrespect is shown by treating a woman with a man as if she were invisible. If a woman goes into a store or hotel with a man, the salespersons and desk clerks automatically focus their attention on the male. Even if it is the woman who asks for information, often the information will still be given to the man. In restaurants, the bill is given to the man, and many waiters and waitresses even ask the man for the woman's order. The treatment is similar at parties, receptions, professional conferences, and meetings.

Two women together are just as likely to get treated as subhumans as is a woman alone. In fact, two women together often get treated worse than a woman alone, because in appearing in public together they implicitly challenge the primacy of men. Women who appear together in public and show interest in one another are often labeled lesbians, and treated with hostility as a result. We were told of numerous instances where when two women out together brushed off the advances of intrusive males, the males responded by calling the women not just mere bitches, but dykes. Radical Lesbians explain the function of this label:

> Lesbian is the word, the label, the condition that holds women in line. When a woman hears this word tossed her way, she knows she is stepping out of line. . . . Lesbian is the label invented by Man to throw at any woman who dares to be his equal, who dares to challenge his prerogatives (including that of all women as part of the exchange medium among men), who dares to assert the primacy of her own needs. . . . For in this sexist society, for a woman to be independent means she *can't* be a woman—she must be a dyke.[6]

Women with physical disabilities get particularly poor treatment in public, too. All women are vulnerable to being ogled as if we were pieces of meat, and that in itself can be humiliating. But women with physical disabilities are frequently stared at as if they were subhuman freaks. Moreover, others often treat them extremely condescendingly, as if they were small children. A woman who uses a wheelchair explains:

> A lot of people don't seem to be able to make the distinction between different kinds of disabilities. Like it's not uncommon for someone in a wheelchair to go out to eat and to have the restaurant staff talk real loud to you and act like they have to help you figure out what's on the menu. They seem to think that if you can't use your legs that's the same as being deaf and retarded.

Women of color also face added obstacles white women don't have to contend with. They are seen by many as less worthy and less human because of race as much as because of gender. A black woman explains how the combination of gender and color causes her to be received when she goes beyond her own home and community:

> Two facts I can neither change nor hide are the facts that I am a woman and I am black. These facts are obvious to anyone who sees me, and it is on

the basis of them that this white man's world draws its conclusions about me. Because I'm a woman, I'm presumed to be inferior. And because I'm a black woman, I must be a welfare mother, a prostitute, a drug addict or a maid—a poor person at any rate. And, oh yeah, illiterate, too. It goes without saying that if you're black and female, you're probably illiterate. And all this affects how you're treated. You should see what happens when a black woman wants to do something simple like cash a check in a supermarket or make a Master Card purchase. Automatically, you're suspected of trying to use rubber checks or a stolen card, and you are given an incredible hassle.

That whites see black women as thieves is often communicated to black women in more subtle but equally unmistakable ways:

> You pick up the distrust directed at you in a lot of ways. I'm walking down the aisle in the supermarket, for example, and there's a white woman dressed real nice that I'm going toward. She sees me and without hesitating she hugs her purse closer to her, tucking it tightly under her arm. As she does this, she smiles a real false smile.

Older women also receive especially disrespectful treatment in public places. The general public tends to be impatient and intolerant of older people who move slowly or need special attention because they can't see or hear as well as they used to. There is a widespread dread of aging in this culture, and this is sometimes acted out against those who remind us of the inevitability of aging.

The Prices We Pay

Our experiences in the public world communicate to us time and again our inferior status in our male-dominated world. When we are constantly put in our place by strangers, it can become that much more difficult for us to hold our heads high and to feel secure in our sense of self-worth.

Street hassling in particular is something women often find difficult to countenance without some cost to our sense of self. Even if a woman ultimately ends up brushing off an episode of harassment as the harasser's problem and as having no bearing on her self-worth, she still has experienced the incident and still must somehow process it and deal with it. We found that for many women dealing with sexual harassment on the streets means splitting themselves in two:

> What I do when some guy on the street verbally degrades me and my body is to cut off my sexual self, to kind of disown it, if you will. My sexual self

is the part of me that the world makes cheap and dirty, my body is what these guys have responded to as cheap and dirty, and so I estrange myself from that part of me. I split the part of me that's been made cheap and dirty from the rest of me, from the *real* me, because if I don't disown it then *I* will have been made cheap and dirty.

But no matter how much a woman tries to disown her body when hassled, somewhere she will likely remain aware that she is her body and that it is she, not just her body, that has been rendered cheap and dirty. Sandra Bartky gives a good description of the terrible feeling of objectification that a woman is likely to feel when, walking down the street and enjoying the flowers, her consciousness is suddenly invaded by a man who calls her "a nice piece of ass":

> Her face flushes with embarrassment; her motions become stiff and self-conscious. Her body, the body which only a moment before she had inhabited with such ease, now floods her consciousness. *She has been made into an object.* The forsythia, the tulips and hyacinths have been driven right out of her head: what she feels instead is embarrassment, rage and shame. Her rage is the rage of someone whose consciousness has been invaded and occupied, her shame the shame of a sovereign self who has been reduced to the state of a mere thing. . . .[7]

Women often pay a high price for the feelings of anger and self-consciousness that our experiences in public can call up. Most of us were brought up to be nice people; we were raised to value kindness, and we want to continue to think of ourselves as caring, warm people. But physical survival in public today requires that we be ever on guard and that we automatically assume the worst rather than the best about many of the strangers we encounter. This puts some women in a bind:

> Whenever I go out, I have to adopt this real tough, wary stance. It's like putting on a mask. Keeping this mask on takes up a lot of energy. I mean, it gets so tiring always being on your guard and having to be aware of every little move everybody on the subway or on the street or in the laundromat makes. And then on top of that, I don't really like the me I have to become out in the world. I don't like having to look at every guy I see on the street or in the laundromat as a potential rapist or mugger. I know that's what I must do, but still it runs counter to my ideal of being a humanitarian who's willing to give everyone the benefit of the doubt.

Equally enervating as the distrust women feel in the public world is the fear. Fear may encourage us to take actions to protect ourselves, and therefore, it's a good thing that so many women today are fearful of crime. But living in fear is not good for us. Even if we never become victims ourselves, we still have to deal with the possibility that we could be, and plan ways to minimize the risk of this happening. Fear, like distrust, eats up our energy, energy we'd probably prefer putting to some other use.

Finally, the fear we realistically feel in today's public world causes us to severely restrict our activities. Although in America today there are no laws decreeing that women can't go to this place or that, the prevalence of violent crimes against women and such practices as street hassling cause many to live as if there were. Certainly, it's terrible to hear of repressive regimes enforcing nighttime curfews in countries like Poland. But equally terrible is that many American women, particularly lone women living in cities, have been forced to live under a nighttime curfew for years now. And some women today are living under a daytime curfew too, for even in daylight many with good cause feel there is no safe place in the public sphere. From the song "Fight Back" by Holly Near:

> By day I lived in terror
> By night I lived in fright
> For as long as I can remember
> A lady don't go out alone at night
>
> But I don't accept the verdict
> It's an old one anyway
> 'Cause nowadays a woman
> Can't even go out in the middle of the day
>
> . . . Some have an easy answer
> Buy a lock and live in a cage
> But my fear is turning to anger
> And my anger's turning to rage
> And I won't live my life in a cage
>
> And so we've got to fight back!
> In large numbers
> Fight back!
> I can't make it alone
> Fight back!
> In large numbers
> Together we can make a safe home
> Together we can make a safe home[8]

BLUEPRINTS FOR CHANGE

I. CONSIDERING OUR ENVIRONMENT

Most of us do not have the option of radically changing our physical environment. If we live in cities, we must put up with large buildings, excessive noise, pollution, and miles of macadam and cement. But while we can't radically change our environment, we can be aware of how it affects us and take action to mitigate the effects when they're negative. A helpful exercise is to take note for a week of how you feel in the different spaces you find yourself in during that week. Do large, glitzy department stores make you feel one way, walking in a park or tree-lined street another? Elevators, subway cars, automobiles, restaurants in high-tech style, and restaurants crammed? The more you become aware of how your environment affects you—if you feel it does affect you—you might want to consider avoiding as much as possible those places where you feel nervous, claustrophobic or otherwise uncomfortable, and trying to spend more time in places where you feel better.

II. BALANCING COMMUNITY AND WARINESS

In today's world, it can often seem as if there's an inherent conflict between feeling a sense of community with the people around us and keeping a "safe" distance in order to protect our well-being and property. But this need not be so. If you live in a neighborhood or an apartment building where people have little contact with one another, and you want more contact, there are probably others who want more contact too, and there are ways to go about creating a sense of community. Block organizations, tenant organizations, neighborhood groups can all bring people together; and whether or not these organizations are formed with the express purpose of watching out for one another and protecting one another from crime, just being involved with your neighbors in some way will increase the likelihood of your being able to get help from your neighbors should you ever need it.

III. PHYSICAL SELF-DEFENSE

No matter where we live, it behooves all women today to know some basic physical self-defense techniques. Many women feel they don't really have the time to spend learning self-defense, and others are simply put off by the idea because self-defense training seems so unladylike and goes against their childhood training. If you don't know self-defense and you live in an area where the risk to personal safety is high, it might be helpful to try to figure out what is keeping you from learning it, then decide if that reason—don't have the time, the idea just feels funny, don't have the money, for example—is really a good enough reason to hold you back. Then, the following guides to choosing a self-defense or martial arts course from *In Defense of Ourselves,* can be helpful:

> If you live in an area which has many resources to choose from, it will probably be worth your time to shop around. If you are considering martial arts training, visit schools of different styles (judo, karate, aikido, kung fu and tai chi) to find the style that interests you most.

> Observe at least one class. How do the instructor and the male students treat the women in class? Are the women encouraged to try defensive moves or are they constantly told that what they try to do won't work against "a real man"? Again, if you are observing a martial arts class, do women hold higher belts? If the women students are treated disrespectfully by the other men in the class, how does the instructor respond? Ask the women students in the class you observe about their experiences of sexism, of being put down, etc. The best recommendation comes from a woman who has attended a class.

> In some areas, all-women martial arts schools or all-women self-defense classes are available. Particularly if taught by women, such training can be an advantage. Again, go on the basis of recommendations and your reactions to what you observe in class.

> The best kind of self-defense training includes both facts about violence against women (so that you are better informed of what to be aware of) and *verbal* self-defense. With information about the dynamics of violence against women, an understanding of the offenders' motivations, and practice in verbally defending herself in the situation, a woman can defend herself sometimes without using any physical force. Be sure this option is covered in your training.

Most women who take self-defense courses not only benefit in their feeling of personal security, but also attain increased competence, self-assurance and respect and liking for their bodies.

IV. STREET HARASSMENT

Feminist activist Vicki Keith, who conducts workshops on responding to street harassment, reminds us that we have three concerns to consider if we are to respond to street hassling or sexist put-downs.

First, we want to insure our physical safety. Second, we want to maintain our self-esteem. Third, we want to educate the offender by responding in a way that will discourage him from harassing or insulting other women. Often these concerns are mutually exclusive. If we tell him to shove it or drop dead, we might momentarily feel better about ourselves, but we may also be in physical danger. It is important that we insure our safety first and foremost.

When expressing ourselves to someone who has put us down, made a sexual comment to us or otherwise demeaned us in public spaces, we might want to use the guidelines in Part Four, Chapter 9 on constructively expressing emotions. Although they are written in a way that relates more to two people who know each other, the guidelines can be just as appropriate for situations involving a stranger. For example, if a woman has been called "honey" in a place of business, she might want to respond as follows:

1. "I heard you call me honey." (Describe the situation.)
2. "I am very offended by this." (State your feelings.)
3. "My name is Ms. (Miss or Mrs.)_____, and I want you to call me that." (Offer an alternative.)
4. "If you ever call me honey again, you will lose me as a customer." (Give the consequences.)

Often in street harassment, the offender is gone before we can think of what to say. The feelings of anger or fear or whatever the harassment evokes in you are valid, so try to get those feelings out in some way. Talk to a friend. Beat a pillow and think of the offender. If the offender harassed or insulted you while doing his job (as in the case of a construction crew), complain to his boss. Whatever you do, don't turn your angry feelings against yourself.

Practicing responses with other women can also be both a release and preparation for the next time you are harassed.

Here is a smattering that we have collected:

> When a man in a crowd molests you, pick up his hand and loudly ask, "Who does this belong to? I just found it on my breasts (or hip or whatever)."

> One woman we know who occasionally gets obscene phone calls asks the offender, "Would you please repeat that—I'm a little hard of hearing." When he does repeat it, she says, "I'm sorry, I still don't get it—would you please speak up." Most offenders hang up on her at this point, but if not, she asks the caller to repeat himself until he does. We hope these men realize how asinine they sound when they have to repeat it.

When hassled by a group of men at a work place, Vicki Keith suggests immediately asking one of them, "What's your name, sir?" He won't volunteer it, but his friends will, and then you have the information you need to file a complaint.

V. Your Right to Report

Women sometimes don't report offenses against them to authorities because they fear they will not be taken seriously or they will be blamed. But in many areas, the antirape movement has helped to change the law enforcement authorities' response to crimes against women. Even if an assault wasn't successfully completed because you prevented it, feel entitled to report it to the police. Often they have received reports, of similar or related disturbances and your information could be helpful. The police may not be able to make an arrest, or you may not want to prosecute, but at least alert them to what happened. The same goes for obscene phone calls. Telephone companies have come up with some effective ways of combating them, so call your customer representative and report any obscene calls. Also, if you are hassled by an employee on the job, consider reporting the incident to his supervisors.

VI. Your Right to Help

If you have been a victim of a violent crime, sometimes it's difficult to know who to turn to. Many communities have rape crisis centers staffed by trained counselors, some of whom have been victims themselves. They are there to listen, to help you if you want medical attention, if you choose to call the police, and if you are presented with the option of prosecuting the offender. If you do not want to report a crime, often rape crisis centers can file a "third party report" for you so that the police get information they can use in investigations of similar crimes. Rape crisis centers will not pressure you to report. Also, many states have Crime Victims Compensation funds which will pay for medical costs accrued to victims as a result to crimes against their persons. If you feel embarrassed about making a call to your rape crisis center, remember it is entirely confidential. You deserve the kind of support and guidance they can offer you.

For the problem of assault against women, some communities now have crisis lines and battered women's shelters (or networks of "safe houses") which can effectively protect a woman from further abuse. They can often also help with relocation, financial aid, legal issues and the like. The phone numbers for either the rape crisis center or battered women's crisis line should be in the phone book, but if they are hard to locate or you aren't sure if you have them in your community, call your mental health crisis line. They should have emotional support information and resources for you.

VII. Showing Concern for Others' Rights

As we move about the public world, we will probably be confronted with situations where someone else is being hassled, treated rudely, or needs aid. It's easy to just look the other way in situations, but we find that women who do pay attention and try to do something often feel better about themselves as a result. Again, maintaining our physical safety needs to be the first priority. But if we can be reasonably assured of our safety, we might want to consider doing things such as offering assistance to another person who is being harassed or taking the time to call the police if that's appropriate. When we see able-bodied people parking in a space that is clearly designated for handicapped people, it is reasonable—and helpful—to politely ask them if they realize that the space is reserved for handicapped people, and that their use of the space is unfair. If they don't move the car, see if you can have them towed.

If you frequent establishments that aren't accessible to the handicapped, ask the managers or owners if they realize this, and tell them you are sure handicapped people would like to patronize their establishments if they were accessible. You can also contact your local or state handicapped persons' rights commission to find out if the establishment is required by law to be accessible. Support of the accessibility-for-all movement through petition signing, letter writing, boycotting and demonstrating is extremely important.

PART FOUR

*

The High Costs of Low Self-Esteem

* 1 *

Introduction

What are the more common ways that low self-esteem manifests itself in the thinking patterns and behavior of American women today? And once low self-esteem affects us in a certain way, what are the further consequences for our self-esteem? These are the questions we address in this section.

In the first six chapters we look at six common negative thought patterns, or ways of thinking that result in negative feelings about the self, that are most common among women with low self-esteem.[1] To the women who have them, these thought patterns usually seem involuntary, as if they had a will of their own. However, we learned to think in ways that reinforce negative views of ourselves, and so we can unlearn these patterns, replacing them with ways of thinking that do not perpetuate our poor opinions of ourselves.

In the other chapters we look at how low self-esteem affects our attitudes and behavior toward our relationships, our life roles, our work, our emotions, our bodies, our sexuality, our futures and, finally, toward others. As we look at the myriad ways in which low self-esteem affects us, an important point to keep in mind is that the precise ways in which we manifest and act out our low self-esteem are determined in large part by our culture. For example, a woman in a culture that does not expect women to conform to ridiculous ideals of feminine beauty and slenderness might have low self-esteem, but she probably wouldn't manifest it by loathing her body, as women with low self-esteem in our culture often do. Similarly, a woman in a culture that does not value work as our culture does might have just as little self-worth as a woman in America, but she probably wouldn't feel driven to make up for it by proving herself through work. Our culture determines the specific ways that we will be affected by our low self-esteem, and our society benefits when we think and behave as the culture encourages us to do.

* 2 *

Can't Get This Out of My Mind: Black Clouds

Dear Ann Landers: For years readers have been unloading their pet peeves on you. Now it's my turn.

Nothing irks me so much as a person who says, "You look tired." In my book it is the same as saying, "You have a nose like a banana."

The message these people pretend to deliver is one of concern for your health. What they are really saying is, "You look beat-up and old. Are you falling apart?"

If you are NOT tired and someone says you look that way, you are bound to wonder if your face knows something you don't. At best, this message can dampen your spirits and ruin your day. Do you agree?—

Well-Rested in Detroit

Dear Detroit: I do indeed. "You look tired" is a bona fide downer. Telling a person he (or she) looks haggard will not encourage that person to get more rest. It will merely create depression.

—Ann Landers column, August 7, 1981.

Both Ann Landers and her correspondent from Detroit appear to have problems with Black Clouds. A Black Cloud is what a person creates when she takes a specific piece of criticism, insignificant mistake or passing comment and blows it up into a reflection of, or attack on, her overall self-worth. Black Clouds are common among women with low self-esteem.

A woman may be walking down the street, enjoying the nice day, when suddenly she trips on a crack in the sidewalk. "Look at what a klutz you are," she tells herself. "One of these days you're going to kill yourself." This is a Black Cloud. Contrast it with saying, "You almost fell there. You better watch where you're going." This is a common-sense reaction. The latter does not diminish the woman's feeling of self-worth or interrupt her enjoyment. The former does.

Any situation will do to begin a Black Cloud, even rudeness from a stranger such as a store clerk:

"Could you tell me if you have this in red?"

"Look for yourself, lady. What we got is all there on the rack."

Rather than be annoyed with the clerk's rudeness, a woman with a tendency toward Black Clouds most likely will take it as a reflection of her own worth. "What's wrong with me?" she wonders. "Don't I deserve to be treated with respect? Did I do or say something to make that clerk rude to me? Why is everyone always so rotten to me?" She takes responsibility for an incident that probably has nothing to do with her, and she, moreover, stews over it, losing all sight of its relative insignificance. In her mind, a major event has occurred, a major event that for that day becomes the basis of her self-esteem—or, rather, the lack thereof.

Black Clouds often begin with a kindly intended comment from a friend or an acquaintance, a comment such as "You look worn out today. Has something been troubling you? Is everything all right?" A woman given to creating Black Clouds will hear this not as the expression of concern it is meant to be, but rather as an expression of doubt about her ability to function: "She must think I'm a real mess, that I can't handle anything in my life. And I thought I looked okay today! Just goes to show how much I know." A small gesture of friendship is transformed into a huge blow to this woman's "house of cards" self-esteem.

Once a Black Cloud mushrooms in a woman's mind, she can react by wallowing in her worthlessness, thus giving others the impression that she is moody and withdrawn, an impression she probably does not want to give. Or she can defend herself vigorously against a nonexistent attack, only to find herself isolated due to what others see as her hypersensitivity. Rarely, however, will a woman with a Black Cloud ask for clarification ("What do you mean, 'is there anything wrong'?") or admit that there is some truth to her friend's observation ("Yeah, I am tired. I've been worried about getting laid off."). The stakes are simply too high. Of course, it is extremely unlikely that her friend, if asked for clarification, would respond by saying, "If you really want to know, I think you look terrible and are a real mess. I don't want anything to do with you anymore." Yet a woman with a tendency toward Black Clouds won't recognize how small the likelihood of getting such a response actually is. Once the Black Cloud has mushroomed, the put-down is as good as said, and it seems oddly comforting to assume the worst without ever hearing it voiced aloud.

Another reason women given to Black Clouds do not ask for clarification or recognize that some situations have nothing to do with them (maybe the store clerk hates his job, feels sick, or is always rude to everyone) is that they believe they can read minds. Convinced in their own hearts that they are flawed, inadequate and worthless, they know others see them that way, too. They *know* what others are really thinking. It doesn't occur to them that many people say exactly what they think. Nor does it occur to them that others may not be thinking about them at all:

> I did some typing and editing for a woman I really respect, and when I gave it to her, she didn't give me any feedback for a couple of days. I was sure she thought my work was terrible, that I'm a real moron, and I knew that she was telling everyone how stupid I was. For two days I felt terrible. Then, on the third day, she called me and said she had just read my work and that she liked it a lot. She was sorry she hadn't gotten to it earlier, but she had been too busy with other work. You know, until then it hadn't occurred to me that this woman might have had other things on her mind, other work to do. Because my work was in the forefront of my mind, I assumed it was in the forefront of her mind. All the terrible things she was thinking and saying about me—I manufactured them all.

Obviously, Black Clouds involve considerable egocentricity. Women who have them assume that judging them is the foremost priority in everyone else's life. This assumption is not only inaccurate, it also tends to limit the woman's ability to develop her own sense of worth, because she is too busy reacting to other's alleged judgments.

By manufacturing reasons to feel bad about themselves, women given to Black Clouds pass the blame for their feeling of worthlessness and inadequacy onto others. David Burns, a cognitive therapist, uses a technique to show his clients that their feelings are not controlled by other people's thoughts:

> You might remind yourself that other people's thoughts do not affect your mood one iota. I have demonstrated this to patients by telling them I will think two thoughts about them for fifteen seconds each. One thought will be extremely positive, and the other will be intensely negative and insulting. They are to tell me how each of my thoughts affects them. I close my eyes and think, "Jack here is a fine person and I like him." Then I think, "Jack is the worst person in Pennsylvania." Since Jack doesn't know which thought is which, they have no effect on him![1]

Burns's comments need clarification. Because what others think of us typically affects how they behave toward us, we can sometimes make fairly accurate guesses about what they are feeling toward us—especially with people to whom we are close. From experience we know that when they can't keep eye contact with us, or when their hands stroke their throat, they are feeling uneasy. Yet they may not be feeling uneasy about anything having to do with us. Again, women prone to Black Clouds do not ask "What's going on with you?" or "How are you feeling?" Instead, they take their friends' familiar gestures as a reflection on them and are off and running with statements such as "I'm making this person feel bad; I'm a bad person," without ever having checked out their perceptions. Huge misunderstandings between people who know each other well can result from the lack of communication and subsequent blaming ("His feeling bad makes me feel bad") that characterize Black Clouds.

Shy people are particularly susceptible to pessimistic speculation about what other people are really thinking. If someone approaches a shy woman at a party and she responds in a perfectly normal but less than witty manner, and the person moves on to meet other people (which, after all, is the purpose of the party), she assumes the person found her to be stupid and boring. She pulls deeper into her shell, allegedly in response to the other person's reaction. No one has said to her, "Are you ever a loser—you just blew that social interaction. Go sit down in that chair and just be quiet for the rest of the night." Again, it was her own judgment which prompted her behavior and made her feel bad.

Women given to Black Clouds generally tend to be excessively concerned with what other people think of them (or what they think others think of them). They also tend not to be able to distinguish between criticism of their specific behavior and attacks on their overall worth. Potentially helpful suggestions are never heard because the intent behind the criticism becomes exaggerated and distorted. When someone interprets specific criticism as an attack on her overall worth, self-esteem can crumble in an instant, and the potential for learning is destroyed. A woman who is unable to hear specific criticism for what it is will not be able to take that criticism, much less take it to heart and learn from it. Hence, her self-concept will remain static, and she will delude herself into thinking that any recognition or acknowledgment of her human failings entails a drastic and permanent drop in self-esteem.

The reverse of a Black Cloud is a Silver Cloud, and it, too, is the result of the same tendencies. Just as what a woman interprets as a negative response from others can ruin her day, what she sees as positive responses can "make" her day. Not only does this leave her vulnerable to insincere flattery, it also puts her self-esteem on a wild rollercoaster ride, depending on who she happens to talk with or what chance experience she has on a given day.

> My boss knows he can manipulate me, and I really resent it. He knows I
> don't like to work late, so if he needs me to, he will pick at me all day, be
> very critical until I feel utterly worthless, and then at the end of the day he
> asks me to stay late. I do it to make up for what a creep I am. Then, after
> he gets what he wants, I am the world's greatest assistant. Funny, but that
> feels good to me, so we keep on playing this game with each other.

This woman has little sense of herself as a worker beyond what her boss tells her she is worth. His criticism precipitates a Black Cloud ("I can't do anything right") and his praise precipitates a Silver Cloud ("I must be competent because he is happy with me"). Until she has a stable sense of herself separate from his opinion, he will successfully manipulate her.

Feedback from others is important to keep our self-perceptions realistic. But there's a difference between being open to taking other people's opinions into account and being entirely defined by them. Moreover, there's a difference between the valid opinions of some and the off-the-mark opinions of others. If a woman exaggerates others' comments and opinions into Black Clouds or Silver Clouds so that they are the definitions of her worth, then her peace of mind will be very unstable. She will always be at the mercy of other's sometimes uninformed or biased opinions of her. Sustained self-esteem is impossible under such conditions.

BLUEPRINTS FOR CHANGE

I. THOUGHT STOPPING

A negative thought pattern, once one has started in our minds, seems to control us. We often say we can't help thinking this way. You can stop, and you can prove it to yourself through this standard behavior modification technique.

Enlist another person to help you with this exercise. You are to sit back in a chair, get very comfortable and close your eyes. Your friend will read the following instructions and lead you in the exercise. *You* do *not* read this exercise beyond this point; what follows are instructions for your friend.

> Tell your friend to think her negative thought—whatever comes into her mind. Tell her to really get into it, to think very hard about it until she really feels terrible about herself.
>
> When you trust she is really immersed in her negative thought and really feeling rotten, pick up a book and slam it down on a table as hard as you can. As the book slams down, yell *"STOP."* Your friend will be startled and will probably exhibit nervous behavior like laughing, clutching her throat or even crying. Don't worry—she is fine.
>
> Ask her now if she stopped thinking her negative thought, if she was able to suddenly snap out of it. When she says "yes" or "of course," point out to her that her thoughts do not have wills of their own, that they can be controlled. She does not need to be controlled by them.

You will most likely have to do this exercise half a dozen times to get the system down. Then you will be able to do it for yourself by simply saying to yourself, loudly and firmly, "STOP," when a negative thought pattern tries to take over. Once you say "STOP," it is important to replace your previous thought with a different one. Further instructions follow in each section.

Exercises such as this may seem silly and trifling. But this simple little technique does work and can make a large difference.

Again, practice the sudden STOP technique. When you catch yourself in a pattern of self-deprecation, saying to yourself "Oh, there I go again running myself down, I'd better stop" will not be effective. A firm and loud "STOP" will give you the physical sensation of pulling yourself up short, and is the most effective method of snapping out of a pattern in progress.

II. THOUGHT-STOPPING MODIFICATION FOR BLACK CLOUDS

When someone makes a specific comment which you transform into a Black Cloud, use the thought-stopping technique, then immediately tell yourself that you are not a mind reader and need to ask for clarification. Here is an example of the process:

> Your neighbor comes over for a cup of coffee. When she enters your house, she looks around and asks in passing, "Is something wrong, have you not been feeling well? The house doesn't look as organized as it usually does." Instead of thinking, "She thinks I'm a pig," and saying to her, "Yeah, I guess it looks messy today," or "There's nothing wrong—what makes you

think that? The house looks fine, just like it always does," try using the thought-stopping technique and responding differently:

> She thinks I'm a pig. STOP. She asked about the house and inquired about my well-being. She didn't say I'm a pig. I can't read her mind, so I need to ask her why she is asking.

"Oh, you notice the house looks different today. How so?"
"Well, it looks like my house. You're such a neat person and I feel like such a slouch next to you. I just thought you may have been busy or sick, you know, not had as much time for it as usual. That's all."

Not only is there no value judgment against you in her statement, you find out the concern came more out of her own sense of inadequacy, which has nothing to do with you. When we create a Black Cloud, we act as if everything someone says or feels is a valid reflection of us. If the criticism is real, then the same approach will work:

"Oh, you notice the house looks different today. How so?"
"Well, it looks like my house after your son has been over playing with my kids. I just can't keep up with it."

> She thinks I'm a terrible, irresponsible mother. STOP. I don't know what she is trying to say—this is very roundabout, confusing, so I'd better ask.

"I'm not following you. You're saying there is a problem with the way Bill plays at your house?"
"Well, yes. He's really messy and he leaves without picking anything up, and now my kids are following his example and it's getting out of hand. I get sick of reminding them."

> She hates Bill and thinks he's a bad influence on the kids. STOP. She didn't say she hates Bill, but she does seem to be having a hard time handling this situation. I'd better find out why.

"Have you reminded Bill or made it clear to him that if he is going to play at your house, he needs to be responsible for picking up after himself?"
"No—I feel funny doing that. He's not my kid, and my kids probably aren't perfect over here. I like them playing together, except for this one thing, and I've just felt hesitant to say anything."
"Please don't be on my account. I'll support you, even if you get cross with him about it. He does need to be reminded of a lot of things, and I want him to be courteous when he goes to other people's houses. Feel free to set those limits with him, and if it doesn't work, then let me know. I want to know if he continues to be messy at your house."

"Okay, I feel better about it now—it isn't that big a deal. You know with so many kids, the little things sometime get you down."

By short-circuiting the Black Cloud, you can understand the person's point more clearly and use your energy to resolve the issue rather than wasting it on self-denigrating thinking. Sometimes people do not say exactly what they mean. We all need help from time to time in expressing our worries, concerns, feelings, etc. It is not always the case that the other person is judging us or thinking horrible thoughts about us. We do a great disservice to both ourselves and others by always assuming so.

III. RUDENESS FROM STRANGERS

When you create a Black Cloud from a stranger's comment or behavior (remember the example of the rude store clerk), use the thought-stopping technique and find a replacement statement, in your own words and style, to the effect of:

"What's wrong with me—why was she so rude? STOP. I have no way of knowing what is on her mind. Furthermore, I *don't care* because as far as I know, it has nothing to do with me."

The point here is that we cannot "work through" every comment with every human being we encounter. The responsibility is ours not to create Black Clouds. We make them happen; other people do not. So when there is no opportunity for clarification, we must tell ourselves that we are autonomous enough to know that it is likely the other person's problem and therefore no reflection on us. Strangers particularly may find a request for clarification to be an imposition, and we can never be assured, even with friends, of receiving a totally honest answer. The ultimate decisions about the significance of brief encounters is ours; we decide what impact they are to have on our self-esteem.

IV. CONDITIONAL LOVE

Can you think of any areas where love was conditional for you as a child? Schoolwork? Sports? Arts? Relationships with siblings and parents? If you feel love was conditional, try to think of three areas of experience where love was withdrawn most often.

Are there any analogous situations in your life now where you feel more prone to create Black Clouds? Think about this very carefully. If you are keeping a journal, do some writing about some specific childhood experiences and try to think if they have been relived in adulthood. If you can pinpoint some problem areas, then add to your

"STOP": "I know this is a loaded area for me. This other person doesn't know he (or she) is 'pushing my buttons.' I need to know more about what he (or she) is saying."

V. THE POWER OF WORDS

Sometimes specific words set off Black Clouds. Thinking back on those childhood experiences which have carried over into adulthood, are there any words which were used often to indicate the withdrawal of love? Again, think carefully. It is not unlikely they are related to (or the same as) the negative labels we discussed in Part Two. What are these words?

Can you tell the people you are close to that those words are very difficult for you to hear? If they want to tell you something about yourself that relates to those words, give them suggestions for descriptive yet not so emotionally laden words to use instead.

If you encounter the word(s) with either someone close to you or someone not close to you and it triggers feelings of worthlessness in you, use the thought-stopping technique:

"I'm not worth very much. STOP. He just described me as being lazy, which always has made me feel absolutely terrible about myself. Being lazy is not the worst thing in the world. If I want to change this, then I can ask his opinion then I will decide for myself."

Or, in the case of someone not close to you:

"I'm not worth very much. STOP. He doesn't know how strongly I react to the word 'lazy.' It means something different to him. I can either tell him how I'm feeling right now, or decide for myself whether or not I've been lazy and what I want to do about it."

In this way we control our own self-concept. It is not at the mercy of unintentional or passing judgments.

* 3 *

Can't Get This Out of My Mind: Critical Tapes

> In a real sense through our own self-talk we are either in the construction business or the wrecking business.
>
> —Dorothy Corkille Briggs, *Celebrate Yourself*

In the mind of someone with low self-esteem, powerful, negative statements about the self or equally powerful and negative visual images often run constantly. We call these Critical Tapes, and they are common cognitive manifestations of low self-esteem. Many women describe these tapes as "parasites" or "monsters," and it often seems that they cannot be stopped. As opposed to Black Clouds, no external event is needed to set a Critical Tape off. A woman may be thinking relatively happy thoughts, or no particular thought at all, when a Critical Tape begins to unwind:

> "I'm so ugly I should be in a circus freak show. . . ."
> "Everyone hates me—I don't know anyone who cares. . . ."
> "I'm so lazy I never finish anything. . . ."

Patterns of thinking such as these often have their origins in one or two deeply imbedded and inaccurate labels left over from childhood. Because they have been in her consciousness so long, a woman with Critical Tapes would probably never question their validity. To do so would be akin to questioning that the grass is green:

> For years I have told myself what an oaf I am. You know, I think of myself as this really big, heavy lumbering person. I am tall—five feet eight—but I only weigh 126 pounds, so I simply couldn't be that massive. I think I've finally convinced myself of that.

If the Critical Tape concerns a less tangible aspect of the self, it might be harder to counteract, but not impossible.

> I've always told myself that no one likes me. I go out, but I couldn't really figure out why people wanted to spend time with me. I assumed no one really cared about me. Then I had my thirtieth birthday and everyone made a big deal out of it. I guess I wasn't as unpopular as I thought, but it makes me think, if I stopped acting like I was, maybe I'd have even more friends.

Self-punishment is the primary function of Critical Tapes. Any woman can very effectively make herself miserable with them. She becomes a name-calling, self-denigrating self-scourge, always ready to dash any hopes of enjoyment or peace of mind.

Critical Tapes do not always take the form of "I am . . ." statements, or any other verbal form. Visual images of dead animals, horrific accidents, the death of a loved one, violent crimes, blood or excrement serve the purpose of making oneself miserable just as well. Behind the upsetting image often is a verbal statement about the self. For example, believing she is bad, a woman may make herself feel bad by conjuring up disturbing images. Chances are that they appear when a glimmer of a happy thought tries to intrude.

Previous mistakes or unpleasant experiences from the past frequently live on as Critical Tapes. A woman reruns a scene in her head and ruminates about how it should have gone differently, as if the outcome influences her inherent worth:

> It was against the rules to go off campus when I was in junior high, yet everyone did it. I was real timid, but one day my friends, who usually didn't do this type of thing, decided to go, and they cajoled me into going along. All we did is go to a nearby shopping center and buy gum, but I was so nervous about getting caught that I wet my pants in the checkout line. No one said anything, but it was still humiliating. I think about that incident an awful lot.

Much time and energy is wasted in rerunning horrific scenes from our past. Even if the Critical Tape concerns a fairly recent incident, usually not much can be done about it now. Everyone at one time or another has said something offensive or stupid, done something mortifying (such as throwing up at a party or falling down in public), or generally made a fool of herslf to some degree. But whereas many people eventually forgive themselves their embarrassments and learn to forget or laugh about them, a woman with Critical Tapes makes her embarrassments the cornerstone of her self-esteem. Even years afterward, she may continue to relive a painful and humiliating experience, and it overshadows what is happening for and to her in the present.

Critical Tapes can serve many purposes. For example, they can help us not deal straightforwardly with rejection:

> Every time someone leaves me, I refuse to listen to why. I figure, they are going anyway, so what's the use. Over and over again I tell myself, "See, no one will ever love you, I told you so." I don't know the specific reasons for any of the rejections—I can't bear it—but sometimes, a few months later, I do start to wonder just what made that person leave.

This woman might learn how to behave in a way that does not invite the dreaded rejection. But like an old friend, her Critical Tape reassures her that "all is right" in her world and she does not have to face the rejection. She would rather listen to herself than hear what others have to say.

Misguidedly, many believe that Critical Tapes actually help them to learn from their mistakes or to correct their flaws. Because Critical Tapes undermine a person's belief that she can be different, they are not as much motivation for change as one might think. To constantly repeat old, self-deprecating statements or replay scenes of bad experiences (probably not as unique to the individual as she believes) is far different from honest, searching self-appraisal, and can actually prevent it. Rollo May observes:

> . . . the emphasis upon self-condemnation is like whipping a dead horse: it achieves a temporary life, but it hastens the eventual collapse of the dignity of the person. The self-condemning substitute for self-worth provides the individual with a method of *avoiding open and honest confronting of his problems of isolation and worthlessness,* and makes for a pseudo-humility rather than an honest humility of one who seeks to face his situation realistically and do what he can constructively. (Emphasis added.)[1]

As an example of how an obsessive and exclusive concern with self-condemnation can preclude honest and open confrontation with the real problems at hand, imagine this scene: A woman whose friend has been imposing upon her is asked directly by that friend whether she feels "put upon." Instead of honestly saying "Yes," she says, "Oh no, don't worry about it. I really don't mind." Her Critical Tape ("I can't do anything right—what's wrong with me?") begins playing over and over. An honest confrontation with the specific situation ("I had my chance and I could have been far more direct with her. Why didn't I tell her how I feel?") could have led to a solution (such as taking an assertiveness training course). By contrast, the Critical Tapes just drain energy, reinforce the problematic behavior and diminish self-esteem.

"So, who's happy?" is some women's response when their Critical Tapes are pointed out to them. "Everyone has those thoughts." To a small extent that is true—we all have deprecated ourselves over specific situations. But Critical Tapes tend to run repeatedly and, once started, can seem almost incessant. Happiness exists in relative states, but the less frequently Critical Tapes obliterate positive thoughts, the happier we will be.

BLUEPRINTS FOR CHANGE

I. IDENTIFY YOUR CRITICAL TAPE

What is your critical Tape? What were your childhood negative labels? Are they related? Was the label ever an accurate description of you? If there are other people to ask (siblings, aunts, uncles, friends, neighbors, even parents) about its accuracy, consider taking that risk. Is it an accurate description of you now? Are there other people's opinions you trust more?

II. STOPPING CRITICAL TAPES

Now that you've identified your Critical Tape and can recognize it when it begins to drone on, run it, say "STOP" to it and then replace it *immediately* with a more positive and accurate statement. Here are some examples:

"I'm so ugly, I can't stand myself."

"STOP. Well, I do like my hands, they are long and slender and I make nice things with them."

OR

"STOP. Maybe I don't look so good today. Other days I look just fine."

"How could anybody love me—I'm such a terrible person."

"STOP. Being awful isn't the point—I'm not awful. How can anybody love me when I hate myself like this? That's the question I should be asking."

OR

"STOP. There's another inaccurate statement. _____ loves me and has really known me over the years. Maybe I don't understand why (I could ask specifically), but that doesn't change the fact that I'm loved."

Do *not* engage in a dialogue with yourself once you have replaced a Critical Tape. When first using thought stopping, it is not unusual for women to rebut their replacement thoughts. These second-wind responses are not so cleverly disguised Critical Tapes. To avoid them, have a storehouse of pleasant images and memories or value-neutral topics ("What am I going to have for dinner tonight?" or "I wonder if there is anything good on TV?") to concentrate on immediately after you've used your replacement thought. If a variation on your Critical Tape sneaks in before you can switch to pleasant or value-neutral thought, then begin again. Say "STOP," replace the thought and think about something else.

III. UPSETTING VISUAL IMAGES

If you have a Critical Tape which is a visual image as opposed to an "I am . . ." statement, carefully describe what it is, perhaps in writing. "I am . . ." statements are sometimes easier to recognize. Try to focus on which image makes you feel unhappy or worthless.

When you recognize the troubling image in the course of daily life, stop yourself and replace it with a calming, pleasant *image*. One woman used the fields of flowers shown in the film *Doctor Zhivago*. Have two or three scenes which have meaning to you (the view of the ocean on one of your vacations, your new kittens, a dramatic sunset) and focus intently on them when your upsetting image appears. It will take practice and time to find the most effective pleasant scenes for you. Choose pleasant scenes which have nothing to do with your Critical Tape. For instance, a woman who has trouble with images of run-over animals should probably not try to use a live-animal image. Upsetting images tend to creep up, so be sure to stop them immediately and crowd them out by concentrating on an image which gives you pleasure.

IV. PREVIOUS MISTAKES

If your Critical Tape is a rerun of an old, unpleasant experience, use thought stopping and replace it with a statement like:

> "STOP. That was a long time ago. Everyone makes mistakes like that. There is nothing I can do about it now. It was bad enough living through it the first time, but reliving it now, by choice, is a waste of my time and energy and I am not going to do it."

OR

> "STOP. I will learn from that mistake whatever I can. Dredging it up again is not helpful; I cannot change what happened. Instead, I choose to

put my time and energy into correcting my behavior so it won't happen again. I like the fact that I can do that."

Then *immediately* switch to a pleasant or value-neutral thought.

V. HONEST SELF-APPRAISAL

Ask a trusted friend for feedback about your specific Critical Tape. For example:

"Hey, look at my body. Now, would you describe me as a big woman?"

"On a scale of one to ten, how would you rate my competence in everyday life? I mean, do you think I barely scrape by, do okay or sometimes do more than okay?"

"Do you think I'm unlovable? Tell me honestly."

In our Self-esteem Enhancement Groups, the members received some very helpful and interesting responses when they risked exposing their Critical Tapes. Although the tapes seem very private to the woman with them, they turn out not to be so secret. Through a woman's attitudes and behavior others were usually aware that she disliked herself in this way, even though she had never said it out loud.

Whether those asked for feedback had recognized the self-doubt or not, they usually offered a different perspective than the tape. Some common reactions were: "I think you are *tall*, but that's not *big* to me. I think you're really well-proportioned for your height." "I think you have a lot to deal with . . . and given all that, I think you do very well. I don't know if I could do as well. Perhaps if you got less excited in a crisis, could try to stay calmer, you wouldn't feel so inadequate." "I think *you* doubt that you're lovable, and until that changes, it probably won't happen for you, but yes, I think you're lovable." In very few cases was the punitive nature of the Critical Tapes confirmed.

In response, many of those asked for feedback began talking about their own self-doubts and invited the group member to give her feedback in return. When this happened, everyone increased the accuracy of their self-concept to some degree. Furthermore, the conversation became part of the replacement thought for the Critical Tapes. Once exposed, a new arsenal of contradictory and informed perspectives was obtained to eradicate the self-denigrating tape.

* 4 *

Can't Get This Out of My Mind: Chronic Comparisons to Others

> and here we are again, folks, a table of women, seven of us, and the
> first thing i do . . . is look around at all of you to see who is prettier
> than i. my lover used to say how i was prettier than the other women
> in my women's liberation group and i would feel better while feeling
> worse and i wish it weren't a consideration in anybody's mind includ-
> ing mine, because it drives me crazy and actually prevents me from
> enjoying social situations.
>
> —Alta, "Pretty"

Many women with low self-esteem constantly compare themselves to others. A woman with this thought pattern sees the world as a rigid hierarchy, and spends a good deal of her time and energy figuring out how she rates in comparison to those around her. Having no sense of her inherent worth, her level of self-esteem fluctuates wildly. It rises when she is around people she compares herself favorably against, but it falls when she is around those against whom she feels she doesn't measure up.

It would be practically impossible to go through life without ever comparing ourselves to others. Indeed, much important information about ourselves and how we fit into the world is gained by looking at ourselves in comparison to others. If we did not compare ourselves to others, we would not be able to make statements such as "I am tall," "I am a good swimmer" or "I am smart." Moreover, comparisons to others can be beneficial. By comparing ourselves to others who possess traits and principles we admire, or who have achieved things we want to achieve, we can be inspired to live up to our goals and ideals and may also be able to get information that will help us do so.

Comparisons are not beneficial when they become habitual. The problem for many women with low self-esteem is not that they occasionally compare themselves to selected others, it's that they compare themselves to everyone they encounter and they do so all the time. For the woman who chronically compares, comparisons are never-ending. She will go to great lengths to find reason to feel bad about herself:

> When I go to a party, I'll spot a woman with great-looking earrings, or something else equally trivial, and I'll focus on that and will immediately feel rotten. She can be a real blob, have horns growing out of her head and bad breath, but all I'll be able to see are those terrific earrings. And what I'll think is, *anyone with earrings like that has got to have it all over me.*

A further problem for women who chronically compare is that when they compare, they typically do so with only one purpose in mind: determining how others are different than they, and then using the differences they perceive as the basis for deciding whether the other person is superior or inferior, better or worse, than they. A woman who chronically compares usually does not look at others with an eye toward the way they are similar to her. She looks only at the way in which they are different, and then assigns herself and the others a rank accordingly:

> When I meet another woman, I don't look at her and say to myself, "Hey, she's got brown hair and a big nose like me." I automatically zoom in on the things that set us apart—like her being skinnier or my being smarter than her. If she's skinnier, I feel like she's better than me. So then I focus on being smarter, because having an edge in smarts will balance out the edge she has in skinniness, and I need that edge or I'll feel really bad about myself.

Still another problem for women who chronically compare is that the value judgments they are always making about themselves and others are usually completely unsubstantiated. A woman who chronically compares is incapable of looking at someone very different from herself and thinking, "So that person is more (or less) accomplished than I. Big deal. That doesn't mean she is better (or worse) than I." In the mind of a woman who chronically compares, there is no room for the possibility that two very different people or things can have the exact same worth.

Chronic comparisons are encouraged by the methods of hierarchical thinking that are taught in our culture. In our culture differences between people are magnified to obscure commonalities and these magnified differences are then used to rank people as better or worse, superior or inferior. From the earliest age, we are taught to compare and rate ourselves and others in such areas as athletics, academics, material wealth, job status, and sex appeal. Were ours a world in which equality prevailed, there would not be such an emphasis on ranking. But hierarchical thinking and constant ranking is necessary to preserve the status quo in a world where people have been rigidly divided into distinct and separate castes on the basis of race, sex, class, intelligence, education, and other factors.

For some women, the childhood home was a place where they learned not to be swayed by the larger culture's constant encouragement to always compare and rank. But others unfortunately grew up in homes where constant comparing and ranking was a way of life. Some women grew up in homes where the parents were obsessively concerned with not just "keeping up with the Joneses," but outdoing the Joneses in order to prove their superiority to them. Others grew up in homes where the parents were unable to keep up with the Joneses, and bitterly lamented their inferiority.

Actress Grace Kelly grew up in a home where her parents made constant comparisons between her and her sisters. No matter what she did, it was never enough:

> She was sandwiched between two sisters—Peggy, who was her father's favorite daughter, and Lizanne, the baby of the family. . . . No one supposed that little Grace would amount to anything, but she had other plans. Even when she had won an Academy Award for her performance in "The Country Girl," her father rather unfeelingly told a reporter, "I always thought it would be Peggy. Anything Grace could do, Peggy could do better."[1]

Chronic comparisons are particularly problematic for women, because when we women compare ourselves to others, we more often than not see ourselves as the inferior ones. G. W. Allport states that inferiority feelings arise when a person feels herself to be "deficient in her personal equipment," and his work shows that women are particularly susceptible to persistent inferiority feelings. Among the college students he studied, 50 percent of the women and 39 percent of the men reported persistent feelings of physical inferiority; 57 percent of the women and 52 percent of the men reported feeling socially inferior; and 61 percent of the women but only 29 percent of the men felt intellectually inferior. Overall, 90 percent of the women reported feeling inferior in some area, and only when it came to the area of morality did most women not feel inferior.[2]

When a woman compares herself unfavorably to others, she runs a good chance of feeling nothing but envy. This envy has a tendency to be acted out against those she compares herself to, as she needs everyone to feel as weak and inadequate as she does. Gloria Steinem explains:

> . . . the women most likely to police others into weakness are those who feel themselves, rightly or wrongly, to be the least strong or who have the lowest self-esteem. That lack of self-esteem leads to a voracious need for approval and recognition from others. . . . Unfortunately, no amount of praise or credit from others can make up for the corroding nonconfidence and self-hatred within the person herself. On the contrary, any prize seems to be turned to ashes by the very fact that its winner sees herself as worthless; thus in her eyes, the prize becomes worthless too.
>
> And that leaves only one recourse. Since the self-hating woman cannot achieve the recognition she craves (at least, not short of a very basic and long-term change in self-image), then by god, no other woman is going to have it either.[3]

Women are fairly adept at tolerating and even understanding weakness in other people. This is not an inherent skill: It is the function of so much compulsory training to nurture others. Clearly, it is a skill that needs to be balanced by supporting each other's strengths as well. Moreover, we need to be able to recognize our respective strengths and weaknesses as natural without ranking them in totally contrived hierarchies which ultimately diminish everyone's self-esteem.

But not all women who compare themselves unfavorably to others feel envy. Some women who see themselves as worse off than others feel a sort of moral purity as a result and use this as a means of propping up whatever self-esteem they have. In their minds the worse off you are in some respect (financially, for example) the better a person you are; and the better off you are in some respect, the worse a person you are:

> This new woman came to work in our office—the filing department for a big corporation—and she wore tailored suits and jewelry and had what seemed to the rest of us a real upper-class air. We started putting her down for being so privileged and slumming with us. We thought we had it all over her—we'd worked hard to support our families, we all had lots of troubles we shared with each other. Our opinion was that she was pale, a big zero in life experience and "soul" compared to us. We looked down on her until we found out that she'd been placed at this job through the battered women's shelter, that she and her three young kids were living

there and her husband had tried to kill her. We didn't feel so superior any
more.

Comparisons to others are often hastily made and based on inadequate
information.

Women who come off well in their own estimation when they chronically compare themselves to others don't do much better in terms of
self-esteem than those who feel inferior. First, many women who see
themselves as better than others can't experience any feeling of superiority without immediately feeling guilty. No matter how well a woman
masks her low self-esteem with exterior bravado, underneath she's
likely to have a dread of being conceited. If she meets someone and
thinks, "I'm better (or prettier, smarter, more successful)," her next
private thought may well be, "Wait a minute—who do you think you
are? How dare you think you are better than someone else! That's a
terrible thing to think!" One momentary feeling of superiority is instantly squelched by guilt and moral condemnation.

Self-esteem that's based on superiority is bound to be shaky. To be
sure, a woman may be able to derive plenty of self-esteem from the fact
that she's the prettiest woman on the block, the wittiest conversational-
ist at the party and the most accomplished person in her crowd. But
since comparisons are never-ending, there's always the chance that
she'll find another even prettier, wittier and more accomplished woman
to compare herself to. The actress, Jill Clayburgh, for example, could
compare herself to millions of women and come out looking good. But
to whom does Clayburgh compare herself? One of the few women
above her in the hierarchy of stars, as Clayburgh explains:

> People think about me, "This wonderful lucky woman, she's got it all."
> But gee, that's how I feel about Meryl Streep. I'm always thinking, here's
> this neurotic mess who's never going to get another job.[4]

The healthy alternative to chronic comparisons to others is to make
note of the differences between us and others and then let them go. A
judgment need not follow. There is a world of difference between saying, "She seems so happy in that relationship—I wish I had a relationship like that. Well, maybe it'll happen for me someday," and saying,
"I'm such a jerk—I could never be in a relationship like that and I'll
never be happy," or "She's cheap—that's how she got him or her."
Other people's successes and failures are not reflections of our worth.

BLUEPRINTS FOR CHANGE

I. EARLY COMPARISONS

Does a time stick out in your mind when you were compared favorably as a child to other children? How did you feel? Can you remember a time when you were compared unfavorably to other children? How did you feel? Within your family, did your parents make value-laden comparisons between you and your siblings? How much is comparison to others a source of your self-esteem today?

II. THOUGHT STOPPING

Pay special attention to your comparative statements. Immediately use thought stopping. Replace the comparison/negative thought *about* your self with a comparison *with yourself.* For example:

> "That mother really disciplines her child well. I wish I could do that. I'm such a bad mother. Why can't I be more like her? What's wrong with me?"

> "STOP. Well, I'm getting better at recognizing this problem and taking some action. That is really good."

OR

> "STOP. Remember how I used to react to his fussing when he was an infant. I have learned much self-control and am getting better at it."

OR

> "STOP. Maybe if I asked her for some ideas on discipline, she might be able to help me along in this. And undoubtedly, there are some ideas I can share with her. What have I got to lose?"

If you still persist in your comparative statements, then use the question, "So what?" as your replacement thought.

> "She's so petite, next to her I feel like an Amazon—I wish I could be feminine like her."

> "She's so petite. STOP. So what?"

Then immediately switch to value-neutral thoughts which involve no comparisons: Plan your next vacation, what you would like to do on the weekend, what you will have for dinner tonight. Do not entertain any responses to "So what?"

III. QUESTIONING THE VALIDITY OF COMPARISONS

If you find you are comparing yourself incessantly to one other person, ask yourself if your lives are truly comparable. How are your lives similar? Different? How much of her background do you know about? If you are making comparisons in a specific area, do you understand how her success in that area affects other parts of her life? If appropriate: Can you ask her how she came to be so successful and what advice she has for you?

* 5 *

Can't Get This Out of My Mind: Expectations of Perfection

> Having to be absolutely right all of the time makes us feel wrong all of the time.
>
> —Theodore Isaac Rubin
> *Compassion and Self-Hate*

Many women with low self-esteem look at themselves and their lives with expectations of perfection. A woman demanding perfection of herself measures everything she does by what was not accomplished rather than by what was. Furthermore, she shows a tendency for all-or-nothing thinking. In her mind, if she is not perfect, then she must be utterly worthless; there is no middle ground. In this way, she robs herself of both the enjoyment of what she has accomplished and her self-esteem.[1]

Expectations of perfection can begin during childhood in a variety of ways. If parents had standards of perfection for their daughter and she was eager to please them, then it is likely she would have internalized their perfectionist standards in order to please herself as an adult. And if parents labeled their little girl "perfect," then as an adult she will probably believe she is nothing unless she lives up to this expectation:

> My parents kept on telling me I was the daughter they always wanted, that I was perfect and that other kids were not as good as I was. I believed that for years until it finally sank in that I was lonely, estranged from everyone but my parents and that I really wasn't perfect at anything, no matter how hard I tried. I was making myself miserable until, finally, I found some other things I wanted to be besides perfect.

The process by which expectations of perfection are passed on is illustrated by the classic example of the girl who comes home to proudly show her parents that she got eight out of ten correct on a math test. Instead of sharing her joy or asking her more about the test, her parents ask, perhaps harshly, "So why did you miss two answers?" She *should* be able to get all ten right. If this or similar scenes are repeated enough times, the child not only internalizes the expectations of perfection in order to please her parents, she also learns to distrust her own sense of accomplishment and thus to look to others for confirmation of her worth.

For most things in life, there is no uniform standard for what is perfect. Popular culture, however, belies this. Myriad self-help books, diet books, "beauty systems" and exercise programs instruct in the ways of becoming more perfect, and endless products are advertised with the promise that they will make us more perfect. Our grading system in school is usually measured against a standard of perfection few people achieve. Most women shown in advertising look perfect. So what is wrong with us that we can't smell, perform or look perfect? Probably, there is absolutely nothing horribly wrong with us. But all of this input, along with early learning, can convince us that perfection is an attainable day-to-day reality and that, furthermore, those of us who fail to attain perfection are somehow unworthy.

Perfectionist thinking usually leads to belief in rigid "if-then" schemes. Advertisers tell us if we buy their products, then we will be perfect. Our education system tells us if we make good grades, then we have truly learned. When a woman's parents told her "if you please us, then you will be loved," they primed her for her own "if-then" scheme. Every woman develops her own "ifs," but the "thens" all tend to be variations on the themes of love, acceptance and power over one's life. Both as a child and an adult, the perfectionist tries to fulfill the conditions set by her "if" so that she can enjoy the "then." Here are just a few common "if-then" schemes devised by women in our groups:

"If I am really generous and nice and helpful, then everyone will like me."

"If I am beautiful and sexy, then I will never be alone."

"If I am really smart, then I will be valued."

"If I can make people laugh, then they won't dislike me or get angry with me."

"If I am supercompetent, then all career opportunities will be mine."

These schemes are problematic for many reasons, not the least being that they are not realistic. Often the "if" and the "then" are at odds. For every example we gave, we can think of a valid response which would shatter any illusion that perfection is a guarantee of success and happiness:

"Lots of people take advantage of generous people—they don't like them at all; they think they are foolish."

"Even beautiful, sexy people end up alone."

"Not everyone values intelligence, especially in women. A lot of people resent it."

"Everyone's idea of what's funny is different, and it is easy to unintentionally offend someone with certain types of humor."

"Promotions often have nothing to do with competence. There are such things as ageism, racism, religious and class persecution, and nepotism. There are no guarantees in the work world."

But most women who have invested heavily in their "key to perfection" would beg to differ. If they end up exploited, alone, resented, misunderstood and/or ignored (and who hasn't at some time in her life?), it is because they didn't try hard enough and weren't good enough. With a little more effort, with more success in the area of their "if," all will go well.

Certainly, we want to consider our own contribution to any success or failure, but perfectionists ignore the reality of the world by insisting on total responsibility for whatever happens to them. They allow themselves only one way to enhance their self-esteem (perfection) and feel guilty and worthless when things do not go well. If they could let go of control they never had and consider the influences of an imperfect world, they would give up the illusion of absolute power and gain peace of mind in the bargain.

One of the most problematic aspects of "if-then" schemes is that they frequently prevent a woman from developing a full personality and a wide range of interests. A woman who focuses most of her energy on being physically beautiful and well-dressed, for example, will likely miss out on opportunities to develop herself intellectually. A woman who concentrates almost exclusively on being brilliant in a specific field may not learn how to relax and have fun. And a woman who directs most of her attention to being the perfect lover, wife or mother, always focusing on other people's needs, will probably not have a chance to find out about her own needs.

Moreover, belief in "if-then" schemes often means a woman will postpone her "real" life until the condition set by the "if" has been fulfilled. Until the desired goal is met—whether it is the goal of getting a degree, getting married, having children, landing a great job—a woman may tell herself that her experiences don't really count because her real life has not yet begun. Women with weight problems, real or perceived, are particularly prone to this "before and after" type of thinking, as Marcia Millman observes:

> A woman [with a weight problem] may distance herself . . . from her present life. Because her unacceptable body comes to stand in her mind for everything wrong in her life, she also imagines that being fat is the cause of all her troubles. Her response is to cease living in the present. Instead, she turns all her thoughts and attentions to the future when she shall be slender. Her present self and her present life circumstances are discounted as temporary, preparatory, not the real thing. Real life, she reasons, will start after she loses weight.[2]

The kicker here is that when, if ever, a woman does achieve the condition set by her "if," she will probably find it is not all it was cracked up to be. Often, losing that weight, getting that job, finding that mate will not make the revolutionary difference in the long run that the woman imagined.

"If-then" schemes are especially problematic in intimate relationships, even though the perfectionist may protest that her idea of perfection is a successful relationship. Part of the problem is that the scheme exists *only* in the woman's head. People around her do not understand that they are supposed to love her unconditionally because she has a generous nature (along with a demanding nature) or that they are never supposed to reject her because she is beautiful. If they did know what was expected of them, they would probably choose to do without the generosity or beauty; the price is too high. And although the perfectionist secretly blames herself ("I'm not getting what I want because I haven't given enough" or "If I were more beautiful, if I lost some of this weight, he or she would have never left"), she may also lash out at the person who does not come through with the "then" part of the scheme:

> Sometimes the man I live with acts uninterested in me. He seems to go through these stages. No matter what I do, it doesn't make any difference. I really try hard to be more attractive and pleasing, but nothing works. I feel like dirt and I end up getting furious with him for making me feel that way.

What *really* makes this woman feel like dirt is her own expectation that she always has to be attractive and pleasing, combined with her delusion that her lover's moods are reflections of *her* worth. Most people do not expect perfection of others. Most, in fact, would be put off by someone perfect—and are put off by those who believe they must be perfect, or could be.

Many perfectionists fail to understand that they may be the only ones who expect them to live up to perfectionist standards they internalized long ago. They believe other people expect perfection of them when this is not usually the case. The woman quoted on page 310 believes it is her boyfriend who expects her to be attractive and pleasing all of the time and she resents him as a result. Only by realizing that impossible expectations come from themselves can perfectionists have a chance of successful relationships.

Expectations of perfection can be a barrier to genuine intimacy for other reasons as well. Many try to attain intimacy through achievement (their individual "if") rather than through vulnerability. They cannot understand how their imperfections could be endearing to anyone, and they are convinced that affection would be withdrawn if they were exposed. As a result, they present only limited parts of themselves. But as talents or beauty or intelligence are usually only part of what an intimate values, friends and lovers become frustrated in their attempts to know the deeper aspects of the perfectionist. Eventually, they quit trying and the relationship remains superficial, or they leave. The perfectionist once again has proof that she isn't perfect, she believes it is all her fault ("if only I had tried harder"). Natural feelings of confusion and sadness are compounded by feelings of absolute worthlessness.

Further complicating the perfectionist's life is the prominence of "shoulds" in her thinking. Ironically, "shoulds" are relied on to reduce gray areas of judgment and uncomplicate complicated matters:

> I work with this very rigid woman client who puts every experience or person she meets into one of two baskets: good or bad, according to how she thinks things should be. I'm trying to get her to give herself more baskets, like "doesn't really matter," or "pretty good," or "not so bad." Her life will be much easier and much less painful once she understands that the world isn't categorized so easily. She's missing a lot.

Perfectionists can be notorious bullies when imposing their "shoulds" on other people. It makes for anything but perfect harmony:

> I used to have this thing—it was sort of compulsive—about being honest. My family wasn't too honest, so I thought things would go better, that I would be real different from them if I was honest. So I was, all the time. No situation was too small to escape my honest assessment of it—out loud, of course. Not only was this obnoxious, it was wearing me out, although I was supposed to be happier because of it. Well, someone pointed out that

my ability to be direct was good, but not everyone valued that. Most people didn't really care about honesty, so I just threatened them or made them angry. That made sense, because it didn't matter how nice or reasonable or correct I was, it often didn't work out. So he suggested I look upon my honesty as a gift to give those who want it. He didn't suggest that I be dishonest with anyone else—just that I be quiet more.

One of the rationales behind the adoption of perfectionist standards and the subsequent imposition of "shoulds" is that they motivate us. But unrealistic and rigid standards don't inspire us to soar to our highest potential. As any perfectionist knows, expectations of perfection limit our knowledge about ourselves, narrow our options and generally make us miserable. In contrast, realistic standards, within our reach, can motivate us to try and, when met, can enhance our self-esteem.

Many differences exist between expectations of perfection and realistic standards. Women with expectations of perfection often feel compelled to be "the best" in virtually *all* areas as opposed to having realistic goals in a few carefully chosen areas. Although they put most of their time and energy into one particular "if," they must be perfect in all other ways as well. As a result, self-satisfaction is generally impossible for a woman with expectations of perfection. Because nothing in the world is ever perfect, her jobs are never done. She does not know the peace of mind that comes with completion of a task or attainment of a goal. She will either punish herself with perpetual dissatisfaction, or, as ironic as it might seem, she will never finish tasks, thus avoiding the judgment of "imperfect." This college counselor tells us:

> So many times I see these kids who were at the top of their class in high school. Then they come here and there is more competiton. Now they are somewhere in the middle. Some kids get involved in other things—sports, social groups, whatever, so the loss of academic status doesn't seem to bother them so much. Other kids can't stand it and drop out. It's sad for them—they're missing a good opportunity to learn that you can survive without being number one.

A woman with cerebral palsy told us she had learned from her experience that "if we are stuck spending all of our time and energy on our shoulds, then we never get to the coulds and the woulds, to the cans and the wills." Realistic standards can be re-energizing. "I can do it," we say to ourselves as we approach a realistic goal. Expectations of perfection focus much more on the statement "I can't do it," which drains energy.

The perfectionist is likely to become discouraged or eventually depressed and also bored. Because the perfectionist wants a guaranteed outcome of perfection before risking any experience, she will only do what she can do extremely well. Average human capacities being what they are, she will have few options.

The perfectionist also will have difficulty in making decisions because, as with most every other endeavor, every decision must be the right one; there is no room for mistakes:

> I learned a lot about my perfectionism last summer. I went out to the garden to get a zucchini for dinner. It wasn't a big deal—I was going to cut it up and fry it anyway, but I took *twenty* minutes picking the zucchini because I couldn't find the "right" one.

With realistic standards for ourselves, failure is unpleasant, but it is also a momentary state and, what is more, an opportunity from which we can learn something. To the perfectionist, failure is evidence of her worthlessness and can be devastating.

BLUEPRINTS FOR CHANGE

I. STOPPING PERFECTIONIST THINKING

Make some choices about exactly what you want to excel in. Pick three specific areas. When you worry about not being perfect in areas other than these, use thought stopping and tell yourself:

> "STOP. I will only worry about numbers one, two, and three. When I am satisfied with what I accomplished in those areas, perhaps I can worry about this. But for now, those are my priorities and the rest will have to wait or make do."

If you begin to obsess about your lack of perfection in the three designated areas, use thought stopping as well:

> "STOP. I am giving this my most sincere effort. What is important is that I am learning something and/or enjoying this while I try. I don't know what the final outcome will be, but it is no more important than the experience of trying to accomplish this."

You might also ask yourself if whatever you find unacceptable in yourself or your performance would be acceptable to you in *another person*. Chances are you would be satisfied with it. Why are you so much harder on yourself?

II. "IF-THEN" SCHEMES

Think and/or write about your "if-then" scheme. Is it realistic? Where did it come from? What happened when you failed? What kinds of fears have developed as a result? Has the "then" worked out for you? Is it everything you expected it to be? What has been sacrificed for the sake of your "if"? Is it worth it? Can you see yourself living without an "if-then" scheme?

III. CULTURAL PERFECTIONISM

Take one day and pay close attention to the media you encounter. How often is the lure of perfection held out to you in radio, television or print advertising? Counting the number of times you notice this in one day will illuminate the support this culture gives to our perfectionism.

If you are having problems with your self-esteem due to concern over imperfection, then give yourself a break. Avoid magazines featuring "perfect" bodies or contests measuring perfection. Don't watch "Mary Tyler Moore Show" reruns if (like Rhoda) you are concerned about having an imperfect single life. Avoid daytime TV advertising if you are concerned about being a perfect wife and mother. If the imperfect state of the world is getting you down, it is permissible to not watch the news for a week. With a vacation from this stimulus, you are much more likely to be able to find new energy that has not been wasted on worry or fear.

* 6 *

Can't Get This Out of My Mind:
Expectations of Doom

Nobody knows the trouble I've seen—and most of it never happened.

—Mark Twain

During the course of day-to-day life, all women are confronted with nuisances, ambiguous situations, and problems. Most of us do not eagerly anticipate such trials and tribulations; we simply meet them, rise to the occasion, and cope to one degree or another. Often in the process we learn something new about ourselves or confirm that we aren't as incompetent as we may have thought or feared.

For a woman with chronic expectations of doom, however, commonplace problems will not be taken in stride. Each and every challenge, no matter how small, spells disaster for her and poses the threat of devastation to her sense of self-esteem.

When a woman prone to expectations of doom has a headache, she does not think to herself, "I don't feel good today. How rotten. Maybe it's the weather or my period. Where am I in my menstrual cycle?" Instead, she assumes the worst: "I have a brain tumor. I don't want to die. I'm not ready; I haven't even made up my will yet. But then, I don't have anything to leave anyone. And if I did have anything, who would want it? No one wants me. I bet no one will come to my funeral. . . ." She starts with a simple headache, but within a few minutes, she feels bad about her overall health, her lack of assets and loved ones and, most of all, herself.

If the lights go out in her house, a woman who has expectations of doom does not think to herself, "Damn, the fuse blew again. Where is the flashlight? I'd better go into the basement and throw the switch."

Instead, she immediately panics, "Ohmygod, someone's broken into the house and they've turned the electricity off. They're going to kill me. I'll call someone if they haven't already cut the phone wires. . . ." She calls someone, who comes over and fixes the fuse, and she feels foolish.

If her boss unexpectedly asks her to meet with him in the late afternoon, she does not think, "What is this about? I hope it's quick because I want to get home. I'll ask him what it's about so I can prepare notes and shorten the meeting." Instead, she sees disaster: "I'm going to get fired, I know it. What did I do or say? People must be complaining about me." She might ask a coworker for reassurance or she might be obsessed about her pending termination until the meeting, at which she is informed that her health plan is about to change significantly. She has wasted her entire day wringing her hands when asking her boss what the meeting was about could have eased her mind.

Many women envision disaster in specific situations; some of us "freak out" over rodents and snakes, while others imagine scenes of fiery car crashes when friends and loved ones are late in arriving. Expectations of doom differ from these sorts of worries because they are free-floating; this negative thought pattern intrudes in a multitude of situations. The expectations of doom rule the woman's life. When presented with any problematic or worrisome situation, she quickly shifts focus from the situation to her inability to cope with it. Worry replaces resourcefulness; she becomes immobilized; self-denigration takes over. No matter what the outcome—even if the catastrophe is "averted" or she is rescued—her self-esteem and belief in her competence plummets in the process. In short, expecting doom becomes a style of reacting to life itself.

As we have found in other negative thought patterns, expectations of doom originate in childhood, where critical situations or feelings were linked to unavoidable catastrophes:

> Whenever I don't know exactly what I'm going to do—like where I'm going to work and live after I graduate (from law school) or which school to enroll the kids in next fall or whether or not I'll pass the bar for certain, I get paralyzed with fear. I assume we'll be out in the street with no place to live and I'll never get a job—not even a waitressing job—and the kids will turn to a life of crime. I honestly believe this and it immobilizes me. I can't make any decision, which, I guess, increases my chances of becoming a shopping-bag lady. Finally, I figured out where all this was coming from. The feeling has a vague familiarity. My father used to berate us mercilessly if we didn't all have foolproof plans. There was no being uncertain about where you were going to work over the summer, no considering two or

three different subjects to major in. Not knowing what's going to happen next was proof positive that you were stupid and all kinds of horrible things were going to happen as a result. I knew there must be some reason why I wasn't just worried like my classmates.

This woman had to learn the hard way that being unsure is not the same as being stupid and headed for disaster. Once she understood this, she could exert control over her life one step at a time.

While uncertainty can spark some women's expectations of doom, for other women feelings of fear, inadequacy, anger, sadness, even an emotion like love can be the trigger:

My mother's first husband died during the war. Then she married my father and that was a disaster throughout my childhood. A really big deal was made of my mother being a war widow—I always thought it was sad. When things were bad with my father, she would say, "What's the point? I already had one good marriage. It doesn't matter." Of course, things got worse and worse. To this day, I feel dread when I love someone. I never completely let myself go with a man, because I'm convinced he'll either die soon or we'll be miserable.

For many women with expectations of doom, being rescued becomes an integral part of the pattern. Firmly believing she is unable to cope and realizing, on some level, that this makes her a less desirable person, a woman with expectations of doom may find "safety" in relating by crying "Wolf!" and acting in a "help me, help me" mode. Perhaps when she was younger, simple statements of need or requests for assistance were not respected, but falling apart got everyone's attention. If so, she is more likely as an adult to either let situations deteriorate into catastrophes or exaggerate them into appearing so. Then she'll feel she has permission to ask for—or demand—help:

I feel sort of guilty when people are nice to me, like I don't deserve it or something. The only time I can accept kindness from others without getting freaked out or worried about what I'm supposed to give them in return is when I'm at the end of my rope. Then, I can't possibly give back, and I get lots of support and help. Then and only then, when all else is lost, can I feel the support of my friends.

By always imagining things to be so bad that others must help her lest she perish, a woman with expectations of doom sidesteps the risk that her friends could refuse an undramatic request for assistance. "Can I talk to you about that later?" or "Can someone else help you with that?" are fair responses to straightforward requests for aid. But what callous soul could refuse someone who is "falling apart at the seams" or on the brink of disaster? The impending doom and paralysis inherent in this style of reacting all but insures a nurturing response from others. The drawback is, after the woman gets the attention, she will probably wonder if it was for her or the catastrophe. Worse, others will quickly tire of her dramatics and demands.

A woman learns little about her own abilities as she drifts from one rescue to another. The predictability of her life is traded off against increased self-knowledge or self-esteem. The only skills she improves is her skill in worrying, whining and crying for help:

> Choices of strategy are rarely considered consciously but however instinctively or automatically these choices are made, different people clearly do respond in different ways to the same kind of stress. In *Winnie the Pooh,* when a flood threatened the forest, Piglet reflected that among his friends, 'Christopher Robin and Pooh could escape by Climbing Trees and Kanga could escape by Jumping, Rabbit could escape by Burrowing and Owl could escape by Flying and Eeyore (the Donkey) could escape by—by making a Loud Noise Until Rescued.'[1]

When a woman thinks like Eeyore, and others are willing to play the part of the rescuer, she will never learn to climb trees, jump, burrow or fly.

There are payoffs for rescuers as well as the rescued. Rescuers often enjoy the appearance of being a "savior." Unsure they merit friendship in their own right, they encourage others to be dependent on their ability and willingness to rescue. Often rescuers or "knights in shining armor" turn out to be more undesirable than the feared catastrophe. Moreover, victim/rescuer relationships usually leave much to be desired. People who want healthy, reciprocal relationships will soon tire of being a one-person emergency squad. When the rescuer leaves, his or her departure will most likely constitute another catastrophe in the woman's life.

There are other payoffs for expectations of doom, some of which are connected to feeling good. A possible motto for a woman with this thought pattern could be, "Always expect the worst and be pleasantly surprised when things turn out better than you expected." If even minor problems (like a misplaced checkbook) can be turned into a serious matter ("There must have been robbers in the house while I was out"), the woman who expected the worst will be relieved and feel good when it turns out to be nothing at all (the checkbook is found, not in its usual place). Certainly, there are healthier ways to obtain pleasure, and those around a woman who derives pleasure in this way will probably find her manufactured crises tiresome.

Some women feel they can only enjoy themselves after they have survived a threatening experience. Hence, they are always primed for one in anticipation of the good feelings which will follow:

> As a kid, I got lots of strokes for being able to handle a really crazy household, for keeping my grades up while my father was in and out of jail and my mother drank. I took care of my younger sisters then. Especially during times of crisis, teachers and neighbors patted me on the head and told me how wonderful I am. Now I don't feel really alive unless I have a thousand things going on at once. I set up these high-pressure projects at work, and the closer I come to cracking and blowing everything, the better I feel afterward.

Knowledge that one has the capacity to survive adversity or to cope with uncommon stress is a valid source of self-esteem. But for women with expectations of doom, the fact that they are still standing after the catastrophe is their *main* source of self-esteem. As a result, they may create catastrophes where none exist, and other abilities (e.g., to have fun) will remain unexplored.

BLUEPRINTS FOR CHANGE

I. EXPECTATIONS OF DOOM

First, try to identify what this thought pattern feels like to you. Most likely, feelings of panic, shortness of breath, dizziness, and/or disorientation will accompany the sense of impending doom.

Next, during a time when you are *not* in this thought pattern, identify three situations in your life which would be *genuinely serious,* situations which would not be likely to happen every day.

The next time you begin to expect doom and you feel the identified physical manifestations, take three deep breaths and use the thought-stopping technique:

> "I'm so inadequate—this is going to be terrible and I can't handle it. STOP. This situation (my friend being angry with me, my boss wanting a meeting, the car breaking down) is not a catastrophe like. . . ." (Refer to your list of three.) "Since it is *not* the end of the world, I can handle it. I may need to ask for help, but basically, I can handle this."

Even if you do not yet believe it, tell yourself that you can handle the situation. Replace the expectations of doom with an accurate statement (it's *not* a catastrophe) and an expression of confidence, then *act* in a way which is consistent with your new statement. It may seem awkward and risky at first, but after the first few positive experiences, the negative thought pattern will more easily change.

II. EARLY LEARNING

Think back specifically to the last three times you felt impending doom, when you were *sure* a catastrophe was about to happen. If you are keeping a journal, write in detail about those times, answering the following questions:

1. What feeling preceded the "catastrophe"? Fear? Uncertainty? Pleasure? Anger?
2. Did anyone rescue you? How did you get him or her to do that?
3. Looking back on it, was it really a catastrophe? What could you have done to handle it yourself?
4. How did it feel when it was all over? More specifically, how did you feel about yourself?

Write as much as you want; include other questions or issues which will help you to discern your pattern. Now, think back to a time in your childhood that seemed catastrophic. Ask yourself the same questions as above, but also think about who told you (through behavior or words) the situation was catastrophic. Are there any similarities between this situation and the ones that trouble you today? If so, after using thought stopping, add something like this:

"This is the end of the world. STOP. It is *not* the end of the world. It is similar to other times in my past when I was *taught* to believe the world was going to end. The fact that I'm adult now proves the world did not end then and it is not going to end now. This situation is not as serious as others and I can handle it."

Reminding yourself that the expectations of your own demise come from very old, inaccurate learning will be effective in managing those feelings today and eradicating them in the future.

III. BEING RESCUED

If you are someone who relies on rescues, who modeled the need to be rescued for you? Were they rescued because of inabilities to deal with a crisis, or were they rescued from enjoying themselves by someone punishing them? What sex was the rescuer? What kinds of things did he or she do for the person who was your model? If your model had one motto, a philosophy of life (in twenty-five words or less), what would it be? Does this philosophy influence your life today? Would you choose it to be your own? If not, what would you rather have as your motto?

IV. PREVENTING DOOM

If you have one particular feared event or experience, ask for help *ahead of time* so that you can prevent the immobilization that results from this negative thought pattern. For instance, tell someone, "During the last storm, my fuses blew and it really frightened me. Do you know what to do in that situation? Will you please teach me?" Then, take notes which you can rely on when the panic comes. As an example in the interpersonal realm, ask someone, "Will you listen to something difficult I have to say to somebody at work and tell me how it would feel to you if you were that person?" Your friend can give you some accurate feedback and suggestions to alleviate your feelings of impending doom. This will help you to avoid or recognize facets of the other person's reaction which spell catastrophe for you.

* 7 *

Can't Get This Out of My Mind: Inability To Accept a Compliment

> I wouldn't want to belong to a club which would have me as a member.
>
> —Groucho Marx

One common manifestation of low self-esteem is the inability to accept a compliment. When another person tells a woman with this thought pattern something he or she likes about her, the woman's low opinion of herself is challenged; a favorable opinion does not compute. Moreover, because women with low self-esteem tend to rely heavily on external definitions of who they are, a momentary validation from another can even seem threatening. Convinced that she does not deserve the compliment and that the compliment giver will come to know the "real" her soon enough, the woman with this negative thought pattern sets the record straight by refusing the compliment. "That's a nice dress you have on today," a coworker comments. No kind words are too insignificant to be disputed:

"Oh, it's just a hand-me-down, it's really nothing."

"Well, it doesn't really fit me."

"I have much nicer dresses than this at home."

"But look, there's this spot on it—I can't seem to get it out."

"I've had it for years, it's really out of style."

Many times these responses are automatic; a woman says them without thinking. No one has said to her, "Hey, has that dress ever belonged to anyone else?" or "Could you show me the spot on your dress? I know there must be one." Still, she feels compelled to discount the compliment rather than take it for what it is. Simply saying "thank you," letting it in, and then letting it go seems beyond her capacity.

When the compliment is of a more personal nature, such as "You're fun to be with," a woman may feel even more honor-bound to dispute it. "You don't really know me" or "You haven't seen me when I'm really angry" (as if she were a monster lurking behind a "normal exterior") are responses which repudiate the compliment and the compliment giver, and ultimately diminish the woman's own self-worth.

Women become extremely adept at making a compliment offered to them seem totally absurd. Often there seems to be only two lines of response: fight or take flight.

The fight response involves a direct attack on the compliment giver's intelligence, judgment or powers of perception. Obviously, others can't have good taste in clothes if they like anything she would wear, nor could they be good judges of character if they like to be with her. She doesn't mean to intentionally insult them, but those offering the compliments will feel not listened to at best, put down at worst. Deep friendships are not built on such reactions; the compliment giver probably was expecting a simple thank you or some other pleasant response.

An excellent example of the fight response to a compliment happened between the two authors of this book:

> I am overly concerned with my protruding stomach, while my coauthor is worried about having large hips. Anyway, one night my coauthor had to stay at my place unexpectedly because her car broke down. I lent her some pajamas. The next morning, at breakfast, we began to talk about our bodies, as we sometimes do while we eat. I said to her, "You know, I don't think your hips are that large—I was noticing last night that those pajamas fit you much better than me and I think your hips have a nice shape to them and they aren't too big." To this she replied, "Oh, yeah, and I really like how your gut hangs out over your belt." I don't even wear a belt!

Talk about inability to accept a compliment! It's amazing this book was ever finished.

Before long, fights against compliments accomplish their purpose. People around the woman who is unable to accept a compliment, weary of giving unappreciated praise, figure she knows herself better than they could ever know her: "There must be something to her lousy opinion of herself," they say on some level, and they stop giving her compliments. She, on the other hand, takes this as proof positive that her low self-esteem is deserved, because, after all, she never receives any compliments.

The flight response consists of muttering an unintelligible platitude or looking dumbfounded:

> I went out on a first date with this guy, and he was rather attentive—more than most guys. He was asking me questions about my work with special-ed. kids and telling me that he really admired what I did and that he imagined I was good at it. Every time he said something like that, I'd either whisper, "Thank you," or I'd put my napkin to my mouth and say it through the linen. He kept on asking me to repeat myself because he couldn't hear what I said. I wasn't aware of what I was doing, so, pursuant to my training, I asked him if he had a hearing problem and did a rap about hearing impairments in adults. Needless to say, it was a long, awkward evening.

Discouraged with the lack of pleasantness in a situation that should be inherent with goodwill, the person stops offering his or her favorable opinion—or leaves entirely.

Another motivation behind the inability to accept a compliment is the belief that accepting compliments will make a woman conceited. She can hear them but doesn't permit herself to outwardly acknowledge them lest people will think ill of her. Of course, if compliment givers thought ill of the woman, they would not even consider giving her compliments. A straightforward "thank you" not only acknowledges the good intention of the other person, but it is likely to beget more compliments. Again, if compliments are taken for what they really are —one person's perception of us at a given point in time—then it's less likely that they will be generalized or exaggerated to the point of conceit.

Women who can't take compliments might have a running chance at self-esteem if they were just as rigid in their refusal to take seriously the flip side of compliments: criticism. But often this is not the case. Instead, some women go one step beyond rejecting compliments to embracing criticism. Negativity rules, as this woman explains:

> When I first started speaking in front of groups and people came up afterward and said, "I really like what you had to say," I would be very ungracious to them. "That's all over," I'd say to myself. "It doesn't make any difference." It made me nervous, because I didn't know what they expected of me, and I didn't want them to think of me as something that I am not. But if someone had come to me and said, "That was the most ridiculous

thing I have ever heard," he or she would have my undivided attention. I would have wanted to know more.

Many beliefs underlie this reaction. Primary among them is the belief that a negative reaction is more truthful than a positive reaction. This is based on a woman's premise that she is not good and must struggle to be a better person, combined with her conviction that other people are to instruct her in how to become better. Since she is not yet good enough, compliments must be wrong or irrelevant, whereas criticism illuminates the path to perfection.

By embracing criticism and rejecting compliments, some women may be trying to achieve a backhanded self-esteem known as false humility, or in its extreme, martyrdom. This goes beyond not wanting to seem conceited: "See how open I am to others, how vulnerable I am. I am not the least bit afraid of facing my many faults." In fact, though, a woman who acts and thinks this way is so focused on criticism, and her defenselessness invites so much of it, that she rarely has time or energy to change those things about her which need changing.

Considering compliments is one way to gather information about ourselves, to expand our sense of who we are and what we're about. If we have a clearly defined, fairly stable self-concept to begin with, a compliment can be a momentary validation of what we knew anyway. We can never hear the truth enough.

> One of the best feelings in the whole world for me is to have someone tell me something that I think is true about myself already. For instance, I needed a letter of recommendation for a job, and an old friend and colleague wrote a very specific letter. In it he said I was very professional yet always warm. That's rare in my field—I work real hard to maintain that balance. Until that letter, I never knew he noticed and I felt really terrific after reading it. It sort of works the same with negatives, too—if someone points out something I already didn't like about myself—as painful as that might be—I feel they are paying attention, that they've gotten to know the real me.

The development of our self-esteem is not done in isolation. We can benefit from other people's observations, and compliments are often the currency of that important exchange.

BLUEPRINTS FOR CHANGE

I. ACCEPTING COMPLIMENTS

When someone gives you a compliment, and you begin to discount it, use the thought-stopping technique.

> "Oh, it was nothing." "STOP. This person is simply offering me her perspective at this given moment. There is nothing to feel uncomfortable about. Simply say 'Thank you.' "

Then say "Thank you" out loud and leave it at that. If you begin to tell yourself that you don't deserve the compliment or that you are conceited, then use the thought-stopping technique again:

> "Who do I think I am?" "STOP. This is one person's opinion. Who am I to tell them they are all wrong? I deserve compliments as much as anybody else."

As a way to reinforce the compliment you received, write it down or, better yet, if you agree with it, use it as one of your "I like myself" note cards. Keep track of how many compliments you get and see if you don't receive more as you discount them less.

Sometimes an unexpected compliment (or criticism) can take us off guard, so choosing our time and place to practice soliciting feedback can be helpful. We can closely examine how we react and also can work to correct responses that diminish our self-esteem. Instead of waiting for someone to say "That was a lovely dinner" and giving your usual reply, "Oh, it was nothing" (even though you spent hours on it), you might say, "I tried a new recipe tonight and I'd like to know if you enjoyed it." If your friend (choose someone you trust) says, "Oh, I thought it was great, didn't I tell you?" then simply reply, "Thank you." As you get more practice, you can work up to "Thank you, I like it a lot, too." If your friend replied, "It was pretty good, but it had too much curry for my taste," be careful not to misinterpret this honest appraisal as an insult or an attack on your overall worth.

II. WHAT GOES AROUND . . .

Try complimenting other people. Instead of privately thinking a positive thought about someone, say it aloud in a genuine manner. Pay close attention to how they react. How do you feel when your compliment is acknowledged graciously? How do you feel when your compliment is minimized or rejected? Have the roles ever been reversed? Can you think of a compliment giver in your life who may have felt the same?

III. FOR WHAT IT'S WORTH

If you embrace criticism, then learn to balance your talent for hearing criticism with the development of a talent for hearing praise. People probably know you are easy to criticize, so the next time you are asking someone for more and more reasons why you are inadequate, try asking them:

> "I just want to put this in a larger picture. I think I understand what you don't like here. Nothing is ever totally one-sided. Would you please tell me one thing you *like* (about me, about the way I handled the situation, etc.)?"

Then listen to this response as carefully as you listened to the criticism.

* 8 *

This Will Make Me Worthy and Whole: The Search for Completion Through Romance, Motherhood and Work

In a candid interview with *McCall's* in 1981, Academy Award-winning actress Sally Field spoke of her struggle to overcome one of the most common problems among women with low self-esteem. Explained Field:

> I'm trying to shed the thought that unless I'm with a man I don't exist. Because I just hate that other state . . . that scary desperation I feel from the absence of a partner. Maybe all that "I-am-happy-alone/I-fulfill-myself/Now-isn't-that-joyous?" stuff *is* just a bunch of words—but I somehow keep hoping that if I say them enough, I'll get to that place. Because the alternative is walking around listless, without reason to go on. And that can't be it for me. . . .[1]

Some women might think that a woman like Sally Field, with all her talent, spunk and professional success, would be free of the self-esteem problems suffered by other women. But talent, spunk and success do not necessarily bring with them high global self-esteem, and the "scary desperation" Field speaks of is a familiar feeling to many women of all kinds. This feeling comes from the belief, hammered into most of our heads from an early age, that a woman must have her existence validated and justified by someone or something outside herself because women by nature are somehow deficient, inadequate, not quite whole, not quite good enough. It is because of this pernicious belief and the feelings of desperation and self-loathing it understandably gives rise to that so many women spend so much of their lives searching for comple-

tion—as if someone or something besides themselves could ma
feel worthy and whole.

People with high self-esteem are generally able to come to grips with
the fact that each of us is alone, that between even the closest of people
there exist chasms that never will be bridged no matter how intimate
they become. They know that two people can never merge no matter
how great the urge to do so. They also know that while they can look to
people and activities outside themselves for some validation of their
lives and worth, the final—and most important—say about whether
they are whole and worthy must come from within themselves. They
will look for *connections* to other people or a larger purpose (work,
religion, family, political and social change, for example), because it is
through connection that they can express and most fully experience
their inherent worth.

People with low self-esteem often have a much greater difficulty accepting their aloneness and the often frightening responsibilities it entails. They turn to another person or larger purpose in the hopes of
finding *completion;* they will look to anyone or anything, except to
themselves. Nathaniel Branden explains:

> Aloneness entails self-responsibility. No one can think for us, no one can
> feel for us, no one can live our life for us, and no one can give meaning to
> our existence except ourselves. For most people, this fact is terrifying. It
> may be the most fiercely resisted, the most passionately denied, fact of their
> being.
>
> The forms their denial takes are endless: refusing to think and following
> uncritically the beliefs of others; disowning one's deepest feelings in order
> to 'belong'; pretending to be helpless, pretending to be confused, pretend-
> ing to be stupid, in order to avoid taking an independent stand; clinging to
> the belief that one will "die" if one does not have the love of this person or
> that; joining mass movements or "causes" that promise to spare one the
> responsibility of independent judgment and to obviate the need for a sense
> of personal identity; surrendering one's mind to a leader; killing and dying
> for symbols and abstractions that promise to grant glory and meaning to
> one's existence, with no effort required on one's own part save obedience;
> devoting all of one's energies to manipulating people into giving "love."[2]

The Search for Completion Through Romantic Love

Although women can and do search for completion via a wide variety
of routes, female searchers in our culture are probably most readily
inclined to look to love to make them feel worthy and whole. The love

may be that of that one special person who will erase the searcher's feelings of estrangement, desperation and self-dislike and make her complete. Or the love may be that of children, who by their very existence will stand as proof of their mother's worth, and who will require so much time and energy that she will be distracted from the feelings of aloneness and worthlessness that she so wants to disown. It's not that women have any innate inclination toward searching for completion through love (as opposed to religion, politics, money, status); it's that for women, love is the most culturally sanctioned and encouraged form.

Although low self-esteem is a problem women have had for centuries, it's only been within the past century that women in large numbers looked to romance as the solution for their feelings of inadequacy and incompleteness. True, loving relationships like that of John and Abigail Adams have existed in the past. And true, many women in the past had extremely passionate relationships with other women. But neither of these types of relationships was typical for the vast majority of women. Prior to the popularization of heterosexual romance in the twentieth century, most marriages were entered into for practical rather than emotional reasons; while the two partners may have come to love one another deeply over the course of the marriage, they rarely were passionately enamored of one another at the start, and they also did not expect one another to meet a wide array of emotional needs. Similarly, although women did rely greatly upon other women to meet their emotional needs, they often relied on a number of women, relatives and friends, rather than just one woman. In short, any one relationship with any one person was not expected to be the end-all and be-all that would sweep a woman off her feet and make her feel worthy and complete.

In our time, of course, all this has changed dramatically. Not only are romantic relationships valued above all others, romance is looked upon as something everyone can and should want to experience, and romantic relationships are expected to fulfill a wide variety of deeply felt needs. Females in particular are raised to be in love with love. Over and over again from the earliest age, girls and women are told that "you're nobody until somebody loves you," and eventually the insidious message sinks in and the search for that one special somebody begins. But according to the rules of our culture, the love of just any somebody won't do to make a girl or woman whole and worthy. No, only the love of a man or boy can make a female person worthy and whole: She is nobody until somebody *male* loves her.

Unfortunately, many women today do believe this. Taught from an early age that her duty in life is to attract and please men, and taught also that her very survival is contingent upon this, the average female reaches adolescence addicted to male approval. She preens, she primps, she wears uncomfortable clothes and crippling shoes, and she waits, waits ever so patiently for that comment, passing glance or telephone call that will inform her that she makes the grade and therefore is worth something. But just like the habits of any other addicts, her appetite and dependence grows: Where once an occasional compliment sated her, with time she becomes insatible in her need for male approval, and she asks constantly, "Do you think I'm pretty? Am I prettier than her? Why do you love me? Do you still love me? You don't really love me anymore, do you? . . ." In *Blooming* Susan Allen Toth recalls how she experienced an intense craving for male approval even as a preschooler. Of males, she writes:

> I can't remember when I didn't want one. Walking timidly for the first time into my sunny kindergarten room, I noticed immediately two play areas, one with a complete toy kitchen . . . the other with a miniature carpenter's shop, filled with wooden blocks, hammers, glue. Although I delightedly fussed in the elaborate cardboard kitchen, I kept sneaking curious glances at the boys who were hammering real nails in their adjoining shop. I wanted one of them to notice I was there.[3]

Some women today are quick to criticize other women's need to be noticed by men. But it's important to remember that no woman ever made a conscious choice to become dependent on male approval and that kicking addiction to male approval is no simple task. The need isn't magically whisked away once a woman reaches an intellectual understanding of it and decides, "I don't want to live like this anymore; it's not good for me." Easy as it is to say only unintelligent or politically incorrect women are dependent on male approval, the fact is that no amount of intelligence, feminist consciousness or intellectualization makes a woman immune. Even the most intelligent and seemingly self-sufficient and self-satisfied woman can be a male approval junkie. Marcia Millman interviewed one such woman, an accomplished scientist who said:

> Well, I have plenty of success in male-associated areas, but I would trade it for being a sexually attractive woman. I'm hooked to the most superficial things and need sexual confirmation in a way that's really sad. A woman who's truly beautiful in men's eyes can walk away from the pain and the ridiculousness of sex-stereotyping in that area much more freely than I can. Someone who is vulnerable in stereotypic roles will cling to them longest because of the forever unsatisfied need to be confirmed. . . . I take

all the work success for granted. I've always been good at work. What I'd give my right arm for is to be good at what I'm not good at—at being a sexually attractive woman.[4]

Like most of those who search for completion, this woman has the problem of keeping all her self-esteem eggs in one basket, so to speak. She has devoted plenty of time and energy to her career, and probably to other endeavors, too. But when it comes to measuring her worth she feels the only thing that *really* counts is her attractiveness to men.

The idea that women need men to validate us is so pervasive in our culture, even direct exposure to women who represent a far different reality may not be enough to dissuade children from believing the myth. Even if our own mothers were divorced, abandoned, widowed or otherwise without men, and even if they were happily so, we probably came to look upon the woman with a man as the norm and the ideal. Many black women in particular were raised by single women who needed no men to validate their worth. But belying the reality, the idea that a woman needs a man was communicated to every small girl who heard Billie Holiday sing "My Man" and later heard Diana Ross of the Supremes lament that "My world is empty without you, babe."

Not just pop music, but literature since the story of Lancelot and Guinevere has glorified the female search for completion through romantic love. When we read about such classic couples as Romeo and Juliet, what is never mentioned is that such all-consuming passions were seen as exceptional, and for most of human history the ideal of romantic love was *not* seen as something most people could or should achieve in real life. Moreover, when we read the great love stories of our literature, we often overlook or dismiss as irrelevant the gruesome results. So big deal that Anna Karenina put her head under an oncoming train and died. She loved, and loved passionately, didn't she?

Biographies and autobiographies of real-life women exalt as ideal women who surrender, if not their lives, at least their identities, to love. Sheilah Graham, who sought completion through F. Scott Fitzgerald, was one such woman. She described her relationship with Fitzgerald in breathless style:

> I looked into his face, searching it, trying to find its mystery, its wonder for me, and I said, almost prayerfully, "If only I could walk into your eyes and close the lids behind me, and leave all the world outside" . . . he held me close and I clung to him. . . .[5]

Such torrid prose masks the fact that Graham's relationship with Fitzgerald (as well as his relationship with his wife, Zelda) was notoriously destructive.

Lest Sheilah Graham seem a dated example, we should point out that the idea that it's romantic for a woman to surrender herself entirely is still around many decades later. At the same time that many women have valiantly made names for themselves in the world of work, in their private lives some have still been tempted to say to their lovers, in effect, "Tell me who I am, what to think, what to do, what I am worth . . . and I'll follow you anywhere." This is precisely what Sally Field did. As she explained in her *McCall's* interview, for a period she affected an "I don't need men" attitude, because in the past she had let herself become consumed by them:

> That Scarlett O'Hara act is a big defense. It comes from anger at myself for years of as much as saying to a man, "I love you, so from now on you carry the ball and I'll be a body walking around without a head." It's so strange: I have such constant sureness of myself with my acting. If a director tells me to do something that I know isn't right, my heels just go in and I don't care if he likes me or not. But in my personal life, with men especially, it's "You like red? Then I'll like red."[6]

Heterosexual women are not the only ones who search for completion through romantic love. Lesbians, too, can feel compelled to be in romantic relationships because they feel worthless without one. Lesbians may not be hooked on male approval, but some can be just as addicted to the approval and love of that one "significant other":

> I've never spent any significant amount of time not being in a couple since my first love affair when I was in college, and that was eleven years ago. When a love affair breaks up I want to die, and the only way I can deal with those awful feelings of terror and worthlessness is to crawl into the arms of another woman who will heal me and make me into one piece again. . . . In a lot of ways, I've done with my life exactly what girls are traditionally raised to do—I've given up homes, jobs, friends and pets for lovers just so that they wouldn't leave me.

Psychologist Penelope Russianoff uses the term "Noah's Ark principle" for our culture's dictum that the only proper way to live is in pairs.[7] Another word for it is "couplism."

Couplism belies the reality that most women will spend a significant portion of their lives living without partners, whether through choice or because of other circumstances. Yet few girls growing up were prepared to live alone, and fewer still were told that it's okay to be alone. Instead, we were frightened by stories about destitute widows and frustrated, lonely spinsters, and we learned to pity or suspect women who were alone. Even women who were encouraged to build careers and live independent lives still were taught to look upon single women not as admirable models but as pathetic examples of a fate too horrible to contemplate:

> Growing up, I got these very mixed messages that I still haven't completely reconciled. On the one hand, I was taught that I was okay on my own and that I should do something with my life beyond and apart from attaching myself to a man. But on the other hand, all through childhood I was always taken to visit these maiden aunts I had, and it was made quite clear that the only stance to take toward these women was one of pity—as if they were really sad freaks. They even encouraged this themselves. They always gave me this big plate of cookies, and I'd always eat them until I got to the last one. When I got to the last one, they'd take my hand and say, "No—don't eat the last cookie. If you eat the last one, you'll become an old maid *like us.*"

For most women who are adults today, the indoctrination into couplism went hand in hand with indoctrination into the heterosexual way of life. Instead of being trained for active participation in the process of finding out who we are and how—among all the many options—we could live, many girls were told to do nothing but sit pretty and wait for a prince charming who would bring us out of our deep sleep. This prince charming would not only make us feel good about ourselves, he would—more fundamentally—make us feel alive for the first time ever. Real living, we were told, would begin after that magical moment we snared a man. And in order to prepare ourselves for this real life, we were told to defer developing our own personalities until we had found our man.

If a girl's mother seemed happy as a woman who deferred her sense of self to a man's validation, then perhaps the daughter will have come to reason that "what worked for her will work for me":

> I used to think my mother was happy—she was so cheery all of the time. She always voted the way my father voted, fit her entire schedule around his, never made a move without his approval. My first marriage was like that and I had high expectations for it. But, God, was it boring. I became so depressed. When it got really bad for me, and when my mother was trying to help, she told me she had never been all that happy either, but she was resigned to it. But I couldn't be—I knew there was more to life than wasting my days waiting for this man to come home, living in his shadow.

The least she could have done is been realistic with me about all the lousy stuff that goes with marriage.

This woman's anger about her mother's failure to be realistic is understandable. But would it have made a difference had her mother told her the truth? Most people today are familiar with the fact that few marriages entered into this year will be intact ten years from now. Yet the multimillion dollar wedding industry is booming, and each day thousands of earnest young couples promise to love, cherish and honor one another until they die. Clearly, sky-high divorce rates have not soured many on the idea of marriage. In fact, the mythology of the eternally happy couple can have its greatest adherents among those with firsthand exposure to the most unpleasant reality:

> I looked at my parents' violent marriage and I said it would never happen to me. I made it my life goal to do what they couldn't do. I wanted a caring, committed, monogamous relationship more than anything in the world. Without it, I felt like a failure. It never occurred to me that I might make a mistake and end up with someone wrong for me, or that I would look and look and look and still not find anyone at all. . . .

Marrying or having a relationship with a man can solve money problems, too, and this advantage cannot be underestimated or overlooked. For many women, marriage means the difference between being well off and being on welfare, and for most women members in the middle and upper classes can only be maintained or obtained through marriage. For other women, having a man may mean the difference between barely getting by and having a few luxuries. A welfare mother explains:

> I think being poor really puts women in a bad situation with men. A lot of times the only way you'll get to use a car, get to go out to dinner, get to take the kids to the beach, get to buy them Christmas and birthday presents is if you have a man. When you're on welfare, a boyfriend is your only access to that little bit of spending money that makes life less hellish. . . .

This woman's situation is not at all unusual; some women want to be with men for financial reasons and only financial reasons. But this woman is also not representative of all women: There are those whose need of men is only psychological, not financial, and sometimes it can be an unhealthy need. For example, Lenore Walker in her extensive study on battered women interviewed professional women (some lawyers and doctors) who were battered by the men in their lives and remained with them.[8] Clearly, economic dependence on the batterer was not the issue for them. Most valued being in a relationship with a man above *all* else, including their own physical well-being.

In *The Cinderella Complex* Collette Dowling relates how her feelings toward herself and her lover, Lowell, were affected once she decided to give up her work and rely on Lowell to support her and her children:

> Inevitably, deference developed: I started to feel intimidated by the man who was supporting me. It was then that I began finding fault with him, carping and criticizing him for the most ridiculous things. I resented Lowell's greater ease with people, the smoothness with which he could swing back and forth in a give-and-take, whether socially or in business. He seemed to have so much confidence. I found myself hating him for it.[9]

While it's possible that emotional dependency and feelings of inadequacy and resentment might arise any time a woman relies on someone else for financial support, it's also possible that Dowling's negative feelings were exacerbated—or even caused—by the dishonest and manipulative nature of her relationship to Lowell. Unlike many relationships in which one person agrees to provide the financial support and the other agrees to provide the nurturing, homemaking and child care, the arrangement Dowling and Lowell had originally agreed to was one in which both would financially support themselves. Dowling's later decision to give up her work and mooch off Lowell was made unilaterally; indeed, she never even informed him of her plan to renege on their agreement. She did, however, cook up a self-serving theory that Lowell had an obligation to support her. The end result was that she did much damage to her self-esteem and her ability to see herself and her relationship clearly:

> . . . Certainly my relationship with Lowell—with him the provider and me the protected—was distorted. So was my relationship with myself. For some reason I was seeing myself as less strong than Lowell, less competent. That was a major distortion, and consequent upon it was another: Lowell "should" take care of me. Yes, that is the twisted morality of the weak (or those who persist in seeing themselves as such). It is the "burden" of the strong to drag us along; if they don't, we keep telling them, in so many ways, we won't survive.[10]

Collette Dowling's story is interesting because it so well illustrates how extremely distorted the views of a woman who searches for completion through relationships can become. It's bad enough that Dowling rationalized her mooching by telling herself that Lowell "should" take care of her. Even worse, though, is that she then invented a woman-hating theory that *all* women have some innate and vague "fear of independence" that causes *all* women to expect "others to do the hard stuff of life." To be sure, some women do seem to fear independence, some women think men should support them financially and some women make suckers out of men. Yet many women do not do any of these things, and feel no compulsion to either. Whether or not a woman was raised with the expectation that men will do the "hard stuff of life," if she opens her eyes, she will see that "the hard stuff of life" is what the majority of women end up doing, and always have done:

> What is all this crap about women being so dependent on men? How many households are supported by women alone with no man even to take out the garbage? Even in the households I see where there is a man around, the women are usually contributing financially, and even if they're not, they are doing the bulk of the hard work of keeping that household together and going. Money aside, in the households I see, it's the woman who is contributing most, not the man. She's the one who provides all the nurturance, the strength, the compassion to keep everyone going. She makes sure the man and the kids feel good about themselves, and in an emotional sense the man usually seems much more dependent upon her than she is on him.

All human beings whether male or female are dependent upon one another to some degree. For all our culture's mythology about male independence and "self-made men," the truth is that male and female alike exist in a web of relationships, and no man has ever "done it all on his own"—always there has been a network, usually hidden, of people, usually women, giving him support and sustenance. Despite the ease with which a Collette Dowling can assert that "psychologists have known for some time that women's affiliative needs are stronger than men's,"[11] the fact is that psychologists have long known nothing of the kind. There is no concrete evidence to support the idea that women have a monopoly on the need for and dependence upon relationships. On the contrary, in a long-term study of 231 young heterosexual couples in the 1970s, psychologist Zick Rubin found that the men fell in love more quickly and easily than the women, and the men also had more desire to fall in love when they entered their relationships. What is more, when the couples broke up—which 45 percent did over the course of the study—the women were slightly more likely than the men to have initiated the breakups, and, of greater interest, after breaking up, it was the men, not the women, who reported feeling more unhappy, lonely and depressed.[12] Clearly, then, it is erroneous to label one sex or the other "the dependent sex." And clearly, too, it is ludicrous to condemn members of either sex for being dependent. Everyone needs other people and is dependent upon others to some degree and there is nothing wrong with that.

The Search for Completion Through Motherhood

A second common way women search for completion is through motherhood. A woman who searches in this way looks to her children to make her worthy and whole, and typically judges herself a failure or success as a human being according to whether she has been a success or failure as a mother. This middle-aged woman interviewed by Lillian Rubin is a case in point:

> My only career has been my children. If I can't find success in raising them, then what? Where am I going to look for any sense of pride or fulfillment? There's nothing else I've done that I can judge myself by. My husband has his career, and he finds success and fulfillment in that. He's proven himself someplace, so he doesn't feel the disappointment the way I do. For me, it's the only thing I tried to do, and I failed.[13]

The problem here isn't that this woman cares about being a good mother; wanting to be a good mother is admirable. The problem is that motherhood is this woman's *only* source of self-esteem. As with those who search for completion through romance, it's a matter of a woman putting all her self-esteem eggs in one basket.

Several generations of American women have been primed almost since birth to look for completion through motherhood. From the earliest age many of us were told that motherhood is our natural calling, and that it alone should be enough to make us feel worthy and whole. But this conception of motherhood is relatively new. Just as our expectations of sexual relationships have changed over time, so have our expectations of motherhood. In colonial America, child-rearing manuals were addressed to both parents or the father alone, and no one spoke in exalted terms of "motherly love" or the "maternal instinct."[14] While mothers often came to love their children deeply as they grew up, only rarely did a woman approach childbirth with the expectation of being consumed by love for her child. On the contrary, as a woman approached childbirth, she was most likely to be fearful of her own death, and fearful of the infant's death. With maternal and infant mortality rates so high, such fears were very reasonable. Also reasonable—and common—was guarding against becoming too emotionally involved with an infant too soon, lest the baby should not survive its infancy.

How different ideas about motherhood and the mother-baby relationship were in colonial America is illustrated by Mary Ryan:

> Statistics available for the eighteenth century indicate that the typical colonial woman could expect to spend some twenty years with an infant under her charge, almost forty years rearing children. These functions decreed by woman's anatomy did not, however, confer upon her a peculiarly feminine nature and temperament. No mystique of motherhood congealed around the time-consuming and oft-repeated physical ordeal of childbearing. The biological intimacy of mother and child did not ordain an instinctive emotional attachment between the two. The first act of a devout mother symbolized detachment from the fruit of the womb: "Give up your New-born Child unto the Lord." A woman of Puritan upbringing could not vainly presume that a child was her private creation and personal possession. Neither was any colonial woman likely to merge her identity with a child torn from her by the pain of parturition and in great danger of infant mortality.[15]

It used to be believed that children were born with fixed personalities, and that the best parents could hope for was to raise a civilized human being. This changed in our century with the increasing promotion of the idea, greatly influenced by Freud, that personalities are made, not born, and that mothers have the power to shape their children's psyches down to the last detail. This new conception of personality formulation developed as the total responsibility for child rearing was shifting from both parents to the female parent alone, and the end result was that an incredible burden was placed upon mothers. Now mothers weren't just responsible for producing children, they were responsible for quality control as well, as Philip Slater observes:

> . . . the American mother has been told: "You have the capacity to rear a genius, a masterpiece. This is the most important thing you can do, and it should rightfully absorb all your energy." With such an attitude, it is easy to expand childrearing into a full-time job. . . . We are a product-oriented society and the American mother has been given the opportunity to turn out a really outstanding product.[16]

It is no coincidence that the view of motherhood as a manufacturing process became particularly popular in the years after World War II. Women who were forced out of their wartime jobs to make room for men had found in those jobs considerable satisfaction and a sense of competence and accomplishment. They didn't want to give all that up for nothing, and so as they were forced to give up their jobs, it behooved many to believe that where they had previously found satisfaction in building a superior nation, now they could be of use building superior children. Child-care experts such as Benjamin Spock were happy to do their part to convince women to see fulfillment and completion through full-time devotion to the making of human masterpieces.

The belief that a woman is incomplete unless she has had the experience of motherhood goes hand in hand with the belief that a woman is nothing without a man. And these two beliefs, in turn, give rise to the idea that marriage and motherhood are everything any woman needs to be happy, and a woman who needs more is deeply flawed and maladjusted. This is a culturally created myth designed to keep women from demanding more opportunities for self-development than the few limited ones our society provides.

For many women, education and employment options still remain severely limited, and for some, motherhood may still be the only route toward social respectability and higher self-esteem. We see this especially among teenage women from economically deprived backgrounds. Among white, college-educated women of the middle and upper classes, the search for completion through motherhood appears to have declined in popularity and the birth rate has dropped accordingly. But among teens with few options, there has been no similar decline. Among this group the search for self through motherhood is as popular as ever. More than one million teenage girls in the United States currently get pregnant each year, and forty percent of the girls turning fourteen this year will become pregnant by the time they are twenty. Half these girls will have their babies, joining the 1.1 million teen mothers now raising more than 1.5 million children.[17]

For a teenage girl, having a baby can fulfill a variety of purposes. Instead of going through the long and often painful period of adolescence, by having a baby she seemingly jumps immediately into adulthood and automatically obtains an identity: "Who am I? I am this baby's mother." And because motherhood is at least more highly valued than the other roles she sees available to her (e.g., student, salesgirl, waitress, unemployed high-school dropout), she may see having a baby as her best bet for social respectability. Within a girl's own family and peer group she often finds that in becoming a mother, for the first time in her life she becomes somebody important—at least for a while.

Another reason many teens have babies is that having a child provides some excitement and a hedge against boredom. Fed by the drama of TV soap operas, many girls feel their own lives are terribly dull—and what better way to liven things up than by bringing a new life onto the scene? And finally, becoming a mother may seem to be the answer to loneliness. Many girls look to their babies with the expectation of the perfect, all-fulfilling human relationship. In her imagined scenario, she will love her baby as no mother has ever loved, and the baby will love Mother back in kind. It will be "me and my baby against the world," the young mother thinks, and—unlike so many boyfriends and girl friends—the baby will never let her down, nor leave her.

Even older women whose education and class background afford them more opportunities than other women can still build up unrealistic expectations of motherhood as a life-transforming experience that will suddenly make them feel worthy and whole. Some women are attracted to motherhood when their dreams of "making it" in the professional world don't pan out. If the world won't reward her for her intelligence and competence as a worker, it might reward her for being a mother:

> I wanted a baby for a lot of reasons, but what really triggered the decision in the end was that I got to the point where I really hated my job. I had worked my tail off for years, but I wasn't getting anywhere. I quit my job with the hopes of getting another, but after six months of looking I still couldn't find anything other than office work. So when I got pregnant, I was thrilled. Having a baby was something meaningful to do—and being a mother was something I knew I could be a success at.

Even women who have enjoyed success in the professional world are not necessarily immune to the lure of the search for completion through motherhood. In fact, in our self-esteem groups we found that some women were actually more prone to the search for completion through motherhood after they had experienced success in other areas. These women had proven themselves in school, in work, and often in romance as well, but typically they found success in these areas did not make them feel worthy and whole as they had originally hoped. Perennial searchers, they would begin to wonder, "What next?" And for many, the answer was motherhood.

For many women, the search for completion through motherhood is additionally fueled by the confusion of the capacity to nurture with the need to nurture. Most women have been trained to be good at nurturing. Moreover, we've been trained to believe that because we can nurture, we must nurture—it is an intrinsic part of us. And, at the same time, many of us were taught that we are not to need nurturance ourselves. Hence, it is quite common for a woman to expect others to need nurturing, and to accept that need in them, but to feel selfish or even repulsed when she has this same need. A woman in this situation may be tempted to get busy giving of herself in order to sublimate her own needs; and what better way to do this than by having a baby?

Whatever the motivating factors, the search for completion through motherhood rarely, if ever, ends up making a woman feel worthy and whole. One reason for this is that what constitutes success or failure in a mother is a highly subjective matter. Some may praise the mother of the excellent student or athlete as a good mother; others may condemn her for driving her children too hard. Some may see the mother of the little boy who plays with dolls and wants to be a nurse as a model of love and tolerance; others may see her as a sick woman making her son into a sissy. A woman with mid to high self-esteem will be able to put her child's success and failures into perspective, understanding that there were other forces which influenced the child—like father, siblings, peers, school and church, just to name a few. But a woman who had children as a way to prove her worth and bolster her self-esteem will be more vulnerable to blame.

When we look at the judgments placed on mothers in our culture, we find that often mothers are in a no-win situation. If a child turns out to be what is perceived as a failure in some way, then blame is usually placed upon the mother. If, however, the child turns out to be what others perceive to be a success, then the credit is more often than not placed on the father:

> My son is involved in politics, just like his father. Our son is doing very well—he might well outshine his dad. All I ever hear about is how lucky he was to have the father he had. Well, one of the reasons our boy has been so successful is because he's articulate and a good leader and real pleasant to be around. Where does everyone think he learned that? His dad was at meetings most of the time. What do they think I was—an uninvolved party?

At least this woman is able to recognize the part she played in having a positive influence on her son, even if others don't. But some women who search for completion through their children end up so devaluing themselves that they completely discount their contributions:

> I look at my daughter and I literally can't believe that she is mine. She is pretty and smart and well liked. How could someone like me have raised a person like that? It just doesn't make any sense. I tease her that she was raised by a band of gypsies and brought back to me later in life.

Grown children can be just as likely as anyone to devalue their mother's contribution and blame her for their faults. No mother feels good about her children rejecting or blaming her, but a woman whose children are her only source of self-esteem will be devastated by the experience.

Unfortunately, the stereotypical "smother love" is prevalent among women who search for completion through their children. It is unfair to burden children with the responsibility of making their mother feel worthy and fulfilled. Moreover, for the children this responsibility interferes with the development of a self of their own. Also, as the children grow up and develop a degree of selfhood in spite of their mother, they are likely to resent her overinvolvement in their lives.

Another reason the search for completion through children inevitably fails to pay off in high self-esteem is that the children eventually leave—and with them goes the mother's only source of self-worth. In her study of 533 women hospitalized for mental illness for the first time, Pauline Bart found one overriding pattern: The women became depressed when their children left home. These women fit the classic pattern of the search for completion through motherhood; Bart described them as conventionally selfless, martyr-ish and overprotective.[18]

The search for completion through children works no better than the search through romantic love because we can't borrow *self*-esteem from another person. It is a contradiction in terms.

The Search for Completion Through Work

Work and love have been said to be the two pillars upon which happiness can be built. Some women today are de-emphasizing the importance of love—whether romantic or motherly or both—proving that, contrary to the old myths, female happiness does not revolve solely around love relationships. This would be an incontrovertibly healthy development were it not for one unfortunate fact: Many women today get into the same trouble with work that other women get into with romantic love and motherhood. They look to work to make them feel worthy and whole. They look to work to justify their existences. They throw themselves into their work as if their lives depended on it, just as other women fear they will die without love. They put so much emphasis on work that they agree with one well-known actress's assertion that "it's not what you feel that matters. It's the work that you do."[19]

As in other types of searches, the woman who searches through work has *one* source of self-esteem. Although she may spend time and energy doing other things, when it comes to deciding whether she is worth something, she bases her decision on how much work she's done and how well she has done it—whether that work is writing ads or scrubbing floors. Just as the previously quoted scientist discounted her work accomplishments, basing her entire worth on her lack of sexual attractiveness instead, so the woman who searches for completion through work will discount factors like success in relationships, telling herself that when it comes to her worth, the only thing that really counts is her performance at work.

Although the woman who searches for completion through work may look outwardly different from her relationship-centered sisters, the primary motivation is the same lack of self-esteem, a sense of not being good enough, or whole enough. Marilyn Machlowitz's description of career-oriented workaholics has bearing here:

> Although they appear assured to the point of arrogance, they secretly suspect that they are inadequate. No matter how undeserved and/or suppressed these suspicions are, they still inspire insecurities. Working hard can be a way of concealing or compensating for such suspected shortcomings.[20]

The image of a woman who seeks completion through work that comes most readily to mind is that of the single career woman who wears man-tailored suits, carries a briefcase, eats lunch at her desk and has little life beyond her office—an office she has been careful to decorate in a way that communicates that while she may be a woman she is a no-frills type who means business. Although many women who search for completion through work fit this stereotype, many others do not. Among such women are the waitress who hangs around the restaurant after her shift is over and even on her days off, helping out as much as she can because when she takes off her uniform she feels a loss of identity, and when she leaves the restaurant she feels a loss of purpose. Then there is the secretary who goes in early and stays late without compensation just to make sure she's done the job right; and the nurse who volunteers to work extra shifts, supposedly because she could use the money, but really because she feels best about herself when she's doing something—something for others. In addition to women who search for completion through paid work, countless others search through unpaid work, as Machlowitz points out:

> While women have been almost completely overlooked in the little that has been written about workaholism, there have always been women workaholics. If housework, for instance, were rightfully regarded as work, generations of compulsive cleaners could be considered workaholics. And so would the tireless organizers of charity events.[21]

In her study of upper-middle-class women in their middle years, Lillian Rubin found many for whom volunteer charity work meant a chance to use their skills without compromising their femininity or undermining their husband's role as provider. Another advantage was that it gave them an opportunity to pay the dues for their family's class status. According to Rubin, such women fill the bill of "Lady Bountifuls whose services buy off the family's guilt for its privileged position."[22]

Some women assume they were born feeling they had to work to be worthy of existence. Yet no one was born feeling she must work to justify her existence; she may find she needs to work to *enable* her existence, but she won't feel her worth is contingent upon her working unless someone tells her so:

> I was too little to remember this for myself, but we fled Poland right before the Nazis invaded. I have no grandparents or uncles or aunts or cousins. My parents told us we had to prove that we were worth saving. They worked hard at their small business, giving other immigrants jobs, and they worked hard in the synagogue. I've spent my life in public health, never feeling I had done enough.

One need not to be a descendant of Holocaust survivors to have gotten the message that she must work, work and work some more in order to justify her life. Given that our nation and culture were founded on a work ethic that equates a person's worth with the amount of work success achieved, it's virtually impossible to grow up in America without making a connection between the two. In a preindustrial, gathering-hunting society, a person would come into the world, live a life and die without ever being told that she must work to have worth, for in such cultures leisure time is highly valued, and work is seen as a means to an end, the less done of it the better. But a highly industrialized capitalist economy such as ours requires that people devote themselves to work, and so children are trained to believe that "to be is to do," and their worth is measured by their achievements as soon as they are capable of amassing achievements. From then on, the child learns her worth is directly tied to her accomplishments, at first in school, and later in the world of work. According to Thomas Carlyle, "work is alone noble,"[23] and according to Calvin Coolidge, the President whose portrait Ronald Reagan hung in the White House in place of Thomas Jefferson's, work is "the only means to manhood, and the measure of civilization. Savages do not work."[24]

Many find the search for completion through work appealing because work has a tangible aspect and is also somewhat subject to the worker's control. The woman who searches for completion through romance must wait for her lover to say "I love you—you are worthwhile." And the woman who searches through motherhood must wait even longer for her children to turn out right and redeem her as a human being. But the person seeking completion through work can measure her worth directly by the number of customers, students or clients served, the number of sales made, the amount of money raised for the cause, the roar of the applause after a performance or the jangle of tips in the apron pocket. Whether she is loved or not, she has a well-defined activity and concrete outcome she can rely on to provide her with tangible proof of her worth.

For some women who search for completion through work, the dedication to the job can act as a buffer against intimacy. The searcher sends out this message: Know and admire me for my accomplishments, but don't get any closer. Sometimes the searcher has set up for herself a deferred-gratification/deferred-intimacy scheme as well. In such cases the reasoning is usually this: I don't deserve love now, I must do more to earn it; and when I have done enough to have earned love, I won't be afraid of intimacy anymore because by then I'll have enough accomplishments to compensate for—or even eliminate—my failings and vulnerability. Unfortunately, many extremely accomplished people have earned the esteem of their peers, been admired by thousands of fans, won every award in their field and still have died lonely and longing for love and closeness with someone who loves them for who they are rather than admires them for what they've done.

Others find the search through work appealing because it can provide a sense of closeness and community. For many women devoted to work, staying at the office until the wee hours of the morning or hanging out at the restaurant after punching out can serve to stave off the loneliness that becomes suffocating in an empty apartment or a home where meaningful communication with a partner or children seems to have ceased a long time ago. In some cases, a work family can take the place of a real family and might be chosen intentionally for this purpose:

> My work won't leave me, it won't reject me, it won't hurt my feelings and it gives me enough money to live on. . . . I have friendships with my office mates—in fact they are my only friends—and that's the way I want it. My own family is a bust and I never meet any interesting men I'd want to get involved with.

Although some women can, and often do, find in their work a sense of purpose, belonging and temporary satisfaction, rarely do they find in their search what they are truly looking for—a genuine sense of self-worth. One reason for this is that few workers in our economy have access to those sorts of jobs that provide enough status, attention and power to be a sufficient basis for self-esteem. Most workers need to find sources of self-esteem outside their work—as in family, clubs, possessions, religion, etc. If a woman looks for completion in her work, she may have to delude herself about the nature and importance of the work. There is no other way for her to feel good about herself:

> When I had everything invested in my work, I had myself convinced that the entire department (where I was secretary) would fall apart if I missed a day or failed to finish some project on time. I truly believed I was irreplaceable. Beyond that, I had myself convinced that this job I saw myself as irreplaceable in was of earth-shattering importance, that the world would cave in if I missed a deadline or bungled a report. It took a friend a long time to get me to honestly look at what would happen if I did miss a deadline. I finally said, "Well, people would be annoyed, and we'd get behind schedule for a few days, I'd have to make some phone calls to explain the delay and there'd be a chance we'd lose the account—although we probably wouldn't." And she said, "Yeah, that's probably just what would happen. Now is that the same as the sky falling in?"

Women who search through work are usually unable to relax on weekends, to enjoy vacations or to ever fully wind down. Even when seemingly relaxed, they are often working, planning work projects, or feeling bad for not working. And even when playing they end up transforming play into work:

> I was laid off for a while, collecting unemployment, and I decided I would take up bicycling. It was a beautiful summer, but I couldn't enjoy what I was doing. I kept thinking, "You're not doing this right—you can't afford really professional equipment." I kept berating myself because I wasn't being serious and racing, and unless I was going to commit myself to that, I felt I had no business riding a bicycle.

For the woman who in the guise of "liberation" gives up everything traditionally female to pursue the traditionally male values of career success and achievement, the pain of failure can be particularly hard, as Gail Sheehy observes:

> What becomes of aspiring women who fall short? To be consigned to a limbo between dependent wife and independent achiever, unvalued in either realm, no children for an excuse, no man to take care of her, the

charms of her twenties spent—this is a fate too punishing even to contemplate.[25]

Even success does not guarantee a life without disappointment, worries, conflict and difficult choices. Among those few women who do make it among the professional elite, many eventually come to ask, "Is this all there is?" There is no substitute for a well-balanced life, one in which a woman can say, "Among many things, I am a good worker, too":

> I always said I hated my father because he spent so much time on his law practice that he ignored us children, and then he used having to support us children as an excuse for having to work all the time. But I ended up going to law school too, and then devoting myself day and most of the night to my career—just like him. But now that I have a baby, I've had to stop and reconsider things. I thought at first that I'd take a few months off, then jump right back to work full-time. But working all the time is boring, and it makes me into an automaton. It didn't make my father happy, and it certainly didn't make his kids happy. So I don't see why it will make me happy, or my child happy either.

In our self-esteem groups we asked those women who search for completion through work to contemplate for a moment how they would cope if they suddenly found themselves in a situation where they could no longer do the work they have relied upon to justify their existences. The women consistently reacted with horror to our question; they had never thought about the possibility of losing their ability to work, and they couldn't imagine such a terrible thing happening to them. This woman, however, could imagine it because she had been through it:

> On TV there are always shows about some guy who was a brain surgeon or concert pianist, then in a freak accident gets his hands run over by a train and his ego is shattered and the whole reason for living is taken away. Or else the guy has been a really successful executive type who suddenly has a heart attack because of all the stress he puts himself under, and he feels worthless as a result and has to reevaluate the meaning of his life. I had seen lots of shows like that, but like everyone else I had never seriously thought about that type of thing happening to me. So when I was in a car accident and ended up incapacitated for a long period, I was really devastated. I broke nearly every bone in my body, I was in the hospital for nine months, and then after that there were still months and months of physical therapy to get me walking and fully functioning again. I had been a phys. ed. teacher before the accident, but right away it was pretty clear that that wouldn't be an option for me anymore. For a good two years there, it was all I could do to get better—working at anything was out of the question.

It took me a long, long time to regain a sense that I had some worth, because I felt that if I wasn't able to take care of myself and contribute to my family and to do something useful in the world, I didn't have a right to be. . . .

It would be maudlin to dwell on it, but the fact remains that each of us could suddenly lose our ability to work and achieve tomorrow, and this is a fact we might do well to contemplate briefly. If we could not work or contribute something useful to our world, either permanently or for a while, would we be able to consider ourselves persons of worth? With the motto "to be is to do" prevailing in our culture, it is difficult to separate being from doing, and to accept that there is value in just being —that being is enough.

Making Peace

A notion popular in America until fairly recently was that true emotional maturity in a woman meant being able to sacrifice her own needs and sense of self in devotion to a man and "his" children. Recently, a new myopic ideal has developed: The true mark of emotional maturity in a woman is the ability to set aside emotional needs and attachments and concentrate fully on a career, thus proving herself an equal in a man's world. Both of these ideals are unrealistic, and both are detrimental to women's self-esteem. No one measure of emotional maturity suits all women. Nor will any one path lead to self-esteem.

Unlearning the belief that our worth is defined by who we are involved with, how many children we have, and what we do requires making peace with being in and of itself. We need to believe that our life has some intrinsic meaning and need not be justified by anyone or anything external. Many of the women we interviewed replaced one search with another, only to find in the end that self-acceptance came only when they finally stopped looking to their relationships and activities with the hope that "if I succeed at this, then once and for all I'll have proved my worth." Ceasing this sort of thinking enabled them to live more in peace, and also to reorder their lives so that there is more balance between work, pleasure and various relationships.

Ending the search for completion also means making peace with being alone. The word "alone" is a contraction of two words: "all" and "one."[26] To be at peace with aloneness does not mean having a chip on one's shoulder, arrogantly convinced that we are all that matters and we can get along in life needing no one else. Rather, it means realizing we cannot get self-worth from someone or something outside ourselves; what we need to be of worth is what we have within. Aware of our inherent worth, it is easier to connect with other people, not out of needy desperation, but with the confidence that our relationships and work will add more to what already exists.

We also need to make peace with ourselves as we are now, and with our lives as they are now. At some point (preferably not during a crisis) a woman needs to ask herself, "What if my dreams never come true—if the perfect lover, child or job never materialize? What if this is it? Can I still accept myself?" Unless she is forever to feel inadequate and incomplete, the answer needs to be, "Yes, I am still okay. I have dreams and am working toward goals. But in the meantime, my life is still worth living."

When a woman comes to this point of self-acceptance, it means a stop to the endless waiting that the search for completion engenders. Too many women spend their lives waiting to find someone or something to put them at ease with their existence, waiting for someone or something to ward off their fears of aloneness. But to wait through life is to waste it. To live fully we need to confront the moment we are in now and to be responsible for finding our own happiness within it. As Sally Field said:

> . . . When you're thirty-five, as I am, you suddenly realize you have a history, that you're not waiting any more for a guy to come around and ask you to go steady so your life can begin. My life is now.[27]

BLUEPRINTS FOR CHANGE

I. PILLARS OF LIFE

What are *your* pillars of a happy life? Is there only one? If you have more than one and were to draw each one in scale according to its importance to your sense of worth, would one pillar dwarf the others? Perhaps you want to scale down one pillar and expand another.

Do your pillars of a happy life reflect your own values or are they borrowed from other people's expectations? Are they reflections of other's ideas of what life should be about? Do any of your pillars include something that is *fun?* Do they reflect self-expression in the areas of your spirituality, physicality, intellectual and emotional needs?

II. Assessing the Search

If you are not sure whether or not you are searching for completion or simply holding someone or something very dearly, ask yourself the following questions (whichever are appropriate to you):

1. What if my lover or mate died or left me?
2. What if my children died or were estranged from me?
3. What if I was fired, laid off or physically unable to do my work?

There is a difference between feeling sad, grief-stricken, angry or disappointed and feeling as if you no longer have a self, as if your purpose for living is gone and your life has no more meaning. If we have a balance of a variety of relationships and interests, we can endure a loss in one area without being totally devastated.

III. If-Then Schemes

Searches for completion are sometimes tied to expectations of perfection. Specifically, we found the "if-then" schemes of the following varieties give the searchers their momentum:

IF I find somebody who loves me and I devote myself to him (or her), THEN I will finally like myself.

IF I place my children's well-being above all else, THEN I will feel good about myself when they turn out right.

IF I devote myself to my work, THEN my existence will be justified to everyone and I can like myself.

Each of these entails endless waiting for affirmation that will probably never happen. Each drains a woman's energy and precludes her self-knowledge as she tries to satisfy the requirement set up by the "if-then" scheme. But these schemes don't work because the self-love has to come first.

IF I love myself, THEN I will be able to more successfully love another person.

IF I love myself, THEN my children are more likely to learn the self-love they need to turn out right.

IF I love myself, THEN I will be more likely to *enjoy* my work, find satisfaction in it, and succeed at it.

IV. Justifying Your Existence

Who told you that you have to justify your existence, that it wasn't okay for you just to be alive? Probably there is more than one source of this message (e.g., family, schools, religion, friends, etc.). Consider each one separately. Are these still symbols of authority to you? Are you willing to consider that they might be wrong?

V. BEING ALONE

We do not need to leave our lovers, children, jobs or whatever in order to make peace with our aloneness. We can begin to do this on a smaller scale. Try to set aside a few hours where you can go someplace quiet and safe to be alone. Structure no activities during this time. Pick a place where you will just exist, perhaps a beach or park (again, where you will be safe). Perhaps you will watch other people, but try to resist the temptation to talk a lot with them to distract you from your aloneness. This is an experiment, and you will need to be as much on your own as you can be. Going to the movies alone, taking a long drive alone, etc., may be good half steps; we interviewed a few women who have never done these things. But the distraction of the movie and paying attention to driving tends to diminish the sense of aloneness.

Although you want to keep your time unstructured, you might want to think about what, specifically, is so difficult about being alone. Was there an important person in your life who was alone and seemed unhappy? Was there someone who lived alone and did fine? As a child, did you spend time alone? How did you feel about that then? Certainly, that would influence your feelings about being alone as an adult, but do you think it would be different today? After all, you aren't that powerless child anymore. Maybe the experience of being alone today could be more positive. You may find you have *all* you need in your *one* self to be at peace.

* 9 *

From Not Feeling Good About Ourselves to Not Feeling at All: Emotional Expression versus Depression

> I must be ready to confront feelings and ideas within myself that are ugly, evil and discrediting, if I am to receive the lovely, tender, decent aspects of myself. All of the good/bad, strong/weak, divine/ridiculous Janus faces must be seen, if I am to have any time to live with my mask off. And should I wear my mask too long, when I take it off and try to discard it, I may find that I have thrown my face away with it.
>
> —Sheldon B. Kopp
> *If You Meet the Buddha on the Road, Kill Him!*

One of the most distinctive and unfortunate characteristics of our culture is the strong bias against emotions that runs through it. In order to have self-esteem a person needs to be able to accept that she is emotional, to say to herself, "I am a feeling being, and that's okay." Yet this is usually easier said than done, for we have been taught to presume a split between the head and the heart, the mind and the body, and to consider cerebral functions superior to emotional ones. Consider for a moment René Descartes' famous words "I think, therefore I am." Just as easily, and with just as much truth, Descartes could have said, "I feel, therefore I am." Better yet, he could have said, "I think *and* feel, therefore I am." But in our culture the trait we are taught to admire and aspire to is complete rationality, and rationality is associated with manliness. Irrationality and emotionalism, by contrast, are associated with women, and to be called irrational or emotional is to be insulted in the worst way.

Given the anti-emotion bias of our culture, it is no wonder that one of the most common ways a woman's lack of respect for herself is expressed is through lack of respect for her emotions. Many women believe emotions are unseemly, silly, signs of weakness or otherwise bad. Many also look down upon emotions and any expression of them as embarrassing, undignified and immature. And many find emotions terrifying as well, fearing that if they allow themselves to feel any emotion at all, they will be overwhelmed and soon become out of control. Ironically, the sentiments against feelings many people have are often extremely intense:

> One of the women I work with was going through a really rough time—her little girl was seriously ill and the strain was putting her marriage on the rocks—and she was really showing her pain. It wasn't like she was overdramatizing or being a martyr or anything, it was just that she wasn't pretending everything was great and she was tough and strong. She got her work done fine, but several times a day she'd take a break and go into the bathroom and cry some. . . . People at first were sympathetic, but after a while they got real judgmental, saying she wasn't handling the crisis correctly, that she shouldn't be acting this way. . . . What was really weird about it was that as people put down this woman for being so upset, they got all upset and worked up themselves. They didn't seem to realize it, but they were getting incredibly emotional about this other woman being emotional.

Reacting against the centuries-old anti-emotion bias, many in the 1960s and 1970s adopted a new pro-emotion bias. Sadly, many of the changes ushered in with the "get in touch with your feelings" era were insidious. Along with the rise of a largely vacuous language that R. D. Rosen has aptly dubbed "psychobabble,"[1] there came in the sixties and seventies a blurring of moral distinctions and the skirting of responsibility with such mottoes as "if it feels good, do it" (even if what makes you feel good makes someone else feel horrible). Moreover, with the new emphasis on emotions it became more and more acceptable, even fashionable, for people to use emotions to manipulate or even hurt others:

> The hardest thing for me to deal with is when someone uses their emotional vulnerability as a weapon or cop-out. I have this one friend who's real good at it—she pulls a lot of shit, but you can't call her on it because she's so sensitive, and she'll start crying and saying how it really hurts to hear what you're saying. . . .

Not all the changes brought about by the "get in touch with your feelings" era were insidious. Some were positive, and some people did emerge from the era with an increased level of emotional awareness and an increased recognition of the need for emotional expression. For the most part, however, these positive changes were superficial.

The general bias against emotions in our culture often merges with biases against certain ethnic and racial groups. Among certain groups certain emotions are considered particularly offensive. A Jewish person who is ambitious, for example, is automatically lambasted for being "a typical greedy Jew." If a Jewish woman is assertive, she's branded pushy and loud-mouthed. Assertive black women are "uppity." Hispanic people are condemned for being hot-blooded. Italians can't show anger without being called hot-tempered. In each case the general anti-emotion bias in our culture is transformed into a specific bias that feeds into prejudices against a specific group.

A main reason for our culture's anti-emotion bias is economic and social expediency: Commerce and social relations would crumble if everyone went around emoting all the time, and so each day most of us are forced to squelch our feelings to some extent—as when we swallow anger, hold back tears, stifle urges to laugh or cry out, and suppress feelings of sadness by "putting on a happy face." This makes for a more orderly and efficient world, but the physiological and psychological costs to individuals are high. For since modern life provides us with few built-in ways of releasing the energy emotions generate (through hard physical labor such as farming, chopping wood, scrubbing laundry by hand, etc.), it often happens that when an emotion has been suppressed, it stays suppressed. And when emotions stay suppressed, they can increase our likelihood of headaches, exhaustion, ulcers, heart problems, asthma, hay fever, insomnia and even cancer. All these maladies have been linked to (among other things) a lack of healthy emotional expression. So, too, has a disease that is now epidemic in America, particularly among women—namely, the disease of depression.

Depression and low self-esteem usually go hand in hand: One study, for instance, found that 80 percent of depressed persons disliked themselves significantly.[2] Precisely how depression and low self-esteem are linked is often difficult to determine, and the question of which came first—the low self-esteem or the depression—can be a fuzzy one in specific cases. But two things are clear. First, depression can only lower self-esteem; it never leads to higher self-esteem. Second, low self-esteem predisposes a person to depression. A person who doesn't feel good about herself isn't likely to feel good about her emotions, and if she doesn't feel good about her emotions, she'll be that much more likely to suppress them. In sum, it's often a direct step from not feeling good about yourself to not feeling at all, which is the hallmark of depression.

Understanding Depression

Another question we've often been asked in our self-esteem groups is, "Just what is depression?" Depression has come to be an umbrella term, used to describe a variety of feelings from disappointment, boredom and listlessness to grief, extreme sadness and despair. But when used correctly, the term depression refers to a specific condition. True depression is characterized by a waning of feeling, eventually leading to complete numbing—or deadening—of the emotions. In its early stages it is characterized by the loss of ability to experience positive emotions such as joy and a loss of the will and ability to act in one's best interest. If allowed to progress, depression in its later stages brings the loss of the ability to feel anything at all, even pain:

> I was depressed for about three years while my marriage was breaking up, but I didn't know I was depressed because I was like someone out of *The Night of the Living Dead.* . . . During this time I had a bad fall on the ice on a sidewalk. I guess it must have hurt, but I really didn't feel anything, and so I ignored it. It was only when I started having noticeable difficulty moving my limbs that my friends dragged me to the hospital, and it was then that I found out I had been walking around with a broken back. I've had several operations, and the doctors said that if I had delayed any longer, I probably would have ended up totally paralyzed. As it is, two years later I still have to wear a brace, and I have no feeling in my feet or fingers. . . .

This woman was severely depressed: she did not feel bad, she felt nothing.

As depressed people eventually lose all their ability to feel, so as depression progresses people eventually lose all ability to act. Whereas in the early states of depression a woman may have trouble getting out of bed or "getting moving" in certain areas of her life, as she becomes more and more depressed, she will have trouble moving at all. Again, we are not talking about occasional lethargy or listlessness; we are talking about a state of chronic immobilization. This woman describes how her depression increasingly immobilized her:

> I wanted very much to leave my husband, and everytime I would bring up divorce, he would reduce my allowance or take my car away or restrict me in some way. One morning I got my two little girls off to school and sat

down, in my bathrobe, with a cup of coffee, to think about the problem. Literally before I knew it, the girls were home. I hadn't moved in seven hours and I had the same cup of coffee.

David Burns elaborates on the immobilizing aspect of depression and how it diminishes self-esteem:

> One of the most destructive aspects of depression is the way it paralyzes your willpower. In its mildest forms, you may simply procrastinate about doing a few odious chores. As your lack of motivation intensifies, virtually any activity appears so difficult that you become overwhelmed by the urge to do nothing. Because you accomplish very little, you feel worse and worse. Not only do you cut yourself off from your normal sources of stimulation and pleasure, but your lack of productivity aggravates your self-hatred, resulting in further isolation and incapacitation.[3]

Theories abound as to why and how people become depressed. For some it is believed to be due to a chemical imbalance within their bodies. For many, however, depression is the result of insufficient emotional expression—or, rather, excessive emotional suppression. As psychiatrist Henry Paul puts it, feelings are not like the keys of a piano—we cannot push one down without pushing them all down.[4] If a woman, for whatever reasons, suppresses a specific feeling she finds problematic (anger, lust or aggression, for example), she will end up unintentionally but effectively suppressing all her feelings, even the ones she wants to experience (joy, for example). This is because all our feelings are interconnected, inextricably so. In order to be able to experience pleasure and joy, we must be able to experience pain and sadness.

Learning To Become Depressed

In spite of the debilitating effects of depressing feelings, people still ask, "But isn't depression a natural response to life?" The answer is a resounding no. Grief is a natural response to the loss of a loved one. Disappointment is a natural response to not getting a hoped-for promotion or failing an exam. Anger is a natural response to having been treated unfairly or cruelly. While we are grieving, disappointed or angry, we can also feel happy that a friend cared enough to call and express concern or we can feel relieved to share our feelings with others who are supportive. This ability to feel a variety of different emotions in succession or even at the same time is what's natural. Depression is not. Early on, most of us learned to be quite adept at suppressing our feelings. Usually, we began by learning to suppress one or two feelings our parents, teachers and other authoritative adults found intolerable in children. The first feeling we were taught to suppress may well have been anger, an emotion many grown-ups find particularly hard to deal with in children. Anne Lamott in her novel *Hard Laughter* gives a good description of the process by which children learn to suppress anger, and other emotions with it. The novel's protagonist is angry about the fact that her father has a brain tumor, and she has written to an old family friend, telling him she is planning to release her rage through some "shouting therapy." The friend replies:

> Of course you're pissed off about the tumor, all of us are. Every so often we are reminded of how sad and shitty the world can be. Part of the secret, as you know, is to siphon anger's self-destructive qualities into a sense of humor, a sense of comic irony, and when that fails to cry and scream and shout. . . . You were better at being mad when you were a young child . . . and in fact most of us were. You had a joyful side at three, and you had a shy retiring side where your voice would become very soft and you would seem almost near tears, and I mostly thought you were great, *except* when you screamed in anger. Then most of us adults wanted to shut you up. You were punished, non-physically of course, when you were pissed off and loud: many small children are beaten when they express anger. Many children are denied their meals (read: love) when they are angry, but as you know, the anger festers inside us when we don't get it out of our systems. Your so-called shouting therapy sounds like just what you need.[5]

The most common defense against feelings is intellectualization. In-tellectualization is the process by which we seek reasons to explain, analyze, judge and censor our feelings. A popular form of intellectual-ization for women is to tell ourselves that certain feelings are bad and wrong and therefore we shouldn't feel them. The dualistic way we have been taught to think makes it seem only natural to categorize some feelings as good, others as bad. Yet moral labels do not really apply to feelings. We can *do* things that are right or wrong, bad or good. But there is nothing that's wrong or bad to *feel*.

We have heard women say, "Well, I just don't allow myself to feel. . . ." This is denial, another common defense against feelings. Those who practice denial may not allow themselves to consciously admit what they're feeling, but the feeling is involuntary, it already exists.

Often we have heard women say, "I shouldn't feel this way—it's really stupid." But the truth is, just as feelings are neither moral nor immoral, feelings have no IQ. Nor, moreover, is there any correlation between a person's IQ and her emotions. A woman with a genius IQ may be terrified of spiders, extremely fond of a pet others find a nuisance, and nervous to the point of panic about the idea of having to face a crowd and give a speech. None of these feelings is dumb, and none is evidence that the woman having the feelings is dumb either. Each, rather, is simply evidence that she is human.

Another common belief among adults which serves to inhibit the experience and expression of emotions is that feelings are "childish." This judgment can be leveled against positive feelings as well:

> As kids we weren't supposed to be noisy about our delight. In fact, we were supposed to be supercool about it, act as if nothing very special was happening. Like one time an old girl friend just appeared on my doorstep. I was in the tenth grade and she had moved away when we were in the eighth. When I opened the door, with a high-pitched voice, sounding surprised, I said, "Sue!" and hugged her. Did I ever hear about that from my mother. She said people would "get the wrong idea," whatever that meant, and that it was an undignified way to act. She said I should have said, "Oh, hello Sue." She even made me practice.

Carried to its extreme, the belief that feelings are childish can become a barrier to expressing the feeling to any degree lest we look foolish.

Some women also believe that feelings, rather than being a natural part of their lives, "get in the way":

> Last week I paid this jerk four hundred dollars to fix my car, and it immediately broke down again—near my friend's. I went to her house to use the phone and I told her what happened. Instead of saying "That's too bad" or "What a jerk," she says, "Don't bother to get upset. It doesn't do any good." I told her it wasn't a bother. Getting upset over this came quite naturally to me.

Certainly feelings can be unpleasant, confusing, untimely and disruptive at times. But so can other body functions, such as being thirsty. We cannot ignore our thirst for a very long time without our body insisting on its need and doing some harm to our total being. So it goes with not expressing feelings. This woman, who had chronic problems with depression throughout her life, finally came to this conclusion:

> depression is the closest you can get to being dead while still being alive. I figure I'm going to be dead soon enough, I don't need to rush the experience. In the meantime, I want to live my life with feeling.

Mislabeling

Many women have problems accurately naming exactly what it is they feel. Indeed, many of us were never taught any specific names for our feelings at all, just as we were not taught names of our sex organs. Instead of being helped to identify and distinguish such feelings as frustration, grief, sadness, loss, anger, annoyance and joy, serenity, satisfaction, fondness, admiration and love, many were taught to distinguish only between feeling bad and feeling good. Like sex, emotions constituted a taboo topic, the specifics unmentionable.

Consequently, a wide variety of feelings get mislabeled as depression. Often we hear or say, "It's been raining for so long—I'm so depressed," or "I just paid all my bills—I'm really depressed," "I just had a fight with my roommate—am I ever depressed." In fact, the person making these statements might be feeling other feelings such as boredom, restlessness, worry, upset, anger.

Women often mislabel various emotions as depression partly because of the imprecise way most of us speak and the misusage of the word "depression." Some women also do it because it seems safer and more desirable to feel depressed than a specific feeling we are uncomfortable or unfamiliar with. Some further mislabel unpleasant feelings as depression because depression in women is accepted as normal; indeed, it is often rewarded:

> If I tell my husband there is something I am upset about, he won't listen. He busies himself around his workshop or maybe he'll walk out on me. But if I tell him I'm depressed, he'll listen to me because he wants to "help" me. I hate it—it's a silly game, but it works.

A woman cannot feel good about herself if she is constantly telling herself she is depressed. However, she can eventually impose the barriers of genuine depression upon herself. There is much a woman can do about being bored, restless, worried, upset, etc. But if she tells herself she is depressed, there seems little she can do, and so she convinces herself that she is trapped, immobilized. A woman who says "I am lonely," for example, has many options. She can say to herself, "I'm really feeling lonely—I'll try to find someone to be with for a while," or "I'm feeling lonely—I guess everybody feels that way from time to time." She can express her feeling to her friends, and they might respond with their companionship or stories about times they had felt lonely, too. If she says "I'm depressed," though, she may see no options. She might even end up doing something we have seen too many women do—getting "depressed" about being "depressed."

Women's Special Problems with Anger

Women in general tend to find anger the most problematic emotion of all. It is the one women feel worst about experiencing, the one we are most likely to deny or suppress, and the one we are most likely to mislabel—particularly as depression.

Depression in women is often "anger turned inward." We have been told that we "shouldn't feel that way," and so we keep our anger inside, where it eats away at us. In fact, anger is a natural response, at times, to the reality of our lives. We need to accept our right and ability to feel anger if we are to be healthy, as Helen De Rosis and Victoria Pellegrino remind us:

> In order to express anger, you have to believe that anger is natural. You have to believe that it is as much a part of you as your sudden feelings of gaiety when you hear a joke, as regret at unintentionally inflicting hurt, as your sorrow at a loss, as your joy in greeting a friend, as your disgust at smelling a bad odor. You have to accept anger as a human emotion. It's not a feeling to be ashamed of, to deny, rationalize, or hide. For no matter what you try to do, if your anger is aroused, it is there whether or not you express it, and it will have certain effects on your psychic and physical being.[6]

In young children anger is usually not tolerated regardless of gender, but as the children grow up, boys are generally given much more freedom to feel and express anger than girls are given. One of the favorite figures of American folklore is the "angry young man." There is no corollary "angry young woman" for girls to admire and imitate. An angry woman is despised as a bitch, or put down as maladjusted or sexually unsatisfied. Meanwhile, thanks largely to the sanction our culture gives to male expression of anger, American males commit more individual acts of violence than males anywhere else, making ours the most violent of all industrialized nations. Philip Slater comments on the consequences of the double standard that disapproves of anger in women but approves of no other emotion but anger in men:

> What does a person do with feelings that are disapproved by his or her society? To some extent, they can be released under the guise of some other feeling that carries no disgrace. In our society, for example, women often

dissolve into tears instead of raging in anger, while men get angry when their feelings are hurt and they feel like crying.[7]

Many women we interviewed had difficulty admitting and expressing anger because, in addition to feeling it is unfeminine, they confused anger with the cessation or withdrawal of love. Never taught to accurately label their feelings, they see anger and hate as one and the same. Thus they have difficulty distinguishing between the two very different statements "I'm angry with you" and "I hate you":

> It was only recently, after a failed marriage, that I finally got it through my head that someone could love me and be angry with me at the same time and that the anger didn't mean a lessening of love. . . . It was only after I was able to hear "I'm mad as hell at you but I love you" that I could begin to own up to my own feelings of anger. Anger is less scary for me on both ends now that I know being angry doesn't mean being hateful.

Another reason many women have difficulty with anger is that most of us have been exposed to too few—if any—examples of constructively dealing with anger. We grew up seeing only two ways of handling anger —holding it in or letting it out explosively in a way that irresponsibly hurt others. As a result, for many it is difficult to find a middle ground between swallowing anger completely and coming out swinging.

Escaping Our Emotions

For some women it's not enough to suppress problematic feelings; they need to escape them entirely. There are three common ways to "kill the pain": through alcohol and/or drugs, oversleep, and suicide.

Approximately five million women in this country are alcoholics. In *The Female Fix,* her study of alcoholic and drug-addicted women, Muriel Nells found that although chemically dependent women came in all shapes and sizes and from all social classes, they all had in common the belief that their feelings were abnormal and dangerous and turned to alcohol and/or drugs to suppress them:

> For a long time, I took Valium and Librium as a way to stop negative feelings. And I had no trouble getting prescriptions from doctors. None of them said feeling anxious or sad or irritable was normal. Eventually, I needed more and more in order to stay in that "mist" where I felt safe. Then I needed downers to get to sleep and then drank to take the edge off. After I crashed and went through detox, I finally understood that in keeping the genuinely bad feelings away, I was keeping the genuinely good

feelings away, too. I was trying to manufacture good feelings. Now the real ones are going to have to be good enough.

Without the aid of any chemical substance, some women are adept at avoiding their feelings through sleep. Gabrielle Burton writes of doing this while a full-time housewife in *I'm Running Away from Home, but I'm Not Allowed to Cross the Street:*

> I read most of the time—in between sleeping. I wasn't working. I had stopped that when we were married, knowing it would undermine my husband's role as the PROVIDER. I lay around for nine months and ten days, waiting for my first fulfillment to come. I insisted that I loved being a housewife. Roger suggested once, in between my sobbings, that maybe I'd be happier if I went out and did something. What did he know? I knew with my extraordinary sensitivity that his ego would be shattered if I brought in a buck. Besides it would all fall into place when the baby was born.
>
> I slept inordinate amounts. It made me very guilty, but it also made the day go away and that was important.
>
> Daytime sleeping is a form of suicide. Amazing numbers of women resort to it. Everybody knows it and pretends it is a necessity when raising small children. When a woman telephones another in the afternoon, she often says, "I hope I didn't wake you." It is common to hear, "Don't call between one and three. That's my naptime."[8]

A woman need not be housebound to feel the need for escape through exhaustion:

> I keep myself busy with work, volunteering, a rigorous exercise program. I go nonstop from the moment I wake up until I literally collapse into bed at night. I don't want to be able to feel anything but exhaustion.

The sleep some women seek is sleep of a permanent kind. Suicide is a question for many people at some point in their lives. Sometimes suicide is seen as a way to gain relief from intense feelings. As a passing thought, suicide may not be dangerous. But when considerable energy begins to go into planning the circumstances of the suicide, or if a woman finds herself living her life as if nothing matters because she knows she will die soon, then the time has come to seek professional help.

Unfortunately, a certain glamor has come to be attached to suicide. A macabre folklore romanticizes the suicides of women like Virginia Woolf and Sylvia Plath, and the alleged suicide of Marilyn Monroe. This is compounded when women who commit suicide are hailed as extraordinarily gifted yet misunderstood, and their deaths are celebrated as proof of their genius. It may seem romantic that Joe DiMaggio sends roses to Marilyn Monroe's grave every week for two decades. But for most people, suicide brings neither romance nor admiration: It only brings death. It is the ultimate statement of self-hatred.

Allowing Ourselves To Feel

The process of beginning to fully experience feelings is not always smooth. It may be confusing or even frightening at times. De Rosis and Pellegrino believe that during these times, we may believe we are going crazy when in fact we are "going sane."[9]

Women often worry that if they let themselves get more "in touch" with their feelings, they will become mindless "feeling junkies." Some women do go overboard in the discovery of their feelings and needs, and for a while they may talk about nothing else. And some women first experience their feelings in exaggerated form and are prone to dramatics. But most women quickly balance out. As feeling becomes more natural to us, as it should be, there is no longer the need for the feelings to be bigger than life to be felt:

> At first I thought I'd lose myself in the feelings I was beginning to allow. It was so different, so disorienting. But I find now I *do* get through them and feel better on the other side. When I was depressed, it was always the same numbness. Now, when I feel sad, there is a purity to it, and I know I will feel differently, better in time. When I'm mad, there isn't the old confusion that got in my way, and I can work it out and let it go. And the happier feelings are that much heightened in contrast. I don't beat myself up for having these feelings—I take them as part of myself, not as alien invaders. I feel less disjointed—more whole—as a result.

As we often say in our groups, "First you feel more, then you feel better."

When a woman begins to allow herself to feel what she has previously expended energy in denying or suppressing, the quality of her life will change. Often those around us are comfortable with our numb old selves and do not welcome the change. For example, a woman's friendships may become less satisfying when she begins to feel better about herself and no longer has the common bond of self-hatred and depression to share with her friends. But eventually she will find new friends with the same evolving sense of self-worth.

We do not have to act on every feeling, but it's usually a wise tack to consider our feelings when deciding what to do. Anxiety might tell us

that we need to change something in our lives or that we need to prepare for some aspect of reality in the future. Sadness might be a signal
that we have suffered some kind of loss and perhaps need to mourn.
More favorably judged emotions like joy and excitement might spur us
on toward gaining more of the same.

Even when we decide it is not a good idea to take direct action on our
feelings, we still have something to learn from them. After receiving
criticism from a coworker, we wisely might refrain from sobbing or
punching the critic in the face. But we also might recognize we are
feeling raw around the edges and need some time to ourselves or perhaps begin to explore why our feelings get so hurt so easily.

BLUEPRINTS FOR CHANGE

I. FEELINGS ABOUT FEELINGS

We tend to judge some feelings as good or bad. The connotations we
apply to certain feelings affect our likeliness to feel them. This woman
found this to be true of vulnerability:

> I always thought of being vulnerable as being bad, open to hurt. So I went
> out of my way to be invulnerable to everyone and everything. But being
> vulnerable is just plain being open. If I'm open to being hurt, I'm also open
> to have something good happen.

Not all feelings fall neatly into good/bad categories. It might be helpful
for you to think about the judgments you have about your feelings and
how they influence your daily living. What feelings do you judge as
being bad or wrong in other people? In yourself?

II. BODY/MIND PARTNERSHIP

List all the emotions you can recall ever having felt. There might be a
few dozen, and they may encompass a wide range (from despair to joy,
for example). Next to each feeling, try to describe the physical sensations normally associated with it. Be as specific as possible. There might
be slight variations from feeling to feeling, or many feelings might seem
similar. Whatever you come up with is okay.

Also think about the ways you stop some of those feelings. What do
you physically do to stop them? Do you hold your breath, numb out,
get dizzy? What do you mentally do? Do you think, "This is a bad way
to feel," "I shouldn't feel this way," or otherwise intellectualize and

judge ("It's not fair")? Try to imagine using your mind and body together to experience the feelings and accurately name them.

III. MISLABELING

Look over your feelings list. Do you mislabel any as depression? As hunger? Do you mask one feeling as another? What are your earlier experiences with this feeling? Did anyone tell you you shouldn't feel that way? Or do you just lack experience with this emotion?

Now that you have thought of some of the whys and wherefores of your mislabeling a problematic feeling, think about alternatives to calling it depression next time you feel it. Often when we are in the middle of experiencing a problematic feeling, we get confused or overwhelmed and cannot think of alternatives, so do it now while you are not affected by it. To combat the immobilization that comes with believing you are depressed, think of what you could do, how you could act, beyond accurately labeling it. Some examples from our groups:

> Sadness: "I could call up a friend and tell her I'm sad."
>
> Worry: "I could sit down and do some constructive planning, put my worry to good use, try to come up with a plan of action to solve the problem I'm worried about."
>
> Boredom: "I'll keep a list of 'rainy day' things that I need to do or would like to do—that way I don't get sidetracked on what a horrible person I am for being bored."
>
> Anger: "If I can't talk to the person, I can write a letter that I would never send. Or I could beat the rugs or chop and stack wood or go running until my mind clears."

Some of these methods may seem simplistic. But if we can deal with what we feel simply and straightforwardly, our energy will go toward expressing and resolving the feeling rather than suppressing it.

IV. NONVERBAL EXPRESSION OF FEELINGS

Sometimes it is not in our best interest to express our feelings directly to the person we have the feelings toward. This would be the case with a boss who is threatened and retaliates against any statement of dissatisfaction with him or her. It also would be the case when we are angry with our lover, but also aware that much of our anger has nothing to do with our lover—it is "spillover" anger stemming from other things. Our feelings in such cases are valid. We don't need to hide or swallow them; we just need other outlets for them. Are there any types of *physical exercise* you can use to express your feelings (pounding pillows, running, swimming, racquetball, dancing, etc.)? Are there any *artistic outlets* for you (painting, writing, music, etc.)? Are there any *spiritual ways* in which you can connect with or express your feelings (religious faith or ceremony, fantasy, meditation)?

Remember, it is as important to find outlets for the expression of what we consider *positive* feelings as well as for sadness, anger, etc.

V. ALLOWING YOURSELF TO FEEL

If you recognize that you expend energy suppressing feelings, try letting them up for a short period of time. At the first opportunity, choose a private place, then sit quietly, perhaps with your eyes closed, and just let the feeling come up in your body. Try not to think about anything except allowing yourself to feel. Use thought stopping to end any intellectualization or judging you tend to do. Try to allow whatever happens (crying, yelling, sighs of relief, jumping up and down in excitement and joy). You can stop after five minutes. Each time, try to extend the amount of time you can allow the feeling to be expressed.

If you are concerned that you will not be able to control this experiment, that the feeling might overwhelm you and "get the best of you," be reassured that for months or even years you have stopped that feeling and that talent isn't going to immediately disappear. You can stop when you need to. It might also be helpful to think of other feelings you do allow yourself to express, or other times in your life when you were more expressive of the problematic feeling. You are still alive today—such expression didn't finish you off.

Carefully notice how you feel after this experiment. Is there any change in the sensations of your body? How you perceive the world? Feel or behave toward other people? Most importantly, in how you feel about yourself? At first, it might feel silly, awkward or even somewhat frightening to allow your feelings to be experienced, even for a short and controlled period. But remember, your feelings exist for a good reason and, as De Rosis and Pellegrino said, it's often the times when you think you're going crazy that you're really going sane.

VI. COMPASSION FOR OURSELVES

There are some feelings women are encouraged to feel toward others but discouraged from feeling toward ourselves. Compassion is a good example. Most of us have no trouble doling out sympathy for another person when that person is sick, but we berate ourselves for not being up to par when we are sick. We find it easy to forgive another person's mistakes or shortcomings but cannot forgive our own. Some women lack compassion for themselves to the point that they don't believe they have the right to exist. Others feel they have the right to exist, but only if they change themselves—only if they lose weight, achieve some sought-after goal, or otherwise improve themselves.

Do you believe you lack compassion for yourself? The next time you are aware that you are berating yourself, stop and think how you would feel toward *another* person in the same situation. If you think you would have more compassion for that other person, try to express that same compassion for yourself.

* 10 *

If It Weren't for My Body, I Might Be Okay: Self-Esteem and Body Image

> You are ugly. You are fat. Your breasts are too small (or large). Your thighs are too fat, your calves are too thin. Your eyes are too small. Your hair is mousy-colored. Your nose has a bump. You are too skinny. You have hair on your face. Your hair is too curly. Your hair is too thin. You have midriff bulge. You have vaginal odor. You wear glasses. Your face is covered with pimples. You compare yourself to almost every woman you see, even ones you pass on the street . . . but no matter who you compare yourself with, you never really feel good about your body.
>
> —Susan Friedman, *A Woman's Guide to Therapy*

Nearly every woman in our Self-esteem Enhancement Groups had a negative body image. Some initially saw this as linked to their low global self-esteem, others did not. But as time went on, it became clear to everyone that it is difficult to dislike your body or a specific part of your body and still like yourself. We tend to dislike our bodies as we dislike ourselves.

When we speak of body image we mean the picture a person has of her body—what it looks like to her and what she thinks it looks like to others. A woman's body image can be clear and detailed or fuzzy and vague, it can encompass her entire body or only certain parts, and it can be accurate or inaccurate. Body image is as subject to change as is the body itself, and it usually does change with aging, pregnancy, disability, illness, surgery and other major physical events. Often, too, a woman's body image will change over the course of the month, with a woman seeing herself as bloated and balloonlike as menstruation approaches, and as thinner and more acceptably shapely in the middle of her cycle. Despite these changes, however, most women have body images that are negative or positive with considerable consistency.

The relationship between self-esteem and body image is a complicated one, and the specific dynamics will vary from person to person. For some women, low self-esteem follows in part from a negative body image. But for other women it is the low self-esteem that comes first and the negative body image that follows from it. For them, abstract negative feelings about the self become manifest as concrete body hatred.[1] Instead of saying "I'm worthless" or "I'm unhappy," a woman says, "I'm fat" or "I'm so ugly." In this way, her pain or self-hatred becomes less nebulous and free-floating, and she obtains a perverse sense of solace and, more important, a sense of control. She knows exactly what is wrong with her: Her body is what is wrong with her, and if only she had a better body, she would have a much better life.

Most of the women we interviewed had negative body images not because they have unattractive bodies, but because they saw themselves inaccurately. Their images of their physical selves were distorted, usually in one of two ways or both. First, many women distorted images of their overall size and shape—for example, they saw themselves as much fatter, larger and rounder than they are. Second, many women's images of specific body parts were extremely distorted, and they saw these distorted body parts as dominating their entire physical selves, so that their body images became caricatures. Thus, not only did women inaccurately describe themselves to us as "oafish," "sausagelike," "built like a house," and "grossly enormous," they saw their "oafish" and "sausagelike" bodies as being dominated by such specific features as big feet, bushy eyebrows, wide hips, thin hair, acne, pointy noses, "tree trunk legs," fat asses, "thunder thighs," knobby knees, sagging breasts, flabby stomachs, etc.

Many of the women we interviewed also felt to some extent alienated or estranged from their bodies. This seems inevitable considering that we have been taught to regard the mind as separate from the body, and to think of ourselves not as bodies but as intellects who own or have bodies the way we own or have cars. Some express this visually, seeing themselves as heads with no bodies or bodies with no heads.

The extent of a woman's estrangement from her body is made most apparent when she becomes ill. Rather than perceiving her mind and body in partnership to comprise her important self, she sees her body as a "spoiler," the enemy of her intellect, career, relationship or whatever else is being disrupted by the illness. It is almost as if the other team has won:

> I always hated my breasts; they were, or are, I guess I should say, flat and hang down—like vacuum cleaner bags. Well, then I had cysts which had to be removed surgically. I was so afraid of having to have a mastectomy. Now that I didn't, and I'm still in one piece, I like my breasts better—or at least I don't let them bother me as much. I think the cysts were my breasts' revenge for all those years of hatred I focused on them. It was a lot to go through to finally get over that.

The Ridiculous Ideals

Adrienne Rich has commented that she does "not know a woman for whom her body is not a continual problem."[2] A principal reason so many of us perceive our bodies as problems is that we live in a culture that says women must be beautiful to be worthy, and then sets up standards for female beauty that are not only impossible for most women to live up to, but are unhealthy as well.

To be worthy we are supposed to be tall and extremely thin, with large womanly breasts but boyish hips, and flawless in our facial features. If through luck a woman has a less than perfect body, she might be allowed to compensate with extraordinary talent, as Barbra Streisand and Liza Minelli have done, but her appearance will still be something people feel entitled to comment on and compare to the ideal.

Today's American ideals of female beauty are particularly irksome in that there is never just *one* clear-cut image of perfection: There are usually many equally ridiculous and often diametrically opposed ideals operating simultaneously. For instance, today we have the voluptuous sex goddesses Loni Anderson and Bo Derek contrasted with top fashion models Kristine Oulman and Brooke Shields, whose adolescent bodies more resemble the bodies of preadolescent boys than the bodies of grown women. No woman can live up to—or even strive for—both these heavily promoted ideals at the same time.

Given the choice of which ideal to live up to—bosomy, curvaceous Type A or boyish, skinny Type B—the most popular one today is the latter. Many of the same women who would scoff at the idea of taking a Mark Eden bust development course think nothing of going on self-abusing diets. Today, getting and staying thin have become principal female pastimes, consuming a significant portion of women's time, energy and money. According to Judith Stein of the Fat Liberation Movement, the emphasis on thinness in our culture not only oppresses over-weight women, it also serves as a form of social control for all women:

> Fat oppression doesn't just affect fat people or fat women. It really works to keep everyone in line. It's a whole system of social control that keeps thin women absolutely terrified of being fat or thinking they are fat, and a whole lot of energy goes into dealing with fat. It keeps women who are medium-sized absolutely panic-stricken because they are right on the bor-der. Those of us who are fat are over that border into some state of evil, basically, very much outside of what is permissible within white American culture. If you are fat, then what you are supposed to do is strive desper-ately to get non-fat. . . .[3]

Just how oppressive the injunction to be thin is becomes painfully evident when we consider that nearly 50 percent of all women are clini-cally overweight,* and that Americans spend $10 *billion* each year on diet aids and strategies, 95 percent of which have been proven to be ineffective over a five-year period.[4] What is more, many diets and all surgery to control weight are physically dangerous.

In addition to being unhealthy and unrealistic, our culture's stan-dards of feminine beauty are racist: To be beautiful is to be white or to have white features if your skin is the "wrong" color. Poet Nellie Wong recalls the pain of growing up under the tyranny of Caucasian stan-dards:

> when I was growing up, I felt
> dirty. I thought that god
> made white people clean
> and no matter how much I bathed,
> I could not change, I could not shed
> my skin in the gray water[5]

Even when nonwhite ideals of feminine beauty have been developed, those ideals are just as likely to be unattainable for most real women. Although the ads in the magazine *Ebony* feature only black women, they feature only slender, young black women.

Our cultural standards of beauty are ageist, too. In fact, we have no cultural standards of beauty for older women. A woman is either young and beautiful or old and frumpy. There are exceptions, like Katharine Hepburn or Lena Horne, but rarely do we consider older women to

---

* Clinically, overweight is defined as being 20 percent over one's ideal weight. How-ever, the charts for ideal weight developed and used by insurance companies have been attacked for being unhealthily biased toward thinness, and were recently revised.

even be "in the running." In our culture, ageing is an obscenity to be prevented at all costs:

> When I was a little girl, I was fascinated by my grandmothers' and great-aunt's faces. They were so wrinkled, but had so much character. Now in my sixties, I like the lines in my face—they are like no one else's. But it drives me nuts to see all these commercials for oils and facials to prevent wrinkling. The models who demonstrate the products are only twenty-five or thirty years old, and already wrinkling is supposedly a big life issue for them. Even worse, every magazine now has ads or articles on cosmetic surgery, on face lifts. Some of my friends have had them. After a while, I wonder if I'm perverse for liking my wrinkles.

Older men are distinguished, whereas older women are just old. Men often increase in public esteem when they age; women do not.

Most of all, our ideals are cruel and oppressive to people with physical disabilities. Because their bodies perhaps look or function differently, it is assumed that they do not care about being attractive:

> Growing up, I was told that I couldn't be pretty like the other girls so I had to make up for it by being nicer than them. I didn't wear a dress until I was an adult. My family insisted that I *always* wear pants to cover the braces on my legs. I missed that real important experience of dressing up in something real pretty, fussing over my appearance with makeup and coordinated outfits and feeling great because I looked so good. Until I was an adult, I thought only "normal" women were entitled to that feeling.

Another problem with the American standards of female beauty is how quickly and radically they change. The full-bodied women Rubens, Degas and Renoir immortalized in paint were considered beautiful in their time, but today such women would be condemned as ugly and banished to fat farms for starvation diets and cellulite treatments. Marilyn Monroe, although held up as the prototypical perfect woman in the early 1960s, would be considered unpleasantly plump by today's standards.

Kim Chernin suggests that the cultural definition of the ideal female body type changes—or rather, shrinks and expands—due to political reasons. According to Chernin, voluptuous and rotundly female bodies are in when women are clearly subordinate to men and not challenging male authority. But when women agitate for equality and start gaining independence, the culture calls for a body type and fashions that "reflect a distinct male fear of a mature woman's powers, particularly as it expresses itself through a woman's large body."[6] Hence, when numbers of women stayed home having babies in the 1950s, the womanly and fecund female body was in style. But when women left home and demanded equal rights, as in the 1920s and 1970s, the ideal female body type became thinner and more and more boyish.

The Pernicious Moral Equation

In America today, attractive people are seen not just as more attractive than others, they are seen as smarter, more compassionate and morally superior. To be beautiful is to be good. The moral values we attach to attractiveness become especially evident when we look at the condemnation and scorn heaped on overweight women. Marcia Millman explains:

> Clearly obesity has become mythologized in our culture into something more than a physical condition or a potential health hazard. Being overweight is now imbued with powerful symbolic and psychological meanings that deeply affect a person's identity in the world . . . an overweight woman is assumed to have a personal problem. She is stereotypically viewed as unfeminine, in flight from sexuality, antisocial, out of control, hostile, aggressive.[7]

The moral judgments made against fat people translate into treatment, indeed into social policy. Not only are overweight people put down for failing to be thin, they are punished, as Deborah Larned Romano points out:

> In America, one's weight is as much a measure of one's social desirability and status as the car one owns. Fatness is regarded as a disability in society rather than as the social adaptation it seems to be. Fat high school kids have a harder time getting into college than thinner ones, despite good grades and SAT scores. A fat army recruit is considered a bad soldier even if he or she is a typist. According to some personnel agencies, for every pound overweight, a worker stands to lose $1,000 a year in potential income, assuming he or she has managed to land a job in the first place.[8]

The proscription against being fat is not applied equally to both sexes. In men, fat is often construed as an appropriate symbol of power. However, fat never symbolizes power in a woman; it symbolizes inferiority and worthlessness. Consider how fat on Luciano Pavarotti is considered attractive and his food intake is celebrated in photos in national magazines, while the public has shown much contempt for the extra poundage carried by Maria Callas and Elizabeth Taylor.

Even if a woman does have the looks of the cultural ideal, she still must cope with the fact that she will not fit the ideal forever. Women who fit the ideal of beauty pay a price in that beautiful women are not taken as seriously as less attractive women. We rarely, if ever, hear a handsome man say, "Just for once I'd like to be appreciated for my mind." But women say it often, because there is no allowance in our culture for a woman to be both beautiful and intelligent. If a woman is beautiful in a conventionally feminine way, she will not be seen as a full human being; if she is not beautiful, she may be taken seriously as a full human being, but she will also be denigrated for failing to be sufficiently female. It's a no-win situation.

Learning To Be Dissatisfied

None of us came into the world believing we had to be attractive to be worthy. Nor did any of us come into the world with the idea that being attractive means being thin or having particular looks. We had to be taught to equate our worth with our attractiveness, and we had to be taught just what it is that's considered attractive in our culture at this particular point in history.

In teaching us about our bodies, our parents played a major role, and often they started teaching us to dislike our bodies before we were old enough to talk.

This is changing somewhat today, but when most of us were young, little girl's bodies were judged on how they looked, while little boys were judged on how they perform. Instead of actively controlling and testing her body for her own satisfaction, a girl was put in the totally passive stance of waiting for validation from others. Not all girls were forbidden the power, self-knowledge and delight that comes from being athletic and pushing the body to its maximum, but even for the "tomboy," agility and comfort with the body is short-lived and can be unlearned once the pressures of pubescence and the arduous struggle to be a desirable object begin:

> I look at old home movies of me running and jumping and swinging on ropes, and I mourn the loss of that part of me in the same way I would mourn the death of a friend. Now I feel so restricted by my body—particularly by what I have to wear to go to work—nothing feels "right" to me. And even when I'm on vacation or in a situation where I could use my body, let it run free, I've forgotten how. That graceful, fearless little girl is not even a memory to me—I don't think I'd know her at all if it weren't for the movies.

Within the family, it was hard for our mothers to give us accurate and positive perceptions about our bodies if they were preoccupied with faulty body images of their own. A poor body image often begins with such overemphasis on the dreaded body:

> My mother was real concerned about body hair. She always shaved her underarms and legs—everyday in the summer—and cut her pubic hair so it wouldn't show around the crotch of her bathing suit. I don't remember how I knew this, because it was all done in great secrecy. I wasn't nine years old yet before I was plucking my eyebrows, and in junior high I was saving up for electrolysis for hair on my forearms. The time of greatest self-disgust for me was around puberty when my pubic hair was sort of there and sort of not there. Although I wasn't happy when it all came in for good either. I've stopped pouring my money into electrolysis, but during the summer I wear long-sleeved blouses to hide my hairy arms.

Fathers often instilled body hatred in their daughters, too. Some women report that they liked their bodies until puberty, when their fathers' rejection of them or lurid teasing of their developing bodies translated into self-disgust. Common double binds such as "Grow up into a sexy woman—but stay my little girl" can render a girl less than pleased with her womanly shape.

If a woman was physically or sexually abused as a child, she is especially likely to have a problematic body image:

> Both my parents would punish us by flailing at us, banging our heads against the wall. Often we would be dragged in front of a mirror and told, "Look at how ugly you are, look at how your face is contorted. I can't believe how you look—you look like a monster." Part of me believes I don't look like a human being, that my face is like an outer-space alien or really repulsive. I think people don't tell me I look like this because they don't want to hurt my feelings.

As the family was—and often remains—a major force in shaping our body images, so were our peers. Insults such as "Beanpole," "Crisco in the Can," "Blimpo," "Slant Eyes," "Ironsides," "Nigger Lips," and "Spaz" were often hurled early in life when the recipient was unable to fight back and the insults ended up taking a prominent place in the girl's self-concept.

For most of us, body dissatisfaction developed as much as a result of what we weren't taught as what we were taught. Never having been taught—at home or in school—the facts about what a healthy, functioning female body is like, women tend to question ourselves rather than the cultural ideals:

> My whole life I've compared my stomach to little boys or physically fit men. Mine sticks out a lot and theirs are flat. I really hated my stomach a lot. In college a friend of mine who was in nursing school told me our pelvic regions are constructed totally differently in a way that causes women's stomachs to protrude some. That was like someone turning on the lights for me. From this I went on to look at how in other times, in other cultures, they valued the Botticelli-type body, and I'm beginning to accept my body more.

No wonder *Our Bodies, Ourselves,* which finally offered women understandable information about our bodies, was an overwhelming success.

Advertising, television and fashion magazines are not only promoters of the cultural ideals, but often in the absence of other sources of information, the entertainment and advertising media become our teacher of what a normal and healthy woman's body should look like. But the information we receive is often neither normal nor healthy. A case in point is the woman who sees herself in severed parts. In advertisements, male models are usually shown from head to toe, or at the very least, from the waist up. Women are *cut up* with the same consistency. Only her legs are shown to sell the panty-hose, when a whole woman could sell the product just as well. Female models' hands, breasts, mouths, hips and genital regions, eyes, etc. are severed from their entire selves.

The same mentality carries over into daily discourse. We hear statements such as, "He's a leg man" or "I'm a breast man" or "I like 'em with small waists and curvy hips." Rarely in reverse do we hear women say, "I am a pectoral woman," or "They have to have hairy legs for me." Certainly some women have preferences for certain body characteristics in men, but they tend to value the man for his entire self as opposed to one severed part of himself.

Continuing To Be Dissatisfied

What we learned within our families and from our culture plays an enormous role in causing women's body hatred, body obsession and desire to "make over" our bodies. But we can and sometimes do play a major role ourselves in conforming to our culture's ridiculous ideals. We are the ones who buy the fashion magazines, cram ourselves into designer jeans and make diet books best-sellers. Sometimes the continuing pressure is motivated by the urging or outright ridicule of someone in our adult life:

> In the heat of battle, my lover would tell me that I was a fat slob, repulsive-looking and that I smell, and he was looking to leave if I didn't "shape up." I tried for so long to look better, thinking that would save the relationship, but since I really wasn't any of those things to begin with—and my looks weren't what was wrong with the relationship—it was all for naught.

And then again, sometimes we are the most unrelenting in our opinions that our bodies are flawed and that we must do something to eradicate those flaws:

> I've never gotten any complaints about my body from any of the men I've been involved with. I've projected a lot of my own complaints onto them. I always assumed that they must think my ass is too fat and my thighs too chunky and my breasts too small because that's what I think, and whenever they told me my body is just fine, I dismissed it—like they were trying not to hurt my feelings or they were really blind. It took me a long time to realize that I had some stake in seeing myself as too fat and ugly.

As we are often our own severest critics when it comes to our bodies, so we are often one another's worst critics as well. Men in our society have license to visually inspect women from head to toe, and then to pronounce their judgments in language loud and often obscene and insulting. This alone poses a threat to women's self-esteem. But also threatening is the perhaps more subtle but still as demeaning way in which we women do a very similar thing:

> I've been in a lot of situations where I've felt real bad and self-conscious because of the way men look me up and down, but the worst feeling for me is when this happens with women. . . . When I see old friends I haven't seen for years, it's not the men's approval I worry about as much as the women's. The men I kind of blot out, but the women I look at carefully, thinking, "Is she thinner than me? Does she look older? Is she getting more wrinkled?"—and I know the other women are doing this to me, too. It's the same thing when I go to church on Sundays. The men don't check me out—they don't care about what I'm wearing or whether I wore it last week or if it's in style and expensive. But the women sure do.

How great a role women can and often do play in upholding the idea that beautiful people are better people is unfortunately well illustrated by many of today's female proponents of physical fitness. In her best-selling exercise book, for example, Jane Fonda complains at great length about "male-defined" standards of beauty, but she is as firm as any male fashion designer in her insistence that a lean, well-muscled body is something every woman should strive for—even if it means spending several hours a day working at it. What is worse, Fonda equates physical fitness with moral soundness and political purity, suggesting that a person who is in good shape will be more receptive to progressive and humane social ideas than someone who is not in shape.[9]

When we look at why women are so often unwilling to give up body hatred and body obsession, we find that for many of us, being hung up on our bodies serves several important purposes. First, devoting ourselves to the pursuit of thinness and beauty may help fulfill the human craving for excellence that in most cases is stunted in women. Men have many areas they are allowed to excel in—athletics, technology, business, wealth, etc. But in general, women are allowed to excel only in very narrow areas, among them being nurturing and being beautiful and thin. By being beautiful and thin, a woman may get a feeling of accomplishment men can get in other areas, and she may be able to channel an urge for competition as well.

Our families can teach us to derive a sense of self-esteem through control of our bodies. Psychiatrist Hilde Bruch explains the extreme form of this mentality, the disease of anorexia nervosa, to her anorexic patients:

> The main thing I've learned is that the worry about dieting, the worry about being skinny or fat, is just a smoke screen. That is not the real illness. The real illness has to do with how you feel about yourself. . . . You have one great fear, namely, that of being ordinary or average or common—just not good enough. This peculiar dieting begins with such anxiety. You want to prove that you have control, that you can do it. The peculiar part of it is that it makes you feel "I can accomplish something." It makes you feel "I can do something nobody else can do," and then you start to think you are a little bit better because you can look down on all those people who are sloppy and piggish and don't have the discipline to control themselves.[10]

Overeating can serve the same purpose: to gain control over one's life. The heroine of Margaret Atwood's novel *Lady Oracle* is a five-foot-seven, 245-pound teenager who is intent on rejecting her mother before her mother rejects her. While the mere sight of this girl's frame makes her mother miserable, everyone else who encounters her, including her father, pities her.[11] It was the quintessential Pyrrhic victory.

The same compulsion for control, complicated by a striving for excellence, can often be found in the adult followers of the body-beautiful mania in our country today. Kim Chernin elaborates:

Of course, we strive for a balance—the old Greek standard of a healthy mind in a healthy body. And many a woman who rises early, drinks a glass of protein liquid and jogs out to play tennis is living out that ideal, in tune with the modern emphasis on sports and diet. There are, however, many thousands of American women who perform those same activities for very different reasons. Sports and diet have taken over their lives. In their obsession with weight, they are alienated from the bodies they perceive to be ugly. *They are driven by the compulsion to impose their will upon these offending bodies.* [12]

For others, a body which defies cultural ideals affords some control over how this culture effects them in some specific ways:

> In all honesty, my extra twenty-five pounds has gotten me out of a lot of things I never was comfortable with anyway. In high school I didn't have to compete with other girls. By virtue of my fat, I was out of the running. I had friends who were boys—mostly because I was smart and helpful with home work—but I didn't have to hassle with being sexually active. I just wasn't, and no one expected me to be. Now, in my office, I see my attractive female coworkers being sexually harassed. They say no to these creeps, but the men assume they really like being leered at. And while I'm sorry for them, I'm glad I'm automatically out of the whole sordid mess.

For some women, estrangement from their body is a useful survival mechanism. Vicki La Motta, the ex-wife of boxer Jake La Motta (the subject of the film *Raging Bull),* explains how repeated beatings at the highly trained hands of her husband affected her sense of her body:

> When a woman encounters violence, a terrible fear sets in. It is a fear beyond sweating, beyond screaming. There is a kind of a shock. You are so frightened, you freeze. So frightened that you don't feel your body. You don't feel anything because you are actually frozen. You want to grab hold of someone. But there's no one there. [13]

Stopping the Dissatisfaction

There are easier and more healthy ways for a woman to take control of her life through her body and body image. On an individual level each woman must decide if that change in her body, be it a loss of pounds, a nose job or face lift, will really make a difference in her feelings about herself. Would what usually amounts to cosmetic changes really make her more of a worthy person? How much time, energy and money does she want to spend striving for the ideal and how much does she want to spend on other parts of her life? Each of us would do well to formulate her own compassionate ideal.

Collectively we can take control by questioning and rejecting the ridiculous ideals, by refusing to judge ourselves by them and by refusing to spend money on products which reflect ideals that are not our own. For example, when women in large numbers decided we ought to be able to wear stylish pants, the fashion industry met the demand. And in a few cases women have banded together to protest advertising that dismembers or humiliates our bodies and had such advertising removed. There is still a long way to go, but if all the time and energy and money we put into trying to make our bodies conform to ridiculous ideals were redirected toward social change, the world could be altered significantly. In the process, we might also learn that just as the body can be a tangible source of self-dissatisfaction, it can be a tangible source of self-acceptance:

> You know how when you first meet someone and you think they are as homely as mud, but three months later, after you get to know them, you think they are interesting-looking, or funky, or something good? That's how I've come to feel about my body. I started to exercise more—I joined a volleyball team and swam after every game—and my body works real good. I always thought I had the "wrong" breasts and the "wrong" shape, but when I just cool out and look at my body, I see it all goes together pretty good.

BLUEPRINTS FOR CHANGE

I. BODY IMAGE REAL AND IDEAL

This exercise has worked well in Self-esteem Enhancement Groups. Make a collage or find some symbolic representation (object, photograph, etc.) of how your body looks to you and how you think you look to other people.

Now do the same for your *ideal* body image—what you think you *should* (not wish or hope) look like. Now ask yourself these questions:

1. Do you think there are negative and inaccurate parts to your real body image?
2. Do you recognize your body image as being distorted or disembodied?
3. How large is the gap between your real and ideal body image?
4. What parts of your body *can* be changed to lessen the gap between the real and ideal?

5. Given all the other things you have to do in your life, how much of your
time and energy (remember, they are limited resources) are you willing
to spend on this?

If you are worrying instead of acting to lessen the gap, refer back to the
chapter on Black Clouds and try applying the Thought-stopping Technique to this situation.

II. COMPASSION FOR YOURSELF AND YOUR BODY IMAGE

Remember that our body image has served some purpose in our lives.
Perhaps body hatred or distortion gave us something in common to a
person we wanted to be close to. Perhaps body estrangement protected
us from very real pain. Perhaps labeling ourselves as "having a weight
problem" made us feel comfortable in a group of people who labeled
themselves the same. In working with overweight women, for whom the
extra weight served a purpose, feminist therapist Susie Orbach encourages her clients to understand:

> The fat was an attempt to take care of herself under a difficult set of
> circumstances. As she moves towards a conscious acceptance of this aspect
> of the fat, she can utilize the self-protective impulse in a different way. As
> she is able to understand that she became fat as a response—to mother, to
> society, to various situations—she can begin to remove the judgment that it
> was good or bad. *It just was.* . . . An understanding of the dynamics
> behind getting fat can help remove the judgment. When the judgment is
> given up and you can accept that the fat just was, you can go on to the
> question of, "Is it serving me well now?"[14]

Is your poor body image serving you well now? Do you hate your body
as a way to bond with people, cope with other pain, or resolve nonbody
self-esteem issues in your life? For instance, a fear of intimacy might
translate into a distorted belief that your body is so ugly that no one
would want you anyway. As long as you believe this, your fear of being
close to someone will not be resolved.

How would your life change if you came to see your body in an
accurate and at least neutral, if not positive, way? Are you prepared for
these changes? Who can help you get ready? What can you do to prepare yourself?

III. QUESTIONING THE LABELS

There is much you can do on your own to re-examine the labels and
judgments which permeate your body image. In her Body Image Trans-

formation groups, psychologist Marcia Germaine Hutchinson worked with many women who

> . . . perceive themselves as being eating disordered, as indulging in "serious binge eating." When questioned further they described a binge as anything from eating a cookie when they "really don't need one" to eating more than they "should eat." There are many men in this culture who engage in similar and far more extraordinary eating excesses but are not pressured to hang the label of pathology on themselves. In a culture that makes thinness tantamount to godliness and at the same time bombards its members with constant food stimuli through the media and through an endless supply of eating opportunities, . . . it is no wonder that eating has become an "issue" rather than a simple pleasure that supports life.[15]

If you believe food is becoming an "issue" for you, it is important for you to seek accurate information about your eating habits. For instance, some women we interviewed gave up the label of "binge eater" when they learned that some genuine binge eaters can consume up to fifty thousand calories per day. Other women mislabel themselves as "anorexic," berate themselves for being anorexic and distract themselves from other life issues even though they are only a few pounds under their normal weight and have been consistently so for a long period of time. It is important that we question our labels before we put much time and energy into questioning ourselves, or trying to change something that was never a real problem to begin with.

Other people can be helpful in questioning the labels we put on ourselves and our body images. Carefully choose a friend and show her your real body image collage or symbol, tell her what it is about, and get her feedback about how realistic your body image is. Share any labels like "eating disordered" that you have for yourself. The friend should be someone you trust, who will be sensitive to you and won't use this opportunity to "get you" on a very vulnerable issue.

IV. GETTING TO KNOW YOUR OWN BODY

Many women we've worked with have never really looked at their bodies closely. They are too shy or embarrassed. How realistic can your body image be if you don't really know what your body looks like?

For some of us, it is asking too much to stand nude before a full-length mirror and check ourselves out. Begin slowly and really concentrate, one part at a time, starting with your feet. Look very closely at them, touch them, get the sense of their texture. The next time you take time to do this, do the same with your calves, then your thighs, then hips, buttocks/genitalia, then stomach, etc. Massaging with lotions is a good way to both become familiar with that specific part of your body *and* do something nice for it.

In suggesting this exercise, we do not mean to encourage a body image of severed parts, or disconnection in the sense that we focus dislike (or approval) on a specific part of the body at the expense of the whole body. The goal in this exercise is to finally be able to look at, and accept, the entire body.

V. FINDING A PLACE ALONG THE RAINBOW

Gloria Steinem wrote in the April 1982 issue of *Ms.* about a consciousness-raising, self-esteem-enhancing experience of spending a week at a health spa with ninety other women. She describes her own history and relationship with her body image, and it sounds very similar to others we have heard. At the end of the week, she concluded:

> I doubt that fat or thin, mature or not, our bodies could continue to give us such unease if we learned their place in the rainbow spectrum of women and humanity. Even great beauties seem less distant—and even mastectomies and other realities seem less terrifying—when we stop imagining and begin to see. . . .
>
> Probably, grown up women also must see and experience—personally, unself-consciously—real female diversity if the stereotype of what-a-woman's-body-should-look-like is to lose its power. Now, like the heroine in *Gypsy* who becomes aware of her teenage body only when she becomes a stripper, too many of us experience female bodies—our own and others, in social settings and private bedrooms—only when they are on display for men.
>
> A little natural togetherness might convince us that we are each unique members in the Family of Women.[16]

Read Steinem's article if you can get hold of it. And begin to look around. Obviously, women's locker rooms and saunas are great places to see other women's bodies and to get a sense of our own unique place along the rainbow. If nudity causes you problems, looking at women on the beach or in photography and art books might be less threatening. However, avoid magazines like *Playboy,* where the air-brushed beauties are bound to make you feel you don't measure up.

VI. THINK WHATEVER YOU WANT

Dr. Hutchinson asks her clients to think "beautiful" or think "tall" or whatever their ideal is. Project yourself as if you were the ideal. If your ideal can be managed on more than a cognitive level (for instance a "frumpy" woman whose ideal is "stylish" could get very dressed up for a day), then try it. What happens? How do people respond to you? Does it really make a difference in how you feel about yourself?

As an example, one of Dr. Hutchinson's clients thought "beautiful" for a day and found she was harassed on the streets much more often than usual. Two questions followed from her experiment: First, how much was her ideal of beautiful tied up in "sexy"; were there other kinds of "beautiful" that she preferred? Second, did she really want to be "beautiful" after all—was it worth it?

* 11 *

Why Is Pleasure So Much Work?: Sexuality and Self-Esteem

> Even in some utopian, guilt-free state of nature, it's doubtful sex
> would ever become just some healthy bodily function. . . . Even for
> the most cynical sexual gymnast or the celibate, sex represents an act
> of vulnerability—a momentary loss of self—that can call up the deep-
> est feelings of connection, transcendence or exploitation.
>
> —Judith Coburn in *New Times* magazine

For many of the women we interviewed, sexuality constituted the last
frontier of self-acceptance. They might have been able to describe themselves accurately as competent, loving and worthy people, but when it
came to their concepts of themselves as sexual beings, they were either
more tentative or more negative. Some stated that their sexuality remained unexplored because they believed they were not allowed to explore it, or just didn't want to explore it. Others knew but did not like
their sexual selves: Some felt they were "too ignorant and uptight for
this enlightened age—I should have been born fifty years earlier," while
others felt they were "too promiscuous—I've been picked up so many
times I'm growing handles." Moreover, we found that many women
think sex is good but still *feel* uncomfortable with it.

Such discontent is ironic given that our bodies were made to experience sexual pleasure. While all other parts of our bodies have primarily
utilitarian functions and perhaps the additional potential to feel pleasure, the clitoris exists *solely* for the purpose of giving women pleasure.
But this physiological fact does a woman little good if she believes she
does not deserve pleasure (perhaps of any kind) or that there is some-

thing wrong, shameful or "icky" about her genitals and her sexual pleasure.

Low self-esteem can affect our sexual attitudes and behavior in a variety of ways. If a woman does not like herself, she might shy away from sexual involvements with others because she sees sexual intimacy as entailing the threat of someone getting too close. Or she might have sexual relationships but be in the habit of holding back in experiencing pleasure because she thinks she doesn't deserve it or it makes her feel guilty. Similarly, she may also be averse to masturbation because she believes she is undeserving of pleasure, or her pleasure is not worth the time and energy. Still other women with low self-esteem will become involved in one unhappy and exploitative sexual affair after another. For them, the sexual arena is a testing ground. Uncertain of their worth, they may feel driven to constantly prove their sexual attractiveness and prowess. But perhaps also believing they do not deserve to be treated well, the sexual partners they are drawn to most strongly are those who do not treat them well, and their affairs thus leave them with less self-esteem at the end than they had before.

Although human sexuality is one of the most written-about subjects of our time, we found in the literature surprisingly little that is of genuine help in illuminating the links between sexuality and self-esteem. Most of the recent popular books written about sex fall into one of two categories: books that provide statistics and tallies pertaining to how many people engage in what kind of sexual activity how often; and "how to" books intended to improve technique and the ability to experience sexual pleasure. Only a handful of all the books on the subject of sexuality tell us much that is insightful about the meaning of sex in our lives and the relationship between a woman's sexuality and her sense of worth.

Many contemporary books on the subject of sexuality do, however, presume a certain link between self-esteem and sexuality. The unquestioned assumption behind much of the current literature is that sex is good and that the more pleasurable sex a person has, the greater her self-understanding, self-esteem and general happiness. Basic to many books, particularly the "how to" variety, is the notion that sex is somehow a great panacea that will not only cure all anxieties about our worth, but will also bring "the revelation of truth, the overturning of global laws, the proclamation of a new day to come, and the promise of a new felicity."[1] And if all that weren't enough, much of the popular literature on sex—as well as the works of such literati as D. H. Lawrence, Norman Mailer and John Updike—presume that sex is the key that can unlock the mysteries of the self as nothing else can, thus making ourselves intelligible to ourselves. As Michel Foucault has pointed out, where once Christianity taught that the body and sexuality were detestable, today there is as much cultural pressure "to make us love sex, to make knowledge of it desirable and everything said about it precious."[2]

One of the most problematic aspects of today's cultural campaign to make us love sex is that it contains an implicit condemnation of anyone who finds sex boring, unpleasant or repulsive. This extends even to those who find sex pleasant but not that terrific, or important but not *that* important. The logic of today's sexologists and sexophiles goes something like this: Sexual activity should be emphasized in a person's life because sex leads to higher self-esteem, to self-understanding, to freedom, happiness, truth, etc.; and therefore anyone who does not emphasize sex in her life is doomed to have low self-esteem and to be unhappy and forever uninitiated in the great truths of the universe and the self.

We take issue with the idea that pursuit of sexual pleasure will inevitably lead to all it is supposed to lead to, and we take special exception to the notion that greater sexual activity and pleasure will necessarily lead to higher self-esteem. For many of us, greater knowledge of our sexuality and greater and more pleasurable sexual experience can indeed enhance our self-esteem; by expressing the sexual aspects of ourselves we may become more aware of ourselves as tender and multifaceted, and by learning to give ourselves and others pleasure we may increase our feelings of significance, connectedness and competence. However, this does not mean that those who do not express themselves sexually or who do not feel competent at giving themselves and others sexual pleasure are inadequate, flawed or of less worth than those who do. Nor does it mean that if a woman has low self-esteem she should go out and learn to become an orgasmic sexual gymnast and then all her feelings of worthlessness will be magically whisked away. *Sex is not a substitute nor a quick means to self-esteem, and the two are not one and the same.* It's entirely possible for a person to have a life full of sex, and to have no problems experiencing orgasms, and still have low self-esteem. Similarly, it's possible to go through life and not have much sex or much satisfying sex and to have high self-esteem all the same.

Those "Icky" Feelings

Many speculate that infants experience sexual feelings. But no one was born thinking sex is bad, or thinking sex is the greatest thing in the world either. Our attitudes toward sex, positive and negative alike, all were learned later from our culture.

Over the course of our lives most of us have been influenced by a variety of cultural attitudes toward sex, attitudes that are often contradictory. The earliest messages we got about sex, however, reached us when we were the most impressionable, and they may stay with us well into adulthood—even when we wish they wouldn't. Unfortunately, those early messages were more likely than not negative ones. These probably included the following:

> Sex is dirty, to be sexual is dirty.

> Although sex is dirty, it's not so dirty for men. Sex, in fact, is good for males. Boys are supposed to be sexually curious and sexually experienced. Good girls, however, are supposed to be neither. We aren't supposed to want sex or to have interest in it until we are married, and then our husbands will teach us all we need to know.

> Female genitalia are dirty, smelly, mysterious, icky, and the natural cause of female shame. Male genitalia, by contrast, are none of the above. The penis is a magnificent invention, the natural source of male pride.

> Although sex is dirty, it is permissible for women to be sexual under certain conditions: within the context of marriage, for the purpose of procreation, for the purpose of pleasing men, and as long as the women don't enjoy it.

> Although sex is dirty and it's best if women don't enjoy it, sometimes even sexual pleasure is permissible. Again, however, certain conditions must be met. A woman can have sexual pleasure only as long as her husband has equal or greater pleasure, if she has earned the pleasure, or she pays for it in some way afterward.

Even though the sexual atmosphere we live in today may seem radically different, these are the lessons which influenced our sexuality:

> What I remember most vividly about sex growing up was the language used to describe it. In our family, we had silly names—my vulva was a wee-wee or just "down there," and my brothers had ding-dongs. No one talked about intercourse, but it wasn't too long before I learned about it in the streets. There were either these passive terms like "sleeping together," or vague ones like "do it"—do what? I wondered for years—And then

there were the more harsh, violent terms like "hump," "fuck" and "bang."
I remember the first times I heard "cunt," then "gash" and "slit" and
"beaver." I felt so ashamed—not of the kids saying those things but of
myself as a female.

When most of us learned about sex, we were at a distinct disadvantage, because adults probably did not discuss sex with us in open, understandable and calm ways.* That in and of itself was enough to give
us the message that sex was bad. The majority of parents gave only
cursory attention—if any at all—to explaining the mechanics of sex and
even less attention was paid to the responsibilities sex entails. We were
supposed to wait until marriage, and then all we needed to know would
magically fall into place.

Of course, a lot of us didn't wait. And most of those who did found
that things didn't automatically fall into place on the wedding night.
More likely than not, our first partners were as ignorant and fumbling
as we were. Lack of information about sex, then, shaped our first sexual
experiences with another person, and that experience—good or bad—
often colored our general feelings about sex:

> I'll never forget this boy I went with for a long time in high school. I really
> wanted to please him, and he kept on pestering me for a blow job. I wasn't
> sure of what it was, but I didn't want to ask and I didn't want to appear
> stupid. I made good grades in school so I figured it out for myself. The first
> time he took his penis out, I puffed up a storm. I blew on his penis. I
> couldn't understand why he didn't get an erection. I felt so stupid when I
> later found out what a blow job is. I am still always afraid I'm getting it
> wrong.

Not every woman's early sexual experiences had such a humorous
side:

> My boyfriend told me I couldn't get pregnant because we did it standing
> up. I wasn't all that sure how you got pregnant anyway, so who was I to
> argue? Of course, I got pregnant. He told my parents and his he didn't do
> it and bragged to his friends he did. I had an illegal abortion; it was really
> traumatic. But the worst part of it has been not trusting men—I don't
> know if I ever will.

A woman's first sexual experience with another person can set the
tone for her sexuality. If her first experience was tender, loving and
essentially positive, then perhaps she will not be so devastated by later

---

* Some women we interviewed who were raised in "rough" city neighborhoods said
they were warned about sexual violence, but there was little discussion of sex between two
people who care for each other.

negative sexual experiences. However, if a woman's first sexual experience with another person was painful or exploitative, she will be more likely to believe that sex is a negative experience.

Even after we have corrected the misinformation and learned otherwise, early lessons can still linger on:

> Intellectually, I know now sex isn't dirty. But when I was a kid, the girls—and only the girls—had two washcloths each: one for the genitals and one for the rest of our body. And in Catholic school we were told to put talcum powder on the top of our bathtub water so that we couldn't see ourselves naked. I no longer confuse sex with bodily functions like urination. I no longer use two washcloths, and I feel fine about the nudity in the sauna I go to. But I worry about how my genitals smell, and I don't want anyone to get their nose near them or else I feel guilty and ashamed—like they are putting up with something really awful.

Our earliest attitudes toward sex were probably influenced and complicated by the cultural image of females as either whores or madonnas. We were trained to be sexy and seductive, to derive our self-esteem from winning male approval and being male "turn-ons," yet we were supposed to stay virginal and untainted. Although sex was dirty and our genitalia were enigmatic and perhaps even repulsive to us, we were supposed to see our virginity and access to our genitalia as our greatest gift to our prospective husbands:

> I remember thinking it was so odd that I was supposed to save my "nasties" for someone who loved me, for the person I was going to spend the rest of my life with. It would have made more sense to give them to someone I hated.

Growing up, the whore/madonna complex gave us one standard of sexual behavior for boys, another for girls. Although we were supposed to hope and pray for a man who knew what he was doing on the wedding night, he was not supposed to gain that experience with us. So a few girls had to be sacrificed as whores for the betterment of female virgin's first sexual experience. Madonna-types rarely expressed gratitude to "bad" girls for this sacrifice—they were very damning of them. Girls were guaranteed a bad reputation for being sexually active and satiating their curiosity, while boys were guaranteed admiration for the exact same behavior.* When researchers polled married couples, 70 percent of the husbands said they had had premarital sex with their

---

* It is interesting to note that there is no male counterpart to the concept of the whore in the context of hetereosexuality. (The male homosexual counterpart is the "trick.") Although men who have sex for money with women are "gigolos," they are seen as a

wives while only 30 percent of the wives said they had had premarital sex with their husbands.[3] The truth probably lies somewhere in between, but obviously the men felt pressure to appear sexually adventurous while women felt pressure to feign virginity.

Right Paths to Pleasure

As we grew older, we probably learned that some sexual pleasure for women was permissible, and it did not necessarily have to be for the purpose of procreation or even in the context of marriage. There was, however, one requirement: Women could experience sexual pleasure only through heterosexual relations. As therapist Sanford Jason states, "Women have not been taught that they have any intrinsic sexuality of their own. They were only taught to respond—to say yes or no—to male sexuality."[4] According to the lessons most of us were taught, there is only one right path to sexual pleasure—and that is through a man.

Most of us learned that masturbation should be avoided because, in addition to being "disgusting," it will drain our energy and interest in "real sex," meaning sex with a male partner. If we masturbate too often, obviously something is wrong with us. The celibate woman, too, is seen as someone with a big problem, either being unable to attract a man or selfish, frigid and neurotic, not a "real" woman. But considered the most deviant of all is the woman who prefers women as lovers: She will be labeled immature, going through a stage she will grow out of. Or, if she doesn't grow out of it, she will be labeled narcissistic and said to be motivated solely by hatred of men rather than by love of women. The bisexual fares no better, as she is assumed to be a confused traitor to both sides. And popular opinion has it that she, like the lesbian and celibate, can be "cured" by contact with the right man.

The lesbian who is a woman of color, Jewish or of another non-Christian faith, disabled, or older is hit by a double whammy of condemnation. Falling short of the dominant culture's ideal to begin with (even if she started out as heterosexual), she also often experiences additional oppression both from within and outside her group because she defies the heterosexual norm.

In reaction to such ridiculous negativity, some lesbians have countered with a new "right" path to pleasure which is just as limiting and judgmental of women. Some separatists believe that the oppression of

---

higher class of people than female prostitutes. They make more money, enjoy a higher standard of living and live freer of danger of arrest or physical violence from customers.

women will not end until we all live in a lesbian nation. Although the hard work and courage of countless lesbians who have been open about their sexuality have opened options for sexual expression for women, we believe it would be a mistake to assume that any kind of genital contact is a prerequisite to political change. A woman's choice of sexual expression is a function of her heart, body and head: it does not adapt well to any externally imposed political dogma. The problems compulsory heterosexuality caused women should have taught us that much.

Not only were we taught that sex with a man is the right path to pleasure, we were also taught that when we have sex with men, there is a right and a wrong way to go about it. The right way to have sex is male-initiated and male-dominant/female-submissive. Few women can remember where they learned this rule: It seemed we learned it by osmosis, through our parent's example, other adults, movies and romance novels, perhaps even from a marriage manual. When we became sexually active, we were afraid to be assertive because that would be breaking the rules. And if we were assertive, we may have been rejected, blamed or otherwise punished by a male partner who wanted sex "the right way":

> When I was in college, I dated this guy, and the first time I slept with him, he was impotent. He was real freaked out by it, so I did everything I could to help out. I was very giving and tried everything I knew to excite him. Later he told me it was all my fault, that guys like it better if you just lay there passive, and I shouldn't have been so "aggressive" because that turned him off. I was dumb enough at the time to accept that blame.

Here, too, there can be added pressure because of ethnicity:

> In college, black men would tell me to my face that it was easier to get sex from a white woman than from a black woman anytime, and they did not mean this as a compliment to us black women at all. It went along with the belief that we are castrating, aggressive, selfish, ambitious, and not supportive of our men, because we work while he is unemployed and we won't readily sleep with him. As for working, they never seemed to understand that the jobs we have gotten—domestics, baby-sitters, factory workers—didn't make us feel too terrific. And when I said I wanted to get to know a black man before I slept with him, to make sure we were compatible and that he was going to do something with his life, their reply was, "There you go again, thinking about yourself first and not taking care of your men."

Closely tied to the idea that the right kind of sex is heterosexual sex that conforms to a male-dominance/female-submission model is the belief that the right way to have an orgasm, if we are to have orgasms at all, is through penile penetration of the vagina. Although many women prefer clitoral stimulation, we were taught that the clitoris is a deformed, dwarfed penis, and that we should prefer vaginal penetration with a real penis to rubbing our stunted, malformed ones.

Followers of Freud deemed clitoral orgasms "immature" and vaginal orgasms "mature." But given that the vagina has relatively few nerve endings, having a "mature" vaginal orgasm is for many women an impossibility. Ann Koedt writes:

> Perhaps one of the most infuriating and damaging results of this whole charade has been that women who were perfectly healthy sexually were taught that they were not. So in addition to being sexually deprived, these women were told to blame themselves when they deserved no blame. Looking for a cure to a problem that has none can lead a woman on an endless path of self-hatred and insecurity.[5]

We were also taught that real sex begins when the penis penetrates the vagina, and that any other activity, even if it culminates in orgasm, is just foreplay or afterplay—terms which presume that intercourse and sexual relations are one and the same. As pleasurable as many women find "foreplay," if we stop there, it's presumed that we're cheating the man at the very least.

Another rule many of us learned is that if we are to allow ourselves sexual pleasure, we had better have earned it first:

> I can have an orgasm and I like to, but only after my husband has his, or else I feel like I'm being selfish.

Sexual pleasure not only has to be earned, it has to be paid for. Many of us fear that if we have sexual pleasure, we will in some way be punished as a result. Adding to this are realistic fears of such negative consequences as out-of-wedlock pregnancies, venereal disease, bad reputations and losing the respect—or even earning the contempt—of male lovers. Another realistic fear is fear of genital herpes, which now afflicts twenty million Americans. Herpes is physically painful, and psychologically damaging, too, with sufferers reporting side effects of depression, social isolation, a loss of control over their lives, and diminished self-esteem. Much of this is due to the superstitious beliefs about herpes, beliefs such as it's "the wrath of God," "the wages of sin," and nature's way of telling us "to bring a close to an era of mindless promiscuity." Another pernicious moral equation has been set up: Morally superior people don't get herpes—or other sexually transmitted diseases either. According to Nora Gallagher, the self-blame, guilt and misery the infected person already feels is "reinforced by the overreactions of others." Of one woman she interviewed for an article on sexually transmitted diseases, she writes:

> Linda's roommate used to scrub out the bathtub with Comet after Linda used it and before she herself stepped in. . . . Doctors would say things like, "Well, that's what you get for screwing around. If you were a good girl . . ." or, "You may as well join a convent; no man will want you now." Sometimes the advice offered is physically punishing: many doctors have prescribed pouring alcohol on open sores; one suggested injections of water moccasin venom.[6]

Since sexual pleasure is not always—or even most of the time—followed by negative consequences, some women punish themselves. A common way to inflict self-punishment is by flagellating ourselves with guilt after sexual pleasure. Another common way is by telling ourselves that what we find pleasurable is somehow indicative of our flaws. For example:

> Occasionally, I masturbate, but only when I have to. I can have orgasms easily this way and I do it as a release, but I usually feel worse afterward. I see masturbation as a sign of weakness. I do it because all my relationships are failures.

Since a woman's sexuality has traditionally been defined in response to male sexuality, a woman is supposed to want sex whenever her male partner desires. If she desires less sex than him, she is frigid. If she desires more, then she is a nymphomaniac. In fact, most of us have fluctuating cycles of sexual interest, and this is completely natural. Yet many women cannot help feeling guilty when their level of sexual interest is out of synch with their partner's.

Some women were also taught that it is wrong to be sexual at particular times, especially during menstruation:

> My lover and I have never talked about this explicitly, but whenever either one of us is having our period, we just don't make love. I feel most self-conscious then. Part of it is that my body is bloated and I feel like a lot of positions make my stomach and breasts sag and look unattractive. But more, it's that I don't want to be intimately close to someone during that time.

Most of us probably also learned that certain kinds of people, most notably people with physical or developmental disabilities, should never be sexual—that they were, in essence, born without sexual selves. If a woman is disabled in some way, our culture's total denial of her sexuality can have a profound impact on her self-esteem:

> People are very uncomfortable with someone like me in a wheelchair—I'm always having to put them at ease. You see this especially around sex. Automatically, people assume that I'm not a sexual being. It's as if the lower half of my body isn't there to them. I can remember swallowing those kinds of attitudes. I tried to think of myself as just a head, neck and arms because I couldn't deal with the rest. It wasn't just that others wouldn't recognize that, hey, I'm a human being—it was that I wouldn't admit it either. Sex was something I thought of as only normal people having.

Pleasure Chic

For those of us who grew up learning negative things about sex, our early learning has been compounded by a recently developed but equally tyrannical cultural attitude we call Pleasure Chic. Today, sex is no longer dirty, it is a wondrous cure-all. The new ethic tells us we should not worry so much about being "good girls." Instead, we should be ready to have "a zipless fuck" with a stranger on an elevator at a moment's notice. Once taught that nice girls don't, we are now told that nice girls do—a lot. We have new unrealistic ideals against which to measure our actual sexuality, as sex therapist Lonnie Barbach comments:

> . . . If a woman learns that multiple orgasm is possible, she feels somehow deficient if she has only one orgasm at a time. If she learns that some people make love for an hour, she thinks she must lack sexual energy if she prefers shorter episodes. If she finds anal sex painful, she wonders what is wrong with her. Some women become sexually aroused very quickly; others respond slowly. Some women require intense and direct clitoral stimulation to reach orgasm whereas others react to subtle pressure and indirect clitoral stimulation. Lack of acceptance of the physiological differences among women (as well as men) creates a personal sexual Olympics; there is no other human activity in which everyone expects to be a gold medal winner or regard herself as a total failure.[7]

We have seen the tyranny of this all-or-nothing thinking in books for women who are preorgasmic (often written by women). Although they give cursory endorsement of sexual pleasure that stops short of orgasm, the thrust of these books is goal-oriented: to enable a woman to match males' ease of reaching orgasm. Now the message is that any progressive-thinking female should be able to be multiorgasmic, if only she's willing to work, as Gabrielle Brown writes:

> Anthropologist Margaret Mead observed that female orgasm is not a problem in most primitive cultures, where men are trained to bring women to orgasm as part of their social responsibilities. But in our culture until very recently, while male orgasms were thought of as inevitable, female orgasms were depicted as rare, mysterious, and difficult to achieve, requiring hard work and concentration. Today a woman is advised to take responsibility for her orgasms and her task-orientation can be just as grim as any of woman's "traditional" chores—with perhaps a more pleasurable but not much more fulfilling ending than a clean house.[8]

There is a "use it or lose it" mentality at work today, too. This says that if we do not have a lot of sex when we are young, we will have missed our chance, and we will damage our physical well-being. Again from Gabrielle Brown:

> Besides its mental health value, we are also led to believe that sex is "good" for us in the same way that healthy foods, exercise, meditation, and other things have been found to raise the quality and longevity of life. But this, too, is misleading. Biologically, we don't lose the ability to be sexual by not being sexual. And unless one is in a weakened physical condition, one has the potential to be sexual all one's life. Yet the deceptive impression has been created that one must be sexually active to remain healthy.[9]

In fact, many women middle-aged and older report that although there are a few physiological changes to be reckoned with, their freedom from fear of pregnancy and the time-consuming task of raising children allows them to enjoy sex more than ever.

Pleasure Chic makes interest in a variety of sexual activity mandatory. And it makes many women feel guilty. There is absolutely nothing wrong with *choosing* to learn to enjoy oral sex or wanting to learn how to have an orgasm. But if a woman sees no reason to change her feelings about oral sex or doesn't need orgasms to feel sexual pleasure, then that needs to be just as acceptable. We must be able to say, "I have specific sexual likes and dislikes and that's okay—I am still worthwhile."

Is That All There Is?

While we interviewed some women who were sexually content, we interviewed many who did not understand what all the fuss is about.

Some women avoid sex altogether. Given the unpleasant or at least unsatisfying nature of most women's early sexual experiences, it is no wonder that this is so. Avoiding sex can be an effective way for a woman to obtain a measure of control over her life. Particularly for women who have been sexually abused, sex can conjure up feelings of helplessness, humiliation or despair. Those who tell us sex is the great panacea would have us believe that not wanting sex is always indicative of a serious psychological problem. But lack of desire for sex should not always be considered a problem:

> There is no safe and effective form of birth control for me right now, and I don't meet many men who are willing to take responsibility and use condoms. But it's more that I need some "time out." Bad affairs are a drain on my time and energy. Until I figure out what would make a good affair for me, I need to stay on the sidelines for a while.

While some women avoid sex altogether, other women focus on sex as if it were the most significant area of their lives. By projecting life's other problems into the sexual realm, they can create the illusion that they understand what's wrong with them, and thus can control it. Just as a woman can reason, "If only I had a better body, my life would be terrific," she can also reason, "If only I had a lover," or "If only I was a more skilled lover, my life would be better." Such investment in sexuality precludes examining other parts of the self that may be curtailing happiness. This can happen in a relationship, too:

> When my husband and I split, the only kind of therapy we had done was sex therapy. My not being orgasmic became the dumping ground for everything bad in the relationship. We never talked about the fact that our values changed over the years, that I was monogamous and he wasn't, that I was ambivalent about children, that he was a wild man with money. No, it was set up—by me as well as him—that if only I would enjoy sex more, then the relationship would be better. With all the pressure put on that, and with that not being the crux of the issue anyway, you can bet I never learned to come and the relationship never got better.

As it can be used to give us the illusion of control over our lives, sex can also be used as a way to control others. Particularly if a woman feels generally powerless in her life, she may sell sex as her only form of power:

> My husband is a tyrant. He would call himself a benevolent dictator, but I'm the one who is stuck at home with the kids, bored out of my mind, feeling like life is just passing me by. When he lets up on his controlling, sometimes I'll give him sex, but most of the time I don't—and he doesn't like it. But it's the only thing I can do, the only way he hears that I'm unhappy.

Ironically, sex can be a way to control other people in another way, to keep them at a distance out of a fear of intimacy:

> I used to think I got bored with sex easily. Now I see that that my supposed need for variety and excitement was just a way to keep the people coming through, keep the turnover high. Mostly I thought they'd leave eventually anyway and I wanted to do the leaving. But most of all, I didn't want them sticking around, getting to know things about myself that I didn't even know yet.

Because many of us have been taught to derive self-esteem from male approval, some women, not surprisingly, use sex with men as a primary way to gain validation or affirmation. This is reflected in the quotes of some heterosexual women interviewed by Shere Hite:

> Sex is important to me as a reaffirmation of my worth that a man would take time to be gentle with me.

> Having a man love me and want to have sex with me is necessary to my happiness. It gives me the feeling of being worthwhile if I can turn a man on.

> I've never heard a word of praise from my husband in twenty-one years except when having intercourse. While I resent this, I still love him and I enjoy sex with him—but only for this reason.[10]

Women can also use sex as a way to demonstrate that they are "good" women. As we know, a good woman is one who gives constantly yet never takes. Hite found this to be a prevalent pattern in her survey of female sexual response:

> . . . heterosexual sex usually involved the pattern of foreplay, penetration and intercourse ending with male ejaculation—and that all too often the woman does not orgasm *[sic]*. But women *know* how to orgasm *[sic]* during masturbation, whenever they want. If they know how to orgasm *[sic]* whenever they want, why don't they feel free to use this knowledge during sex with men? *Why do women so habitually satisfy men's needs during sex and ignore their own?*[11]

Perhaps the answer to Hite's question is that when a woman tries to fulfill her role expectations in the sexual arena, it behooves her to be nonassertive. Although we found women who were uncomfortable with oral sex, we found by far the most prevalent "oral phobia" concerned talking with one's partner about sex. This is due, in part, to the cultural image of "good sex" as something that happens spontaneously, with no communication between the lovers:

I fake orgasms mostly to make him feel better, but also to make myself look like a real woman, a fully functioning sexual being. Now the problem is that every time I think about telling him that sex isn't really that pleasurable for me, that I need different kinds of touch, I remember this lie I have been living. He thinks he's doing all the right things. I'm stuck—it would do too much damage to the relationship and to how he sees me sexually to tell him how I really feel.

Some women fear that if they spoke up about their sexual likes and dislikes, they would be obligated to hear their lover's likes and dislikes as well. Perhaps they would discover their lover has not been ecstatic all along either, and this is something they don't want to risk finding out. Also, some women believe, "If he really loved me, he would know what I want. If I have to tell him, it doesn't mean as much."

Often not knowing what we want or not knowing how to ask for it, we settle for less. And then we begin to believe we *deserve* less. Not communicating about sex may serve to keep up our appearances as giving women who need nothing back in return, but it inevitably curtails feelings of sexual pleasure and competence.

Especially today, sex often serves as "mock intimacy" for some women. Particularly in the "early morning stranger" variety of sex, where we attempt an intimate connection to someone we do not know, sex is bound to fall short of our expectations. Of this Elisabeth Haich writes:

Sexuality mimics love. It compels tenderness and embraces, it forces the lovers to hug one another, to allay one another's pain through the revelations of sexuality, as when true love is exchanged. What follows such experiences? Disappointments, a bitter aftertaste, mutual accusations of bleak loneliness, feelings of exploitation and defilement. *Neither of the two gave true love but only expected to receive it, therefore, neither received it.* [12]

For others, the need is more global, for a sense of more caring in the world, as Nora Gallagher explains:

Whereas a person once felt a warm, truly intimate connection to his or her community, today living isolated is the norm. But the need to be touched by another human, to be warmed by flesh, is still there. . . . This desire for others is rarely satisfied by one night with a stranger, but for many of us, it was all we had. Thus, we lost our ability to make the distinction between a desire for sex and a desire for a warmer world altogether. We also may have lost a sense of the difference between what a stranger can give and what is given between trusted lovers. These confusions led to a pain in many of us whose source we were not sure of: some tried to eliminate the pain again and again until sex became very like a drug; others retreated, helpless and uneasy.[13]

No matter what the original motivation, "mock intimacy" does not enhance self-esteem:

> I used to get involved in a lot of instant intimacy. I would sleep with someone on the first date and have a lot of expectations that go with sex. But we'd never develop skills like learning to communicate with each other, and we wouldn't have a history of good feelings to fall back on. The relationships never could survive under the weight of my expectations and invariably they ended badly. . . . It wasn't until I got more comfortable with myself, less in need of that instant intimacy, that I was able to be successfully involved with someone.

Sexual Evolution

Neither the anti-sex lessons most of us were taught as children nor the pro-sex propaganda that surrounds us today ultimately does much to aid us in expanding our self-knowledge and self-acceptance. We needed to question what we were taught as children, and through questioning to come to our own conclusions about what sex means to us and how we will behave sexually. Instead, we got a so-called sexual revolution and a new set of standards just as rigid and oppressive as those we were raised with.

There are two main lessons we learned from the women we interviewed. First, sexuality can be experienced *not* in relation to another person. Second, a woman's sexuality extends well beyond her genitals. If we define sexuality as feelings emanating from a woman's genitals, then we are disembodying ourselves. No human behavior is motivated by one need alone, and our sexuality is a function of a myriad of feelings. What makes us feel "sexy" or sensual is different for everyone:

> Swimming in warm water, dressing in silks, exercising until I feel high—all of those things are sexual feelings to me. Even if I'm not involved with someone else, I can still feel sexually alive.

In learning to like herself, a woman may want to work toward a positive concept of herself as a sexual being. This means unlearning rigid ideologies and lies, discovering what gives her pleasure, and taking the risk of pursuing this self-discovery. It is no easy task, but for a fuller sense of self, she may decide it is worth the effort.

BLUEPRINTS FOR CHANGE

I. EARLY LEARNING

Certainly our early learning and experiences can influence our adult sexuality. Were there any lessons taught or experiences you had in any of the following areas which you think play a role in your sexuality now?

> —masturbation (in childhood and adulthood)
> —sexual contact with an older authority figure or trusted person (see Part II, Chapter 6)
> —first sexual experience with a boy (if you had one)
> —first sexual experience with a girl (if you had one)
> —nudity in the home
> —physical affection between parents
> —sex education (by whom? content?)
> —pornography

Can you question what you learned? Have you replaced it with new beliefs? Do you feel guilty or chastise yourself instead? To undo very powerful early lessons, we might need the help of professional or friend(s).

What kind of messages did you get about female sexuality specifically? How were sex symbols regarded in your home? What double messages were directed at you? For example, were you taught to act seductively, then told that you should pretend not to want sex? Were the contradictions exacerbated by racism or other kinds of oppression? Are there any ways in which these double standards are operating in your life today?

II. STARTING WITH YOURSELF

A woman's sexuality does not have to be experienced in relation to another person. Just as we often form our body image according to how we think other people see us, we often develop a sense of our sexuality according to how other people respond to it. And just as a woman can unlearn a negative and inaccurate body image by really looking at her body and disregarding the cultural ideals and personal criticism on which she has previously based her body image, so can a woman explore her own sexuality on her own. First, however, a woman must decide whether she wants to. If she does, that's fine. If she doesn't, that's fine, too.

For those who do, begin by asking yourself if you are aware of what gives you pleasure sexually. The specifics need not be confined to touch alone. Are there elements of atmosphere, music, mood, etc., that can make a sexual encounter (of any kind) more pleasurable for you? How often do you "indulge" yourself in what is pleasurable for you? Is it possible to do this more often? Do you want to?

How would you describe your sexuality? Don't feel confined by the rigid labels of homosexual or heterosexual. Use any words you want to describe your individual sexuality. One woman who did this exercise felt that "monogamous" and "playful" were more important characteristics of her sexual expression than her sexual preference. Try to be more precise about yours.

One of many ways to explore what kinds of touch give a person pleasure is masturbation. Of course, many women masturbate, but not always with the attainment of self-knowledge in mind, and it isn't always guilt-free. The same activity with a different focus can have an entirely different meaning to a person. From *The Hite Report:*

> Masturbation is one of the sacred rituals that women can enjoy amongst themselves. I say it is "sacred" because it is *self*-initiated, *self*-controlled, and *self*-gratifying—coming from a position of strength. It is not only about a physical or emotional (they are inseparable) closeness to one's body, but a conquest of all the fears that families and men have instilled in women about their bodies and sexual dependencies.[14]

Masturbation for self-pleasure is valid in and of itself. If a woman wants to attain more pleasure with a partner, masturbation might be helpful in learning what feels best. Once we know what we want, we will be better able to communicate with a partner.

By the same token, we can often learn more about what we want in a sexual relationship by taking some "time out" sexually within our relationships. In *The New Celibacy,* Gabrielle Brown explains:

> Becoming celibate for a time is not closing off but an opening up. It allows women to break old patterns of behavior, dependencies, limits. Women find that becoming celibate enables them to experience a greater degree of self-sufficiency and freedom while at the same time offering a chance to explore new dimensions in relationships. It can be a time to free a woman from the frantic nature of sexual activity and its narrow focus. And it can be a time to sort out feelings about a particular relationship without the mask of sex

—to allow the deepening of a love relationship to occur in a more un-
bounded field.[15]

If there is something to be gained in celibacy for you, perhaps it is a
valid option you want to consider.

III. FANTASIES

Fantasies are also another one of many ways to explore one's sexuality. However, as with masturbation, we found much guilt and other
negative emotions linked to fantasy among the women we talked with.

We found fantasies became problematic under two conditions. First,
when fantasies became ideals against which the real is judged. For example, the notion of the "zipless fuck" immortalized in Erica Jong's
novel *Fear of Flying,* or the image of spontaneous and overwhelming
passion that culminates in perfect sex scenes in romance novels, are fine
as fantasies. But if a woman adopts these as ideals and measures her
own sexual performance against the heroines, or expects her lover to
sweep her off her feet and know exactly what she wants without any
communication, then she is bound to be at the very least disappointed.

Second, when fantasies are judged as good or bad, politically correct
or incorrect, etc., they can be problematic. For example, some women
have rape or abuse fantasies and feel terrible about themselves, as if only
a regressed, secretly victimlike woman would have such fantasies. But,
by virtue of the fact that she is creating the fantasy in her mind, she is *in
control* of the situation, unlike a woman in a real rape or abuse situation. Moreover, if we have a fantasy about something, it doesn't mean
it's something we would really want to have happen.

Guilt over a fantasy can compel a person to return to the fantasy in
hope of resolving the guilt. But both the guilt and the compulsion to
return to the fantasy deepens each time. First, remember that fantasies,
like feelings, just are, and ought not to be judged. Then try using
Thought Stopping on your guilt and perhaps the fantasy will become
less relentless and problematic.

IV. ONE OF MANY KINDS OF FEELINGS

Because sexual feelings are connected to other kinds of feelings, our
sexuality can serve either to control or repress those feelings (by re-
pressing our sexuality) or express them. Sex therapist Carmen Kerr
became aware of this interconnection in her own personal experience:

I remember when I first began letting myself experience the feelings that accompany sexual arousal. I felt many emotions I hadn't expected and didn't really want to have. . . . I decided to let myself experience whatever was there because when I stopped feeling them, I stopped feeling everything. I'd cry a little and then diddle a little. It turned out to be a cleansing, relaxing experience and accustomed me to the fact that my feelings, no matter what they are, are normal. I even began to use masturbation to get in touch with feelings I couldn't quite fathom. My anger, fears, unhappiness would suddenly all come into focus this way.[16]

Are you aware of any connections between your sexual feelings and other kinds of feelings?

V. POWER AND COMPETENCE

In what ways do you feel like a powerful person? Is sex one of them? Is it the only way in which you feel powerful, or the way in which you feel *most* powerful, or is it one of many ways in which you feel powerful? Do you feel more or less powerful in sexual relationships as compared to nonsexual relationships? If you use sex as a way of manipulating others to meet your needs, perhaps you want to experiment with a different approach, such as being assertive rather than manipulative.

VI. SEXUAL ASSERTIVENESS

When you feel secure, at ease with yourself and confident enough so that a sexual rejection would not devastate you, try asking your partner (if you have one) for one specific change in your sex life. Ask for something you want—a certain type of touch, sex at a different time of day, "foreplay" without intercourse if you are heterosexual. Don't start with the change you want most. Work up to that after a few successful experiences. It's okay to tell your partner that you are nervous or even frightened about being straightforward about your needs. What is the worst that could happen? Also, it might be helpful, if you genuinely feel like it, to ask your partner if there is anything he or she would like to change. Give him or her the opportunity to be assertive, too. Remember, though, that it's perfectly all right for you to ask for something without immediately giving back.

VII. HOMOPHOBIA AND OTHER PREJUDICES

If you are a woman who has chosen a sexual life-style that is not heterosexual, do you have other women talk with about the stresses of living in a homophobic society? Celibates also can benefit from knowing others who have made the same choice, with whom they can talk about living in a culture so concerned with sex. In larger cities, various support groups are often run through gay community centers, YWCAs, mental health clinics, college campuses, etc. Groups are not for every woman; some do not want to be so public about their sexuality. For such women, talking with a trusted friend can make a difference in alleviating the sense of isolation.

* 12 *

I'd Rather Be Right than Happy: Self-Fulfilling Prophecies

In classes on literature we are taught that "character determines action." I would paraphrase that to say self-concept determines destiny. Or to speak with greater restraint and precision, there is a strong *tendency* for self-concept to determine destiny.

—Nathaniel Branden,
The Psychology of Romantic Love

Human beings have an undeniable desire for consistency. When our internal thinking does not match our external experience, we have an uncanny way of manipulating the external until it aligns with our expectations. Women with low self-esteem are often extremely adept at this sort of manipulation. Beginning with a self-hypothesis such as "I am unlovable" or "I have to do everything myself, no one will help me," a woman may set out to test and prove that hypothesis through experience. On general principle, of course, everyone would rather be proven right than wrong, so the woman who is sure she is unlovable or has to do everything herself will gather evidence that reaffirms her belief that, yes, indeed, she is unlovable or entirely on her own. She has created for herself a self-fulfilling prophecy. She gets what she most wanted—consistency—but only at the cost of her self-esteem and happiness.

Self-fulfilling prophecies are scripts based on seemingly intractable beliefs about the self and backed up by past experience. Through the repetition of a specific experience (rejection, failure, abandonment, quarreling) which reinforces a specific message about the self ("No one will ever want you"; "You screw everything up"; "You'll always be left alone in the end"; "You can't get along with anyone"), many people come to believe that what has happened in the past is bound to happen again in the future. And in order to legitimize the belief that the future will conform to the past, they behave so as to eliminate any other possibility.

Self-fulfilling prophecies can be constructive, too. A woman who believes "I am lovable" and "I am competent," for example, will likely arrange her life and behavior to align as much as possible with those beliefs. Unfortunately, though, self-fulfilling prophecies of the destructive sort are far more common among those with low self-esteem.

Negative beliefs about oneself and one's life acquired in childhood set one up for a destructive self-fulfilling prophecy that can last a lifetime. But even those women who escape childhood without having acquired a set of predominantly negative beliefs about themselves can still find themselves playing out a self-destructive script. If a woman has enough bad experiences over a relatively short period of time, she may find herself thinking and acting in ways that help to insure more bad experiences in the future:

> I grew up feeling pretty good about myself, and my life was going along just fine until my late twenties. Then suddenly, a whole bunch of terrible things started happening: My apartment was robbed three times in nine months, I got mugged, my lover and I broke up, my mother died, I got passed up for a promotion at work, and then to top it all off, about a month after my lover and I split up, I found out I was pregnant. I had an abortion and felt awful about it, really hated myself for it, and somewhere in the midst of all this I broke out in psoriasis all over. I remember sitting in my apartment, scared to death of being broken in on again and itching like crazy, and suddenly thinking, "Well, maybe this is how it's gonna be. Maybe you're just one of those people who's bound to have a shitty life." For about two years after that I was in a complete rut. Having decided that I was one of those people who's gonna have a shitty life, I gave up attempting to make my life less shitty. I did a lot of incredibly self-destructive things. It took me a long time to free myself from the belief that because I had had a couple of bad years I was sure to have a bad life.

A woman with a negative self-fulfilling prophecy is often so convinced that all her future experiences will further prove her negative beliefs about herself that she develops a prepatterned and extremely rigid style of perception. Often, it simply does not occur to her that there may be many different ways to perceive and explain the same experience or situation:

A couple of months ago I met a man I really liked at a party. He asked for my phone number and said he'd call me. Well, weeks and weeks went by, and he didn't call. This didn't surprise me. I don't think I'm very attractive, and so I knew that this guy really wanted nothing to do with me and would never call. Finally, though, he did call. I was real cool toward him, and in a real flip manner said, "So what's been keeping you so busy these past few months?" I felt terrible when he told me that his father had died, and the reason he hadn't called sooner was that he was too overwhelmed with grief. It just hadn't occurred to me that there might be something else behind his not calling than my unattractiveness.

Sometimes the inability to recognize that there are numerous ways to perceive and interpret a situation or experience can blind a woman not just to external reality, but to internal reality as well:

I used to be so convinced that no one could really like me that when I first met someone or was just beginning to get to know them there would be a funny feeling, like things weren't going really terrifically. Right away I'd assume they didn't like me, so I'd feel real hurt and slink away and feel bad about myself—it had happened again. Then one time, my sister asked me how I felt about someone this was happening with. Honestly, I'd never thought about it—*I* didn't like *them*. And that was what my uneasiness was all about. Before I was always so quick to assume that it was the other person who didn't like me!

The desire for consistency is not the only reason people cling to destructive self-fulfilling prophecies. Happiness anxiety, too, often factors in. Happiness anxiety is common among those who believe they don't deserve happiness and is encouraged by such clichés as "Happiness never lasts" and "Suffering is what gets you to heaven." Among people with happiness anxiety, Branden observes,

Often there is the feeling that if they are happy, either happiness will be taken away from them or something terrible will happen to counterbalance it, some unspeakable punishment or tragedy. . . . While they may long for it on one level of consciousness, they dread it on another.[1]

Again, what was learned in childhood has an influence. If someone has not experienced sustained, repeated periods of relative happiness, she can't possibly know how to embrace it.

For some women the most attractive aspect of their prophecy is that it gives them the illusion of control over their lives. Believing they can predict future outcomes on the basis of past experiences, they believe they can prepare themselves for what will happen. The pleasure of being comfortable with what we know is preferred to the pain of the unknown. This woman relates a classic example:

> I get into relationships, but I know they aren't going to last too long. My most recent relationship seemed to be going better than most, but I knew it would end eventually. I didn't want to take a chance of breaking up over Christmas—that would be awful—so I broke it off before. One thing I do well is heal after relationships. I've had years of experience. But what if we had gotten closer and closer, then maybe lived together? I wouldn't know what I was doing—it really scared me, and I knew breaking up then would hurt even more.

The control issue here is obvious: Hurt first before being hurt. In addition, this woman resolved her happiness anxiety by terminating the relationship, and restored her sense of congruency and competence by allowing herself to do what she knows best: putting the pieces of her life back together.

Some women need the illusion of control so much because deep inside they feel very out of control and it frightens them. This contradiction can be bewildering to the people who work, live or are friends with a woman with a destructive pattern. She can seem not only controlling, but downright mean at times:

> When I thought someone would leave me, as they always would once they got to know me, I would often strike out and say terrible things to them. Then I was so surprised when they acted hurt. As I matured some, I realized that I had rationalized, "They don't care about me anyway, so nothing I say has any meaning to them," when in fact, what I said really did hurt them. It did make a difference to them.

Branden explains the difference between the "pseudo-control" of the self-fulfilling prophecy and authentic control:

> . . . the desire to be in control of our lives is entirely human; it is hardly irrational. But it can lead to irrational behavior, when we are unconsciously manipulated by our self-destructive and self-sabotaging beliefs. To be "in control" means to understand the facts of reality that bear on our life so that we are able to predict, with reasonable accuracy, the consequences of our actions. Tragedy occurs when, out of a misguided notion of control, we attempt to "adjust" reality to our beliefs, rather than to adjust our beliefs to reality. Tragedy occurs when we cling to our beliefs blindly and manipulate events without awareness of doing so, insensitive to the fact that alternative possibilities exist. Tragedy occurs when we would rather be "right" than happy, when we would rather sustain the illusion

that we are "in control" than notice that reality is not the way we have told ourselves it is.[2]

Fear of responsibility also contributes to the tenacity of a self-fulfilling prophecy. If a woman noticed that reality is different than she had thought (that she could be competent at work or successful in a relationship, for instance), a tremendous amount of responsibility might befall her.

Consider a woman whose self-fulfilling prophecy is that she will never succeed in a job. Life for her is a series of predictable short-term jobs, each ended in disrepute. While she has a job, she relies on the knowledge that some coworkers will learn to adapt and will cover for her incompetence. With others she is quick to apologize for her mistakes; she disarms them with self-deprecation before they criticize her. Most important, she knows when to leave (before she actually gets fired) and is practiced at finagling jobs without many references.

But imagine now that she takes some classes and increases her skills. Based on a few initial successes, she begins to rewrite her scenario and becomes a valued employee rather than someone who has to be tolerated for the time being. Her style of relating to her coworkers definitely would have to change. She might even be assigned more responsibility, or be considered for a promotion. This can be extremely frightening for someone who has long considered herself incompetent and who does not want to lose what little apparent "control" and predictability she has had in her life.

Destructive prophecies do force one to develop skills and resources that could enhance self-esteem if put to use in a positive context. The resiliency cultivated in the process of recovering from many broken affairs, for example, can be an asset in a stressful but challenging job, and can help one in coping with the strains encountered in an ongoing relationship. The ability to listen to criticism that comes as a result of resigning from numerous jobs can be used effectively on a job one wants to keep. But just because a woman can survive dismal situations does not mean she has to; she can take her strengths and skills and apply them elsewhere:

> My parents were alcoholics, and I learned how to take care of myself in that situation. I did it so well that I married one and was miserable—but surviving—for years. Finally, I had enough. Through some counseling, I found some things about myself that I liked a lot—things which had been useful to me during those times, like being responsible and caring and being able to keep my sense of humor when things don't seem all that

funny. Now I'm putting the determination I used to cope with the alcoholism to work in another way, by going back to school—for me. And I work with teenagers who have alcoholic parents a few hours a week. I still use those old skills, to help myself and other people, but I no longer go home to the stench of scotch at night.

This woman did not discard the skills she acquired to endure her early bad experiences, nor did she change herself. She looked at her skills in a more self-enhancing light and replaced her old prophecy with one built on a better understanding of herself.

Changing a prophecy does not come easily, but it is possible. Our self-concept has only a tendency to determine destiny; it is not a hard-and-fast rule.

Women with self-fulfilling prophecies are adept at manipulating their perceptions of external events to align with their inner views toward themselves and life in general. But in order to change a self-fulfilling prophecy, it's necessary to reconsider and most likely change one's perceptions of oneself. Simply manipulating external events in the opposite direction will not suffice to turn around an old prophecy. A change in the self-concept is needed, too. This woman, who conceived of herself as someone who had to give of herself constantly, found this out:

> My parents were really children, and I did a lot of taking care of them. Now, I find men whom I can take care of, but just as with my parents, I feel I never get anything back, and I feel resentful. I encourage them to feel dependent, then they see me as controlling and not needing anything from them, and they get angry and leave. . . . Finally, through lots of help, I began to believe that I didn't have to give all the time and that it was okay for me to want something back; it didn't mean certain death.

Perhaps the most difficult part of giving up a self-fulfilling prophecy is giving up the illusion that the world is consistent, predictable and individually controllable. If a desperate need to be in control rules someone's life, she is not truly in control; the need controls her. To be genuinely in control means being able to tolerate feelings of fear, uncertainty, inadequacy or self-doubt from time to time without manipulating everyone and everything into our singular view of the world.

BLUEPRINTS FOR CHANGE

I. HAPPINESS ANXIETY

If you suffer from happiness anxiety, you can help yourself by setting up controlled situations where you learn to experience happiness without anxiety. Decide on five activities that you enjoy but rarely do. Do not try to tackle too much happiness at once. For instance, if one of your activities is to sit in the sun or go for a walk in the snow, and you are not accustomed to this type of leisure activity, begin with only fifteen or thirty minutes of it. When you feel more comfortable, slowly increase the time.

It would also be helpful if you constructed a hierarchy of pleasurable experiences that seem unattainable. You might begin with sitting and doing nothing for half an hour because that seems the easiest. From there, you might graduate to taking yourself out to a nice dinner. Your ultimate goal might be to go away for the weekend with a friend and be able to ask for private time as well as shared time together. Ten potential sources of pleasure, ranked by their likelihood of attainability, should keep you busy for a long time.

II. LIFE SCRIPTS

Write out your self-fulfilling prophecies in as much detail as you possibly can. Begin it like a story, "Once upon a time," and include your global assumptions, such as "The world is a
place,"   "Men   always   ,"   "Women   always
                ." In parenthesis, write how you feel about yourself as a result. It may take up to five pages to complete—some prophecies are more complicated than others. You might find it painful to write things like this out, but it will help in gaining a perspective on the destructive script.

Once written out, leave the prophecy alone for two weeks, then go back and reread it. Examine each of the original sentences and feeling statements. Do things *really* have to be this way? What can you learn or change so the story will have a more positive outcome? Can you remember times when the story was entirely true? Would your life be different—and how—if you changed the script? What frightens you about doing this? What positive feelings or outcomes could come of changing it? Do the risks outweigh the potential good?

After you have thought about these questions, perhaps written your answers in a journal or discussed them with a friend, you are ready to rewrite the prophecy. Do not rewrite it in one sitting. Consider each sentence over the period of at least one day and carefully choose how you want to change it. Don't forget the feeling statements in parentheses.

The new script does not have to be unqualifiedly positive; horror stories rarely turn into fairy tales. Strengths can be highlighted and reinterpreted in a more self-enhancing light. If we make changes in a destructive script, our experiences will be expanded and greater self-knowledge will probably result. Energy no longer will be wasted on the destructive self-fulfilling prophecy. It may take a long time for all of this to happen, but it will be worth the effort.

* 13 *

Distract Me from My Dreaded Self: I'd Rather Hate You than Me

It has always been a mystery to me how men can feel themselves
honored by the humiliation of their fellow beings.

—Gandhi

Believing they are inadequate, people with low self-esteem find the
world overwhelming at best and downright threatening at worst. Often,
their fear and self-hatred lead to hostility toward others: this can seem
like a necessary defense when one's world constantly reminds someone
of his or her inadequacy. The talent one develops for self-hatred can
easily be applied to the hatred of others—especially certain groups
(Jews, women, Hispanics, etc.), but sometimes the whole world.

Some people who feel hostility toward others keep it pretty much to
themselves; they don't act it out. In fact, they may even feel ashamed of
being misanthropic, racist, sexist, anti-Semitic or the like. But hostility
is a powerful emotion, and so low self-esteem which translates into fear
of the world and then into hostility toward others is likely to be acted
out against others eventually, either through hurtful judgments or oppressive behavior.

Sometimes people hate in others what we cannot or will not accept in
ourselves. By hating we attempt to smash the mirror that reflects the
dreaded image rather than trying to accept or change that image. We
see this in people who berate others for showing emotion because they
feel especially ashamed of and overwhelmed by their own emotions.
Hate serves the purpose of distracting us from ourselves. It is conve-
nient for us to have someone against whom we can ventilate our negativity. With all that time and energy going into finding fault with others,

there is little time or energy left over for self-reflection or self-acceptance.

Not all people who hate do so out of a wealth of low self-esteem. It is almost impossible to grow up in America without acquiring prejudices, and there are those who hate people different from themselves simply because they have been taught to do so and have not learned another way. Others hate also because hostility against certain people is sanctioned by their class, gender, and race. For instance, many white men are oppressive to women and people of color not because they secretly feel bad about themselves (although perhaps they should) but because they believe they are entitled by divine or natural law to treat women and people of color as inferiors. Historically, this type of oppressive person often has used the rationale that he is the "protector" of these inferior people who cannot fend for themselves. At least partially under the guise of such paternalism, blacks were enslaved, Native Americans were "relocated" onto reservations, and women were relegated to subordinate, second-class status.

Those who try to bolster their own self-worth by denigrating and oppressing others practice the bully approach to self-esteem. Often this goes along with blaming or scapegoating, and we can see it at work in many homes. Dad suffers injury to his self-esteem at work where his boss has been picking on him lately, and so he attempts to make himself feel better by punching out his wife, saying all his problems are *her* fault. Mom, in turn, feels pretty rotten about having been punched and scapegoated, so she slaps the kids and screams that it's all *their* fault. Being scapegoated makes the kids feel angry and powerless too, so they kick the dog, or each other, or go beat up the neighborhood "sissy." And on and on it goes. In this way, the young are trained to fit into a society where many believe that the only way to obtain self-esteem or to repair injured self-esteem is to set yourself up as superior to and more powerful than others.

Most of us were taught to hate people for differences over which they have no control: skin color, gender, age, physical disabilities, ethnic identity, sexual preference, the social class or religion they were born into. Economic circumstances often fan the flames, giving people perverse justification for lashing out at those whose differences they have been taught to despise. Anti-Semitism had existed in Europe for centuries, but when Germany's economic system was failing, Jews were first stripped of their economic holdings, then millions were interned and murdered. We have waged three wars against Asian peoples in less than forty years—two of them with questionable justification. And now the

Ku Klux Klan is terrorizing Vietnamese refugee fishermen off the Gulf Coast because they believe they are "taking all the fish." White people have never respected the different cultures of the Native Americans, but now that profitable minerals are found on the reservations they were forced onto, attempts to take away their land *again* have escalated. Homophobia has always been rampant, but the appearance of the fatal Acquired Immune Deficiency Syndrome is now being used as an excuse to further condemn, scapegoat and oppress homosexuals. It has been the experience of most immigrant groups in America that they started out as workers in the lowest-paid, least valued jobs and later became targets of scapegoating and bullying as their eventual upward mobility threatened those who not so long before were also targets:

> During the Boston busing riots, I went down to pick up the kids one day, and I saw at least fifty white men taunting and throwing things at these little black kids. My first reaction was, "What in the hell are these men doing out at two in the afternoon picking on eight-year-old black kids for?" Knowing that neighborhood, a good bet is that most of those men are unemployed. They wouldn't dare throw tomatoes and yell slurs at the men who laid them off, so instead, they're down here taking it out on little black kids. If poor white people and poor black people ever joined forces to fight the ways they are kept down, this whole country would change. But I don't think it'll ever happen, because racism is what keeps them apart. Racism benefits the white men in power—keeps the poor from going for their throats—so it's encouraged. Then we're told racism is an inevitable fact of life, that there's nothing you can do about it.

People who hate, scapegoat, and bully cannot afford to see the similarities between themselves and their victims. Cherríe Moraga explains:

> . . . it is not really difference the oppressor fears so much as similarity. He fears he will discover in himself the same aches, the same longings as those of the people he has shitted on. He fears the immobilization threatened by his own incipient guilt. He fears he will have to change his life once he has seen himself in the bodies of the people he has called different. He fears the hatred, anger, the vengeance of those he has hurt.[1]

In order to avoid seeing any similarities between themselves and their victims, haters must *exaggerate* the differences between themselves and their victims. Not only are any disconcerting similarities obscured, but it's then easier to rank-order the differences and to use them as "proof" of overall inferiority or superiority and as justification for unequal treatment. In our culture, for example, the differences between the sexes have been so exaggerated that traditionally women have been viewed as members of a different species from men, and the belief that women are an inferior group has been used, in turn, to justify treating women as less than fully human. The differences between various races and ethnic groups have been exaggerated in the same way, for similar ends. And the differences between people with and without obvious physical handicaps are also often exaggerated to the point of obscuring all similarities, as this woman explains:

> As a disabled person, I think a lot of able-bodied people make a bigger deal out of my disability than it really is because they want to believe that being disabled is *so* foreign an experience that it'll never happen to them. Maybe they are afraid they don't have what it takes, they couldn't cope if it did happen to them. They don't think, "But for the grace of God go I," and focus on the similarities between us—like the interests, the feelings, the fact that life is hard for everyone. Instead they treat me like a freak who must be totally alien, someone they couldn't have anything in common with. I think part of it may be that most able-bodied people don't want to be reminded that they are just a car accident or fall down the stairs away from being in a wheelchair too.

Women can be as misanthropic, racist, anti-Semitic, classist, ageist, homophobic and cruel to people with disabilities as men can be. Women also can be as misogynist as men, because like all oppressed groups, we are encouraged to disown our own kind. Just as some light skinned blacks disdain those with darker skin and some homosexuals disdain gays who are "too swishy" or lesbians who are "too butchy," women often disdain other women. Flo Kennedy explains:

> It's women's sense of their own lack of worth that makes sibling rivalry and horizontal hostility so easy. *If you have a sense of your own worthlessness, then somebody else from your own class or race or religion is clearly not to be looked up to.* This is one of the bases for the pathology of women saying, "I don't get along with women. I get along with men; they're superior, so if I get along with them, I'm superior. I've left my class behind." (Emphasis added.)[2]

We see this phenomenon in women who strive for acceptance from the most powerful group by trying to be "honorary men":

> I hope I would never do this again, but I remember distinctly starting in a corporation as a mid-level manager and agreeing with men that women were limited and too emotional and unreliable to do certain kinds of sales and marketing work. I didn't see how I was cuting off my nose to spite my face. I actually *liked* being the only woman there. It made me seem more like "one of the boys." Only after the "boys" passed me up for promotion

after promotion, and threw my own antiwoman stuff back in my face, did I wise up.

A woman who believes she is an "honorary man" does not see herself merely as "different" from other women; she sees herself as better than other women. But since the biological fact of her femaleness is inescapable (and moreover is the most defining aspect of how other people perceive her), any pride she takes in being different eventually will be canceled out by the inevitable shame of being the same in that she is female. Moreover, when a woman makes damning generalizations about women while excepting herself, it's likely that somewhere deep inside her lurks the fear that what she says is really true about herself as well.

Whether it's women or a certain ethnic or religious group they hate, some women who hate others excuse their hostility by telling themselves that because women are relatively powerless in our society no one gets hurt when women hate. To be sure, women do not have access to power as men do, and thus women cannot marshal armies and governments in the service of hatred as men often have done. Still, women can and often do hurt others when we hate, and we are accountable for it.

It is easy to try to make ourselves feel better about ourselves by putting others down and venting rage at them. And for some, hating, scapegoating and bullying others does lead to a fleeting feeling of self-worth and satisfaction. But in the long run, it doesn't transform us into more self-accepting people, nor does it challenge the social systems that are at the root of many people's feelings of powerlessness and inadequacy.

It would be naïve to suggest that the human race do a total turnabout, and that we all come to love each other for our differences. But there is such a thing as neutrality, learning to live and let live. After all, most of the differences between us really don't make a difference. A person is not more or less worthy because of her skin color, ethnic identity, religion, class, body-type, sexual preference or age. There is much room between love and hate for all of us to live. We can make note of our differences—as well as our similarities—and not waste our precious time and energy passing judgment on them. We can also remember that hating and oppressing other groups is a symptom of low self-esteem, not a solution.

BLUEPRINTS FOR CHANGE

I. FEAR OF DIFFERENCE

Often, blaming and hating others stems from the need to escape parts of ourselves we don't accept and to escape the feelings of self-hatred generated by those unacceptable parts. However, if people remembered what it is like to be blamed or hated, if they could stay in touch with what it feels like, then perhaps they would be less likely to act in a blaming or hateful manner toward others. From a lecture by Audre Lorde:

> I urge each one of us [here] to reach down into that deep place of knowledge inside herself and touch that terror and loathing of any difference that lives there. See whose face it wears.[3]

Can you remember a time when you were labeled "different" and then judged by it? How did it feel? Was your difference something within your control? If not, how did you feel about being judged by it? How did you want to respond? Was it a difference that could have been acknowledged but not judged? The next time you pass judgment on someone's difference, it might be helpful to remember how this felt. Do you really want to spend your time and energy causing someone else to feel bad?

II. SYSTEMATIC HATING

Do you feel that you are encouraged by such factors as capitalism, patriarchy, racism, ageism, homophobia, anti-Semitism, classism, and prejudices against people with disabilities to hate and blame other people? Chances are good there is a common ground between you and those you hate, in that the social system oppresses you both and benefits from the strife between you. Can you see this? For the sake of undermining that system, consider using your time and energy to join forces with those you are encouraged to hate.

III. HIERARCHIES

The most prevelant and traditional hierarchy of Western culture places God above man, man above women, adults above children, humans above animals, animals above insects, etc. Do you recall being taught this hierarchical world view? Do you ascribe to it today—in part or in entirety? Or do you have your own specific hierarchies? For instance, we interviewed women who thought women were above (better than) men, and we even met one woman who considers cats superior to all other living beings, including humans. What does your hierarchy look like? There is nothing inherent or inevitable about hierarchical thought. How can you break down your hierarchy so that aspects of it can coexist on the same plane, being neither superior or inferior to another? Think about the influence your hierarchy has both on how you view and behave in the world and most importantly, on how you feel about yourself. Do you need to put others down or to think of them as inferior to feel good about yourself?

EPILOGUE:
Self-Esteem and Social Responsibility

No right comes without responsibilities, and women's right to greater self-development and self-esteem is no exception to this rule. Numerous books appearing on the market in recent years have encouraged people to develop their full human potential through relentless pursuit of their individual rights to happiness, liberty, self-development and self-assertion. Yet few of the books and therapies spawned by the so-called human potential movement have paid much attention to the issue of responsibility to others. On the contrary, a number of pop psychologists and best-selling authors in recent years have operated on the assumption that individuals have no responsibility to others at all. Instead of suggesting that we try to find a moral balance between individual rights and social responsibility, many of the gurus of the human potential movement have preached a single-minded policy of "getting yours" even if that means ignoring the rights and needs of others, and of "putting yourself first" even if doing so means exploiting or hurting others. One popular writer has even gone so far as to suggest that in our search for self-gratification we each should "become a shrugger," closing our eyes to injustice, social problems, and the suffering of others.[1]

We think the "put yourself first and forget about everyone else" type of philosophy so popular today is not only morally reprehensible, but dangerous. The self-centered, exploitive behavior encouraged by so many advocates of the philosophy of single-minded self-gratification is precisely what's behind women's oppression, indeed all forms of oppression. Me-ism and the bully approach to self-esteem have been practiced for millennia by men against women, whites against blacks, rich against poor, humans against animals, ad infinitum; and the result is a world in which social ills and injustice abound, atrocities are common, ecological damage is rife, evil is considered banal, and ever growing arsenals of nuclear and biological weapons threaten all the earth's creatures with annihilation. For women to embrace the "put yourself first" philosophy and practice me-ism and bullying will mean only more problems; it will solve none.

Women have a right to self-development and self-esteem, and in a world that historically has denied women our rights we need to be vigilant about protecting this right. At the same time, however, we need to be aware that with our right to self-development and self-esteem come important responsibilities, and living up to these responsibilities requires vigilance, too. Learning to like and value ourselves is extremely important. But in itself it's not enough. If we are able to develop high self-esteem, we have a responsibility to do what we can in ways large and small to make ours a world that recognizes everyone's right to self-esteem and gives everyone opportunities to exercise that right.

One of the most important responsibilities we have is the responsibility not to participate in practices that deny others dignity and encourages their low self-esteem. In the workplace, for example, we can refuse to put down others we work with, even when we are pitted against them in competition for promotions, and even when we are encouraged by peer pressure to be gossips and bad-mouthers. At a party where sexist and racist jokes are told, we can refuse to participate in the laughter. We can refuse to participate in organizations that bar certain groups. We can refuse to participate in the mania for fashion and beauty that foster in so many women body loathing and feelings of inferiority. We can refuse to participate when those in authority over us order us to discriminate against members of certain groups. Activist Barbara Litchfeld-Palmer explains:

> When I do racism workshops with women, what I try to get them to do is stop participating in the practices. For instance, when a white woman's boss tells her not to accept any checks from black people, she should refuse to do it. Agreeing to do what he says just pits the white woman against me. And really the bottom line is that neither one of us have any power in relation to him. That's what we need to change. We need to work together and refuse to let others separate us like that.

We also have a responsibility not to take advantage of others who, because of their low self-esteem and/or lack of power, might be easy to take advantage of, manipulate, bully, blame or otherwise treat unfairly. The manager whose secretary has such low self-esteem that she cannot stand up for her rights might not have caused the secretary's low self-esteem, but the manager has the responsibility not to take advantage of it by treating or paying her poorly with the excuse that "she never complains." The white woman who employs a woman of color as a housekeeper might not be responsible for the fact that her housekeeper has limited job opportunities, but she does have a responsibility not to treat her like an unworthy inferior as a result. A woman who has no physical disabilities might not be responsible for the oppression of people with disabilities, but she has a responsibility not to take advantage of a disabled person's relative powerlessness by treating her condescendingly. An emotionally secure woman might not be responsible for the unhappy life events that have caused another woman to feel insecure, but she has a responsibility not to take advantage of the other woman's vulnerability and insecurity by manipulating her or using her.

Among the most important of our responsibilities are those we have toward the younger generations. None of us came into the world with low self-esteem. And none of us was born believing certain groups of people are better than others. Even if we are not parents, we all teach children by our example, by the way we treat them, through the institutions we participate in. Each of us has a responsibility to stop and think about the messages we are giving youngsters about themselves and their relationship to the world. There is a tendency for us adults to say, "If it was good enough for me, it's good enough for the kids today." But we have a responsibility to do what we can to make the world in which children grow up a better one than the one we grew up in. We have a duty to leave the earth livable for children, not polluted with our waste, depleted of its natural resources or on the brink of a nuclear holocaust. We have an obligation to leave a world that is hospitable as well as inhabitable, not a cruel and frightening place where "winning through intimidation" and "making yourself number one" are the prevailing doctrines and people's response to injustice and suffering is to shrug their shoulders and look the other way.

Notes

PART ONE

Chapter 1

1. Ernest Becker gives a good description of the effects of self-esteem in *The Birth and Death of Meaning*, 2nd ed., (New York: The Free Press, 1971), chaps. 8, 9, 10.

2. The double standard that says self-love is a moral virtue in men but a fault in women is discussed further in Lionel Trilling, *Beyond Culture: Essays on Literature and Learning* (New York: The Viking Press, 1965), pp. 38–39.

3. The notion that *amour de soi* is basic to "man" and in "man" is necessary and good is central to all Rousseau's work, especially the *Discourse on Inequality*, while his belief that woman is a subordinate being whose purpose is to serve man comes out most clearly in *Émile*. For further discussion of Rousseau's ideas on *amour de soi* see, for example, Ernest Hunter Wright, *The Meaning of Rousseau* (London: Oxford University Press, 1929) and J. H. Broome, *Rousseau: A Study of His Thought* (London: Edward Arnold, 1963).

4. Becker, op. cit., p. 69.

5. Alfred Adler, quoted in Heinz and Rowena Ansbacher, *The Individual Psychology of Alfred Adler* (New York: Basic Books, 1946), p. 358.

6. Rollo May, *Man's Search for Himself* (New York: W. W. Norton & Co., 1953), p. 87.

7. We were greatly aided in our attempt to define the self-concept and the different kinds of self-esteem by two books: Morris Rosenberg, *Conceiving the Self* (New York: Basic Books, 1979) and Stanley Coopersmith, *The Antecedents of Self-esteem* (San Francisco: W. H. Freeman & Co., 1967).

8. Thanks to William Appleton for this definition of self-esteem.

9. Rosenberg, op. cit., p. 63.

10. This definition of narcissism is from Maya Pines, "New Focus on Narcissim Offers Insight Into Grandiosity and Emptiness," The New York *Times*, March 16, 1982, p. C-1.

11. John Russell, "How The Arts Mirror the Retreat of Manhood," The New York *Times*, Sunday Feb. 1, 1981, p. 1 of Arts and Leisure section.

Chapter 2

1. Lillian B. Rubin, *Women of A Certain Age: The Midlife Search for Self* (New York: Harper & Row, 1980), p. 52.

2. Most sources on the subject agree that children acquire gender identity

between the ages of eighteen months and three years. For more information, see Irene H. Frieze et al, eds., *Women and Sex Roles: A Social Psychological Perspective* (New York: W. W. Norton & Co., 1978), pp. 125–27.

3. Fay Fransella and Kay Frost, *On Being A Woman: A Review of How Women See Themselves* (London: Tavistock Publications, 1977), p. 42.

4. I. K. Broverman, D. M. Broverman, F. E. Clarkson, P. S. Rosenkrantz and S. R. Vogel, "Sex-Role Stereotypes and Clinical Judgments of Mental Health," *Journal of Counseling and Clinical Psychology*, 1970, no. 34, pp. 1–7.

5. See Eleanor E. Macoby, "Sex Differences in Intellectual Functioning," in Eleanor E. Macoby, ed., *The Development of Sex Differences* (Palo Alto, Calif.: Stanford University Press, 1966), p. 32; and also Caryl Rivers, Rosalind Barnett and Grace Baruch, *Beyond Sugar and Spice: How Women Grow, Learn, and Thrive* (New York: G. P. Putnam's Sons, 1979), pp. 140–45.

6. Dorothy Corkille Briggs, *Celebrate Yourself* (Garden City, N.Y.: Doubleday & Co., 1977), p. 16.

7. This exercise was taught to Linda Sanford in a Music and Imagery workshop led by Stephen Schatz, Ph.D., at Interface in Newton, Massachusetts, in February 1983. We are indebted to him for this insight.

8. Briggs, op. cit., p. 36.

PART TWO

Chapter 2

1. See Karen Horney, *Our Inner Conflicts* (New York: W. W. Norton & Co., 1945) and *Neurosis and Human Growth* (New York: W. W. Norton & Co., 1950).

2. Stanley Coopersmith, *The Antecedents of Self-esteem* (San Francisco: W. H. Freeman & Co., 1967), p. 132.

3. Kenneth Keniston and the Carnegie Council on Children, *All Our Children* (New York: Harcourt Brace Jovanovich, 1978), p. 15.

4. Lois Hoffman and Martin Hoffman, "The Value of Children to Parents," in *Psychological Perspectives on Population*, ed. J. T. Fawcett (New York: Basic Books, 1973).

5. Ellen Gallinsky, *Between Generations: The Stages of Parenthood.* (New York: Times Books, 1981).

6. Nancy Williamson, Population Reference Bureau Study results reported in *Ms.,* May 1978, p. 20.

7. Maxine Hong Kingston, *The Woman Warrior: Memoirs of a Girlhood Among Ghosts* (New York: Alfred A. Knopf, 1976). Quotes are from the Vintage Books edition (New York: 1977), pp. 54–55.

8. Elizabeth Fishel, *Sisters: Love and Rivalry Inside the Family and Beyond* (New York: William Morrow & Co., 1979), pp. 75–76.

9. Ibid.

10. Lucille Forer as quoted in Philip Zimbardo, *Shyness* (New York: Jove Publications, 1978), p. 60.

11. Don E. Hamachek, *Encounters with the Self* (New York: Holt, Rinehart & Winston, 1971), p. 173.

Chapter 3

1. Coopersmith, on page 38 of *The Antecedents of Self-esteem,* states that the four components of success are power, virtue, significance and competence. Our formulation of the childhood essentials of self-esteem was originally based on Coopersmith's formulation, then modified by our research and interviews.

2. Hamachek, op. cit., p. 182.

3. Tillie Olsen, *Silences* (New York: Delta Books, 1978), p. 28.

4. Coopersmith, op. cit., p. 221.

5. Theodore Isaac Rubin, *Compassion and Self-hate* (New York: Ballantine Books, 1976), p. 20.

6. Coopersmith, op. cit., p. 252.

7. Study cited in Eleanor Maccoby and Carol Nagy Jacklin, *The Psychology of Sex Differences* (Palo Alto, Calif.: Stanford University Press, 1974), p. 157.

8. Nancy Chodorow, *The Reproduction of Mothering: Psychoanalysis and the Sociology of Gender* (Berkeley and Los Angeles: University of California Press, 1978); Carol Gilligan, *In A Different Voice: Psychological Theory and Women's Development* (Cambridge, MA: Harvard University Press, 1982).

9. Bernice Lott, *Becoming a Woman: The Socialization of Gender* (Springfield, Illinois: Charles C. Thomas, 1981), p. 81.

10. Jean Baker Miller, *Toward a New Psychology of Women* (Boston: Beacon Press, 1976), p. 32.

11. Jerome Kagan, "The Child in the Family," *Daedalus,* vol. 106 (Spring 1977), p. 34.

Chapter 4

1. Morris Rosenberg, *Conceiving the Self* (New York: Basic Books, 1979), p. 29.

2. Ibid., p. 74.

Chapter 5

1. Don E. Hamachek, *Encounters with the Self* (New York: Holt, Rinehart & Winston, 1971), p. 153.

2. Judith Arcana, *Our Mothers' Daughters* (Berkeley, Calif.: Shameless Hussy Press, 1979), p. 9.

3. Hamachek, op. cit., p. 154.

4. Caryl Rivers, Rosalind Barnett and Grace Baruch, *Beyond Sugar and*

Spice: How Women Grow, Learn and Thrive. (New York: G. P. Putnam's Sons, 1979), p. 21.

5. Dorothy Dinnerstein, *The Mermaid and the Minotaur* (New York: Colophon Books, 1976), p. 84.

6. Carol Tavris and Carole Offir, *The Longest War* (New York: Harcourt Brace Jovanovich, 1977), p. 165.

7. Nancy Chodorow, *The Reproduction of Mothering: Psychoanalysis and the Society of Gender* (Berkeley and Los Angeles: University of California Press, 1978), p. 82.

8. Ibid., p. 128.

9. Mary Lou Shields, *Sea Run: Surviving My Mother's Madness* (New York: Seaview Books, 1981).

10. Nancy Friday, *My Mother, My Self: The Daughter's Search for Identity* (New York: Delacorte Press, 1977), pp. 21–22.

11. Dinnerstein, op. cit., pp. 85–86.

12. Philip Zimbardo, *Shyness* (New York: Jove Publications, 1978), p. 80.

13. Margaret Hennig and Anne Jardim, *The Managerial Woman* (Garden City, N.Y.: Doubleday & Co., 1977), p. 85.

14. Rivers, Barnett and Baruch, op. cit., p. 44.

15. Dinnerstein, op. cit., p. 85.

16. Hennig and Jardim, op. cit., p. 94.

17. Rivers, Barnett and Baruch, op. cit., p. 53.

18. Alfredo Mirande and Evangelina Enriquez, *La Chicana: The Mexican-American Woman* (Chicago: University of Chicago Press, 1979).

19. Paula Nelson, *The Joy of Money* (Briarcliff Manor, N.Y.: Stein & Day, 1975), p. 17.

20. Ellen Gallinsky, *Between Generations: The Stages of Parenthood.* (New York: Times Books, 1981), p. 236.

21. Adrienne Rich, *Of Woman Born: Motherhood As Experience and Institution.* (New York: W. W. Norton & Co., 1976), p. 202.

Chapter 6

1. Evelyn Reed, *Woman's Evolution.* (New York: Pathfinder Press, 1975), p. 243.

Chapter 7

1. Nathaniel Branden, *The Psychology of Romantic Love* (New York: Bantam Books, 1981), p. 111.

2. Rich, op. cit., p. xiv.

3. Muriel James and Dorothy Jorgenwald, *Born to Win* (Boston: Addison-Wesley Publishing Co., 1971), p. 115.

4. Sheldon Kopp, *If You Meet the Buddha on the Road, Kill Him!* (Palo Alto, Calif.: Science & Behavior Books, 1972), p. 80.

5. Jesse Bernard as quoted by Nancy Friday, *My Mother, My Self* (New York: Delacorte Press, 1977), p. 379.

6. Mitsuye Yamada, "Asian Pacific American Women and Feminism," in *This Bridge Called My Back*, ed. Cherrie Moraga and Gloria Anzaldua. (Watertown, Mass.: Persephone Press, 1981), pp. 73–74.

Chapter 8

1. Mary Brown Parlee and the editors of *Psychology Today*, "The Friendship Bond: PT's Report on Friendship in America," *Psychology Today*, October 1979.

2. Carroll Smith-Rosenberg, "The Female World of Love and Ritual," in Nancy F. Cott and Elizabeth H. Pleck, eds., *A Heritage of Her Own* (New York: Touchstone Books, 1979), pp. 311–42. Quote is from pp. 311–12.

3. See, in addition to Smith-Rosenberg's article, Lillian Faderman, *Surpassing the Love of Men* (New York: William Morrow & Co., 1981); Nancy F. Cott, *The Bonds of Womanhood* (New Haven, Conn.: Yale University Press, 1977); and Carl N. Degler, *At Odds: Women and the Family in America, from the Revolution to the Present* (New York: Oxford University Press, 1980).

4. Smith-Rosenberg, loc. cit.

5. See Faderman, op. cit., and Smith-Rosenberg, loc. cit.

6. See Degler, op. cit., and Mary P. Ryan, *Womahood in America*, 2nd ed. (New York: New Viewpoints, 1979), especially chap. 5.

7. Faderman, op. cit., p. 314.

8. Louise Bernikow, *Among Women* (New York: Harmony Books, 1980), p. 144.

9. Paule Marshall, "From Poets in the Kitchen," the New York *Times Book Review*, January 9, 1983, p. 34.

10. Toni Morrison, *Sula* (New York: Bantam Books, 1975), pp. 51–52.

11. Simone de Beauvoir, *Memoirs of a Dutiful Daughter* (New York: Harper & Row, 1974), p. 112.

12. Joel Block, *Friendship: How to Give It, How to Get It* (New York: Macmillan Publishing Co., 1980), p. 33.

13. Ibid., p. 82.

14. Bernice Lott, *Becoming A Woman: The Socialization of Gender* (Springfield, Ill.: Charles C. Thomas, 1981), p. 268.

15. Virginia Woolf, *A Writer's Diary*. Quoted by Tillie Olsen in *Silences*, p. 235.

16. Karen Lindsey as quoted in "Friendships of the Platonic Kind," by the Los Angeles Times-Washington Post News Service, appearing in the (Lebanon, N.H.) *Valley News*, March 18, 1982.

17. Jesse Bernard, "The Paradox of the Happy Marriage," in Vivian Gornich and Barbara K. Moran, eds., *Woman in Sexist Society* (New York: New American Library, 1971), p. 154.

18. Block, op. cit., p. 36.

19. Philip Slater, *The Pursuit of Loneliness: American Culture at the Breaking Point.* (Boston: Beacon Press, 1976), p. 42.

20. Daniel Goldstine, Katherine Larner, Shirley Zuckerman and Hilary Goldstine, *The Dance-Away Lover.* (New York: William Morrow & Co., 1977), p. 7.

21. David Finklehor and Kersti Yllo, *License to Rape* (unpublished manuscript, 1983), chap. 1.

22. Karen Barrett, "Date Rape: A Campus Epidemic?" *Ms.,* September 1982, pp. 48, 49, 130.

23. Finklehor and Yllo, op. cit.

24. See Lenore Walker, *The Battered Woman* (New York: Harper & Row, 1979).

25. Barrett, op. cit.

26. Barbara Cain, "The Plight of the Gray Divorcee," New York *Times Magazine,* December 19, 1982, pp. 89–95.

27. Sheldon Kopp, *If You Meet the Buddha on the Road, Kill Him!* (Palo Alto, Calif.: Science & Behavior Books, 1972), p. 188.

28. Bernikow, op. cit., p. 196.

29. Block, op. cit., p. 203.

30. Block, op. cit., pp. 175–97.

31. Personal conversation with Trina Beck.

Chapter 9

1. See especially Sheila Kintzer, *Women as Mothers* (New York: Vintage Books, 1978), chap. 4.

2. See Elizabeth Fisher, *Woman's Creation, Sexual Evolution and the Shaping of Society* (Garden City, N.Y.: Anchor Press, 1979), pp. 211–14.

3. See Kintzer, op. cit., Fisher, op. cit., and Elise Boulding, *The Underside of History: A View of Women Through Time* (Boulder, Colo.: Westview Press, 1979).

4. Ibid.

5. In Julia O'Faolain and Lauro Martines, eds., *Not In God's Image.* (New York: Harper & Row, 1973), p. 240.

6. Cited in Kintzer, op. cit., pp. 54–55.

7. Quoted in Landon Y. Jones, *Great Expectations: America and the Baby Boom Generation* (New York: Ballantine Books, 1980), p. 24.

8. Adrienne Rich, *Of Woman Born* (New York: W. W. Norton & Co., 1976), p. 253.

9. Elaine Heffner, *Mothering: The Emotional Experience of Motherhood after Freud and Feminism* (Garden City, N.Y.: Anchor Press, 1978), pp. 9–10.

10. Suzanne Arms, *The Immaculate Deception* (Boston: Houghton Mifflin Co., 1975), cited in Kintzer, op. cit., p. 74.

11. Michelle Harrison, *Woman in Residence* (New York: Random House, 1982), p. 87.

12. Ibid., p. 125.

13. Numerous sources on primatology report on male participation in child rearing among some primates. For a good summary, however, see Naomi Weisstein, "Tired of Arguing About Biological Inferiority?" in *Ms.*, November 1982.

14. See Fisher, op. cit., p. 172.

15. Judith Arcana, *Our Mothers' Daughters* (Berkeley, Calif.: Shameless Hussy Press, 1979), p. 177.

16. Madonna Kolbenschlag, *Kiss Sleeping Beauty Good-Bye* (New York: Bantam Books, 1981), p. 68.

17. Lillian Rubin, *Worlds of Pain: Life in the Working-Class Family* (New York: Basic Books, 1976), pp. 168–84.

18. Lisa Cronin Wohl, Book Review, *Ms.*, April 1982.

PART THREE

Chapter 1

1. Sheila M. Rothman, *Woman's Proper Place: A History of Changing Ideals and Practices* (New York: Basic Books, 1978), pp. 48–49.

2. Ibid., p. 18.

3. Carl N. Degler, *At Odds: Women and the Family in America* (New York: Oxford University Press, 1980), p. 151.

4. Rothman, op. cit., pp. 18–21.

5. Stuart and Elizabeth Ewen, *Channels of Desire: Mass Images and the Shaping of American Consciousness* (New York: McGraw-Hill Book Co., 1982), p. 54.

6. Ibid., p. 214.

7. Ibid., p. 212.

8. See James J. Farrell, *Inventing the American Way of Death* (Philadelphia: Temple University Press, 1980).

9. Susan Moller Okin, *Women in Western Political Thought* (Princeton, N.J.: Princeton University Press, 1979).

Chapter 2

1. Wong as quoted by Mike Granberry in "Nun: Why One Woman Left the Convent," Los Angeles Times-Washington Post News Service, in the (Lebanon, N.H.) *Valley News*, October 15, 1982, p. 20.

2. Carol P. Christ, "Why Women Need the Goddess: Phenomenological, Psychological and Political Reflections," in Charlene Spretnak, ed., *The Politics*

of Women's Spirituality (Garden City, N.Y.: Doubleday & Co., 1981), pp. 72–73.

3. Many recent books on women's spirituality and the history of the Judeo-Christian tradition trace the development of patriarchal religions from their roots in goddess religions and pantheism. However, for an especially succinct discussion see Peggy Reeves Sanday, *Female Power and Male Dominance* (New York: Cambridge University Press, 1981).

4. Elaine Pagels, *The Gnostic Gospels* (New York: Vintage Books, 1981).

5. Ibid., pp. 58–59.

6. Ibid., pp. 48–50.

7. Paul, First Epistle to the Corinthians, 11:3–9.

8. Adrienne Rich, *Of Woman Born* (New York: W. W. Norton & Co., 1976), p. 81.

9. Tertullian, quoted in O'Faolain and Martines, *Not in God's Image,* p. 132.

10. See Matilda Joslyn Gage, *Woman, Church and State* (Watertown, Mass.: Persephone Press, 1980), chap. 5.

11. Jean Baker Miller, *Toward a New Psychology of Women* (Boston: Beacon Press, 1977), pp. 56–58.

12. Max Weber, *The Protestant Ethic and the Spirit of Capitalism,* trans. Talcott Parsons (New York: Charles Scribner's Sons), p 113.

13. Quoted in Carolyn G. Heilbrun, *Reinventing Womanhood* (New York: W. W. Norton & Co., 1979), p. 65.

14. Mary Gordon, "The Unexpected Things I Learned From the Woman Who Talked Back to the Pope," *Ms.,* July/August 1982, pp. 65–69.

15. See Max Weber, *The Protestant Ethic and the Spirit of Capitalism,* op. cit., p. 3. Weber's book has been central to our understanding of American attitudes toward work and the role of religion in shaping them.

16. See Mary Daly, *Gyn/Ecology: The Metaethics of Radical Feminism* (Boston: Beacon Press, 1978).

17. Sheila E. Thompson, *Misogyny in the Sweetest Story Ever Told* (Madison, Wis.: Freedom For Religion Foundation, 1979), p. 1.

18. Ibid., pp. 1, 8.

19. In Pagels, op. cit., p. 152.

20. Alice Walker, *The Color Purple* (New York: Harcourt Brace Jovanovich, 1982), pp. 166–67.

Chapter 3

1. See Phyllis Stock, *Better Than Rubies: A History of Women's Education* (New York: Capricorn Books, 1978).

2. Stock, op. cit., chap. 1.

3. Ibid., p. 36.

4. Ibid., p. 106.

5. Ibid., p. 73.

6. Ibid., p. 73.

7. Women on Words and Images, "Look Jane, See Sexism," in Judith Stacey, Susan Bereaud, and Joan Daniels, eds., *And Jill Came Tumbling After: Sexism in American Education* (New York: Dell Publishing Co., 1974), p. 160.

8. Marsha Federbush, "The Sex Problems of School Math Books," in Stacey, ed. op. cit., pp. 178–84.

9. Casey Miller and Kate Swift, *Words and Women: New Language in New Times* (Garden City, N.Y.: Anchor Press, 1977), p. 21.

10. Ibid., p. 21.

11. Ibid., p. 19.

12. Ibid., p. 33.

13. Maxine Hong Kingston, *The Woman Warrior* (New York: Alfred A. Knopf, 1976), p. 165.

14. Tillie Olsen, *Silences* (New York: Delta Books, 1978), p. 29.

15. Elise Boulding, *The Underside of History: A View of Women Through Time* (Boulder, CO: Westview Press, 1979); Elizabeth Fisher, *Woman's Creation: Sexual Evolution and the Shaping of Society* (Garden City, NY: Anchor Press, 1979); and Frances Dahlberg, ed., *Woman the Gatherer* (New Haven: Yale University Press, 1981).

16. See Joan Kelly Gadol, "Did Women Have a Renaissance?" in *Becoming Visible: Women in European History* (Boston: Houghton Mifflin, 1982). Also see Joan Hoff Wilson, "Hidden Riches: Legal Records and Women, 1750–1825," in Mary Kelley, ed., *Woman's Being, Woman's Place: Female Identity and Vocation in American History* (Boston: G. K. Hall & Co., 1979), pp. 8–9.

17. Lila McCourtney, "I Wish I Could Learn to Talk Indian," in Jane B. Kate, ed., *I Am the Fire of Time: Voices of Native American Women* (New York: E. P. Dutton, 1977), p. 109.

18. For example, in her unpublished 1978 study of the sex makeup of educational administrators in New England, Frances Kelsey found that nearly all administrators in high-level posts are men.

19. Adrienne Rich, "Toward a Woman-Centered University," in *On Lies, Secrets and Silence: Selected Prose, 1966–1978* (New York: W. W. Norton & Co., 1979), p. 139.

20. See Mary Wollstonecraft, *A Vindication of the Rights of Woman* (1772) and John Stuart Mill's *The Subjection of Women* (1869).

Chapter 4

1. A good discussion of the attitude toward women held by the framers of the U.S. Constitution can be found in Linda K. Kerber, *Women of the Republic: Intellect and Ideology in Revolutionary America* (Chapel Hill: University of North Carolina Press, 1980).

2. David Finklehor and Kersti Yllo, *License to Rape* (unpublished manuscript, 1983).

3. Burt Schorr in the *Wall Street Journal,* January 26, 1983, p. 33.

4. Vicki Gregory in *Ms.,* July/August 1982, p. 221.

5. Cited by Barbara Ehrenreich and Karin Stallard, "The Nouveau Poor," *Ms.,* July/August 1982, p. 217.

6. Ehrenreich and Stallard, op. cit., p. 220.

7. See the New York *Times,* January 31, 1983, pp. A-1, A-8.

8. See Joseph Alsop and David Joravsky, "Was the Hiroshima Bomb Necessary? An Exchange," *The New York Review of Books,* Oct. 23, 1980; and McGeorge Bundy, "The Missed Chance to Stop the H-Bomb," *The New York Review of Books,* May 13, 1982.

9. For a discussion of the psychological impacts of the nuclear arms race see Robert Jay Lifton and Richard Falk, *Indefensible Weapons: The Political and Psychological Case Against Nuclearism* (New York: Basic Books, 1982).

Chapter 5

1. Quoted by Joyce Wadler, Los Angeles Times–Washington Post News Service, in the (Lebanon, N.H.) *Valley News,* September 13, 1982.

2. Reported on "Coping With," a program broadcast by the Source Report, WGIR radio station, Manchester, N.H., Jan. 19, 1981.

3. Elizabeth Fry Moulds, "Women's Crime, Women's Justice," in Ellen Boneparth, ed., *Women, Power and Policy* (New York: Pergamon Press, 1982), p. 207.

4. Julianne M. Malveaux, "Moving Forward, Standing Still: Women in White Collar Jobs," in Phyllis A. Wallace, ed., *Women in the Workplace* (Boston: Auburn House, 1982), pp. 101–27.

5. Rose Laub Coser, "Women and Work," *Dissent,* Winter 1980.

6. Malveaux, loc. cit.

7. Carin Rubenstein, "Money and Self-esteem," *Psychology Today,* May 1981, p. 30.

8. Ibid., p. 39.

9. "Civil Rights Panel Notes Alarming Job Discrimination Rate," Los Angeles Times–Washington Post News Service in the (Lebanon, N.H.) *Valley News,* November 24, 1982.

10. Cynthia Fuchs Epstein quoted in Ann Oakley, *Woman's Work: The Housewife Past and Present* (New York: Vintage Books, 1974), p. 88.

11. Nona Glazer, Linda Majka, Joan Acker and Christine Boxe, "The Homemaker, the Family, and Employment," in Joan Huber, ed., *Women in the U.S. Labor Force* (New York: Praeger Publishers, 1979), pp. 156–57.

12. See, for example, Myra Strober "The MBA: Same Passport to Success for Women and Men?" in Wallace, ed., op. cit., especially pp. 38–39.

13. The CBS Evening News with Dan Rather, February 3, 1983.

Chapter 6

1. Charles Dickens, *Dombey and Son* (London: Bradbury and Evans, 1848).

2. Marc Granetz in the "Washington Diarist" column, *The New Republic,* December 9, 1981, p. 43.

3. Information about home furnishings and the presence of mirrors in American homes during the colonial period is from the 1968 World Book Encyclopedia entry on "Colonial Life."

4. Anthony Brandt, "Self-confrontations," *Psychology Today,* October 1980, p. 82.

5. Elaine Kanzaki Wong, "Asian Women," in Linda T. Sanford and Ann Fetter, *In Defense of Ourselves* (Garden City, N.Y.: Dolphin Books, 1979), pp. 158–59.

6. Carol Krucoff, reporting on Screen Actors Guild findings in the TV section of the Boston *Globe,* February 17, 1980, pp. 18–19.

7. "Children's TV Found Dominated by White Men," New York *Times,* July 15, 1982, p. C14.

8. Krucoff, loc. cit.

9. "Children's TV Found Dominated by White Men," loc. cit.

10. Isabel Wilkerson reporting on findings of the NAACP study in "Blacks Left Out of Movie Boom," Boston *Globe,* August 29, 1982, p. 93.

11. Rita Moreno as quoted by Jack Hicks in "The Cutthroats Almost Got Her," *TV Guide,* January 15, 1983, pp. 26–29.

12. Kim Hayes as quoted by Krucoff, loc. cit.

13. See Joyce Flynn, "Women of the Eastern Dawn," an interview with Anita Neilsen and Linda Jeffers, *Sojourner,* January 1983, p. 9.

14. Mary P. Ryan, *Womanhood in America,* 2nd ed. (New York: New Viewpoints, 1979), p. 155.

15. Kathryn Weibel, *Mirror, Mirror: Images of Women Reflected in Popular Culture* (Garden City, N.Y.: Anchor Press, 1977), p. 142.

16. Stuart and Elizabeth Ewen, *Channels of Desire* (New York: McGraw-Hill Book Co., 1982), p. 4.

Chapter 7

1. Statistics of the Health Care Financing Corporation, cited in "New War on Health Costs," *Newsweek,* May 9, 1983, pp. 24, 29.

2. See Claudia Dreifus, ed., *Seizing Our Bodies: The Politics of Women's Health* (New York: Vintage Books, 1977), p. xviii.

3. Miriam Greenspan, *A New Approach to Women and Therapy* (New York: McGraw-Hill Book Co., 1983), pp. 5–6.

4. See Sheila Kintzer, *Women as Mothers* (New York: Vintage Books, 1978), p. 99.

5. Barbara Ehrenreich and Deirdre English, *For Her Own Good: 150 Years of the Experts' Advice to Women* (Garden City, N.Y.: Anchor Press, 1979), pp. 33–34.

6. Ibid., p. 97.

7. Quoted by Kay Weiss, "What Medical Students Learn About Women," in Dreifus, ed., op. cit., p. 218.

8. Ibid.

9. David R. Reuben, *Everything You Always Wanted to Know About Sex but Were Afraid to Ask* (New York: David McKay Co., 1969), pp. 292–93.

10. Diana Scully, "How Residents Learn to Talk You into Unnecessary Surgery," *Ms.,* May 1980, pp. 89–90.

11. See Claudia Dreifus, "Sterilizing the Poor," in Dreifus, ed., op. cit., pp. 105–20; and such articles as "Sterilization is Forever—Are Indian Women Victims of Loose Medical Policies?" Arizona *Daily Star,* December 19, 1976, p. K-1.

12. Reported in "Frontlines," *Mother Jones,* August 1979, p. 10.

13. Gena Corea, *The Hidden Malpractice: How American Medicine Mistreats Women* (New York: Jove Publications, 1979), p. 15.

14. Robert S. Mendelsohn, *Male Practice: How Doctors Manipulate Women* (Chicago: Contemporary Books, 1982), p. 111.

15. Corea, op. cit., p. 16.

16. Mendelsohn, op. cit., p. 148.

17. Ibid., p. 61.

18. Corea, op. cit., p. 17.

19. Mendelsohn, op. cit., p. 157.

20. Lawrence K. Altman, "Hospital Patients Can Suffer Twice As Much When Staff Adds Insult to Injuries," New York *Times,* February 24, 1983, p. C1.

21. Frances Farmer, *Will There Really Be a Morning?* (New York: G. P. Putnam's Sons, 1972), p. 144.

22. Greenspan, op. cit., presents this as *the* reason more women seek psychotherapy than men do. See chap. 1, pp. 3–38.

23. Ibid., p. 19.

24. Reported in "News in Sojourner" column, *Sojourner,* January 1983.

25. Barbara Gordon, *I'm Dancing As Fast As I Can* (New York: Bantam Books, 1979).

26. Greenspan, op. cit., p. 231.

Chapter 8

1. Jamake Highwater, *The Primal Mind: Vision and Reality in Indian America* (New York: New American Library, 1981) p. 124.

2. Barbara Cameron, "Gee, You Don't Seem Like an Indian from the

Reservation," in Jane B. Katz, ed., *I Am The Fire of Time: Voices of Native American Women* (New York: E. P. Dutton, 1977), p. 46.

3. Cheryl Benard and Edit Schlaffer, "The Man in the Street: Why He Harasses," *Ms.,* May 1981, pp. 18–19.

4. Ibid.

5. Gail Brewer quoted by Carol Krucoff in "Women Travelers: Those Who Go Alone Encounter Many Problems That Men Don't," Los Angeles Times–Washington Post News Service, in the (Lebanon, N.H.) *Valley News,* January 14, 1983, p. 13.

6. Radicalesbians, "The Woman Identified Woman," in *Notes from the Third Year: Women's Liberation,* 1971, p. 81.

7. Sandra Bartky, "On Being Hassled in the Street," in *Open Forum,* a women's publication of Dartmouth College, February 25, 1980, p.1.

8. "Fight Back," words and music by Holly Near, copyright 1978 by Hereford Music. All Rights Reserved—Reprinted with permission. We are grateful to Holly Near for her permission to use these lyrics.

PART FOUR

Chapter 1

1. We would like to thank Janice de Lange, Ph.D., who presented six common negative thought patterns among women and the thought-stopping technique in a workshop on self-esteem at the University of Washington School of Social Work in July of 1977. Since that time, Linda Sanford has researched and modified the thought patterns in her clinical practice. We encourage our readers to read Dr. de Lange's forthcoming work on self-esteem.

Chapter 2

1. David Burns, *Feeling Good: The New Mood Therapy* (New York: William Morrow & Co., 1980), p. 103.

Chapter 3

1. Rollo May, *Man's Search for Himself.* (New York: W. W. Norton & Co., 1953), p. 100.

Chapter 4

1. Stephen Birmingham, "Princess Grace: It Never Really Was All Fairy Tale," in *TV Guide,* February 5, 1983, p. 8.

2. G. W. Allport, *Patterns and Growth in Personalities* (New York: Holt, Rinehart & Winston, 1961), pp. 130–31.

3. Gloria Steinem, "Forum/The Mail on Trashing," *Ms.*, October 1976, p. 65.

4. Glenn Collins, "Jill Clayburgh—Acting on the Edge," New York *Times,* March 7, 1982, p. 1 of Arts and Leisure section.

Chapter 5

1. Dorothy Corkille Briggs discusses all-or-nothing thinking in *Celebrate Yourself* (Garden City, N.Y.: Doubleday, 1977), p. 60.

2. Marcia Millman, *Such A Pretty Face: Being Fat in America* (New York: W. W. Norton & Co., 1980), p. 192.

Chapter 6

1. Goldstine et al., *The Dance-Away Lover* (New York: William Morrow & Co., 1977), p. 7.

Chapter 8

1. Sally Field as quoted by Sheila Weller in "Sally Field is Learning to Please Herself," *McCall's,* January 1982, p. 78.

2. Branden, *The Psychology of Romantic Love* (New York: Bantam Books, 1981), p. 60.

3. Susan Allen Toth, *Blooming: A Small-town Girlhood* (Boston: Little, Brown & Co., 1981), p. 39.

4. Marcia Millman, *Such a Pretty Face* (New York: W. W. Norton & Co., 1980), p. 127.

5. Sheilah Graham as quoted in Stanton Peele with Archie Brodsky, *Love and Addiction* (New York: New American Library, 1975) p. 77.

6. Sally Field as quoted by Weller, op. cit., p. 107.

7. Penelope Russianoff, *Why Do I Think I Am Nothing Without a Man?* (New York: Bantam Books, 1982).

8. Lenore Walker, *The Battered Woman* (New York: Harper & Row, 1979), p. 182.

9. Collette Dowling, *The Cinderella Complex: Women's Hidden Fear of Independence* (New York: Summit Books, 1981), p. 22.

10. Ibid., pp. 23–24.

11. Ibid., p. 102.

12. See Carol Tavris and Carole Offir, *The Longest War: Sex Differences in Perspective* (New York: Harcourt Brace Jovanovich, 1977), p. 46.

13. Lillian Rubin, *Women of a Certain Age* (New York: Harper & Row, 1980), p. 21.

14. Mary P. Ryan, *Womanhood In America,* 2nd ed. (New York: New Viewpoints, 1979), especially chap. 1.

15. Ibid., p. 26.

16. Philip Slater, *The Pursuit of Loneliness* (Boston: Beacon Press, 1976), p. 71.

17. Statistics provided by the Alan Guttmacher Institute, 1982.

18. Pauline Bart, "Depression in Middle-Aged Women" in *Female Psychology: The Emerging Self* (Chicago: Science Research Associates, 1976), pp. 349–69.

19. This remark is attributed to Glenda Jackson by Madonna Kolbenschlag in *Kiss Sleeping Beauty Good-bye* (Garden City, N.Y.: Doubleday & Co., 1979), p. 74.

20. Marilyn Machlowitz, *Workaholics* (Boston: Addison-Wesley Publishing Co., 1980), p. 28.

21. Ibid., p. 140.

22. Lillian Rubin, op. cit., p. 170.

23. Thomas Carlyle, quoted by George Seldes, *The Great Quotations* (New York: Pocket Books, 1970), p. 985.

24. Calvin Coolidge, quoted by George Seldes, op. cit., p. 986.

25. Gail Sheehy, *Passages: Predictable Crises of Adult Life* (New York: E. P. Dutton, 1974), p. 91.

26. Dorothy Corkille Briggs, *Celebrate Yourself* (Garden City, N.Y.: Doubleday, 1977), p. 143.

27. Field as quoted by Weller, op. cit., p. 107.

Chapter 9

1. R. D. Rosen, *Psychobabble: Fast Talk and Quick Cure in the Era of Feeling* (New York: Atheneum, 1977).

2. Aaron T. Beck, *Depression: Clinical, Experimental and Theoretical Aspects* (New York: Paul B. Hoeber, 1967).

3. David Burns, *Feeling Good* (New York: William Morrow & Co., 1980), p. 82.

4. Henry Paul on "The Phil Donahue Show," 1982.

5. Anne Lamott, *Hard Laughter* (New York: Signet Books, 1980), pp. 154–55.

6. Helen De Rosis and Victoria Pellegrino, *The Book of Hope: How Women Can Overcome Depression* (New York: Macmillan Publishing Co., 1976), p. 282.

7. Philip Slater, *The Pursuit of Loneliness* (Boston: Beacon Press, 1976), p. 4.

8. Gabrielle Burton, *I'm Running Away from Home, but I'm Not Allowed to Cross the Street: A Primer of Women's Liberation* (New York: Avon Books, 1975), p. 23.

9. De Rosis and Pellegrino, op. cit., p. 325.

Chapter 10

1. We are indebted to psychologist Marcia Germaine Hutchinson for her clarification of this dynamic as well as many other dynamics in this chapter.

2. Adrienne Rich, *Of Woman Born* (New York: W. W. Norton & Co., 1976), p. 292.

3. Pam Mitchell and Robin Newmark, "The Political History of Fat Liberation: An Interview," ed. Jennifer Parnell, *The Second Wave,* vol. 6, no. 1 (1981), p. 33.

4. Deborah Larned Romano, "Eating Our Hearts Out," *Mother Jones,* June 1980, pp. 20–24.

⌐ 5. Nellie Wong, "When I Was Growing Up," in *This Bridge Called My Back: Writings by Radical Women of Color,* ed. Cherrie Moraga and Gloria Anzaldua (Watertown, Mass: Persephone Press, 1981), p. 8.

6. Kim Chernin, *The Obsession: Reflections on the Tyranny of Slenderness* (New York: Harper & Row, 1981), p. 136.

7. Marcia Millman, *Such a Pretty Face* (New York: W. W. Norton & Co., 1980), p. xi.

8. Romano, op. cit., p. 23.

9. Jane Fonda, *Jane Fonda's Workout Book* (New York: Simon & Schuster, 1981), p. 49.

10. Hilde Bruch, *The Golden Cage: The Enigma of Anorexia Nervosa* (New York: Random House, 1978), p. 135.

11. Margaret Atwood, *Lady Oracle* (New York: Simon & Schuster, 1976), pp. 87–88.

12. Chernin, op. cit., p. 90.

13. Marian Christy, "Vicki La Motta's Life With Jake," Boston *Globe,* February 4, 1982, p. 39.

14. Susie Orbach, *Fat Is a Feminist Issue.* (New York: Medallion Books, 1978), p. 60.

15. Marcia Germaine Hutchinson, "The Effect of a Treatment Based on the Use of Guided Visuo-kinesthetic Imagery on the Alteration of Negative Body-cathexis for Women" (doctoral thesis, Boston University, 1981), p. 108.

16. Gloria Steinem, "Feminist Notes: In Praise of Women's Bodies," *Ms.,* April 1982, p. 32.

Chapter 11

1. Michel Foucault, *The History of Sexuality,* vol. 1 (New York: Vintage Books, 1980), p. 7.

2. Ibid., p. 159.

3. Cited by Lonnie Barbach at "Female Sexuality" Workshop at Interface, Newton, Massachusetts, November 1982.

4. As quoted by Victoria Pellegrino, *The Other Side of Thirty* (New York: Rawsom Wade Publishers, 1981), p. 108.

5. Anne Koedt, *The Myth of the Vaginal Orgasm* (Boston: New England Free Press, 1970).

6. Nora Gallagher, "Fever All Through the Night," *Mother Jones,* November 1982, p. 39.

7. Lonnie Barbach, *Women Discover Orgasm* (Garden City, N.Y.: Doubleday & Co., 1980), p. 40.

8. Gabrielle Brown, *The New Celibacy: Why More Men and Women Are Abstaining from Sex—and Enjoying It.* (New York: McGraw-Hill Book Co., 1980), p. 106.

9. Ibid., p. 8.

10. Shere Hite, *The Hite Report: A Nationwide Study on Female Sexuality* (New York: Macmillan Publishing Co., 1976), p. 426.

11. Ibid., p. 536.

12. Elizabeth Haich, quoted in Brown, op. cit., p. 212.

13. Gallagher, op. cit., p. 43.

14. Hite, op. cit., p. 69.

15. Brown, op. cit., p. 114.

16. Carmen Kerr, *Sex for Women Who Want To Have Fun and Loving Relationships with Equals.* (New York: Grove Press, 1977), pp. 141–42.

Chapter 12

1. Nathaniel Branden, *The Psychology of Romantic Love* (New York: Bantam Books, 1981), p. 131.

2. Ibid., p. 130.

Chapter 13

1. Cherrie Moraga, "La Guera," in *This Bridge Called My Back,* ed. Cherrie Moraga and Gloria Anzaldua (Watertown, Mass.: Persephone Press, 1981), p. 22.

2. Florynce Kennedy, *Color Me Flo: My Hard Life and Good Times* (Englewood Cliffs, N.J.: Prentice-Hall, 1967), p. 87.

3. Audre Lorde, "The Master's Tools Will Never Dismantle the Master's House" in Moraga and Anzaldua, eds., op. cit., p. 101.

EPILOGUE

1. See Wayne Dyer, *Your Erroneous Zones* (New York: Funk & Wagnalls, 1976).

Index